Jefferson's Sec

Also by Andrew Burstein

The Passions of Andrew Jackson

Letters from the Head and Heart:
Writings of Thomas Jefferson

America's Jubilee: How in 1826 a Generation
Remembered Fifty Years of Independence

Sentimental Democracy

The Inner Jefferson: Portrait of a Grieving Optimist

> A death-bed adieu. Th:J. to MR.
> Life's visions are vanished, it's dreams are no more.
> Dear friends of my bosom, why bathed in tears?
> I go to my fathers; I welcome the shore,
> which crowns all my hopes, or which buries my cares.
> Then farewell my dear, my lov'd daughter, Adieu!
> The last pang of life is in parting from you!
> Two Seraphs await me, long shrouded in death:
> I will bear them your love on my last parting breath

Thomas Jefferson's deathbed adieu. Original in a private collection, photostat from James Monroe Museum, Fredericksburg, Virginia.

Jefferson's Secrets

DEATH and *Desire*
at *Monticello*

ANDREW BURSTEIN

BASIC
BOOKS

A Member of the Perseus Books Group
New York

Published by Basic Books,
A Member of the Perseus Books Group

Books published by Basic Books are available at special discounts for bulk purchases in
the United States by corporations, institutions, and other organizations. For more
information, please contact the Special Markets Department at the Perseus Books
Group, 11 Cambridge Center, Cambridge, MA 02142, or call (617) 252-5298 or (800)
255-1514, or email special.markets@perseusbooks.com.

Cataloging-in-Publication data for this book is available from the Library of Congress.

ISBN 0-465-00812-7

05 06 07 / 10 9 8 7 6 5 4 3 2 1

TO
Peter Onuf

Reputation is worthless; trial is best.
Many have good repute who are untried.

THEOGNIS OF MEGARA

The aim of the dreamer, after all, is merely to go on dreaming and not to be molested by the world. His dreams are his protection against the world. But the aims of life are antithetical to those of the dreamer, and the teeth of the world are sharp.

JAMES BALDWIN
from *Another Country*

CONTENTS

Active Memories

Jefferson Dying

ILLUSTRATIONS

Postmortem

"Why start at death?" asks the eighteenth-century poet Edward Young, once considered a genius on the order of Milton and Shakespeare, and a favorite of Thomas Jefferson's from his early years through retirement. Why start at death? Because many mysteries find their solutions in longings expressed at the end of life.

Young's most famous poem, *The Complaint: or, Night-Thoughts on Life, Death, and Immortality,* was published around the time of Jefferson's birth. In it, the poet avows that the foreboding sensations we routinely associate with death torment us only if we feel compelled to nourish them from within:

> *The knell, the shroud, the mattock, and the grave;*
> *The deep damp vault, the darkness, and the worm;*
> *These are the bugbears of a winter's eve,*
> *The terrors of the living not the dead.*
> *Imagination's fool, and error's wretch,*
> *Man makes a death which nature never made;*
> *Then on the point of his own fancy falls;*
> *And feels a thousand deaths in fearing one.*[1]

The poet's point is simple: To fear death is to resist life and misinterpret nature. Jefferson copied Young's lines into his *Commonplace Book,* a scrapbook of quotations, sometime in the late 1760s or early 1770s; this was about the time he met his wife and moved to the mountaintop where he had already begun the brightly conceived mansion of Monticello. He built, experimented, redesigned, and brought new life to that reputable prominence, occasionally having to bury friends and loved ones in its shade.

No stranger to sorrow, an elderly Thomas Jefferson was still quoting Young's verses a half-century later. In a letter he wrote to John Adams from Monticello in 1822, he lamented the worn and weary feeling of old age. Every act felt to him like a pointless repetition, wherein "with lab'ring step / To tread our former footsteps."[2] He had been granted long life. His eighty-three years made him, in 1826, one of the last three surviving signers (among the original fifty-six) of the Declaration of Independence. He would tread heavily in former footsteps, as the poet put it, until July 4 of that year. The day Jefferson died was America's fiftieth Fourth of July, its jubilee as a nation.

He was a zealot, supremely self-confident, extremely well read, a visionary proponent of natural rights, and the moving spirit behind America's first opposition political party, the Democratic-Republican, which challenged upper-class rule. Born April 13, 1743, at Shadwell, on the Virginia frontier and directly below Monticello, he was thirty-three when he wrote the Declaration of Independence; forty-one when he journeyed to France to take Benjamin Franklin's place as America's minister to the Court of Versailles; forty-seven when he joined George Washington's cabinet as the first secretary of state; and fifty-seven when he took the oath of office as president. As he built his national reputation, he impressed upon the citizens of America an unassailable ideal that we take for granted in the twenty-first century: participatory democracy.

This book addresses deep and delicate questions about a figure from our national past who looms so large in social memory that he is primarily evaluated on the basis of selective re-readings of familiar texts. My aim is somewhat different. Distrustful of smooth biographical narratives that question only so far, I am interested in the *unfamiliar* that was familiar to Jefferson. This study is built upon an appreciation for the particular spectrum of knowledge and feeling that characterized the eighteenth and early nineteenth centuries: an alien medical environment, sexual attitudes unlike our own, literary and aesthetic considerations, as well as the more obvious (and more prominent in modern minds) aspects of political competition and race relations. I want the reader to grasp, as fully as possible, what conditioned Thomas Jefferson's mind.

Throughout his life, Jefferson used language in a distinctive manner. His consciousness of his audience has a lot to do with why, these many generations later, we continue to appreciate his democratic political genius and his lively, comforting expressions. But what if we are only scratching the surface of his meaning? DNA connecting his genetic material to that of the offspring of one of his slaves has recently suggested that key facets of his life remain poorly understood. His revolutionary romance with the written word is only one part of what binds us to him. For reasons having to do with the risks he took, both as a private man and as a public figure, everyone, it seems, wants to discover Jefferson's secrets.

We start at death and move backward through his retirement, because that is how an emotive Jefferson is to be found, and how, consequently, we can add meaning to many of his earlier writings. In the lesser-known texts of his postpresidential years, he presents a retrospective few have ventured to study until now.[3] He looks back on his long life in the decidedly sensual terms of enjoyment and suffering, ease and dis-ease. Most critically, I find, he invokes a comprehensive language of medicine past that historical investigators have tended to ignore. We have been shut off from that vocabulary, and it is one that will make Jefferson appear less secretive when we better understand it.

No label is all embracing. We must take care in describing Jefferson, because his tendencies vary: Like a poet, he cannot dismiss mortality when he writes of community. Like a philosopher, he is involved with systems of knowledge and morality; and least familiar of all, like a physiologist, he looks elementally at the body's natural responses—pain and pleasure mechanisms, drives and motivations—and tries to comprehend how human beings can thrive in such a stormy, yet fertile, environment as the Earth we know. Politics is much the same for him: an environment both stormy and fertile. He constantly inquires about conditions. When, as a political leader, he draws upon his (and his society's) deep concern with neurophysiological symptoms, he invariably describes psychological effects. Invoking the "agonizing spasms of infuriated man," or the "agitations of the public mind," "tickled nerves" or "frigid insensibility," Jefferson manifestly lets us know how he is feeling about America's prospects. This is an encompassing theme within the pages of *Jefferson's Secrets*.

In attempting a closer examination of Jefferson's mind, I am introducing two conspicuous methods of discovery: reading and interpreting the consciousness-raising, sympathy-generating language of eighteenth-century health science that he relied on so heavily; and, in a broader sense, emphasizing the relatively uncensored Jefferson that exists in the least-studied writings of his retirement years, 1809–1826. His large body of papers for the postpresidential period have been selectively reprinted; Jefferson left a treasure trove of unceremonious writings yet to be compared to those already published.

This book will not bring an end to all arguments about Jefferson, but it should help distance him from the mounting prejudices of modern biographers. I resuscitate Thomas Jefferson long enough to pose certain questions that he has answered subtly in the personal documents of his late years: What did this prodigious reader and ruminator take from books? What kind of America did he envision? How might we, from so great a cultural distance, be misjudging him? In short, what was the extent, and what were the limits, of his imagination? We have lost touch with Jefferson's imagination, and that is a shame.

Of course, Jefferson cannot partake of *our* imaginations. On the high-priority, rather touchy subject of race, for instance, some read his sensitive words about human rights, which we take to define the democratic ethos, and conclude that Jefferson lost a good deal of sleep over slavery; others believe that, with cowardly abstention, he turned his back on black America—indeed, on all of us in the twenty-first century. We need to find a way to approach historical problems without allowing our own emotional baggage to overwhelm the discussion.

On the equally interesting, and related, subject of his sexual imagination, we need to consult at-home medical guides and the popular literature he and his family owned; we need to contend with unquestioned class privilege and the understood options men possessed, as well as the disjunction (common to all periods of history) between what people said and what they did. This is a complex subject that necessarily takes us beyond the limits of Jefferson's Virginia surroundings, and yet it was as close to his heart as his reading and writing in Greek. What we might consider indelicate, or an unpersuasive logic, might have been entirely defensible when Jefferson lived.

The reader should approach this book with an open mind. Too often, the stubbornness that directs modern ideologies shuts off valuable discussion. I hope to launch a more honest conversation about Jefferson, race, and sex than historians and others have engaged in of late. When DNA testing in 1998 sexually linked "a Jefferson" to Jefferson's slave Sally Hemings, two extreme opinions emerged: Either Jefferson and Hemings were in love in a way we should be able to recognize or a relative of Thomas Jefferson's had slept with Hemings, because the president was morally above such behavior.

Good historical inquiry should never stop. That is what law professor Annette Gordon-Reed believed in challenging a consensus in 1997. In her dogged and timely analysis, *Thomas Jefferson and Sally Hemings: An American Controversy,* and unaware that a DNA "solution" was about to be attempted, she reopened the door to this discussion. Just because DNA appears to have made our task ("Did he or didn't he?") easier, we should not close the door now.

There is much we do not know about the Jefferson-Hemings relationship, and the last thing we should do is to impose twenty-first-century views of sex on eighteenth-century people so that their relationships "make sense." First, the unusual emotional considerations facing a mixed-race couple in, say, the 1950s or 1990s, cannot be compared to those of Jefferson's time and place. Second, there is no universal structure for human sexual response: We do not share in eighteenth-century sexual attitudes, and we should not guess at Jefferson's or Hemings's feelings according to modern notions of love and sex. It is silly to deny that sexuality has a history. Third, we should admit that part of what impels the popular imagination today is the desire to protect the historical reputation of Thomas Jefferson or to construct one for Sally Hemings—or both at once, by concluding that they were a "romantic" couple. As a slave, she had only a limited range of options; and all we know about her is what her son told a newspaper reporter decades after her death: He referred to her as Jefferson's "concubine." He made no allusion to affectionate feelings of any kind. Thus, the conversation begun by Gordon-Reed should continue.

In the pages that follow, Jefferson writes about politics, sex, race, and religion in ways that complement, but in significant ways alter, his better-known writings. The musings of his later years, Jefferson's lost words, as it were, offer valuable insights into his inner life. I wish to suggest that our knowledge of him is incomplete if we fail to obtain a clearer picture of these years. We shall see how intensely conscious he was of his role in history, though he was retired from politics, and how fearful he was that his persistent political opposition would put its imprint on the age. And in exploring the medical vernacular, a metaphorically rich subset of eighteenth- and early nineteenth-century writing, we shall see beyond the harried frame and physical aches and pains of an old man and discover, at the crossroads of politics and religion, what he experienced as the medical Enlightenment.

Jefferson was body as well as mind. In the texts he left behind, Body gestures to us no less than Head and Heart imaginatively "speak" to us. Body tells us about his appetites and desires, his fears of contamination. As quotable as Jefferson's observations tend to be, his most memorable statements do not often place him inside a world of physicality. This is misleading, because physical nature did not simply amuse him; it preoccupied him. He was marked by an enthusiastic confidence in the existence of a scientific truth that he could apply to human society. The design of nature was a lifelong problem that loomed before him, and he thrived on the creativity scientific study invited.[4]

Through literature on the body, we also learn how flawed the eighteenth-century scientific construction of nature was. From our perspective, Jefferson's ideas about sex and race suffer, of course, because his world saw gender differences and power as natural rather than cultural formulations. When he conceived, for example, that "all men are created equal," as lovingly as these words are still received, Jefferson restricted equality to a minority of his countrymen, based on a "natural" hierarchy of race and gender. He also tended to group taste and temperament in natural rather than cultural categories—because that is what the science of his day preached.

To ask "What did life really mean to Jefferson and his generation?" is not ridiculous. The question can be broken down into its component parts, as we have already begun to do here.

Recent writing on Jefferson infers that his sensual side was most dominant during his political prime, and particularly when he served as American minister to France (1784–1789). But we must, with equal attention, plumb the depths of his later years' reflections. Just to take one long-since published example, and one of the most comprehensively revealing letters of his retirement years, Jefferson answered John Adams's request for his judgment on whether life was worth living over again. This exchange occurred in 1816, as the Virginian was nearing his seventy-third birthday, and Adams had just turned eighty. The two were, at this point, ten years from death.

"I cannot be serious!" Adams opened his appeal. "I am about to write You, the most frivolous letter, you ever read." Jefferson obliged him fully, as he tended to do in these years, by using a curious kind of medical imagery to distinguish the dull protestations of others from his own determination and sturdy optimism. Here, then, is Jefferson to Adams:

> I think with you that it is a good world on the whole, that it has been framed on a principle of benevolence, and more pleasure than pain has been dealt out to us. There are indeed (who might say Nay) gloomy and hypocondriac minds, inhabitants of diseased bodies, disgusted with the present, and despairing of the future; always counting on the worst to happen. To these I say How much pain have cost us the evils which have never happened?[5]

There is more here than meets the eye. Jefferson was claiming an almost prophetic moralizing power; he did so on the basis of his particular concern with bodies, healthy and diseased.

We see, too, that he attributed pain and pessimism to an abnormal psychology. He was realist enough to know that physical deterioration belongs to the processes of nature, but it did not follow for him that the soul ought to wallow in anxious anticipation of what might occur. Mind and body worked in tandem: those of "gloomy and hypocondriac minds" were "inhabitants of diseased bodies." And what is he telling us about the imagination? In Jefferson's day, *hypocondriac* was defined as "disordered in the imagination";[6] he knew the healthy imagination to be productive of clever designs, whereas the sickly or disordered imagination laid waste to all pleasing potential. Happiness can just as easily be said to derive from the life of the body as the mind.

Jefferson's reply to Adams proceeded:

> My temperament is sanguine. I steer my bark with Hope in the head, leaving Fear astern. My hopes indeed sometimes fail; but not oftener than the forebodings of the gloomy. There are, I acknowledge, even in the happiest life, some terrible convulsions, heavy set-offs against the opposite page of the account. I have often wondered for what good end the sensations of Grief could be intended. All our other passions, within proper bounds, have an useful object.

Here the optimist consults the pathologist, and defines the nearly unendurable pains of life in decisive terms of physicality, as "convulsions" and "sensations of Grief," emerging from a cluster of indescribable, unfathomable "passions." Harassments, some visceral and devastating, may loom; yet in Jefferson's vocabulary, life is made tolerable (and worth repeating, if such were possible) through a deliberate pursuit of—as he goes on to tell Adams—"a just equilibrium of all the passions."

Throughout his adult years, Jefferson consistently invoked a desire to live in a state of tranquil ease—"tranquil permanent felicity"—that flowed from a sweet, thriving home life. Indeed, in the most personal sense, this is what Jefferson meant by "pursuit of happiness." He used the word *felicity* consistently and often when he described a situation greatly desired, or an ideal or near-perfect value; *delight* sometimes substituted for *felicity*. The word *happiness* was a more generic and less impassioned version of the same quality.[7]

Under the circumstances of a self-monitored life, death is neither a shock nor a terror, certainly not to one who has studied the human condition as Jefferson had. There was no surprise in the downward slope of his last years. Yet even from an aging man's perspective, sensations—the imaginative faculties— were to be enlisted in the enjoyment of life.

Because we shall be going into greater depth when we examine Jefferson's recurrence to a neurological vocabulary, it helps, right from the beginning, to associate the quality of life Jefferson so famously prescribed with the perspective of a distinguished modern neurologist who has devoted books to capturing "the feeling brain," or how feeling becomes known to the feeling organism.

Antonio Damasio examines what happens inside the sensory portals (delivery of our sight, sound, taste, touch, olefaction) and nerve pathways, tracking automatic emotional responses and individualized feelings, separating nature's self from culture's self. He takes feeling back to its essential electrochemistry by traversing a "body landscape."

"Emotion-induction sites," he writes, "trigger a number of responses toward the body and toward other brain sites, and unleash the full range of body and brain responses that constitute emotion." Thus emotion precedes feeling. Feelings emerge as changes take place in the body's chemical profile, when muscles in the face, throat, trunk, and limbs contract. First we execute emotions, and then we know what we are feeling.

As an experiment, Dr. Damasio asks us to reconstruct through mental imagery what good feelings feel like. He has the subject conjure a warming sun and a breezy siesta at the oceanside. As he describes the physiology of being at ease, he points to less tangible, more diffuse sensations: "You had the energy to move, but somehow you preferred to remain quiet, a paradoxical combination of the ability and inclination to act and the savoring of the stillness. . . . The picture of events you eagerly anticipated as pleasurable came into mind, as did scenes you enjoyed experiencing in the past. Also, you found that your cast of mind was, well, felicitous."

Felicitous stillness, then, is Damasio's novel definition for inner peace and contentment. Backed by the latest neuroscience, the twenty-first-century doctor, by apparent accident, chooses almost the same words Jefferson chose as he elaborates on the Jeffersonian ideal of "tranquil permanent felicity." So, just as there are universally recognizable facial expressions for fear, anger, surprise, sadness, and happiness, there are historically dynamic, if not quite transcendent, ways of comparing vocabularies of emotion and feeling.

As Damasio shows, too, in everything we encounter there is a dynamic engagement of the body. Illustrating the interactive perceptions that we know as good feelings and that Jefferson enlarged into a tranquil, permanent, felicitous lifestyle, the neurologist returns to our imagined moment on the beach: "What you usually regard as 'body' and 'mind' blended in harmony. Any conflicts now seem abated." For Jefferson and eighteenth-century neuroscience, this phenomenon was "a just equilibrium of all the passions."

The mind perceives the body's well-balanced operation. The mind tells us that the flesh is happy. All feeling is, in Damasio's words, "the idea of the body being in a certain way." He is still essentially speaking Jefferson's language, for both are attuned to reactive processes, combining "well-being" and "well-thinking."[8]

In an earlier book, *The Inner Jefferson* (1995), I described my subject as a "grieving optimist"—and the paradox was intentional. Fully sixty of Jefferson's *Commonplace Book* entries concerned death in one way or another. Because he relished the sensations that rendered human beings capable of unselfish commitment to one another, he relished (or should we say withstood) "the joy of grief" that encompassed the poetry of his age. At the same time, he evidenced the most forward-looking perspective among the founders, confident in the educability of an expanding electorate.[9] His reply to Adams's "frivolous" question suggests that he considered death surmountable, though obviously not avoidable, through the power of positive thinking. In this sense, as we can glean from the poem of Edward Young that meant so much to him, Thomas Jefferson held a conception of mortality that was rather *un*superstitious.

In part because he worshipped science and nature, Jefferson never alluded to death with anything but studied calm. As he aged, he professed that he was entirely prepared for a peaceable death whenever it might come, and that life's end did not have to be anything more than the body's exhaustion. Trusting in nature, he gave the passion and mental toil of his last years to the construction of the University of Virginia, in his own neighborhood. He lived to see it open in 1825, and was greeted with near awe whenever he descended from his mountaintop and paid the school a visit.

He first thought that his retirement from the public had come at the end of 1793 when, at the age of fifty, he had completed his tenure as secretary of state and quit George Washington's administration. In "a retirement I doat on," he had fashioned himself "an Antediluvian patriarch among my children & grandchildren."[10] To James Madison, in the spring of 1795, he explained why he could not be persuaded to return to politics: "My health is entirely broken down within the last eight months; my age requires that I should place my affairs in a clear state. . . . The little spice of ambition, which I had in my younger days, has long since evaporated, and I set less store by a posthumous than present name."[11] By 1796, however, he was persuaded to stand for president against his friend Adams, after their political paths had diverged. He narrowly lost, and according to the original constitutional provision, as the second-place vote-getter, Jefferson became vice president.

Politics became nastier, intensifying Jefferson's fear that America's republican experiment would dissolve in the face of a consolidating power at the center. In notes he recorded after a dinner conversation with President Adams, he wrote, somewhat incredulously, that the second president feared democracy: "As to trusting to a popular assembly for the preserv[atio]n of our liberties it was [to Adams] the merest chimaera imaginable." Adams underscored "that anarchy did more mischief in one night than tyranny in an age."[12] In 1800, Jefferson succeeded in unseating the incumbent. After serving two terms at the head of the nation, presiding over what he considered a restoration of the Revolutionary turn of mind, he retired for good in 1809, when he was about to turn sixty-six.

In old age, Jefferson extracted more from life than most do in a lifetime. Though his physical complaints were certainly real and pronounced, when he died, he died possessing more felicitous thoughts than solemn regrets. Still, the thoughts he expressed were bittersweet. Nearly every day, he passed the graveyard where he had buried a best friend and brother-in-law before the Revolution; a wife not long after; a grown daughter during his presidency; and a granddaughter, who had delivered great-grandchildren, in the late winter of 1826, just before his own final illness. It is but a short, sloping walk from Monticello's west portico to the burial ground where the bones of Thomas Jefferson reside. Those who wish to feel closer to history can still make that walk.

A mindful practitioner of the art of living life, Jefferson was every bit as diligent when he scripted his own death. The author of the "Declaration of American Independence"—as the words on his tombstone actually read—left little to chance. During his last months, as he assiduously mapped out the future of the newly established university, he took stock of the contents of his wine cellar; gave his "annual gratuity" of twenty dollars each to his favorite slaves, Burwell Colbert (coordinator of Monticello domestic affairs) and John Hemings (carpenter); and paid his outstanding bills to cover the requirements of daily existence, such as newspapers and bookbinding and repair of his prized "polygraph," the mechanical device that enabled him to produce instantaneous copies of outgoing letters.[13] He made sure that his private papers were perfectly filed and readily accessible to his thirty-three-year-old grandson and executor, Thomas Jefferson Randolph. He knew how he wanted to embark on his voyage into historical memory.

Jefferson died worn down in body but as vigorous intellectually as he was in his prime. He devoted his life to reading, designing, and communicating. The politically uncompromising and distinctly sentimental third president of the United States applied his phenomenal will to every project he undertook. That included the active enterprise of surviving until July 4, 1826. Lanky and lean, and troubled by various internal complaints, he was frail at eighty-three years, two months, and twenty-one days old, when his nation celebrated its fifty-year jubilee. His death is doubly memorable because the ninety-year-old John Adams "chose" that same day to die, outlasting the Virginian by some four hours.

For quite a while, Jefferson had been telling his correspondents that the effects of age were upon him. An old wrist injury made writing extraordinarily difficult, as his friend William Short well knew, for he had been Jefferson's private secretary in France in 1786 when the hand was fractured and poorly set. "I see with some kind of alarm the life which you condemn yourself to lead," Short wrote in 1819. "So much time passed at the writing desk must be unfavorable to health—& I really wish you would consult more your health & less the satisfaction of your correspondents."[14] "My race is run," Jefferson wrote in 1822 to the Marquis de Lafayette. "Weighed down with years, I am still more disabled from writing by a wrist & fingers almost without joints. This has obliged me to withdraw from all correspondence that is not indispensable."[15] That same year, in the somewhat more playful style of address he reserved for women, he philosophized: "Time, which wears on all things, does not spare the energies either of body or mind of a presque [near] Octogenaire. While I could, I did what I could, and now acquiesce chearfully in the law of nature which, by unfitting us for action, warns us to retire."[16]

Yet his pen remained active, his grip firm and hand steady, his penmanship as clear and unmistakable as ever before, right up to the third week of June 1826, when he became permanently bedridden. He could have dictated letters to his daughter or one of the grown grandchildren who lived with him; but he did so rarely, insisting for the most part on managing everything as he always had, maintaining his daily account books and his *Summary Journal of Letters,* in which he made notations about every letter sent and received. By the end of his life, that annotated manuscript extended to several hundred pages.[17]

Despite "paroxysms" of pain, to use his and his doctor's words, the celebrated draftsman pressed on. Integrally concerned with the university he had founded, the layout of which he had personally overseen, he remained attentive and ready to act. At the same time, understandably nostalgic for the Revolution, reluctant to voice publicly that he considered some of its principles in danger of dilution, he deftly prepared the final drafts of what he hoped would be politically definitive letters to friends, the last gifts of his still-agile mind. He did not give in until he was ready.

He died, in his own bed, at 12:50 P.M. on that fiftieth Fourth of July. His keen interest in the affairs of the university at the end of his days did not prove such a distraction that he enjoyed any less the company of the family that surrounded him. On July 2, he informed "the cherished companion of my early life, and nurse of my age," his one surviving daughter, Martha Jefferson Randolph, that he had penned her a particular farewell; she was not to see it until he had closed his eyes on the world, when she opened a certain drawer to which he had directed her. "Life's visions are vanished, it's dreams are no more," went the deathbed adieu *(see frontispiece).* "I go to my fathers, I welcome the shore." Less maudlin than expectant, Jefferson sought a death that promised peace and offered hope—not an assurance but a hope—of reunion with beloved friends in an afterlife.[18]

There is another way to describe Jefferson's strength and vitality. His life was a composition, an unfinished symphony. His never quite complete but well-ordered dreamworld on Earth, the splendid pastoral retreat of Monticello, begun in 1769, did not have its last pillar in place until 1823. But the willful, undiminished composer-arranger (and amateur violinist) gave himself plenty of time to prepare for the next world, and in the spring of 1826 he formulated a serene final movement to life. That is when he put on paper his own cenotaph, a modest obelisk made, he wrote, of "coarse stone." His sketch was folded up with the paper on which he had composed his wife's epitaph forty-four years earlier.[19]

As he kept and chronicled so much of his correspondence, it does not require extensive detective work to discover how Jefferson settled on the obelisk. On February 27, 1826, he received a letter from Robert Mills, an architect and a correspondent of many years. In a P.S. to his letter, Mills remarked that he had designed an obelisk (he underlined the word) for the Bunker Hill monument, the cornerstone of which had recently been laid on the fiftieth anniversary of the battle by their mutual acquaintance, the returning war hero Lafayette. In preparing his reply, Jefferson scribbled in the margin of Mills's letter, just under its salutation, the themes of the letter that most interested him, including the word *obelisk*. On March 3, he answered the architect: "Your idea of the obelisk monument is a very fine one," and proceeded to sketch his own tombstone, tuck it away with keepsakes of his wife's burial, and (within days) write out his final will.[20]

What could be clearer than that Jefferson retained a perfect, passionate sense of order, method, and control to the very end? He was borne through a retirement of seventeen years that was marked by an intense intellectualism and disturbed (if that is the proper word) only by the abundance of visitors to his mountaintop. The Monticello idyll, if it ever truly existed, was broken in his last months. Watchful though he was with regard to his growing indebtedness, that condition suddenly became most urgent in the spring of 1826. Jefferson was more than $100,000 in debt when he died.

As the day of national jubilee neared and the bedridden patriarch lay dying, he called in his grandchildren, one by one, and pronounced parting advice for them. When his mother died on March 31, 1776, at fifty-seven, Jefferson made an emotionless notation in his account book. When his wife, Patty, died on September 6, 1782, at thirty-three, after her sixth pregnancy and a difficult birth, it was simply "my dear wife died this day."[21]

Nowhere did he record for posterity how he missed Patty, though there are hints: A Dutch acquaintance encountering the widower in Annapolis in 1784 termed him "impervious since her loss to the feeble attractions of common society"; but a poignant verse that the couple wrote out together, as she lingered, offers what would seem more than ample evidence of a powerful closing scene. "Time wastes too fast, . . . like clouds of a windy day," Thomas and Patty Jefferson had harmonized, these being the sad words first penned by the author of *Tristram Shandy*, Laurence Sterne. Sterne was the affecting novelist (with a talent for capturing human foibles) whom a young Jefferson looked to for sublime moral sentiments. In the hand of Thomas Jefferson, Sterne's words provide the aching heart with its putative voice: "And every time I kiss thy hand to bid adieu, every absence which follows it are preludes to that eternal separation we are shortly to make!" Thomas outlived the less fortunate Patty by more than four decades, but he kept this souvenir of her death, a square piece of paper, in a drawer by his bedside. There it had lain, presumably unseen by any but him, for the remainder of his life, only to be found by his grieving daughter Martha.[22]

Patty and their other daughter, Maria (she died in 1804), were the "two Seraphs . . . long shrouded in death" whom Jefferson summoned up in his deathbed adieu, written for his surviving daughter. Despite Martha's having produced eleven healthy grandchildren for him, the absence on the mountaintop of her mother and sister had been indescribably felt. These two losses changed Thomas Jefferson most dramatically: After the first, he busied himself away from Monticello, as if memories made it painful to plan a future there; after the second, he was drained of energy and impelled toward retirement.[23]

Certainly this time, when it was Jefferson's end that had come after a long and fruitful career, death arrived with an undeniable appropriateness. We do not know how the grandchildren and great-grandchildren looked as they solemnly paraded into the dying man's chamber, but it is not hard to imagine. It is reliably reported that he addressed "affectionate words of encouragement and practical advice, adapted to their several situations." A few months earlier, before his final illness, Jefferson and his eldest grandson, Thomas Jefferson Randolph (known in the family as "Jeff" or "Jefferson"), had been in conversation about an event likely to occur in midsummer. The grandfather slipped in a remark, with apparent ease, to the effect that he did not expect to be alive in midsummer. He had a good idea about the seriousness of his condition when he spoke with his executor grandson.[24]

To others around this time, he was equally direct. He wrote to the obelisk designer Mills: "My own health is quite broken down. For the last 10 mo. I have been mostly confined to the house. . . . My faculties, sight excepted[,] are very much impaired." By way of a lighthearted refusal to comply with a friendly request from Senator Nathaniel Macon that would have required elaborate historical research on his part, Jefferson told the North Carolina Republican that he was "scarcely able to walk from one room to another, rarely out of pain, and with both hands so crippled that to write a page is nearly the work of a day." Yet he wrote on, several letters each day, some quite lengthy. He remained as sociable as one could in his condition.[25]

Like most of his contemporaries, Jefferson had watched others, young and old, weaken and die from fevers and other agitations that medicine could not yet combat. He had visited the bedside of Benjamin Franklin in Philadelphia in the early months of 1790 and accepted from the dying founder's hand the final installment of his autobiography. He had shuddered at the news that his law professor and mentor, George Wythe, a notably serene and beloved man, had been poisoned by a greedy nephew seeking an early inheritance. Only very recently, Jefferson's eldest grandchild, Anne Randolph Bankhead, had died at Monticello. The thirty-five-year-old succumbed on February 11, 1826, after giving birth prematurely.

As the wife of an aggressive alcoholic, Anne had led a difficult life. Charles Bankhead had gone so far amid drunken tirades as to stab her protective brother Jefferson in his side, on the courthouse steps of Charlottesville. It could not have helped her sick and troubled grandfather to witness another postpartum calamity, a repeat of the heartrending experiences of her Aunt Maria and the grandmother she had never known. Jefferson had been just a few feet away during Anne's final travail, though himself too weak at that time to sit with her. In sorrow and pain, he wrote a short note to his grandson, her brother:

> Bad news, my dear Jefferson, as to your sister Anne. She expired about half an hour ago. I have been so ill for several days that I could not go to see her till this morning, and found her speechless and insensible. She breathed her last about 11 o'clock. Heaven seems to be overwhelming us with every form of misfortune, and I expect your next will give me the *coup de grace.*

The ex-president's doctor, Robley Dunglison, was present at Anne's passing and recorded of his surviving patient: "It is impossible to imagine more poignant distress than was exhibited by him. He shed tears, and abandoned himself to every evidence of intense grief."[26]

The world of medicine that Jefferson subscribed to surmised that those female crises not traceable to uterine structure and function were related to nervous sensibility—feelings and emotions thought more potentially dangerous to the female of the human species. He owned a great many texts relating to medical science that detailed diagnoses and treatments; but, in spite of all he read, Jefferson did not speculate on possible means to save the childbearing women in his family. William Buchan, M.D., the author of *Domestic Medicine*, believed that women who died in labor did so out of a sudden and violent effect of fear. Recovery depended on allowing "necessary evacuations"—that is, for the woman to expel whatever noxious matter or energy remained. "Thus," Buchan instructed, "the [female] sex often fall a sacrifice to their own imaginations, when there would be no danger, did they apprehend none."[27]

Deterministic doctors came up with a host of theories to explain what provoked bodily crises, but interventions were rarely successful, and death was greeted with resignation. It was fairly typical of medical literature at this time for the "thrills" and "vibrations" of the nervous system to be linked to the impressionable mind and metaphorical heart. Prescribing gender roles was just one symptom of the public's desire, under unpromising medical conditions, to sustain health. This thinking led to a flowering of sentimental literature in which delicate women, constantly dying in childbirth, required the equally constant protection of wholesome, self-assured men. Under such conditions, the only chance a woman had to avoid a bitter end was to remain plain and unadorned, to be spiritually healthy and mentally secure, and to make herself immune to seductive promises. Any other kind of literature—such as bold novels in which a wide-eyed young woman is swept away by a dashing hero—or novels that stimulated the female sexual imagination—was thought, in the most literal sense, to be dangerous.[28]

As a national leader, Jefferson had centered his political beliefs on a concept of health and on a quality of sympathy and generosity that extended across the population. He wished to create a democratic society that operated with "harmony and affection" and "a just equilibrium of the passions"—in other words, therapeutic considerations. Today, we continue to relate to his prescription for good government without understanding it as death-defying, that is, without understanding the real force of culture that stood behind it. Neither sentimental literature nor Jefferson's sentimental vocabulary would have existed without the constant presence of death and inconsolable anguish.

The citizens of the United States of America lived with certain understandable fears in 1826. One was that life could cease at any moment, because the state of medical knowledge remained fairly primitive. As their diaries show, they knew well how to grieve, and they expected more of the same. In fact, historians tell us that a migration of population (the broader transmission of disease) caused the life span of the average American to *decline* throughout the first half of the nineteenth century.

As Jefferson's end approached, the republic's founders were nearly all entombed. His own consciousness of the situation emerged in a letter to Maria Cosway, the Anglo-Italian painter whom he had openly adored, many years before, when their paths crossed in Paris. Happily cloistered at the convent school she had established, she wrote to Jefferson in latter days with unfeigned nostalgia, and he responded: "For after one's friends are all gone before them, and our faculties are leaving us too, one by one, why wish to linger in mere vegetation, as a solitary trunk in a desolate field, from which all its former companions have disappeared."[29] This seems a rather morbid view of reality for one so busily occupied with the founding of a great university; still, it reveals Jefferson in the determined grip of time and mortality.

Jefferson never doubted that he had been permitted to live as full a life as was available to one of his generation. He told his surviving daughter, Martha, that he looked forward to whatever condition was to come. This is how his deathbed adieu reads: "I welcome the shore, which crowns all my hopes, or which buries my cares." As life's boisterous emotional sea[30] slowly dissolved into calm and acquiescence, he was ready to leave behind the memory of life's pangs as well as happinesses. In exchange for them, he reached out for the postcorporeal form of his earlier vision, for a different "tranquil permanent felicity."

Medical Concerns

1

Dr. Dunglison's Patient

The most undesirable of all things is long life: and there is nothing I have ever so much dreaded.

THOMAS JEFFERSON TO
DR. BENJAMIN WATERHOUSE,
JANUARY 8, 1825[1]

Thomas Jefferson, who cast a spell over generations, faced his own mortality without flinching, and, at times, with a touch of humor. So was there a bit of caprice in his letter to Dr. Waterhouse of Boston—was he toying with us as well—or did the durable Jefferson really mean it when he described longevity as an "undesirable" outcome?

Yes, he very much meant it. But he also said it for effect. He was referring to life as an accountant might in balancing the "happiness" column against the "pain" column. He had performed similar accounting in the already cited 1816 exchange with John Adams on the matter of his willingness to relive his life, taking the good and bad together. As an octogenarian in 1825, Jefferson was even older than Adams had been when he posed his "frivolous" question. Nothing had altered the Virginian's belief that the world was framed on a principle of benevolence.

Jefferson was still reaping happiness from the constant company of his family; from a university long conceived and, finally, about to commence operation; from a library constantly being refreshed with books of science, philosophy, and the Greek and Roman classics. But even these gifts did not erase the effects of physical debility on the old man's psyche. He had long since exceeded the average life span of an American male, and he was thoroughly convinced that incapacity would very soon outweigh mental acuity, which he still possessed in full. He wanted to avoid living on after he started feeling useless; he wanted to avoid facing a lingering death. With eighteen months of life ahead of him, Jefferson had in mind what we now call "death with dignity." It was his suspicion of what

19

lay just ahead that provoked this statement: "There is nothing I have ever so much dreaded." And to this he added: "Altho' subject to occasional indispositions, my health is too good generally not to give me fears on that subject."[2]

There had been no lessening of his intellectual passion during retirement. In health, he occupied his mind with grand ideas and mass movements, and yet he paid attention to details in such a way that nothing appeared too trivial to be noticed. He responded to any written work that challenged the boundaries of knowledge: a Greek grammar, a dry dock system for the navy. Familiar with the range of his interests, inventors and authors constantly sent along their designs and schemes and productions to the ex-president, requesting comments. And despite his aches and pains, Jefferson eventually obliged them all.

His life of the mind began with an adoration of the natural sublime and extended to aspects of nature that could be measured and modified. As a student of science, mathematics, and medicine, he marveled at the world's endowments and contemplated how human energies could be directed toward improving every quality of life. He insisted that although nature could not be stopped, it could be regulated in small but significant ways—such as flood control. But death was the exception: It held the full force of the oceans, sweeping over everyone and everything. As the philosopher-anthropologist Ernest Becker has reminded us, human values are mental ones, and nature's values are those of the aching, bleeding material body. That Jefferson seems to have intuited as much suggests some of the ways in which his consciousness was a modern one.[3]

Jefferson the worshipper of science was certainly no masochist. And so, getting back to the letter to Dr. Waterhouse, what he feared was not life's termination but the hopeless deterioration preceding it, what the *littérateurs* of his time called "the imbecility of age." It was what correspondents meant when they signed off letters, as the portrait painter and natural historian Charles Willson Peale did in a letter to Jefferson in 1815: "May you, my dear Sir, last until you feel no pain in leaving this world"; and Jefferson did in writing to John Adams in 1820: "I love you with all my heart, and pray for the continuance of your life until you shall be tired of it yourself."[4] In January 1825, Jefferson may not have calculated, with the nearly blind Adams, on the two more Fourth of Julys that the frail ex-presidents would live to greet; but it was his neighbor Adams's declining health that Dr. Waterhouse was reporting on, and that prompted Jefferson to pass judgment on the quality of life generally.

His hair had gone from red to a sandy color; his skin, sensitive to the sun, peeled easily, giving his face what his grandson called a "tettered" appearance.[5] At the time he was writing to Waterhouse, a Harvard medical authority with whom he had corresponded for a quarter century, Jefferson could scarcely take a stroll through his mountaintop garden without fatigue. Yet he still rode his horse, Eagle—a reliable mount with white hind ankles and a white spot on its nose—up to ten miles a day. The old man reckoned that this kind of activity could not last. He awaited the moment, he said, when a slight misstep would "cut short the toughest thread of life." He claimed he was ready, and rather willing, to escape "the evils of dotage." And yet, as his body weakened, he remained a persistent scholar to the end, complaining occasionally of memory loss while in actual fact retaining an impressive mind for detail.[6]

The conscientious Robley Dunglison was Jefferson's physician at the close of this exceptional American life. The twenty-seven-year-old Englishman arrived in Virginia in the spring of 1825, three months after Jefferson had penned his fatalistic letter to Waterhouse. Dunglison had been recruited in London the year before by Jefferson's gifted neighbor, Francis Walker Gilmer, a lawyer and amateur botanist who had been deputed by the Board of Visitors of the University of Virginia to select several of its faculty—including a worthy professor of medicine.

If Dr. Dunglison had been in less of a hurry to win the heart of a young woman, he might never have crossed the ocean. In his matter-of-fact memoir, the doctor says that his destiny turned on the urgency of love: "I was ardently attached to a daughter of Mr. Leadam [a physician], whom I could not expect to be able to marry if I remained in London, for years to come; whilst if I embraced the American offer I could do so immediately." Presenting a pretext for prompt action to his prospective father-in-law, Dunglison made his courtship brief, married Harriette Leadam in London, and set sail for America. In his personal and professional choices, the young doctor was not disappointed.[7]

Nor was Jefferson, who had long expressed deep reservations about inexperienced physicians. On June 24, 1826, which appears to be the last day on which Jefferson picked up his pen to write, this man whose life emerges from his love of the written word finished two meaningful letters: One was an eloquent response to the Washington, D.C., committee that had invited him to be guest of honor at the upcoming Fourth of July festivities; and another, more hastily drawn, was carried down the mountain and over to the university; this letter requested his doctor's presence—"begging me to visit him," Dunglison recorded. The young professor stayed at Monticello, attending his patient constantly during the final days.

It was not just youth that Jefferson distrusted in a physician. He repeatedly told Dr. Dunglison that, as a rule, he put little faith in a profession that meant well but too often did more harm than good. "It is not to physic that I object," he quipped, "so much as to physicians." Though known for his restraint and subtlety rather than direct humor, Jefferson had once joked in front of an uncomfortable medical practitioner (who happened to serve James Monroe and family), that whenever he encountered three physicians together he cast his eyes skyward to see whether a turkey buzzard was hovering nearby.[8]

During his presidency, Jefferson had explained his skepticism to Caspar Wistar, professor of anatomy and midwifery at the University of Pennsylvania, and author, in 1808, of the first American textbook on anatomy. It was generally observable, Jefferson told the distinguished doctor, that mother nature provided relief for most forms of illness: "She brings on a crisis, by stools, vomiting, sweat, urine, expectoration, bleeding, &c., which, for the most part, ends in the restoration of healthy action." The average physician, he went on, "substitutes presumption for knowledge," often taking credit for what nature had accomplished. "I bow to the utility of medicine," he allowed, but only when it was applied to "well-defined forms of disease"; otherwise, in his view, there were too many "adventurous" doctors.

One unnamed physician whose judgment Jefferson trusted had admitted to him that he routinely committed the "pious fraud" of giving out bread pills (placebos) to his patients, rather than take chances with medicines the properties of which were uncertain. Jefferson approved. He was most disturbed by the tendency of the contemporary experimental physician to jump to conclusions on the basis of insufficient data. He called their recourse to "visionary theories" an "ingenious dream." Jefferson allowed that nature's secrets would some day be known, but until then he preferred to leave discovery to the "slow hand of accident" rather than to murderous guesswork. "I would wish the young practitioner, especially, to have deeply impressed on his mind, the real limits of his art," he advised, and "to be a watchful, but quiet spectator of the operations of nature."[9]

The art of humbling doctors was not one that Jefferson indulged in alone. The prominent Philadelphian Dr. Benjamin Rush, his close friend and a signer of the Declaration of Independence, recognized inadequacies in his own medical knowledge when he noted in his *Commonplace Book,* with deadpan humor, the words of a failing patient: "Mrs. Mease told me when dying that among other sins she had to repent of one was too much confidence in my remedies." More cynically, Rush wrote to New York's Dr. David Hosack of the rarity of medical friendships, given jealousy and the competition for business: "Alas! while merchants, mechanics, lawyers, and the clergy live in friendly intercourse with each other, and while even the brutes are gregarious . . . physicians, in all ages and countries, riot upon each other's characters!" It was a common refrain. Benjamin Franklin, as the creator of *Poor Richard's Almanack,* routinely spoofed the medical community with such wonderfully piquant maxims as "He's a fool that makes his doctor his heir" and "There's more old drunkards than old doctors." If physicians held the key to longer and better life, then why did patients who broke all the rules so often survive them?[10]

Jefferson in 1825–1826 confronted a condition that did not allow for light humor. Early in their association, he enjoined Dr. Dunglison to treat him for a painful "irritability of the bladder." His previous doctor, Thomas Watkins, had been unable to afford his patient permanent relief. To Henry Dearborn, his former secretary of war, Jefferson wrote while under his new doctor's care: "My health has become less certain as might be expected with the advance of age. I am suffering at present under an attack of dysury [dysuria: difficult or painful discharge of urine] which confines me to my couch." Dunglison determined that the problem was an enlargement of the prostate gland, and he rode up from the university twenty-one times between May 17 and July 26, 1825, to look in on his patient at Monticello. That summer, he instructed Jefferson in the dangerous self-application of a bougie, a thin metal or elastic gum cylinder that dilated the urethra canal and helped pass urine. By August, Jefferson could write that his health was "tolerably good" and his "senile complaints . . . of uncertain duration" now that he had put himself in the "able hands" of Dr. Dunglison.[11]

The bladder problem had already bothered Jefferson "for some time," Dunglison reported. The gradual intensification of this condition could not but have affected Jefferson's sense of his physical prospects. As he made clear in the 1825 letter to Dr. Waterhouse, if life, with its attendant anxieties, was to be worth living, one's "channels of enjoyment" had to be "in full exercise." A channel was a conduit or passage, and life a different kind of passage—in Jefferson's prose, often a metaphorical journey or voyage. A blockage in the channel of enjoyment, or a blockage or stricture in the channel of the urethra, made life's pain much greater than its remaining pleasures, so that the prolongation of the voyage became an unwished-for thing, and decease the welcome "shore" of Jefferson's deathbed adieu.

He was thankful to his London-trained doctor. The routine Dunglison prescribed did so much to remedy the discomfort that a trusting relationship evolved. When William Short, a diplomat who had commenced his career as Jefferson's secretary in Paris, wrote from Philadelphia urging his ailing friend to see that city's famed urological specialist, Dr. Philip Syngh Physick, Jefferson answered that he had his own Dr. Physick in Dr. Dunglison. The transplanted English doctor years later reflected that, in spite of his suspicions with regard to the medical profession, Jefferson was "one of the most attentive and respectful" of patients.[12]

Politics and Medicine Mix

Before the respected Dunglison arrived in his neighborhood, Jefferson was equally kind and appreciative toward Maryland-born Thomas Gassaway Watkins, a physician known for his very public contentions. Self-defensive and politically opinionated, he had a spotty reputation to which Jefferson was privy, though it seemed to matter little. In an odd way, the doctor's inability to avoid trouble at the hands of ill wishers is what bound the two together. The story of the troubled Thomas Watkins makes it possible for us to understand how tenuous the claims of the medical profession were in post-Revolutionary America. Where it mattered most—among the majority of people who lived outside the reach of those few who were trained in medical schools—medicine was an amateur affair rather than a reputable calling, and for many of its clumsy practitioners a temporary and not always dignified job. Watkins's search, as a man and as a physician, was a search for respectability.

He first drew attention to himself in 1806, as a resident of Nashville, Tennessee. At that time, he became embroiled in controversy with militia general Andrew Jackson, who had not yet been to battle and was not yet considered statesmanlike; rather, in that year Jackson was the unpopular victor in a much publicized duel with a young Nashville attorney. Before this so-called affair of honor, Dr. Watkins had cared for members of Jackson's extended family, having "bled" and prescribed medicines for Jackson's wife, Rachel. But after the sensational killing, Watkins stepped forward to express sympathy for the widow of Jackson's victim.

The hot-tempered general snarled at his doctor: "You . . . have intermeddled in things that common delicacy ought to have prevented you from. Indeed sir, were you not an entire stranger to the feelings of a gentleman and humanity, you would not have wantonly interfered in this business." Accusing Watkins of being "a hypocritical, cowardly assassin," Jackson was prepared to return to the dueling ground. But Dr. Watkins evidently had no interest in a deadly encounter, though in a local tavern he did strike the messenger bearing Jackson's note.[13]

Watkins married into the family of a different Jackson, in east Tennessee, but left the state in 1817 and became Jefferson's personal physician in the autumn of 1819. He lived close by at Glenmore, an estate that had been in the Randolph family, where he sought prominence as a member of the Albemarle County Agricultural Society. Farmer Watkins claimed that he had always wished to make agriculture his "exclusive pursuit," directly stating that his medical practice only got in the way of—"in perpetual confliction" with—his desire to experiment in planting. He sounded a bit like Jefferson himself, who frequently complained that politics kept him from his science, philosophy, and gardening.[14]

Overlooking the soap opera that was Watkins's life, Jefferson quickly gained confidence in the frustrated planter's medical skills, writing to James Madison in January 1821: "As a physician I should put myself in his hands with more confidence than any one I have known in this state, and am indebted to his experience and cautious practice for the restoration of my health."[15] But Dr. Watkins found himself answering critics who got wind of another entanglement, this time concerning his handling of a Tennessee will. The distressed doctor appealed to his old nemesis Jackson, recently retired from the U.S. Army, who, as a presidential hopeful in 1822, was in a forgiving mood. The general wrote directly to Jefferson attesting to the good character of the physician he had challenged to a duel nearly two decades before.[16]

Like his distinguished patient, but with less versatility, Watkins used the language of medicine in taking a political stand. Censuring the banking industry for its role in ruining Virginia farmers' prosperity, he diagnosed the "delirium" that had produced "delusions" and "unhappy paroxysms." And like the physiocratic Jefferson, he assured that it was "from the earth we derived our prosperity and independence, and to the earth, rural and domestic economy, we must return." Watkins added with pungency that an over-dependence on foreign commerce had "ruinous and corrupting consequences" (i.e., "luxury," in the idiom of the day); as the populist he professed to be, he demeaned the "coffeehouse gentry—the windy votaries of commerce." A Jeffersonian maxim followed: "Experiment to be relied on, must be reduced to a science." The ambitious doctor was evidently trying to display what was called "useful knowledge" before his new community.[17]

In 1823, he took an excursion, thinking he had the right connections to insinuate himself into national politics. He cast his eye on the clerkship of the U.S. House of Representatives. In a letter to Jefferson posted from "the road to Tennessee," Watkins requested that Jefferson send him, as Jackson had earlier, a testimonial to his good character—meant to be shown to any Jefferson admirers he should perchance to meet. At the same time, with due diligence, he reported gossip to Jefferson about a plan already afoot to position Jackson for the presidency. Neither of them wanted Jackson to succeed. The doctor's political ambitions were never realized, and he eventually returned to Jefferson's neighborhood.[18]

But not before landing himself in another mess or two. During his absence from Virginia, he learned, "enemies" had been practicing "intrigue and malevolence, directed against my feelings and success." These unspecified efforts were ostensibly intended to impair the doctor's "connexions" to "the Monticello family," and involved, at least in part, his behavior in a case of nonpayment for medical services. He defended himself before his most illustrious patient: "I practiced among you with fidelity and feeling. . . . My first and best feelings and concern were for the lives and salvation of my patients—my last for my necessary fee and fame. Do I deserve to be so traduced!" As far as Jefferson was concerned, no explanation was needed—he understood human behavior, and he fully supported the hypersensitive Dr. Watkins.[19]

The presidential election of 1824 was to be the last that Thomas Jefferson would live to see. And it was the first not to feature a candidate from Virginia.

The South had divided its hopes between Jackson of Tennessee and William Harris Crawford of Georgia, secretary of the treasury under outgoing President James Monroe. Crawford was Virginia's choice—and, in defending the "old republican" embrace of small government and states' rights, Jefferson's as well, though Jefferson refused to make a public declaration. At the core of Jefferson's ideology was a distrust of any (typically northerners) who retained respect for the elitist, pro-growth model of development that seemed British; he had always wished to protect an America that basked in its provincial comforts. Jefferson distrusted Jackson for a different reason: The Tennesseean appeared to him as a militarist lacking a coherent political doctrine.

As the campaign accelerated, Jefferson's doctor found himself in the middle of a new political drama. In September 1823, just before he was due for a visit at Monticello, candidate Crawford suffered an apparent stroke.[20] The ubiquitous Dr. Watkins, though bound for Tennessee at that time, was called to the scene, to the home of the Virginia senator (and former governor) James Barbour. There he treated the ailing candidate for a few weeks when he felt obliged to respond to a "painfully urgent summons" to attend to his family in the west. He had wished to do more for his patient, but when he left he thought that all was as well as could be: Others had wanted to bleed the patient, to draw an additional thirty ounces beyond what had been taken before Watkins's arrival—so as to "save" him. Watkins prevailed on those assembled ("my point carried with difficulty") not to do so.

Nevertheless, Washington was abuzz in rumor, and Watkins learned while in Tennessee that he was being blamed for Crawford's miserable condition. "It is still believed," he wrote to Jefferson a year later, "that the extremity of Mr. Crawford's suffering and danger was induced by excessive bleeding and other maltreatment . . . for which I was responsible!!" Lest there be doubts about his intentions or attentiveness, Watkins declared, "I do not here attempt to defend my medical practice in his case—but only to maintain that I promptly, feelingly & faithfully exerted my best efforts for his benefit." Certain that his insistence on stopping the practice of bleeding had rescued Crawford from deadly medicine, he wrote: "I felt rejoiced at having contributed to so valuable a life."[21]

Jefferson wrote back, reassuring the doctor that he wholeheartedly approved his actions. "That you have met with enemies and backbiters is the lot of all men, and of talents especially. Had you been good for nothing you would have stood in nobody's way and been spoken of as a good creature." Professing not to have heard any of the malicious things said about his personal physician, Jefferson added of his neighbors that they knew better than to fill his ears with such talk: "I hear them not," he reported, referring at once to his self-declared aversion to gossip and to his declining ability to hear.

As to the Crawford matter, Jefferson was even more definitive: "It is entirely understood here that the mischief done him was after you left him. When I visited him I saw that they were killing him by bleeding and mercury and intimated my apprehension cautiously to himself and those about him. . . . I have always lamented he had not been spared one day more so as to have reached us, where under your care he would have been restored in one fortnight. You know that your leaving our neighborhood was a real affliction to us." It may not have been entirely true, but the style was typical of Jefferson's genteel letter-writing posture, and it was the vote of confidence Dr. Watkins had no doubt prayed for.[22]

The much impaired, fifty-two-year-old Crawford stayed in the race and won enough electoral votes to qualify for a runoff in the House of Representatives. Andrew Jackson had earned ninety-nine electoral votes, John Quincy Adams eighty-four, and Crawford forty-one, but Jackson did not have a sufficient number to secure the presidency. In the end, though Jackson had led in popular votes, too, Adams won a majority of the state congressional delegations. Incensed by the backroom politicking that tainted an already convoluted election, the Jacksonians would have to wait four more years to exact revenge. And there was probably nothing that a healthier William Crawford could have done to alter these results—with or without the services of Thomas Watkins and Thomas Jefferson.[23]

The medical practitioners who played so important a role in Jefferson's last years, Watkins and Dunglison, appear never to have met. But the story does not end there: Some years after Jefferson's death, the celebrated Dr. Dunglison would have occasion to treat President Andrew Jackson for a pain in his side—and not before having been called upon by former Presidents Madison and Monroe as well. How odd it seems, then, that Dr. Watkins began his career as Jackson's physician and went on to become Jefferson's intimate; and Dunglison, who came to America at gentle Jefferson's behest, eventually tended to the rough-hewn Jackson.

Dunglison was Watkins's opposite, a professional who was unseduced by the prospect of becoming a Virginia planter and took little apparent interest in national politics. During Jefferson's prime, however, the political and scientific worlds had been conjoined in noteworthy ways. In a tradition established by the proactive Franklin, scientists and physicians held government appointments in the new United States: Mathematician-astronomer David Rittenhouse, a hero to Jefferson, served in the Pennsylvania Assembly and as director of the U.S. Mint; Dr. Rush, a Pennsylvania member of the Continental Congress and the constitutional ratifying convention, was treasurer of the Mint during Rittenhouse's tenure there; William Shippen, a medical doctor, professor of surgery, and member of the American Philosophical Society who helped found both the University of Pennsylvania and Princeton, served in the Continental Congress. (He was well known to Jefferson, having inoculated him against smallpox in 1766.) Josiah Bartlett of New Hampshire was another signer of the Declaration who was trained in medicine; his son, also a practicing physician, served one term in Congress. Dr. Hugh Williamson, surgeon general to North Carolina troops during the Revolution, published on medical matters, and was later a member of the House of Representatives. Dr. David Ramsay, who practiced in Charleston, South Carolina, attended medical school in Philadelphia, served in the Continental Congress, and was the author of the first history of the American Revolution (1789). Jefferson's secretary of war, the New Englander Henry Dearborn, began his career as a physician. The list goes on. As president, Jefferson was famed for inviting congressmen to dinner and directing long conversations about scientific subjects without reference to politics.[24]

Among the friends and correspondents of his late years, Jefferson counted several medical doctors. After Rush and Wistar died in 1813 and 1818 respectively, the most noteworthy was Waterhouse, a pioneer in vaccination, whose work Jefferson championed. As president, he had personally collaborated with the New Englander to set up the first smallpox vaccination clinics in the South, and he maintained extensive records charting the success of their joint project. He saw to it that Lewis and Clark took a supply of vaccine on their westbound journey.[25] As an ex-president, Jefferson shared private thoughts with his physician-correspondents, sometimes venturing into history, politics, religion, and general education, as well as medical science. And though Dunglison and Watkins were themselves very different people, Jefferson appreciated both, or at least made both feel entirely welcome at Monticello.

"whether you may have had gonorrhœa"

As for the matter of succession, there was no ceremonial changing of the guard in the spring of 1825, when Dr. Watkins left and Dr. Dunglison came on. Only a day or so before the steady Englishman's arrival in Charlottesville, the more impulsive Tennesseean left town, prevailing upon Jefferson for the loan of his trusted servant Wormley Hughes to start him off on the road south: "I am under a thousand obligations to you, my Dear Sir," the departing Dr. Watkins wrote to Jefferson. "Since I got so much hurt by a fall from my gigg two summers ago I am timid with an untied horse." He needed Wormley to help him calm the animal; after a day's chaperoned ride, Watkins sent Hughes back to his master with the appreciative letter, "praying for the restoration of your health."[26]

Watkins may have been timid around horses, but he was not timid in the three-page statement he left his patient, which gave suggestions for continued care:

Dysuria, which is the proper denomination of your case, may proceed from various diseased states of any part of the urinary canal. . . . There would seem to be a chronic state of inflammation or ulceration of the prostatic part of the urethra or neck of the bladder or perhaps both. I have not thought it proper to enquire whether you may have had in early life any continuance of gonorrhœa.[27]

Gonorrhea? Was Jefferson's private physician of five years (on and off) freely speculating, or was he making a logical inference on the basis of prior knowledge?

His question appears innocent. The word *continuance* here does not indicate that Jefferson admitted having suffered from a venereal disease at one time, and that it might or might not have *continued* to afflict him after its initial appearance. In the vocabulary of this era, "continuance" could just as well mean "duration,"[28] in which case the question is being posed, without the supposition of knowledge, to mean: "Did you have to *endure,* at any time in early life, an eruption of gonorrhea?" The answer could be yes or no; either way, no answer was forthcoming. Watkins had ceased to serve as Jefferson's doctor, and had not felt comfortable, at any point before his departure, in directly posing this question to Jefferson.

Believing that contracting gonorrhea "might have predisposed the urethra to diseased lodgment" in Jefferson's later life, Watkins noted: "The increased frequency of your promptings to discharge urine, is rather indicative of inflammation about the neck of the bladder—the occasional sprouting of the current—of some obstruction or stricture—spasmodic & temporary or ulcerative and permanent." He called for the application of the purgative castor oil "and warm water fomentations" in the immediate area, as well as abstinence from physical exercise and irritating food and drink, including wine. If this regimen failed, Watkins proposed "half a grain of opium with one grain of calomel [mercurous chloride], every night for a few weeks." He assured Jefferson that his condition was not life threatening.

Watkins was content to yield authority to his successor. "I am happy to reflect that you will have so excellent a resource in professor Dunglison," he wrote at the end of his evaluation. Presumably, his intention was that Dr. Dunglison would read the document and comprehend what Watkins verbosely called "the hystory of your sufferings consequent upon your present indisposition." Dunglison's solution, as above stated, was to teach Jefferson to use a bougie, an early version of the urinary catheter. This instrument succeeded in alleviating his obstructive uropathy, or blockage of urine. Watkins had mentioned the bougie to Jefferson, but had not pursued its use.

As to a younger Jefferson's sex life, we cannot say whether he was a virgin when he married the widow Martha Wayles "Patty" Skelton in 1772, or whether his sexual behavior had exposed him to venereal disease. Obscure references in

Jefferson's *Memorandum Books* in the summer and autumn of 1770, written in shorthand code, give women's names—one is a married woman—and may indicate sexual encounters. (Indeed, the shorthand entries are graphically depicted by the editors of the *Memorandum Books,* with the thought that they might bear such a meaning.) Subsequently, from Paris in 1785, and by now a widower, Jefferson wrote home anxiously to a Virginia acquaintance whose son was about to embark on a European tour. In the letter, Jefferson was exceedingly direct in cautioning American men against exposure to the "luxury and dissipation" of European ways. To him, an impressionable American "is led by the strongest of all the human passions into a spirit for female intrigue destructive of his own and others happiness, or a passion for whores destructive of his health." Were his moralistic pronouncements from Paris the result of a painful personal experience, or observation of the conduct of others around him, or simply formed from stories he had heard? It is impossible to know. And then, of course, there is the speculation about his sexual relationship with his slave Sally Hemings, which, if it took place, began after 1787, after she arrived in Europe. If Jefferson did contract gonorrhea—which is by no means clear and, on the surface, seems less than likely—we cannot determine how or when the disease occurred.[29]

In analyzing Watkins's report, modern medical specialists are generally doubtful that Jefferson suffered a venereal complaint earlier in life. True, this was an age, before antibiotics, when symptoms of the disease could have disappeared, only to lead in later life to urethral strictures causing chronic pain and difficulty urinating. Yet if Jefferson had contracted the sexually transmitted disease, he most likely would have developed urethral and urinary problems much earlier, and there is no evidence of it before the 1820s.

Thomas Watkins might have been a magnet for political trouble, but his medical diagnosis was in the main correct. Jefferson's problem, prostatic hypertrophy, was benign, and did not, at least directly, cause his death. On the other hand, if the condition developed into a bacteriological infection after his repeated use of the bougie, it might have played a role in worsening Jefferson's medical outlook.[30]

"an old crazy carcase like mine"

Jefferson's extant copy of *The Modern Practice of Physic,* published in 1817, opens to the page that discusses intestinal disorders.[31] Though he balanced friendly advice against published clinical studies and medical "self-government," he never quite understood his own digestive ailments.

His medical history is that of a generally fit man who kept to a moderate diet and who exercised regularly. "He was never a great eater," reported Edmund

Bacon, Monticello's overseer during the retirement years, "but what he did eat he wanted to be very choice."[32] His library contained more than a hundred medical guides and treatises on subjects ranging from general medicine and the fairly recent practice of inoculations to dentistry, gout, rabies, venereal disease, and hysterics. For longer than a half-century, each morning upon rising he bathed his feet in ice-cold water, which he believed prevented the onset of colds.[33] He could not recall ever having had a fever that lasted for more than twenty-four hours.

From 1764, as he was becoming a lawyer, through his retirement from political office, Jefferson suffered from what he called his "periodical head ach," or "fits," that were apparently caused by tension; they lasted from sunrise to sunset and were at times so debilitating that he could not function for days on end, choosing to closet himself in darkness while he waited for the pain to go away; and if he worked at all during these episodes, it was in the evening, by candle-light. He never recorded another of his "periodical" headaches after retiring to Monticello at the end of his two-term presidency in 1809. He read constantly, and his eyes remained strong: "I use spectacles only at night," he wrote to Charles Willson Peale in 1824.[34]

Jefferson's worst extended episode as a suffering retiree occurred in 1818–1819, when he endured unremitting rheumatism. He first encountered the disease in a mild form in 1808, when he found walking painful. He next experienced "a total prostration of the muscles of the back, hips and thighs," in 1811. In 1813, he was sufficiently troubled that he was "almost tempted" to permit a "medical gentleman" to try out a new machine on him, invented by a Lynchburg, Virginia, doctor, that was called "a Panacea." A tin tube blew alcohol fumes "into the bed of the patient, under the bedclothes." But, on second thought, as Jefferson explained self-mockingly to Dr. Samuel Brown, "I consider that an old crazy carcase like mine is not a safe subject for new experiments."[35]

In 1818, when his rheumatism returned, Jefferson finally sought relief by traveling to Virginia's fashionable Warm Springs to bathe in the curative waters. He ended up with painful boils over his body. "A large swelling on my seat," he wrote to his daughter, "increasing for several days past in size and hardness disables me from sitting but on the corner of a chair. Another swelling begins to manifest it self to-day on the other seat. . . . Perhaps these swellings may yet disappear, but I have little hope of that." Back at Monticello, his hapless doctor at the time exacerbated the problem by applying mercury and sulfur, so that Jefferson languished for weeks more, unable to leave his house. One of his literate slaves, Hannah, expressed her concern in a note to her master: "I was sorry to hear that you was so unwell." In the summer of 1819, just as financial panic devastated the Virginia economy and put extreme pressure on Jefferson personally, his rheumatism recurred, the swellings more serious than before. He purchased flannel to wrap his shoulders, wrists, and knees, but was only slowly restored to comfort. It was in the aftermath of these events that Dr. Watkins entered the picture.[36]

Although dysuria may have played a role in bringing on his final illness, the official cause of Thomas Jefferson's death was chronic diarrhea. His bowel troubles dated back at least to his first year as president. In 1803, "after all my life having enjoyed the benefit of well formed organs of digestion, and departation," Jefferson confided his complaint in his old friend Dr. Rush, who had bravely, if ineffectively, combated the yellow fever epidemics of the 1790s. Rush in turn wrote to Jefferson about an "old nurse" who, after a three-year stretch of diarrhea, was cured in one month by "drawing the breasts of a woman . . . and swallowing her milk." Cow's milk, with sugar added, would have had the same effect.

Rush provided him with several other solutions: (1) the stomach should never be full or empty; (2) horseback riding is preferred to walking or sitting in a carriage; (3) to avoid "fatigue of body," resist "midnight studies" and go to bed no later than 10:00 P.M.; (4) permit proper excretion through the skin—perspiration—through mid-day bathing: cold baths in summer and warm baths in cool weather. A layer of flannel was to be worn next to the skin, and feet kept warm; for the feet, Rush insisted, were "the avenues of half the paroxysms of all chronic diseases when cold." He also said that he had witnessed "the happiest effects" from a syrup made by boiling "oak galls" and cinnamon in water, straining and combining with brandy and sugar, and reducing over a slow fire.[37]

The model of the human body was thought of as a system of energy and economy. For this reason, evacuations were no less critical to the medical imagination than a healthy appetite.[38] In the first year of his retirement, Jefferson planted rhubarb, which was used medicinally to relieve diarrhea.[39] In 1815, immediately after selling his personal library to the government (to replenish the Library of Congress, which had been incinerated by British troops the year before), Jefferson requested from a Washington bookseller James Ewell's *Medical Companion.* Dr. Ewell, originally from Savannah, Georgia, had set up a practice in the nation's capital and had dedicated his 1808 medical guide to then President Jefferson. Ewell described diarrhea as "a purging without sickness or pain," caused by "acid or putrid elements—obstructed perspiration—acrid bile—drinking bad water— violent passions, or a translation of morbid matter of other diseases to the bowels," and recommended "a dose of rhubarb or castor oil, followed by forty drops of laudanum [the widely available opiate] at night."[40]

In 1822, Jefferson commiserated with fellow sufferer Judge Spencer Roane of Richmond. Euphemistically referring to "the visceral complaint," he expressed his conviction that the stagnant air of the Virginia tidewater was somehow the cause of Roane's diarrhea; without mentioning Rush, Jefferson noted helpfully that the best advice he had received was that of the English physician Thomas Sydenham, who, more than a century before, had prescribed, in Jefferson's words, "long journies on a hard trotting horse, and that he found infallible." (In this instance, the Harvard-trained Dr. William Eustis had referred him to Sydenham, and corroborated the efficacy of the old method from his own experience.) And so, concluded Jefferson, "a couple of hours riding every day relieved me from a case tolerably manifest, although but incipient."[41]

It was common, as a part of daily conditioning, to monitor bowel movements. In 1802, a friend of a friend, Sir John Sinclair, sent President Jefferson a copy of his book on good health. He observed that excess sleep inhibited the desired daily morning discharge, and confirmed that in advanced years "loose and abundant stools" were as much a problem as irregularity; Britain's Sinclair agreed with Philadelphia's Rush that keeping the feet warm and wearing flannel close to the skin not only promoted a healthy perspiration but also strengthened the bowels. In the same mission, he noted, red wine was preferable to white.[42]

Diarrhea was understood to have various causes. According to Dr. Buchan's *Domestic Medicine,* that which was defined as a normal "salutary evacuation" did nothing to weaken the person. Diarrhea proceeding from "violent passions or affections of the mind," however, was best treated, as Jefferson's was, with an opiate, until the antispasmodic effect was felt and "ease, cheerfulness and tranquility of mind" returned. Any diarrhea, normal or abnormal, was to be answered only with certain food preparations: rice, boiled with milk and flavored with cinnamon, was one; "the lighter sorts of flesh-meat" was another. As to drink, the patient could take thin water-gruel, or a weak broth made from lean veal or sheep's head. (Dr. Rush preferred peppermint tea.) But not beef or chicken broth, or meats of hard digestion. Also to be avoided was exposure to "cold, moisture, or whatever may obstruct the perspiration. . . . All violent passions, as fear, anger, &c. are likewise carefully to be guarded against."[43] But how was a president, especially one so embroiled in partisan debate as Jefferson was, to guard against predictable feelings?

"affections of the mind"

Jefferson was, alas, only human, and he responded to his physical and psychological environments. In attempting to understand his introspective personality, we can ask how, over time, he assessed the interactions of his own mind and body. The first record of such reflections occurs at college age, when he admitted to an inordinate fear of the water; and in the 1780s, he would scrupulously study the history of a vessel before he (or a loved one) boarded it for a journey by sea.

If the debilitating headaches of his pre-retirement years were related to stress, then perhaps his diarrhea had a psychological component, too. He worried as much about his public reputation as he did the health of his family; he thought out and painstakingly crafted letters that he knew would descend to posterity; he recorded every purchase, every transaction, and, as an architect, he calculated to the fraction of an inch, though construction crews of this age never even came close; as president, he charted over his eight years in Washington the dates when several varieties of vegetables came to market. In sum, he ordered his daily life with exceptional care and concentration.

Jefferson's generation devoted much attention to the unwanted side effects of mental stimulation. The Swiss medical theorist Samuel Auguste David Tissot (1728–1797) was perhaps the most influential among those who studied the ways in which men wore themselves out, mentally and physically. His detailed anthology concerning human sexuality was the Kinsey report of its day. Jefferson owned his collected works in French as well as the single-volume treatise *Tissot's Advice,* which he owned in English. The Scottish William Buchan produced his highly popular *Domestic Medicine* as a tribute to the Swiss doctor's groundbreaking work.[44]

In his prime, Jefferson the unrelenting natural philosopher and political moralist was himself a candidate for Dr. Tissot's science, as he evidently realized. As a man with a highly structured daily routine, and not known for his spontaneity, he could not escape Tissot's warning that "a strict habit is downright servitude," and that some men of letters became "such slaves to their *régimes* that the spirit became completely dependent upon the body."[45] Tissot was manifestly concerned with the lives of scholars, because he considered their nerves especially reactive, and their digestion poor. Geniuses of the first order were often reduced to objects of pity, listless and forgetful, who suffered severe stomach and intestinal cramps. There was a consensus among clinical specialists that a pathological sympathy existed between the head and the stomach, and we have every reason to believe that Jefferson thought of his own irritable bowel in this way. Tissot went so far as to warn scholars against taking up new subjects in their later years: New ideas that brought into action previously unexercised fibers in the brain would do violence to the nerves generally. The entire mind and body would suffer as a result.[46]

Aside from being known for commanding moderation, Tissot notably warned of the dangers of "self-pollution," or masturbation. Like intensive study, masturbation was seen as draining and unproductive, wasting the vital energy of the body. Why Tissot and others thought that the social elite suffered especially in this way is less clear, though the logic Tissot followed led him to conclude that nervous degeneration among those who studied excessively carried over into their seminal fluid. This explained for him "why it is so rare that great

DE

LA SANTÉ

DES

GENS DE LETTRES,

PAR

Mᴿ. TISSOT, D. M.

De la S.R.de LONDRES, de l'Ac.de BASLE, & des Soc.
Œc.de BERNE, & de Phyſ. exp. de ROTTERDAM.

TROISIEME ÉDITION AUGMENTÉE.

Morbus eſt etiam aliquis per ſapientiam mori.

PLINE.

A LAUSANNE,

Chez FRANÇ. GRASSET & COMP.

Libraires & Imprimeurs.

M. DCC. LXXV.

Title page of famed Swiss medical theorist Samuel Auguste David Tissot's popular study of the mental and physical risks linked to poor diet and exercise, and unfulfilling sexual behavior. This was translated into English as *An Essay on Diseases Incident to Literary and Sedentary Persons.* Jefferson owned Tissot's collected works in French, and appears to have regulated his daily life in line with Tissot's counsel.

men have sons worthy of themselves." One could never be entirely secure about the effects of mental exertions, and Jefferson reflected this belief when he told Dr. Rush that he had retired after two terms not only because of George Washington's political precedent but because, at the age of sixty-six, he feared "the progress of decay"—the relaxation of nerve fibers, the reduction of mental vigor—if he were to remain in office. "The sedentary character of my public occupations sapped a constitution naturally sound and vigorous."[47]

Jefferson's friend Dr. Waterhouse took his cue from the European medical community in repeating that the sedentary life to which intellectuals were prone damaged their health. "Sedentary thoughtfulness will wear out the body and generate diseases that shorten life," he wrote. "A dyspeptic stomach, emaciated body, and irritable feelings, compose the heavy tax, which men of fine intellects and deep study pay for their eminence. . . . Here the body is not *worn* but *rusts* out." In every part of the transatlantic medical community, it was a given that mental exhaustion threatened to bring on every imaginable ailment.[48]

Sedentary men were also said to have a tendency to overindulge in alcohol and tobacco. Dr. Ewell's guide warned: "The lovers of wine and cider should remember that those beverages, however pleasant and exhilarating, have a tendency to aggravate all diseases of the kidneys and bladder."[49] These were two of the main beverages served at Monticello. More sensitive to the dangers of hard liquor, Jefferson wished to promote brewery operations in his neighborhood as a substitute for the ever-increasing popularity of whiskey, which, he claimed, "kills one-third of our citizens and ruins their families."[50]

As he aged, he discovered all too well, if he had not seen long before, what the abuse of alcohol could do. His eldest grandchild, Anne, was terrorized by her violent husband, Charles Bankhead. Early in the marriage, a longtime Jefferson friend, Eliza House Trist, lamented: "Bankhead has turn'd out a great sot always frolicking and carousing at the Taverns of the Neighbourhood. Poor Ann I feel for her." "With respect to Bankhead," Jefferson wrote several years after this, in an attempt at fair-mindedness, "if ever he becomes a sober man, there will be no difficulty of reconciliation on Anne's account, but as long as he is subject to drink, his society is dangerous & we shall reject it."[51]

Waterhouse was particularly harsh on those who poisoned their systems with Virginia tobacco. Whether smoked or chewed, tobacco was "pernicious," a "nasty custom" that turned faces "pallid" and made a person "restless, and dissatisfied with himself." The long-term effects were obvious to him: They led to a sedentary existence. "As a sedentary man advances in life, he perspires less, while his lungs labour more." Jefferson, who reluctantly grew tobacco but never smoked, escaped the pallor and disorder of the smoker's fate by breathing good air and preserving his ruddy features. He approved Waterhouse's denunciation of tobacco, writing realistically of the doctor's treatise: "However sound in its principles, I expect it will be but a sermon to the wind."[52]

In the gendered philosophy of nervous activity, men were thought "naturally" more suited for the stimulation provided by books and scientific investi-

gation, women for the delicate tasks of ordering the home and influencing children. Male and female obsessions were distinguished along similar lines: Men,
filled with public ambition, could excessively crave intellectual accomplishment; women, bound to domestic reality, could succumb to obsessions of the
heart. A woman's temperament was the more readily excitable, vulnerable to
her own feelings; but a man operated under stronger outward passions and
consequently indulged his sexual appetite.[53] Wariness about polluting the body
conspicuously absorbed Jefferson and his physician friends as they speculated
constantly on the natural environment and the interaction of male and female
impulses. The accuracy of their speculations would never be effectively resolved
in any of their lifetimes, however. The best they could expect was to do no harm
to themselves.

Tissot was an eighteenth-century thinker, and Waterhouse began writing
about the smoker's vice during Jefferson's presidency early in the nineteenth. At
the time of Jefferson's death in 1826, a new breed of American moral reformers
was just gearing up to root out contamination in a society that appeared increasingly coarse as it democratized politically. They were something like
cultists, applying methods of religious faith in pursuit of better health. Less
concerned with the body of medical knowledge bequeathed by classical antiquity, the reformers capitalized on Tissot's success by intensifying their concern
with the "solitary vice" of masturbation, at the same time associating human
physiology more and more with the diseased imagination and a subversion of
knowledge. In a combined effort to uphold middle-class respectability and religious discipline, they preached reliance on a self-restraining inner voice. At the
same time, they doubted they could succeed without regulating by legal means
what people read. If the pursuit of happiness was beginning to be associated
with vernacular culture and commercial erotica, reformers forecast the increasing abuse of medical knowledge. Texts that might stimulate, even inadvertently,
had to be suppressed. Victorian values were on the horizon.[54]

But Jefferson was a moralist of a different kind. He supported that which
tended to dignify and promote human happiness. He engaged in a quiet pursuit
of inner contentment, what we have already identified in his phrase "tranquil
permanent felicity." At about the time Jefferson was heading for college, the
Scottish philosophe Adam Smith was explaining the concept that we now think
of as Jeffersonian: "Happiness consists in tranquility and enjoyment," Smith
wrote. "Without tranquility there is no enjoyment; and where there is perfect
tranquility there is scarce anything which is not capable of amusing."[55]

Tranquility was considered a natural, or primitive, state of man, which in advanced society was rather an ideal. In old age, Jefferson related it at once to a
medical state and to happy thoughts ("not to be pained in body, nor troubled

in mind"). This was a dictum of the Greek philosopher Epicurus, which Jefferson expressed simply: "To procure tranquility of mind we must avoid desire and fear, the two principal diseases of the mind."[56] When Jefferson used the word *tranquility* during his retirement, it was as often to appeal for release from political disputation. Though inundated with requests by letter, he would say, as to a Georgia politician in 1815, that he wished for his opinion to be read but not disseminated, and above all to be kept out of the newspapers; for, in this evening period of life, he was striving "to enjoy the privileged tranquility of a private and unmeddling citizen."[57]

By remaining conscious of his duty to exhibit "justice" and "magnanimity," the tranquility-seeking Jefferson was ever conscious of his behavior toward acquaintances, guests, and strangers. This was why he answered so many of the letters that came from correspondents whom he had never met. His graciousness was not just good breeding but a moral quality known alternately as "firmness" and "self-command." Having an active commitment to justice, a predisposition to be magnanimous, and a steady ability to convey firmness and self-command was the sum of eighteenth-century masculinity. These same qualities proved useful, too, in political life, as Jeffersonians showed an inclination to place the adjective *firm* before the word *republican*.

"a keen appetite"

Many medical writers of the age placed emphasis on maintaining a balance between diet and one's nervous constitution. George Cheyne was the first to document the clinical cases of "those whose Nervous Complaints were cured by Medicine, under a common, though temperate Diet." Sir John Sinclair catalogued the qualities necessary for long life: (1) Air (2) Liquid Food (3) Solid Food (4) Digestion (5) Labour, or Exercise (6) Sleep (7) The Government of the Passions.[58]

Jefferson was himself conscientious in trying to live and eat moderately, particularly in the years after his digestive complaints increased in frequency. As Dr. Waterhouse noted: "The first effect of violent grief or trouble of mind is deprivation of the powers of digestion." Observing loss of appetite after a person received sudden "afflicting news," he posed, "Now what connexion is there between a piece of bad news and a man's stomach, full or empty?" He answered the question as follows: "Because the animal spirits or action of the nerves, whatever be the secret cause of their power, are called off to supply and support the tumultuous agitation of the brain, and the stomach with all its appendages and secretions is left powerless and paralytic." Taking a holistic approach, Waterhouse advised: "Perfect health requires the temperate action of the vital influence through every part of the system. In perfect health food is sought with appetite, enjoyed with relish, and digested with facility."[59]

Tempering his scholarly exertions, Jefferson ate little meat (his granddaughter Ellen described his meat as "a seasoning for his vegetables"), exercised daily by walking and riding, took up gardening with his grandchildren, and slept between six and seven hours. As Waterhouse prescribed, "A ride with the cheerful scenery of a new and beautiful country will give you health, vigour, and vivacity, sound sleep, and a keen appetite." No drug matched "a regular course of moderate exercise." The penalty for ignoring the doctor's advice was chronic illness, including "depraved appetite" and "the long and gloomy train of nervous disorders."[60]

In his sixty-eighth year, the year before he died, Dr. Rush described his daily regimen to Vine Utley, a fellow physician:

> I generally sleep about seven hours in the four-and-twenty, and spend from three to seven hours at my desk every day, according to the greater or less hurry of my business. I continue to prefer tea and coffee with their usual accompaniments to all other kinds of aliment. At dinner, but at no other time, I eat sparingly of animal food, with the common garden vegetables of our country, and generally drink one glass and a half of old Madeira wine after them. I never drink ardent spirits in any way nor at any time.[61]

Dr. Utley wrote to Jefferson seven years later, describing Rush's regimen and asking the now seventy-six-year-old Virginian for his own secret to longevity. Here was his reply:

> Like my friend the Doctor, I have lived temperately, eating little animal food, and that not as an aliment, so much as a condiment for the vegetables, which constitute my principal diet. I double, however, the Doctor's glass and a half of wine, and even treble it with a friend; but halve its effects by drinking the weak wines only. The ardent wines I cannot drink, nor do I use ardent spirits in any form. Malt liquors and ciders are my table drinks, and my breakfast, like that also of my friend, is of tea and coffee.

At this point not yet seriously troubled with a recurrence of the diarrhea he earlier complained of to Dr. Rush, he added: "I have been blest with organs of digestion which accept and concoct, without ever murmuring, whatever the palate chooses to consign to them, and I have not yet lost a tooth by age." Dr. Utley was so impressed that he framed Jefferson's "account of your Physical habits," and displayed it where visitors to his home could not miss it. "It is an example of strict temperance," he later wrote.[62]

For Jefferson, a human being was not powerless, and health, more often than not, was a state of mind. Influenced equally by the medical writings of the age and his own experience, he liked to think that positive activity served the heart and cleared the head, just so long as a body did not lapse into sedentary pursuits. For this reason, he thought horseback riding prompted internal as well as external movement, the combined force of the muscles stimulating circulation.

In his personal life, in all Jefferson did, he was conscientious and actively sought to counteract whatever depressive force challenged his accustomed outlook, temperate and optimistic, or threatened to bring on restlessness and inner dissatisfaction. He was so closely attuned to the stealthy threat of nervous disorders in his world—it was apparent in the books on his shelves and in the tone of so many of his written texts—that he *strained* to maintain a moderate means of living, as paradoxical as that might sound. He constantly reassured himself that he was living properly.

He sought advice and gave advice. Well into his retirement years, he retained the high level of confidence and moral self-regard that such self-monitoring had conditioned him to feel, despite the physical deterioration he increasingly reported in his correspondence. His regular diet of vegetables, with moderate portions of meat and wine, bears this out. His friend Dr. Waterhouse insisted that there was "an inseparable sympathy and a beautiful balance" between the processes of breathing and digestion,[63] and Jefferson concurred. The quest to maintain that sympathetic balance was subservient to nothing and, in his mind, only surrendered to the ultimate power of nature over the doomed human organism.

Jefferson believed that he was simply practical and humane in his politics, when his approach to government in fact re-created the personal system (the self) that his study of the human body had led him to prefer. The republic was grounded, then, in a hybrid faith that consisted of the concepts he applied to his health: (1) structured diet and exercise, and (2) a "natural" sensibility.

In the first, daily physical exercise translated as reduced spending (only what was needed), to insure the longevity of the organism/body politic; its opposite, sedentary speculation, or "idleness," led to the growth of immoderate passions, or an unhealthy love of wasteful, opulent display—what was then called "luxury." As for the second feature of Jefferson's medico-political faith, "sensibility," this is a word that tends to be used nonspecifically today, but which encompassed almost every quality of feeling in Jefferson's age. Jefferson understood it as "susceptibility," which was felt as a pleasant or unpleasant disruption within the body—but more remarkably as susceptibility translated into social policy on the basis of philanthropic inclinations. Well-honed nerves led to superior taste and imaginative commitment—socially progressive legislation. Others, across two centuries, have identified Jefferson as a political thinker influenced by pure science and natural philosophy; but no one until now has presented him as a politician who was in effect a medical practitioner.

Medical reality as Jefferson understood it shaped his thinking about a host of ostensibly unconnected issues. As a self-confident man of letters and a discriminating patient, Jefferson as he aged intellectualized what he felt viscerally—his own deterioration. He divided the human experience into cultural categories: pleasure and pain, courage and timidity, calculated temperance and passionate excess, purity and pollution (of the human body and external environment alike). These so-called natural passions are all, in fact, elements of culture.

Despite the humbling experience of physical weakness and decay, Jefferson continued to toil on behalf of the next generation. It seems almost peculiar that the various, and often agonizing, ailments that he endured did not produce an unusual amount of distress among the doctors, friends, and loved ones who interacted with him. Indeed, it tells us a great deal that Jefferson was regarded as an unusually hale and hearty man for his day. He sometimes, though infrequently, meditated on the death that awaited, but he was more preoccupied with comprehending life.

In the self-revealing letter of 1785 in which Jefferson celebrated the "tranquil permanent felicity" with which he imagined his country blessed, he asserted that the tranquil character of American society enabled citizens to follow "steadily those pursuits which health and reason approve." It is significant that he paired "health" with "reason." To a man of the Enlightenment, "reason" harnessed all knowledge; the Enlightenment equated science with progress. And it is just as meaningful that "health" bespoke America's advantages over others in the world.[64]

2

A Sensational Vocabulary

On the basis of sensation, of matter and motion, we may erect the fabric of all the certainties we can have or need.

THOMAS JEFFERSON TO JOHN ADAMS,
AUGUST 15, 1820

Jefferson created a sensation, one might say, as he lay on his deathbed on the morning of July 4, 1826. Nicholas P. Trist, the husband of his granddaughter Virginia, sat beside him, listening to his breathing. The young man began a letter at 9:15 A.M. and finished it at a quarter till noon—just sixty-five minutes before Jefferson would cease to live. "He has been dying since yesterday morning," Trist wrote, "and until twelve o'clock last night, we were in momentary fear that he would not live to see his own glorious Fourth." To give satisfaction to those present (because he was fully aware that his condition was hopeless), Jefferson had deferred to his doctor, taking brandy, a bit of boiled rice, medicine for pain. His due diligence matched the certainty he possessed that the end was near. Over the several days preceding, he had repeatedly prepared his family for this moment. That consciousness of inevitability, his verbalizing that he understood what was happening inside his body, caused those attending him to marvel at the persistent control he exercised over his world, or what Trist called "his wonted inflexibility."[1]

Everything in the written record instructs us that this was how Thomas Jefferson imagined a man of science and philosophy ought to look forward to his final rest. All his life, he had divided his time between speculation on natural phenomena and regulation of human society—in either case, improving the world by achieving a better understanding of it. He studied the human body so as to expand his capacity to reason. But, as I have already hinted, to view his interest in science and his political vision separately is to mislead, because science also fueled the politics of liberation for him. His entire conception of America was predicated on a philosophical purpose that mirrored the function of medical research: experiment leading to the mastery of nature, to health, to moral improvement, to a better quality of life, to greater human dignity.

A British visitor to Monticello during Jefferson's retirement years described the aging president as a man in different guises, and in particular as a man who "shun[ned] none of the humbler duties of private life." During his brief stay, the visitor looked upon an enthusiast of literature, an avid gardener, a "good neighbour," and thought it curious besides that Jefferson served not just as an unpaid local lawyer but also as "physician . . . of his vicinity."[2] It sounds quaint, but should soon make more sense.

Science could not do without generosity. Too few students of history recognize that the Age of Reason was more than an age of abstract philosophy. Jefferson studied and practiced medicine at home, and occasionally gave out advice. The power of sentiment, like the passion that augmented science, gave him something to do as well as to write about. And because he was Thomas Jefferson, when he wrote, or acted, he changed the way people thought; even small things he did were remembered.

Science solved, sentiment enacted. This is the essence of Jefferson's affinity for the Enlightenment. Its language imbued him with confidence, not to be afraid of open dialogue or necessary change that he equated with progress. The Enlightenment armed him against the forces of arrogance, pride, and false piety that he observed in his larger community and called by such names as "despotism" and "priestcraft." He may have pretended to ignore the powerful effect of his own prejudices when he displayed an outward calm meant to convince others that he was somehow immunized from the grip of ordinary passions; but it cannot be denied that he read with the greatest eagerness and relished new ideas.

In retirement, he avidly pursued the "moral sciences"—that was how David Hume classified such forward-looking subjects as sociology, political economy, and education. All depended in some way on research in the field of medicine, and in particular on that which highlighted the sensual nature of the human organism. Jefferson's metaphors drew upon this conviction, as when he courted "a warm visit from the sun (my almighty physician)," or remarked that "books are the best medicine for the ennui of age." His use of a medicalized vocabulary also explains why he grew so disturbed when the powers of life diminished for him. As Peter Gay puts it in his classic study of the Enlightenment, "Medicine was the most highly visible and the most heartening index of general improvement." It was hope for more sustained activity, for the vigorous life, *vita activa,* that raised spirits among the eighteenth-century intelligentsia.[3]

Sensations, Nerve Fibers, Convulsions, and Spasms

The bond between philosophy and medicine was certainly not new. The seventeenth-century physician Thomas Sydenham was a friend of John Locke's, and popularly known as "the English Hippocrates"—a reference to the medical ethicist of antiquity. Sydenham taught medicine on philosophical principles; Locke, who began his career as a doctor, devised his philosophy on medical principles: "What we know of the works of nature," wrote Locke, "especially in the constitution of health and the operation of our own bodies, is only by the sensible [i.e., palpably felt] effects." He credited Dr. Sydenham for pointing him away from speculation and toward experience and clinical study. In Jefferson's day, just as Sydenham was "the English Hippocrates," the tireless Benjamin Rush of Philadelphia was styled "the American Sydenham."[4]

Jefferson the learner, educator, philosophic critic, and defiant political healer acquired many of his guiding principles from medical discourse—the French and Swiss, perhaps, more than the English.[5] One key to understanding his expectations from the vocabulary of medicine is the work of Étienne Bonnot de Condillac, whose landmark *Treatise on Sensation* (1754) is responsive to Locke. Its aim can be summed up in one line: "By observing the birth of sensation, we show how we acquire the use of our faculties." Perceptions, desires, and all thinking and judgment derive, Condillac said, from *inquiétude,* or uneasiness; before there is even "the idea," there is "the will"—choice. In other words, the mind transforms sensation into practical expression. It engages the capacity for feeling and so produces the attentiveness from which memory and judgment are formed.[6]

Breaking down the processes of thought-experience, Condillac considered desire to be merely *"la sensation transformée,"* sensation transformed, or recalled with pleasure to the imagination. Now think for a moment about Jefferson's 1825 letter to Dr. Waterhouse, in which he considered the value of long life. If happiness begins in life with the first pleasurable sensation, as Condillac instructs, and happiness compounds as pleasurable sensations grow in number, then the debility of age (and attendant sensations) heighten awareness of declining faculties: memory, imagination, passions. This was clearly on Jefferson's mind when in 1817 he mused to Abigail Adams that natural processes were "stealing from us, one by one, the faculties of enjoyment." The reduction of sensations "gradually extinguished . . . the wish to stay here," one's impulse to survive.[7]

As an eager student of the Enlightenment, seeing the world through the prism of vital sensations, Jefferson insisted that the most striking impressions (pleasure or pain) were the ones to be recalled through life most powerfully. As we shall see repeatedly, the imprint of sensations—memory, imagination,

> table. Bishops Watson, however, in his Essay on the subjects of Chemistry, lays it down as a principle that wherever there is an internal circulation of fluid, there is life; and where there is life, there may be, and probably is sensation. whence he infers that the vegetable forms of matter are also sensible beings, and he names several plants, as the Dionaea, the Sensitives, those which fold & unfold their petals or leaves, which exhibit evident proofs of sensibility. we may add another to the Bishop's inferences, that where there is *life*, and *sensation*, there probably is thought also. perhaps it would be more exact to make the presence of a nervous system the test of sensibility, and consequently of thought. it is true that the best optical instruments have not as yet enabled us to discover nerves in vegetable bodies. but their improvement is indefinite, and we cannot say to what future dis-coveries their further improvements may not lead. there is a whole Order of animals

"Where there is *life*, and *sensation*, there probably is *thought* also." Evidence of Jefferson's ongoing intellectual interest in nervous sensations. He had read (and apparently reread) the "Chemical Essays" of Bishop Richard Watson, professor at Cambridge, which were published between 1781 and 1787. This excerpt is from a letter Jefferson wrote to François Adrian Van der Kemp, February 9, 1818. Library of Congress.

passions—was a powerful instigator in Jefferson's philosophy of mind and politics alike.

There is a simple way to demonstrate this: Jefferson's literary-epistolary persona was decidedly nostalgic. To women he reflexively sang the praises of old friendship, as he lamented the passage of time; or, as in the above-cited letter to Abigail Adams, he fantasized about their meeting again: ". . . and could I, in the spirit of your wish, count backwards a score of years, it would not be long before Ellen [his well-traveled granddaughter] and myself would pay our homage personally to Quincy [the Adamses' hometown]. But those 20. years, alas! where are they?" To men of the Revolution, Jefferson gave tribute to an eventful moment in history. To his fellow signer of the Declaration, Dr. Rush, he summed up his nostalgia in 1811: "I find friendship to be like wine, raw when new, ripened with age, the true old man's milk and restorative cordial." Reflection on the Revolution was restorative in recalling the human energy applied to the protection of America's natural abundance. Recollection ruled, memory motivated—it is hardly surprising that the nation's birth took on affection (as well as authority) in the collective memory of its midwives. The inalterability of the liberty won in the act of declaring independence became an image of hope and a constant refrain for Jefferson, the solid ground on which his country stood.[8]

Just as plainly, the stamp of sensation upon memory could have a negative impact upon political society. It was Jefferson's overwhelming conviction that blacks and whites were caught in a desperate power struggle that made the emancipation of slaves and their reintegration into American society impossible: Slaves would never be able to overcome the "ten thousand recollections . . . of the injuries they have sustained." Memory, whether appreciative and hope-filled or decidedly fearful, elicited passion and recorded its influence on Jefferson's style.[9]

Jefferson and his circle of scientifically influenced correspondents, one and all, regarded the quality of life, the impact of memory, and the power of imagination by how vividly each sensation formed itself amid constant, necessary, invisible movement in the brain. Health and vigor required "due excitement." When Jefferson reacted to Dr. Rush's letter proclaiming the public's esteem for humane propositions in the president's first inaugural address, he described the effect of Rush's letter itself: "The pleasing sensations produced in the mind by it's affectionate contents." Writing to James Madison on the effect of partisan political galas, Jefferson noted that this kind of event "excites uneasy sensations in some." To John Adams, early in his retirement, Jefferson reflected on the politicization of religion in their age as "the sensations excited in free yet firm minds, by the terrorism of the day." ("Terrorism," at this time, could mean something akin to brainwashing.) But nothing gets the point across better than Jefferson's 1820 remark to Adams about his "habitual anodyne, 'I feel: therefore I exist.'" He went on to clarify: "When once we quit the basis of sensation, all is in the wind." In short, sensations described the primary function of the human brain.[10]

Why is it so important to establish this? To prove that the Enlightenment was not so much preoccupied with the intellect, as it was influenced by an affective psychology. As logical and rational as Jefferson wished to be in applying his knowledge to his world, his letters show that he embraced Condillac's terms and understood desires and passions as the first components of human nature. Events always struck him by their "sensible effects."

In his acceptance of the medical Enlightenment, Jefferson next made the jump from sensationalist philosophy to physiology. Sensations and impressions became less intangible as nerves. Nerves roused heart and arteries into action and produced a visibly "ardent glow over the whole body." This was especially detected on faces because the skin was abundantly supplied with nerves: Frustration begot "paleness" and "tremor," and love was exhibited in cheeriness and "vivacity"—the effect of nervous sensation. Dr. George Cheyne's conspicuous study of "nervous distempers," *The English Malady* (1733), called wide attention to the power of the nervous system. He provided an entire vocabulary to a passionate people in their lifelong search for "Fortitude, Patience, Tranquillity." His very readable three-volume work was subtitled "A Treatise of Nervous Diseases of All Kinds, as Spleen, Vapours, Lowness of Spirits, Hypochondriacal, and Hysterical Distempers." In it, he identified the essential "fibre" behind nervous sensations, which was stimulated into "Spasms and Convulsions." In suggesting that the human organism was delicately balanced, Cheyne explained: "All the *Fibres* of the Body . . . are sensible."[11]

When he referred, as he did often, to the "sensible" or feeling organism, Jefferson was thinking of Cheyne's categories, of the fibrous system, the nerve fibers that traversed the body's sympathetic reactive system that was centered in the "sensorium" of the brain. Eighteenth-century intellectuals were fascinated by states of the body and modes of perception. The Swiss naturalist Charles Bonnet pronounced in 1759 that it was through the body that the mind or soul acted: "We know that ideas are attached to the workings of certain fibers: we can thus reason about these fibers because we see fibers; we can study a bit their movements, the results of their movements, and the connections they have among themselves."[12]

"Fibres" encompassed every imaginable human attribute: from memory to language to abstract ideas of beauty, harmony, liberty, and selfhood. In varying contexts, Jefferson typically wrote that he felt with "every fibre" of his being. He denied his political ambition by saying that "every fibre of that passion has been eradicated." He would also eradicate "every fibre of aristocracy" from American politics; and, as a mark of patriotism he claimed that he had "not one farthing of interest, nor one fibre of attachment" to anything beyond "my country." Female hysteria, "uterine fury," in the language of eighteenth-century medicine, was the result of incompleteness and *inquiétude,* or "fibres" gone mad. It should not be surprising that the term *moral fiber* continues as a part of vernacular English.[13]

To understand Jefferson's imagination, then, we must recover an old vocabulary. We must examine how he linked the physical body and the operations of the mind to the development of a natural amiability and the makings of social policy. His political legacy, in a very real way, has depended on it. The language he drew upon in attempting to fathom human behavior in general and partisan struggle in particular engaged with these connective elements that produced nervous energy. He referred to "vibrations," "spasms," "convulsions," "commotions," "tremors," "irritants," and "agitations." These seven words, individually and collectively, epitomize the peculiar manner in which Jefferson employed nerve-based imagery to influence others.

This is not to say that the nerves gave expression to fearful prospects only. Jefferson's was a time when "nervous" could mean "vigorous," as when the

British orator John Wilkes praised Jefferson for giving the Declaration of Independence a "manly, nervous sense," an effect that moved humanity. In 1819, Jefferson recalled the "nervous" energy of the Revolutionary firebrand Samuel Adams in a similar vein: "I can say that he was truly a great man . . . whose deep conceptions, nervous style, and undaunted firmness made him truly our bulwark in debate."[14]

Whatever the sentiment or interpretation, a nerve-dominated vocabulary generated power. In his first inaugural address, when speaking of political intolerance, Jefferson coupled the "*throes and convulsions* of the ancient world" with the "*agonizing spasms* of infuriated man," metaphors of the agitated body. Writing of European efforts to undo the pernicious effects of arbitrary rule, he claimed he felt "*strong spasms* of the heart" in favor of this movement, and then pronounced: "I am entirely persuaded that the *agitations* of the public mind advance it's powers, and that at every *vibration* between the points of liberty and despotism, something will be gained for the former" (italics supplied in each case). Valuable clues to a lost emotional universe are embedded in this language.[15]

The noun *convulsion* and the verb *convulse* will be shown at key moments to be dynamic and revealing words in Jefferson's vocabulary. They serve as a literary warning mechanism when he contemplates social or sexual dysfunction; they trigger in his anxious mind a rhetorical call to restore stability or balance. This can be said to have begun with his draft of the Declaration of Independence, in which he assessed the threat to the land of America: A suffering people lay "exposed to all the dangers of invasion from without and convulsions within." As well, near the end of his life, when he refused to commit to political debate, Jefferson wrote: "At the age of 82. I have no inclination to volunteer myself into a question which convulses a nation. Quiet is my wish with the peace and good will of the world. With it's contentions I have nothing to do."[16] In Jeffersonian parlance, convulsions disturbed the body politic and prevented affection and harmony from arising out of discord and division.[17]

In Jefferson's metaphorically rich, medically threatening environment, human energy could be used up or wasted, consumption could defeat the will, and nervous convulsion undermined natural serenity or arrested the power to achieve and enjoy tranquil felicity. In his *Notes on Virginia,* published in 1785, Jefferson described the sublime spectacle of southwest Virginia's Natural Bridge, a lofty arch of stone and earth on property that he owned: "It is on the ascent of a hill, which seems to have been cloven through its length by some great convulsion." Crossing on foot and momentarily glancing down, Jefferson suffered "a violent headache." The Natural Bridge was irresistible yet convulsive; the same can be said about Jefferson's attraction to the torment of political life.

This is a significant statement about the Virginian's disposition, if not an explanation for his lack of self-diagnosis. Jefferson's friend Dr. Rush went so far as to attribute all fevers to "convulsive action"—otherwise known at this time as "morbid excitement."[18]

It may have been, at times, a rhetorical strategy, but Jefferson constantly blamed politics for keeping him from his happy pursuit of the sciences and "speculative meditations." Yet, in his mind, the importance of the American experiment to world historical progress demanded that he commit himself. In 1818, he wrote paradigmatically in this regard: "It was my lot to be cast into being at the period of the commencement of a political convulsion, which has continued since to agitate the whole civilized world." Though he had grown old, the "convulsion" continued to "agitate"—and to stimulate his mind. What more is there to say in identifying Jefferson's overriding sense of the world of men? Combining words drawn from the science of nervous physiology was a regular feature of his writing and, as it should be clear by now, not by accident.[19]

In his famous dialogue between Head and Heart, a twelve-page love letter written from Paris to the artist Maria Cosway in 1786, Jefferson contrasted his active Heart to the "gloomy Monk" and the "sublimated philosopher." He marveled at the human capacity to experience "the solid pleasure of one generous spasm of the heart." A heart's "beat," in his lexicon, did not measure up to the more persuasive power of a heart's "generous spasm." In the dialogue, Jefferson's Head vainly reasoned in its effort to overcome primal sensations: "The art of life is the art of avoiding pain." The Heart insisted that reason alone was "frigid," "unsocial," and, in neurological terms, dulling. As he negotiated between Head and Heart, Jefferson expressed himself best and most humanely when he acknowledged the systemic source of contradiction and common anxieties.[20]

If these elements of Jeffersonian language and culture still seem a bit intangible, let us think of what they mean through a straightforward analogy to modern concepts of mind. A few decades ago, more than now, physicians routinely diagnosed "nervous breakdowns." The same phrase could be used colloquially without clinical precision. Someone can be a "nervous wreck" without a distinct pathology, or can remark casually, "My nerves are shot," to acknowledge ineffectiveness. Our cultural vocabulary may have replaced the activity-generated image of a "nervous breakdown" with the less-sudden phenomenon of "depression," in clinical as well as everyday discourse, yet our conception that we face "nerve-racking" choices in life, that nerves retain their amorphous yet influential character, is translatable to conversations of Jefferson's day.

We can appreciate Jefferson's language better by charting subtle shifts over time that signify larger cultural preferences. In the last decades of the nineteenth century, doctors still spoke of the nerves as "impressions" generated by "fibers," and still noted that we feel, move, and think through the nervous system. But they now found equivalence in a mid-century invention: "The construction of the nervous system, and its manner of action, may be compared to the arrangement of a common electric battery used in telegraphy." Nerves had become electrical.[21] Today's scientists tend to describe the nervous system's operation through the unemotional metaphor of communication: Nerves carry *information* to the brain for *analysis,* and the brain generates a *response.* But we still draw liberally on nervous physiology when we use "body language" as part of our cultural vocabulary. We know what someone is referring to when he or she has a "gut feeling." These are other examples of medical referents that have crossed into vernacular speech.[22]

Body Language and the Body Politic

One of the most intriguing facts we retain about the historical Jefferson is this: His dynamic pen often belied his placid disposition. His tenderness is demonstrated in numerous episodes taken from his life, and especially from friends who evoked his simplicity and humility, his modest carriage—his body language. Margaret Bayard Smith, who subsequently grew quite close to the family, was struck on her first encounter by those sensations that "the stranger" Jefferson produced in her: "I know not how it was, but there was something in his manner, his countenance and voice that at once unlocked my heart." He listened in a generous, giving way, "and put me perfectly at my ease." It was December 1800, the season of Jefferson's election to the presidency, and Smith and her husband had put their faith in the willfulness of this unabashed defender of the undervalued citizen; yet in person he appeared "with a manner and voice almost femininely soft and gentle."[23]

His great rival, Alexander Hamilton of New York, interacted with Jefferson in President Washington's cabinet, and marvelously spoofed the Virginian when he published a piece in the newspaper referring to "plain Thomas J—; wonderful humility on all occasions."[24] Clearly, Jefferson used his body, his corporeal style, to convey an aversion to conflict. In a sense, he cheated those who expected (and might have preferred) the directness of a political battler, which Jefferson's pen proved him to be many times over during his career in government.

His most thorough nineteenth-century biographer, Henry S. Randall, had regular access to Jefferson's grandchildren and others who knew the president.

Randall reported on incidents in which everyday people happened upon Jefferson during his travels between Monticello and Washington, started conversations with the "tall stranger," and sometimes berated Jefferson the man or his policies without recognizing him in their presence. In every such vignette, Jefferson is unruffled, even playful, offering no resistance, but perhaps wryly offering a useful homily about withholding censure if it concerns someone you do not know firsthand. Randall shows how in the presence of "servants, and, indeed, of all plain and ignorant men," Jefferson did not appear imposing and formidable, as one might expect a lordly southerner to appear: "His look . . . fell benignantly and lovingly upon the weak, the simple, and the lowly, and they at once felt and returned the sympathy."[25]

Whether the above are exaggerated events or in large measure true aspects of Jefferson's life matters less than the fact that they are consistently reflected in Jefferson's self-projection in letters. As president, he refused to make an official goodwill tour of the northern states, as George Washington had done, because of concern about the sensations such a trip would produce. "I confess I am not reconciled to the idea of a chief magistrate parading himself through the several States, as an object of public gaze, and in quest of an applause which, to be valuable, should be purely voluntary. I had rather acquire silent good will by a faithful discharge of my duties." Traveling as a private citizen, after retirement, would, he said, "better harmonize" with his feelings.[26]

In modern times, the contrast between Jefferson's modest demeanor and fighting words—his partisan personality—has been lost to the great mass of Americans. He appeals broadly across the political spectrum today as the first national leader to herald the concept of "representative democracy." But that is not how he was perceived two hundred years ago. He seized upon *inquiétude* and converted it into political action. He roused ordinary citizens to demand protection from excess power. He was especially sensitive to, and explicitly identified, abuses of authority among the self-satisfied Hamiltonian Federalists of the chronically turbulent 1790s, who questioned the wisdom of the people at large and insisted that society's "better sorts" should direct the course of political improvement. For Jefferson, the hardened Federalists were betraying the Revolution. That is why he, along with the then congressman James Madison, organized a political party to challenge them.

The important thing to remember is that Jefferson constructed a language of body, mind, and sensations that proved to be an integral part of his political message. He fashioned his words so that they effervesced and incited, yet they were meant to be read as advocating harmony and common understanding. The language of sensation helped his words come to life, and penetrate, and stimulate.

Because physical sensation was the vital force behind the human personality, rich drama flowed from human activity. Even when Jefferson's words did not borrow directly from the science of sensation, they were shaped by it. Here are random examples of his literary genius that affect in this manner, the key words italicized:

"The good *sense* of the people will always be found to be the best army. . . . *Cherish* therefore the *spirit* of our people and *keep alive* their attention."

"The *spirit* of resistance to government is so valuable on certain occasions, that I wish it to be always *kept alive*. . . . I like a little rebellion now and then. It is like a storm in the Atmosphere."

"I appeal to the true fountains of evidence, the *head & heart* of every rational & honest man. It is there nature has written her *moral laws*, & where every man may read them for himself."

"Bigotry is the *disease* of ignorance, of *morbid minds; enthusiasm* of the *free and buoyant*."[27]

Read together, we can see how the dramatic, euphonic intermingling of words might appeal to an alert sense of right and wrong. Good sense is an army; spirited rebellion is a natural phenomenon; bigotry is a disease. All in all, Jefferson says about himself: I cherish; I keep alive the spirit of honest, moral introspection; I remain healthy through buoyant enthusiasm.

This is why we still like Jefferson. His words uplift. Of course, they also attempt to justify a political ideology—an ideology now well ingrained, but then quite new. Knowing how easy it was for the careful framers of a new republic to fixate on selfishness and corruptibility in society generally, he delivered instead, in adroit and elegant phrasing, a message far more personal. It was a message of liberality and unselfish commitment that emanated from medical understandings of the moral sense as it related to nervous physiology. He kept saying, in the largest sense, in universal strains: By tapping into our innate sensitivity, we can be better as people; we can do more as a government.

For Jefferson, the American people's essential character was constituted at the precise moment of the nation's birth, when a rhetorical and actual resistance to tyranny were one. In choosing to preserve (or package) the Revolution's earliest, purest, most ecstatic moment of optimism in words that exploited the effect of nervous susceptibility on the popular imagination, Jefferson gave his name to a political faith he knew would never go out of style in America. This was his genius, and his historic success. In a highly conscious effort, and by using the most powerful vocabulary he had at hand, he saw to it that his words kept alive the first promise of the struggle for independence:

common commitment. The Declaration ends with the signers' mutual pledge of "our lives, our fortunes, and our sacred honor."

Jeffersonian democracy was, from the beginning of Jefferson's career, a radical movement based on sympathy for the people at large. "I am not among those who fear the people," Jefferson wrote in 1816, well into his retirement. "They, and not the rich, are our dependence for continued freedom." He was effusive in his remarks on social equality ("I cannot say things by halves"), without ever transcending the *material body* of his democracy. He aligned himself with the emotional health of "the corporeal inhabitants" of "this corporeal globe."[28]

It is important to pause and explain precisely what "sympathy" meant. Certainly, its meaning coincided with the modern definition of emotional support or generosity of spirit; but it was richer than that. Anyone with the least amount of medical knowledge understood nervous sympathies as *constant, perceptible and imperceptible, movement within the body, by which impressions were transmitted from the brain to other organs.* For Jefferson's self-protective Head and outgoing Heart alike, physiological and moral sympathies had considerable bearing on the active imagination. Modern American political life has inherited a Jeffersonian definition of "sympathy" in the public's embrace of humanitarian commitment as an instrument of policy; but we have not inherited the more visceral sense of the word that Jefferson's generation possessed, that is, the body-spirit duality it encompassed.[29]

In his medical school lectures, Dr. Benjamin Rush laid out his thinking on that "certain connection of feeling in the nerves, called sympathy." This was what caused the salivary glands in a hungry person to respond to the smell of tasty food. Rush theorized that sympathies made it possible to recognize diseases in otherwise "insensible parts"; and sympathies enabled diseases to be "diffused over the whole body" rather than concentrated in a certain organ. As for treatment, "knowing the sympathy between the nose and the intestines, we remove the itching of the nose, by dislodging worms in the intestines." The same phenomenon "extends to our ideas," he said, "for [intimate] association is governed by the same laws as [physiological] sympathy."[30]

Sympathy explains how "nervous sensibility" became the "culture of sensibility" that caused early Americans to identify philanthropic urges with notions of republican virtue, thereby consummating the marriage of philosophic medicine and republican politics. It was by means of internal sympathies that the sentient mind could respond, remember, and empathize. Under ordinary circumstances, nerves carried a healthy kind of excitement (a desired level of human susceptibility) to the generous soul. This, then, was "sensibility," the capacity of the soul to find fulfillment in commitment to a cause outside oneself.

And yet, so desirable a quality could also prove disruptive. People (women especially, but also men of uncommon compassion) suffered from having too much feeling. Well-being, therefore, for both the private and political Jefferson, had to mean balanced or harmonious living, brought about by monitoring excitable desires.

A lifetime of letters shows that Jefferson was attuned to the enlarged role of sympathy in human affairs, but he felt the bodily part of its dual nature most particularly as he grew older. "The hand of age has more than begun to press upon me," he wrote DeWitt Clinton of New York in 1815. "And with the diminished vigor of body the mind also has it's sympathy, ardor sensibly abates in those pursuits which were the delight of earlier years." Because of sensation and nervous excitability, sympathy was possible. "In a word," wrote a Philadelphia-trained doctor in his 1799 medical dissertation, "the whole system, mind and body, is one mass of general sympathy."[31]

None of these ideas about sensation, stimuli, and sociability was home-grown. Jefferson's friend Dr. Rush, "the American Sydenham," was, like Caspar Wistar, the other renowned Philadelphia physician in Jefferson's circle, trained in medicine at the prestigious University of Edinburgh.[32] The speculative Rush went even beyond Jefferson in establishing links between the body's active nerves and the spirit of republican politics or social policy. He actually regarded the American Revolution as a medical phenomenon in which liberty, as a condition of life, affected the relationship between an individual's health and the health of all.

In his *Account of the Influence of the Military and Political Events of the American Revolution upon the Human Body*, Rush wrote that oppositional Loyalists suffered mental and physical breakdowns, but hysterical women who welcomed the Revolution were actually cured of their mental condition. After the war, however, Americans' mental state deteriorated when people failed to check the impulse to enjoy liberty; that is, liberty became an unhealthy addiction: "The excess of the passion for liberty," wrote Dr. Rush, "inflamed by the successful issue of the war, produced, in many people, opinions and conduct which could not be removed by reason nor restrained by government. For a while, they threatened to render abortive the goodness of heaven to the United States." This was, he concluded, "a species of insanity," and he gave a name to the syndrome: *"Anarchia."*[33]

Jefferson had his own, more positive way of putting this. In his Head and Heart dialogue, written in 1786 for the benefit (and enchantment) of Maria Cosway, he attributed American independence to passion and imagination rather than to rational thinking. Though British power was indisputable from the outset, "we threw up a few pulsations of our warmest blood: we supplied enthusiasm against wealth and numbers." As it was for *sympathy,* the dictionary definition of *enthusiasm* in this era was markedly stronger than our present usage: It meant "heat of imagination; violence of passion." A passionate, pulsating system explained, in biomedical imagery, the American spirit.[34]

Yet the spirited patriot publicly contained his passions. More than a thinker, Thomas Jefferson was a strategist. He was different from his conservative political opposition in not being afraid, on paper, of the occasional eruption of passion, if employed in a progressive cause. For most in his world, though, the word *passion* (other than as a neutral category of neurophysiological study) implied "excess." Jefferson himself decried "English passions . . . nourished by the newspapers," "vulgar vehicles of passion" that contributed to war fever.[35] Passion served to "distract" or "mislead"; passionate (out-of-balance) behavior was characterized, in more directly medicalized language, as a "deformity," or a "disorder."[36] When Jefferson's old school contemporaries wished to critique Jeffersonian democracy, they noisily branded the third president a social radical who would let loose unhealthy passions.

Using the same nuance of political language, conventional morality demanded an antidote, a cure, for excess passion. It was for a public character to prove "candour" without succumbing to "agitation" or "violent emotions." For Jefferson himself, "candour" was precisely the personal quality that his supporters most warmly attributed to him and that his vocal detractors doubted he possessed at all.

A Salutary Education

Jefferson routinely used the word *salutary* both when he was discussing personal health issues and when he was referring to "republican principles." In his preference for a sound agrarian lifestyle over the unhealthy urban air, he wrote: "The mobs of great cities add just so much to the support of pure government, as sores do to the strength of the human body."[37] (Though Jefferson probably had London in mind, each square mile in New York and Philadelphia in 1800 was home to more than 40,000 people; in the nation as a whole, the number was six per square mile.)[38] If we accept that he did not use such language indifferently, but that the vocabulary he drew from medical studies often consisted of weighty words, then we must link that vocabulary to public conflicts and Jefferson's record on socially disruptive issues, as well as to his private judgments.

America was beginning to separate culturally from England, having already done so politically. The Jeffersonian period, as should already be clear, was a time of profound cultural transformation. As a committed Revolutionary, Jefferson found his enemy in the image of the English aristocrat who loved pomp, craved luxurious living, and enjoyed his pleasures at the expense of others. He gave it as a catechism in 1795: "There is no quarter of the globe so desireable [sic] as America, no state in America so desireable as Virginia, no county in Virginia equal to Albemarle, and no spot in Albemarle to compare to Monticello." To the Marquis de Lafayette, in 1823, the eighty-year-old Jefferson insisted that no matter how political parties named themselves, the world was naturally divided into Democrat and Aristocrat, and that the latter species was, always, unhealthy: "The sickly, weakly, timid man, fears the people." Thus the aristocrat was wasteful in his habits, covetous of power, and unrestrained, thoroughly unhealthy, and as much a "sore" on the body politic as the urban squalor Jefferson found symptomatic of the worst kind of social inequality. As a republican, he contrasted this image to his own occupation: grower. He thought of himself as one who created and distributed commodities of real value. He was, comparatively speaking, a fiscal conservative, a hands-on lover of the land, a generous employer, a family man; he idealized his environment, and dubbed it the most healthful on Earth.[39]

Jefferson learned early on to appreciate the European aesthetic, and he acquired expensive habits. Yet his politics decried the "luxury" attributable to extensive foreign commerce, and the fashions and fineries that ostensibly corrupted a people. The historian Drew R. McCoy offers the following definition of "luxury" as Jefferson understood it: "dangerous forms of sensual excess that accompanied men's indulgence in artificial and superfluous pleasure."[40]

It is that sensuousness—unhealthy appetite—that most concerns us here. Jefferson's premise in opposing "luxury" was that enlightened moderation in all facets of life fed harmony. We can better understand how Jefferson lived when we accept the tension inherent in his situation: He was born to the privilege of America's landowning elite; he was an art collector, wine lover, epicure, and builder who justified expenditures on grounds of taste. At the same time, he insisted that the national wealth was properly thought of as a function of the judicious use of the Earth's bounty, not as a means to material comfort.[41]

The unavoidable problem with Jefferson's political economy and his critical assessment of aristocracy was that he lived well at the expense of others. As much as he feared America's re-creating the British social order under Federalist rule, and as much as he sought to construct a new kind of society predicated on the collapse of inherited privilege, he could not have intended for liberal intellectuals like himself to suffer degradation in their way of life. He had been exposed in the 1780s to the Parisian literati and their opulent liberal friends—noblemen such as Lafayette and the gentle duc de la Rochefoucauld—and he, too, wanted to live the good life. Yet he believed deeply in social justice; that he never feigned, even accepting that his lifestyle required the unpaid exertions of enslaved Africans.

Playing up his rediscovered agricultural identity when he formally retired from politics, the hospitable Jefferson attempted a Virginian's balancing act: to behave fairly and decently toward people of all social ranks, while squeezing all he could out of his farms; to be a republican, without freeing his slaves, and without selling off lands to support a more moderate domestic economy. In this era preceding what might be called "rampant democracy," that instability, mutability, and ignorance Alexis de Tocqueville sneered at in the 1830s,[42] Jefferson lived like an aristocrat without being "known" as an aristocrat, that is, without disparaging the smaller-scale farmer, without denying them their equal rights, without succumbing to aristocratic vices of the dissipated sort that he alluded to in his 1823 letter to Lafayette—the vices thought to bring down empires. His democratic style of aristocratic living was equally a matter of self-definition as publicity. Never mind that his spending appears to us rather extravagant, he would have considered his actions as an effort to achieve the quiet, simple, unostentatious life.

Jefferson could never sustain a life that was truly "simple". As one who did not easily sit still, he presented himself with massive challenges, even in his retirement. Conceiving and constructing the new and very public University of Virginia, he worked tirelessly, first to gain financial support from the Virginia legislature, and later to attract an excellent faculty. Just as Monticello itself was envisioned as a legendary retreat from the tumult of public disagreement, affording ease, tranquility, and the opportunity for undisturbed self-cultivation, his university was meant to provide physical health along with useful knowledge, to show the way to republican happiness and dissuade a younger generation of Americans from hungering after aristocratic excess and overindulgence.

How exactly, then, did health comport with a rejection of aristocratic pretension? The answer lies in the design of Jefferson's university. Many have studied in detail its arresting Greek revival architecture, but something further needs to be said about the inspiration behind Jefferson's ultimate experiment in republican education. It is well known that he made sketches of places he had seen in Europe from 1784 to 1789—the signature dome of Monticello and the Rotunda of the university have their French antecedents. However, far less attention has been given to the medical Enlightenment that animated Jefferson as he contemplated a university suited to his tastes.

As enamored as he was with physician-philosophers during his Paris years, so, too, was Jefferson attracted to the cause of hospital reform that arose among them and flourished just as he arrived there. His friends in France, the liberal intellectuals, shared the view he had expressed in his *Notes on Virginia* (published in France in 1785), that, except when surgery was needed, "nature and kind nursing" in a home-like setting was superior to a stay in a hospital, "where the sick, the dying, and the dead are crammed together in the same rooms, and often in the same beds."[43] Principals of the Paris Academy of Sciences submitted designs for a new, healthier hospital that would be situated away from the crowded center of the city and built on a garden-like plan.

For centuries, the massive, fusty, unwholesome Hôtel-Dieu had been packing sick people together in a death trap they were unlikely to escape. The new, decentralized health care system placed its emphasis instead on an open-air setting, discriminating among disease types (to separate patients suffering from different illnesses), and attending to sanitation requirements. Such a place would be far better for convalescing patients. This was Jefferson's concept of progress, too. In 1786, a close friend, the philosophe Marquis de Condorcet, proposed to the Academy of Sciences a plan that would remove responsibility from the church and instead put health care decisions in the hands of local organizations.

Jefferson approved of both the reform impulse and the architectural model of the French hospital plan. This is readily apparent in his layout of the celebrated lawn of the University of Virginia: its parallel walks, marked by symmetrical pavilions—five on each side, and facing. There is little doubt that Jefferson borrowed his design from the Paris hospital plan of the late 1780s, which consisted of the same idea of neoclassical pavilions, albeit with six, rather than five, facing structures. (The opposite sides were divided into wings for male and female patients.) Open gardens for recuperating patients occupied the middle area that forms the lawn in Jefferson's redesign. At the head of the French archetype was a domed structure similar to Jefferson's Rotunda. In Jefferson's proposal, the pavilions featured distinct classrooms at ground level and professors' quarters above, all connected by a covered porch and walkway to keep the university community dry. Small classrooms made it possible for the air to circulate and promote health; as in the hospital plan, fire and contagious diseases were less likely to spread than they would in a single massive structure.[44]

Even before his project was feasible, Jefferson was excitedly imagining it. In 1800, he wrote to Joseph Priestley, the discoverer of oxygen and a political reformer whom he held in the highest esteem, and contrasted the situation of Virginia's first college, his own alma mater, William & Mary, with the institution he dreamt of building. Thinking medically as well as politically, he called Williamsburg "eccentric in it's position"—residing near the coast, not very far inland—and thus "exposed to bilious diseases as all the lower country is." He had a wholesome alternative: "We wish to establish in the upper & healthier country, & more centrally for the state, an University on a plan so broad & liberal

& *modern,* as to be worth patronizing with the public support, and be a temptation to the youth of other states to come and drink of the cup of knowledge & fraternize with us."[45] A few years later, as president, with his French experience still in mind, Jefferson wrote to his fellow Virginian (and future U.S. senator) Littleton W. Tazewell: "Large houses are always ugly, inconvenient, exposed to the accident of fire, and bad in case of infection. . . . In fact a university should not be a house but a village." To another southern politician, William H. Crawford, he compared America's "pseudo-citizens" to a "disease" for desiring to remake the country into the unhealthful city of London.[46]

The whole finally came to him in 1810, after his first year in retirement, when he envisioned for Tennessee judge Hugh L. White "an academical village, instead of a large and common den of noise, of filth and of fetid air. It would afford that quiet retirement so friendly to study, and lessen the dangers of fire, infection and tumult." Knowledge was not only power, as Francis Bacon famously said, but, to Jefferson, it was the source of a healthy and felicitous existence.[47]

As early as the 1800 letter to Priestley, Jefferson specified that anatomy, surgery, and medicine were absolutely essential to his then visionary policy to advance American higher education.[48] The university took him nearly a decade to realize, and proved to be the great triumph of his retirement years. Beginning in 1816, he managed labor, finance, and curricular affairs, in addition to architectural plans, down to the tiniest details. As a result of his singular efforts, the professors he hired would teach what he wanted them to teach, and the university would function according to his design. It would therefore introduce a path-breaking medical curriculum.

In early 1825, when Dr. Dunglison and two other professors who had sailed with him did not arrive on schedule, Jefferson postponed the university's opening. He feared the men lost at sea, and a fourteen-week voyage, more than double the average, made his concern legitimate. As a result, he greeted Dunglison's appearance in Charlottesville that spring as a particular blessing. Dunglison and his bride were able to move right in to a neoclassical apartment on the lawn of the university. The doctor's first impression of Jefferson was surprise at how energetic he was: In mid-1825, the father of the university was still riding his horse and walking "with all the activity of one twenty or thirty years younger." Their partnership, though brief, proved to be a highly agreeable one. Young Dr. Dunglison was meticulous and hard working, every bit the scholar Jefferson had hoped for in a professor of medicine.[49]

Nor is it a coincidence that Jefferson had already begun stocking the library with a large selection of medical, surgical, and pharmacological texts, and planning a state-supported clinic that would offer free medical care to those who could not afford it. Jefferson's goal was charitable, and his method cunning. As he had put it to Priestley back in 1800, in recognizing America's relative backwardness, "We should propose to draw from Europe the first characters in science, by considerable temptations, which would not need to be repeated after the first set should have prepared fit successors & given reputation to the institution." It was a patriotic conspiracy, and he saw to its implementation.

He wanted to train America's top physicians, and he even designed an "Anatomical Theatre" he called "indispensable to the school of Anatomy,"[50] in which medical students would acquire their skills by learning to perform dissections. His correspondence shows that he scoured the country for preserved specimens of everything from brains to uteruses. To complete his university, he never stopped doing, and it seemed to him perfectly appropriate to "tempt" the first generation of professors away from superior European institutions, with suitable financial incentives to lure them to America. Afterward, their students—Americans—would pass on what they had learned, and in doing so make the initial European connection irrelevant. If the ex-president had his way, the University of Virginia would reach out to meritorious youths, North and South, and bind the nation to the Jeffersonian ideal of liberal erudition.

Just before the start of building, he wrote of the university with a metaphor from nature: "I look to it as a germ from which a great tree may spread itself."[51] As the university opened, Jefferson, almost as the "nature's god" of his immortal Declaration, directed operations from Monticello, sitting high above and looking down upon the academical village he had created. From the beginning, he had been its prime mover, and insofar as his associates understood that success or failure would be assigned to him, he executed his plan without interference.[52]

He was as concerned with the health of the university in its first year as he was with his own sinking health. He continued to oversee the psychological well-being, along with the academic prospects, of the first crop of students. In this mission, he found Dr. Dunglison a useful liaison. Barely a month after his arrival in Charlottesville, and a few days before the Fourth of July, 1825, Dunglison, in his role as secretary to the university faculty, transmitted a request from the student body: The young men petitioned for a Fourth of July vacation.

Although Jefferson protested that as rector of the university he was merely one member of the governing Board of Visitors and did not bear sole responsibility for the decision, he knew otherwise. He made it clear that he took a hard line on time off from studies. As it stood, the only authorized vacation was from December 15 to January 31, to avoid, as he put it, "the common abuse by which 2. or 3. months of the year are lost to the students under the name of vacations. The thread of their studies is broke & more time still to be expended in recovering it." His message was that education was not a divisible but a combinable product, and not empty ceremony either; the student retained what he learned as he added to it.[53]

The students had apparently thought they could take advantage of Jefferson's uniquely sentimental connection to the Fourth of July and so steal a little vacation time. But Jefferson, preoccupied with the future of America's governance, had labored hard on the university and was unmoved. Indeed, for the old man on the mountain, the students' minds were unfinished for as long as America was unfinished.

Jefferson had a view toward philanthropy, but he also felt he knew when to overrule. It was the privilege of a founder. His university had been set up as a laboratory, and Jefferson figured he had earned the right to direct its experiments. He never wearied of building, nor of systematizing his own and others' education. No matter how his physical condition lagged, the search for knowledge never ended. The love of science and the art of living well were one and the same to him.

Domestic Cares

3

An Utopian Dream

I should not care were life to end with the line I am writing, were it not that I may be of some avail to the family. . . . Their affectionate devotion to me makes a willingness to endure life a duty, as long as it can be of any use to them.

THOMAS JEFFERSON TO
THOMAS JEFFERSON RANDOLPH,
FEBRUARY 8, 1826

In 1825 and in the early months of 1826, at Thomas Jefferson's supper table, one might have found Dr. Dunglison seated on his left, the guest of honor on his right. It was, however, his fifty-three-year-old daughter Martha Jefferson Randolph at the head of the table, and the eighty-two-year-old paterfamilias directly across from her. The old man's hearing was excellent up close, so that he could converse easily with the person next to him; but his ear became confused when several persons were speaking. Burwell Colbert, a member of the biracial Hemings family, was in charge of meals, that is, the comings and goings of servants. It was Burwell Colbert, at this time in his early forties, who kept the keys to the wine cellar and the cabinets where imported foods and chinaware were stored. His conscientious ways and sanitary habits were celebrated by the extended family, and Jefferson trusted him completely.[1]

Jefferson's retirement was constantly interrupted by visitors, announced and unannounced. Some, such as the Portuguese botanist Abbé Correa da Serra, a favorite, stayed for weeks and frequently returned; strangers, generally of lesser intellectual attainments, were treated politely but obliged to find lodgings elsewhere. Not surprisingly, Jefferson relished intellectual companionship: Young intellectuals such as Harvard's George Ticknor became regular correspondents after their initial visits. In June 1823, Mr. Miralbe, "a native of Buenos Ayres, but resident in Cuba," patiently answered Jefferson's questions about Cuban popular opinion, and was led to speculate on the prospects for trade between the

Watercolor of Monticello in 1825, by Jane Braddick Peticolas, a young friend of
Jefferson's granddaughters. Monticello/Thomas Jefferson Foundation, Inc.

United States and that charming island.[2] The gala return of the Marquis de
Lafayette in 1824, after an absence of four decades from his adopted country,
was manifest in the tender embrace of two aging Revolutionaries at Monticello.
Though geographically remote, Jefferson's home remained a point of conver-
gence for curious minds.

Jane Braddick's watercolor of Monticello's west lawn was painted in or about
1825, and it is the closest we can come to visually capturing Jefferson's backyard
at the end of his life. It certainly suggests an idealized retirement vista for a cul-
tured man surrounded by his large family. We see three of the grandchildren
and an unknown sketch artist occupying the otherwise empty lawn, which lay
between the house and the family graveyard.

Little of the vegetation that was there then remains now. Overseer Edmund
Bacon, in later years, recalled that Jefferson "would never allow a tree to be cut"
from the acreage about the house. "There were roads and paths winding around
and over it, where the family could ride and walk for pleasure. How often I have
seen him walking over these grounds and his grandchildren following after him
happy as they could be." Bacon remarked that the setting was "beautifully orna-
mented. . . . There were walks, and borders, and flowers, that I have never seen
or heard of anywhere else." It was Jefferson's slave Isaac who encapsulated the
activity that went on at Monticello, with these oft-repeated words: "Monticello
house was pulled down in part and built up again some six or seven times. One

time it was struck by lightning. . . . They was forty years at work upon that house before Mr. Jefferson stopped building." These descriptions suggest a livelier tableau than the watercolor's view, which appears almost deserted and absent of sound.[3]

Henry Gilpin of Philadelphia visited Monticello in the months after Jefferson was buried. "The house is on the loftiest point," he wrote, "surrounded but not obscured by majestic trees, very extensive." From Jefferson's gardens, "where the best views presented themselves, & which Mr. Jefferson had fixed as his favourite spots for walking, reading, or reflection," Gilpin gazed out at the undulating countryside. He expressed amazement at the distance encompassed by the view, the wooded hills and valleys, the "immense plain," the Blue Ridge Mountains. In the near distance was the winding form of the Rivanna River, and Mr. Jefferson's university "with its domes & scattered houses, & the farms[,] buildings & fields green with tobacco, all so near & so directly beneath you, that it seems as if a stone could be thrown upon any object below."[4]

Jefferson's sole surviving daughter, Martha Randolph, gives a sense of how frenetic Monticello's activity could be. She wrote this to an absent daughter in midsummer 1825:

> We have been literally overwhelmed with company this summer. From one Monday to another we have dined one day alone, the other days we had company *every day* to dinner. Ladies 4 days of the 6, and the Sunday 9 unexpected guests in addition to a party invited. To morrow we have Judge [Dabney] Carr's family with [financial agent Bernard] Peyton and his wife. I presume they will stay some days. . . . I have been obliged to get up at 5 o'clock to write to you.[5]

Her father, in retirement, obliged the mother of eleven children to serve as hostess at Monticello when he was at home. The dutiful Martha had performed similar chores, on occasion, at the President's House before that.

Jefferson, who was six feet, two and a half inches tall, was described by the visiting Massachusetts congressman Daniel Webster in 1824 as "thin and spare," with a mild, relaxed countenance, his long, once-red hair now sandy. His walk was "easy and swinging," and he had a "lounging habit of sitting"—the same as it was described in the journal of a Pennsylvania senator back in 1790. His dress, all agreed, was simple and comfortable, suggesting that he was unmindful of the fashions of the day. It was, however, his conversational tone that visitors most remarked upon: polite, indulgent, without affectation, wide-ranging, and captivating without deliberately seeking to be so.[6]

In retirement, the ex-president regularly rode into Charlottesville, a town that he thought had as yet little to recommend it. In 1822, the northern publishers Cary and Lea queried him about it, and he wrote back concerning its modest scale: "The neighborhood is of plain industrious farmers; the town of retail merchants & mechanics, of about 250. free inhabitants. The merchants sometimes have a shelf or two of books, but they are of very slow sale." Jefferson counted on the university to put Charlottesville on the map, and by 1826 he was growing more confident, at least on this score.[7]

This is not to say that he disparaged the place of his nativity. Quite the contrary. To Jean Baptiste Say, a French author of a treatise on political economy, he celebrated a healthful, picturesque landscape: "It's soil is equal in natural fertility to any high lands I have ever seen; it is red and hilly, very like much of the country of Champagne and Burgundy . . . excellently adapted to wheat, maize, and clover. Like all mountainous countries it is perfectly healthy, liable to no agues and fevers, or to any particular epidemic, as is evidenced by the robust constitution of it's inhabitants." Noting that survival into one's nineties occurred "habitually" in his neighborhood, Jefferson went on to explain Charlottesville's chief attraction and its chief deficiency: "The society is much better than is common in country situations; perhaps there is not a better *country* society in the U.S. But do not imagine this a Parisian or an Academical society. It consists of plain, honest and rational neighbors, some of them well-informed, and men of reading, all superintending their farms, honorable and friendly, and speaking nothing but English." Though sacrificing the cosmopolitan flavor of European society, one could still count on frankness and common charity. A turkey or goose cost only fifty cents, and garden peas, strawberries, and cherries "come to table about the 12th of May." It was the ideal setting for an American, who ought to be entirely satisfied, Jefferson thought, just to have a "rational," book-reading neighbor; but for those accustomed to more stimulating society, the plainness of his surroundings might prove disappointing.[8]

Though a noted wine connoisseur and art collector, Jefferson preferred country plainness, especially in dress and manner. After the War of 1812 ended, and trade with England resumed, he wrote to the botanist Benjamin Smith Barton: "The greatest obstacle I apprehend to our manufacturers is our slavish obsequiousness to British fashions." American "belles and beaux" appeared unable to resist the lure. "This is a great evil," he bemoaned, "but I fear an irremediable one. It is the particular domain in which the fools have usurped dominion over the wise." Similarly, to Caesar A. Rodney of Delaware, his former attorney general: "The cities, I suppose, will still affect English fashions, & of course English manufactures. But the cities are not the people of America. The country will be clothed in homespun." Confident that simplicity would continue to thrive among those of his own vicinity, Jefferson clothed his letter in homespun pride: "We are an industrious, plain, hospitable and honest, altho' not a psalm-singing people."[9]

Martha believed her father could do no wrong. She amused her children, as they grew up in the first two decades of the nineteenth century, with morally uplifting anecdotes of her five years abroad with him, tales that the family cherished and passed down. As his precious "Patsy," ten years old in 1782, Martha was witness to her father's grief after the death of her mother and namesake. Two years later, she accompanied him to Paris; there she was schooled amid the intellectual ferment that so affected her father, who took his place at the Versailles court as the worthy successor to America's singular, most affable international icon, Benjamin Franklin. In France, Martha acquired what one of her daughters termed "her highly cultivated understanding and fascinating manners." But she did not learn there how to be a Virginia plantation mistress: She returned home in 1789 a scholar who was behind in needlework and housewifery.[10]

At seventeen, Martha married her cousin Thomas Mann Randolph and proceeded to become what her father wanted her to be: a model Virginia matron, devoted caregiver, able teacher, and eventually a chatty correspondent to her daughters whenever they traveled beyond Albemarle County. She became that proud plantation mistress. A neighbor recorded that she was "tall, loosely made, and awkward," yet also "one of the most interesting persons of the age."[11] Along with her son Jefferson, and her maturing daughters Ellen, Cornelia, and Virginia, she offered regular companionship to her father while directing a socially visible family. Jefferson regarded the diligent Martha and her older children (given that the youngest son was not born until 1818) as his life preservers. After his death, they would go on to prove themselves equally attached to protecting his reputation.

To a French nobleman he had known in the 1780s, Jefferson wrote in 1817 of what was most apparent to him, as he bore his retirement at Monticello:

> I am now feeling the effects of age, enfeebled in body & less active in mind. My daughter, whom you knew, has provided for my old age a numerous family of grand children, and these again begin to add to our society another generation of descendants. I shall die therefore in the midst of those I love.[12]

He felt that political life accorded him an uncertain legacy at best, but he had every expectation of having secured in his immediate posterity a level of devotion only possible among those intimates who depended entirely on his good name.

Jefferson Randolph

"Jeff" Randolph (1792–1875) was the son of the president's daughter Martha and Thomas Mann Randolph, the latter of whom served Virginia as its governor during the financially trying years of 1819–1822. It was the elder Randolph's poor personal management of lands and funds, and not anything he did as the state's executive, that prompted the proprietor of Monticello to groom his grandson, instead of his son-in-law, for the larger business responsibilities he preferred to delegate rather than handle on his own.

By a simple process of elimination, Jeff was, in that sense, "chosen." The older his grandfather grew, the more responsibility fell to him. As executor of the ex-president's embarrassed estate, he would be one of three people who remained close at hand during the days leading to July 4, 1826, along with Dr. Dunglison and the dying patriarch's house servant and traveling companion, Burwell Colbert—whose mother had attended Patty Jefferson at her deathbed in 1782.[13]

Thomas Mann Randolph, though he professed to adore his famous father-in-law, was an ill-tempered man, unsteady in all respects. He gave money away to his siblings and neighbors, as well as to friends bearing empty promises. Thus, his agreeable if less-than-scholarly son Jeff (along with Jeff's older cousin Samuel Carr) had to be called in to manage his mounting debts. Martha was an efficient and economical household manager; it was her husband who parted with money too easily. Jeff began to take over his father's finances soon after the elder Randolph's governorship concluded.[14]

It was difficult for Jeff to live up to expectations. Thomas Jefferson had no sons, and after 1804 Martha was his one remaining daughter. To the eldest grandson thus fell the political as well as financial hopes of the family. When Martha accompanied her father to Paris in the mid-1780s, she was in her mid-teens, and proved both studious and remarkable for the poise she developed as a result of her exposure to European society and learning. When her son was in his mid-teens, he was sent to Philadelphia for an education; she no doubt expected him to represent the family well and display a comfortable self-possession. But the times he was reared in differed somewhat from hers, and things rarely went exactly as a parent wanted. It was challenging, in that sense, for a boy to start out with everything.

When Jefferson Randolph was in Philadelphia, his grandfather, then president, arranged for him principally to study anatomy and surgery, "as well for general information as for utility, in the country where surgeons were not often at hand," the grandson explained decades later.[15] President Jefferson wrote optimistically to Dr. Caspar Wistar, his successor as president of the American Philosophical Society, and Jeff's anatomy professor: "I think he has an observing mind & sound judgment. He is assiduous, orderly, & of the most amiable temper & dispositions."[16] But the next year, living under the roof of the patriotic portrait painter, natural historian, and inventor Charles Willson Peale, Jeff revealed that his temper was not always cool. This lapse elicited a reflective letter from his grandfather urging prudence and "self-cathechising." Young toughs, "fiery zealots," were baiting the teenager by bad-mouthing his grandfather. "Pity them," said the president. "Look steadily to the pursuits which have carried you to Philadelphia, be very select in the society you attach yourself to; avoid taverns, drinkers, smoakers, and idlers and dissipated persons generally; for it is with such that broils and contentions arise, and you will find your path more easy and tranquil."[17]

Years later, Peale was reminded of these trials: "I offended him once or twice highly, while he was with me, by some severe remarks I made on the folly of dueling." Peale had wished to keep the teenager out of trouble, but it turned out that Thomas Mann Randolph, the boy's father, had fought a duel. Jefferson Randolph looked to have inherited not the pacific mind of his grandfather, but the rash, combustible spirit of his father. Still, wrote Peale, "I loved him the more for his filial affections."[18]

In 1814, Thomas Jefferson began to observe a magnet drawing his twenty-two-year-old grandson away: "Jefferson has found a loadstone," he wrote, with a dash of wit. The lad's frequent absences "induce us to conclude the attraction of the two bodies mutual."[19] By the time of his marriage the following year to Jane Nicholas, seventeen-year-old daughter of Wilson Cary Nicholas, another of Virginia's governors (1814–1816), Jeff had acquired an outlook sufficiently mature to cause the retired president to place substantial trust in him. He began managing the Bedford County lands that encompassed his grandfather's Poplar Forest retirement house, and he and his bride otherwise lived in the dome room at Monticello. Jefferson wrote of his maturing grandson to Dr. Wistar: "He always speaks of you with a high sense of gratitude. He is married & become an industrious and skillful farmer."[20]

Jefferson Randolph was not a brilliant man, nor was he at all times in command of his temper, but he was absolutely devoted to removing undue worry from the mind of Thomas Jefferson. Sometimes, however, events were beyond Jeff's control. In 1819, when his alcoholic brother-in-law Charles Bankhead stabbed him, word reached Monticello and, as darkness fell, the seventy-six-year-old grandfather took off on his horse, at night, and rode down the mountain "at full gallop." He feared Jeff mortally wounded, but eventually found him inside a Charlottesville store, "laid on a bale of blankets." Jeff recorded in his later memoir that his grandfather "knelt down at my head and wept," as both men broke into tears.[21]

There is real significance to this story, insofar as men's tears were, at the time, considered remarkable, and revealing of a rare sensibility. As highly susceptible creatures, women were judged so delicate, so prone to tears, that little was to be made of their breakdowns; but less excitable men who cried, not out of bodily weakness but from elevated feeling, were commended for demonstrating this kind of vulnerability. Jeff Randolph is telling the readers of his personal memoir that Thomas Jefferson, though seemingly impassive at other times, was one who refused to be cured of an overpowering affection for family. His sudden seizure in 1819 in downtown Charlottesville served as a testament to the power of love that burned in him.

From his school days through the end of his days, Jefferson Randolph understood his obligation to safeguard his grandfather's legacy. Before 1826, he did so by cultivating a sense of business, negotiating with bankers when debts mounted—"I threw myself more and more into the breach of his affairs"—and doing his best to sustain the pastoral idyll proudly envisioned by the man whose name he shared.

It is crucial to bear in mind that Jeff was plagued, from the time he undertook to stabilize his grandfather's finances, by a notoriously volatile father. Thomas Mann Randolph felt in dire competition with his son for the old man's trust and affections. As he matured, Jeff, too, hardened. By the end of Jefferson's life, Thomas Mann Randolph lived apart from the family. The Randolph women sided with Jeff in their family feud, and Jeff acted publicly with a measure of dignity and less awkwardness than he might have under such unpleasant circumstances. In spite of the way he handled strains within the family, the younger Randolph's lone biographer has overall called him "unimaginative, plodding, and self-righteous."[22] When Monticello's slaves were sold to pay off the debts of the estate, Jeff mourned the human toll: "I was powerless to relieve them."[23]

That last statement more or less sums up his life under the gathering cloud that culminated in his grandfather's passing. Thomas Jefferson Randolph showed a certain amount of perseverance, by which he earned his grandfather's respect and trust. But he spent the prime of his life as his grandfather's attendant rather than partner. Immersed in the unrewarding details of finance, he lacked the creative intellectual spark to rise above being an appendage to the greater man's designing mind.

Grandpapa's Ellen

Jeff's sister Ellen, on the other hand, met every expectation. Jefferson recommended great literature to shape the female mind, and he found an exceptionally willing student in his granddaughter Ellen Wayles Randolph (1796–1876), the next youngest after Jeff. The books that rounded out her education included Shakespeare, Milton's "Paradise Lost," the works of the French literary giants Molière, Racine, and Corneille, Cervantes's *Don Quixote* (in French), the *Iliad* and the *Odyssey* (Alexander Pope's English translations), a selection of sermons, and texts on arithmetic, geography, and natural history. In the parlor at Monticello, she customarily sat in the chair opposite her grandfather, whose own favorite was the curved-seat, high-backed goatskin campeachy, or siesta chair. Especially when suffering from rheumatism, Jefferson could not do without the comfortable mahogany lounging chair, of Spanish-Mexican design and imported from New Orleans.[24]

Ellen and her mother were extremely close. The daughter's responsiveness explains part of that. After the untimely death of his wife, Thomas Jefferson had raised Martha to be hardy and resilient, and Ellen, home-schooled, was every bit as well-read, sober, and dignified as Martha; though she appears to have been, in her grandfather's opinion, the most compassionate of the brood, a jilted suitor knew her as "the cold mountain nymph."[25] Martha did not resist her father's high expectations, but was drawn closest to him when she anticipated his need and felt she could provide comfort. Ellen was a mirror of her mother in that way, longing to prove her love. In his late years, as he planned the curriculum of his university, Jefferson wrote of the young fearfully, much as the parents and grandparents of every generation do. Students no longer thirsted for knowledge, he said, and he took particular aim at "the spirit of insubordination and self will which siezes [sic] our youth so early in life as to defeat their education, and the too little controul exercised by indulgent parents." Whether or not Jeff's earlier experience formed a part of that prejudice, self-sufficient Ellen disabused her grandpapa of the fear that there were no disciplined scholars left.[26]

The "Wayles" of her middle name was the surname of Jefferson's deceased wife. Thomas Jefferson paid close attention to Anne, his eldest grandchild, and to all the other young women of his family; but Ellen was unquestionably the granddaughter who most naturally came by her poise and intelligence. He, and everyone else, marveled at her personality. As a student, she was the most gifted. As a writer, she charmed. As a judge of men, she was confident and discerning.[27]

In May 1825, as her doting grandfather's ailments increased, Ellen married a Harvard graduate, Joseph Coolidge, a merchant two years her junior who had traveled in Europe. After their Monticello wedding, she left with him for his hometown of Boston. Jefferson demonstrably approved of Coolidge, and would not have thought of hindering their removal to New England. In a letter to the Greek scholar and Massachusetts congressman Edward Everett, he attested: "I have not been acquainted with a finer character than mr Coolidge, more amiable, more respectable or more worthy."[28] Younger sister Virginia (1801–1882) wrote to Ellen

Ellen Wayles Randolph, before becoming Mrs. Joseph
Coolidge. She was widely regarded as Jefferson's most
accomplished granddaughter. Monticello/Thomas
Jefferson Foundation, Inc.

just after she had left: "I fear he misses you sadly every evening when he takes
his seat in one of the campeachy chairs, & he looks so solitary & the empty
chair on the opposite side of the door is such a melancholy sight to us all, that
one or the other of us is sure to go and occupy it, though we cannot possibly fill
the vacancy you have left in his society."[29]

It may seem unfair to characterize Ellen as the most prized among Jefferson's
granddaughters, but the historical record bears this out. During the Civil War,
Ellen's sister Cornelia (1799–1871) recalled that "Gran' papa" had never shown
signs of inconsistency, either in his daily routine or in his treatment of the
grandchildren. According to Cornelia, her grandfather was "*always,* in all things
& at all times, with never a shade or shadow of change or variation, and without any one of us ever feeling that there was any difference in what he was for
one from what he was for all & each of the rest." He accomplished this by making the grandchildren feel that he was "a companion" rather than behaving con-
descendingly toward them. He was so good-natured that when young they felt
they could write to him at the President's House and demand his immediate
and serious reply to their letters.[30]

Nevertheless, Ellen was the most like him. It can be observed in her portrait that she had even inherited his distinctive high nose. The style of Jefferson's well-known letter of friendship and love, his 1786 dialogue between Head and Heart, is echoed in Ellen's letter to her future brother-in-law Nicholas P. Trist in 1822. She wrote: "Time as he bears us along with him frequently appears to have a slow and heavy wing, but when we look back to the span over which he has carried us, we are astonished and even dismayed at the rapidity of his flight." Here is its predecessor, her grandfather's appeal to Maria Cosway in Paris, thirty-six years before: "The wheels of time moved on with a rapidity of which those of our carriage gave but a faint idea, and yet in the evening, when one took a retrospective of the day, what a mass of happiness had we traveled over!"

Though impressed with her grandfather's gentle and forbearing disposition, Ellen leaned toward the somber mood of her Romantic generation. Metaphoric similarities aside, she added to her "timely" description: "Every year lessens our enjoyments for every year diminishes the force and elasticity of that spring of hope, which after all I believe is the great good of life." Returning to the evocations of her grandfather's earlier Head and Heart letter: "Retrace all those scenes to me, my good companion, and I will forgive the unkindness with which you were chiding me." Clearly, time, memory, and affections collided poetically in the familiar writings of a grandfather and this particular granddaughter.[31]

There was, as well, something about Ellen's presence of mind that made her unusually adept in social settings. Others (men, mostly) reported that she was an inspired conversationalist. When she traveled to Philadelphia in 1816, at the age of nineteen, Jefferson commented to one of that city's residents, William Short, his one-time secretary in Paris who had gone on to romance a duchess, invest well, and become prosperous: "I am glad you have fallen in with my granddaughter Ellen. . . . She merits anything I could have said of a good heart, good temper, a sound head, and great range of information."[32] That same year, Abigail Adams took note of Ellen, who had impressed certain visitors to Monticello. The former first lady cooed about "your Grandaughter Miss Ellen Randolph, whose praises are in the mouths, of all our northern Travellers, who have been so happy as to become acquainted with her." In his reply, Jefferson fantasized accompanying Ellen on a trip to Boston.[33]

Ellen enjoyed opportunities to mingle in high society, to be seen, to create an effect. In 1821, from Washington, she wrote to tell her grandfather that she wished for more amusements: "Mr. Monroe's unsociable temper closes the President's House against females except on the drawing-room nights, and these will not commence this year."[34] When, in 1823, Dr. Watkins was fretting over the treatment and recovery prospects of the presidential candidate William Crawford, he was willing to leave Crawford's side only after Ellen had appeared on the scene, ostensibly to take charge, render proper judgments, and faithfully represent Jefferson's interests. Watkins expressed relief upon "the presence of E. W. R. [Ellen Wayles Randolph] your most intelligent granddaughter."[35]

She was clever and spirited, even as a child. When her grandfather was in Washington, the two were exchanging frequent, highly affectionate letters. After matters of the family's health, their correspondence ranged from pet bantams to Monticello's tulips and orange trees. Once or twice, Grandpapa even touched on politics. As a five-year-old, early in Jefferson's first term, Ellen applied to him for an appropriation, instinctively transmitting the sort of request that made him happiest: "I hope you will bring me some books my dear grand papa." He made it a habit to send her poetry. By her ninth year, he was prodding her with his philosophy of fine arts. When she was eleven, he sent her sheet music to play ("It was much in vogue when I was your age"), and he familiarized her with useful Latin phrases. Near the end of his second term she cooed, "How I long for the time that you are to come home to live and then we shall all go to Monticello to live with you." And that is precisely what happened. By 1809, Ellen was reading French fairly easily, and had been introduced to Homer. To his faithful correspondent, Jefferson signed with an unusually effusive sentiment: "To yourself I am all love." He recognized that she was special.[36]

In retirement, Jefferson saw Ellen constantly. While he cultivated his Monticello garden, she cultivated her mind. She performed French translations in her teens, and Jefferson wrote in this regard that she was "as much of a mistress of the language as any of us."[37] Year by year, his confidence in her mental powers grew. Once she had nothing more to prove intellectually, he jocularly bade her to carry on careless conversation in her letters to him. "Do not write me studied letters," he told her when she was in the nation's capital, "but ramble as you please. Whatever books you want, desire Milligan [a Washington, D.C., bookseller] to furnish them and to put them into my account."[38]

She responded with something more than a ramble, teasing him in a perfectly free form banter of the sort found in only the most intimate letters of this time. "With congressional incidents and fracasseries [a cacophony of scattered noise] I am unacquainted," she wrote, "because those with whom I associate, either take no interest or forbear to speak of them; and the babble of the coteries of the place I can never remember an hour." The simplest kind of communication can sometimes reveal depth of feeling. Here, in the middle of an election season, Ellen insists that she is capable of delivering political news only in a fractured way, and she chooses not even to attempt it. But even in this, she is stylish. Jefferson adopts the same tone when there is nothing of significance to say, when the unfeigned desire to communicate love is conveyed through wit and wordplay: "I have no other news for you but the thermometrical," he professes, the banality of a weather report effectively substituting for "I love you."[39]

Portrait of Jefferson in 1821, by Thomas Sully. West Point Museum Art Collection, United States Military Academy.

Ellen was with her grandfather at Monticello in the spring of 1821, when the eminent portrait painter Thomas Sully produced a full-length painting, commissioned by the U.S. Military Academy at West Point. Sully had "succeeded admirably," Ellen reported to her first cousin. "The upper part of the face is perfect, the eye is so full of life that you almost expect to see it roll. He is the first painter who has ever succeeded in catching the expression of Grandpapa's countenance, and rendering that mixture of dignity and benevolence which prevails in it." She was not so sure about the lines of the mouth and chin, but overall she approved—it was Grandpapa as she knew him—and she calculated that there would not be a more suitable rendering of one "to whom future ages must look back with gratitude and admiration."[40]

Though Jefferson was pleased with Ellen's choice of a husband, Monticello was shaken up in 1825, when the newly married Coolidges took off for Boston. In the autumn of that year, Jefferson shipped his granddaughter a precious piece of history—the desk, or "writing box," as he called it, of his own design, on which he had penned the Declaration of Independence. "It claims no merit of particular beauty," he demurred, explaining that he was willingly parting with an item he had continued to use routinely at Monticello since 1776. "It is plain, neat, convenient." Knowing what this token of love meant, he added: "Its imaginary value will increase over the years."[41]

Ellen wrote regularly, and with considerable penetration. In the last year of her grandfather's life, she gave a report on her visit to ninety-year-old John Adams:

We found the old gentleman, just as he has been frequently described to you, afflicted with bodily infirmities, lame, and almost blind, but, as far as his mind is concerned, as full of life as he could have been fifty years ago; not only does he seem to have preserved the full vigor of his intellect, but all the sprightliness of his fancy, all the vivacity of his thoughts and opinions. He converses with fluency and cheerfulness and a visible interest upon almost any topic. . . . I am afraid our revolutionary worthies have been succeeded by a race comparatively small.[42]

Adams wrote to Jefferson of the same event:

Mrs. C[oolidge] deserves all the high praises I have constantly heard concerning her. She entertained me with accounts of your sentiments of human life, which accorded so perfectly with mine that it gave me great delight.[43]

One can easily imagine how she commanded in conversation, with delicacy and good deportment in equal portions, and armed with all the qualities of female competence that her exacting grandfather wished for—and felt deeply grateful for—in the young woman he no doubt privately regarded as the principal heir to his tastes and affections.

To Reorient Nature: Jefferson's Imagination

As a man happily isolated from city amusements but often starved for intellectual companionship, Jefferson let the campus architecture going up within his view present a model of multilingual conversation, allowing him to talk to the past as well as the present. As he had done with his mountaintop home, he made the academical village an extension of the pastoral retreat by mixing styles; in this way, the gentleman farmer and classicist in him would both be appeased.

What made Jefferson a Romantic was his conviction that nature was overflowing with vital energy. These two architectural classics, Monticello and the University of Virginia, were conceived holistically, lovingly landscaped with flower gardens and such odd additions as Chinese fences and serpentine walls. Jefferson cherished the natural soil, richened with manure, when he had his labor force remove rocks and sculpt new orchards, or level new winding paths meant to be dotted with flowerbeds. He combined curves and vistas to add sensory surprises, because nature was never at rest, and therefore endlessly capable of astonishing. "Though an old man, I am but a young gardener," he famously wrote Charles Willson Peale in 1811. He sought to produce an effect—he hoped that a calming pleasure would overtake the strolling visitor.[44]

It is easy to see that the university was fashioned with the same eye and the same pencil that had conceived Monticello. As the historian Garry Wills has put it, "Monticello was not simply an observation post for the building of the university. It was in effect the soul of the larger fabric going up within its sphere of influence."[45] Once again, the malleable natural landscape was Jefferson's palette; he mixed pigments as he mixed professorships in establishing the setting he felt best suited to the languages he spoke: medicine, moral philosophy, natural sciences, and belles-lettres.

Across the sweep of Jefferson's letter writing, from the 1770s to the 1820s, the pastoral imagination upheld its right by branding the city as "diseased," a place where work was drab and mechanical. Who would not prefer, as he did, the health of the fresh outdoors? Who would not prefer, as he did, an unencumbered view of the distant horizon? The domestic dreamworld of Monticello stood protected from lowland fevers and urban cynicism. Here, and at the university now coming into being, just as there was good ventilation, there were to be no barriers to intellectual freedom.

His was a fragile world, for sure, but there must have been moments when he glimpsed something poetically close to immortality. As a Romantic, he never tired of the mountainscape he woke to—timeless, deathless, but for the constant reminder of the graveyard of his own arrangement, where he planned for his "old crazy carcase" to be laid soon. When he described his telescopic view of the mountains on three sides, "distant and near, smooth & shaggy," he must have felt not just fortunate but convinced that his vision held the best future for America.

British lieutenant Francis Hall's overnight visit to Monticello in 1817 yields a momentary glimpse of Jefferson's surroundings, as the university was beginning to take form. Hall remarked first upon the patriarch's bearing, finding it just what a predecessor, the French Marquis de Chastellux, had recorded back in 1782: "At first serious, nay even cold," but soon adjusting into a warm and inviting, if elevated and loosely philosophical, demeanor. The host led Lieutenant Hall about the grounds, directing his gaze toward a "looming" mountain on his southern horizon, a peak that played tricks on the eye by seeming to invert. Neither Jefferson nor any man of science had succeeded in explaining the phenomenon.

Jefferson had first written on "looming" in his *Notes on Virginia* in the early 1780s, describing "whimsical shapes." The mountain's impressionistic instability, like Jefferson's constant building and rebuilding of Monticello over decades, tells us that it is all right to define Jefferson in dualistic terms: He admired structures that were solid and enduring, and he bargained with Romantic disorder. He built with utility and occupancy in mind, and he imagined beyond his immediate comfort, beyond his immediate time.[46]

In his way of interpreting nature, this neoclassical architect was an early Impressionist. He was enamored of light, found his harmony in an eclectic, mysterious geometry, and studied forms from a variety of vantage points. With less than a year to live, after designing the Rotunda of the university, he sketched a sundial of "strong hoop iron," L-shaped, "making an eyelet hole . . . for a ray of the sun to pass through." Until a specially ordered clock arrived, this simple and ingenious device was to be placed between the two middle columns of the Rotunda's portico, so that the sun, which he had once called "my almighty physician," would become, impressionistically, a part of the tableau.

With his temporary sundial, Jefferson saw as a Romantic and worked as an experimental physicist. He would capture a pinhole camera image of the sun; then, as the earth turned, his bright shadow-dot would trace a swooping curve, marking the hours of the day. Manipulating planes of light and shadow, he produced new life, new movement. Sensation and imagination combined to communicate the scene. In short, he recaptured nature that it might improve in beauty and deepen in effect.[47]

And let us not neglect the creator's consciousness of human history. The classical style of architecture on the university lawn was, in and of itself, a means for Jefferson to embrace the cause of memory, to show how the genius of antiquity had once given shape to a well-ordered perception of the world. Jefferson championed education, just as he was deeply concerned with health. But his purpose in constructing the academical village was even more: It was a soulful, systematic effort to reorient nature. Bringing his dreamworld of Monticello down to earth, he lined up pillars and pavilions. He elevated the past.

He did not deny that nothing lives forever. But he pledged himself to a future of greater promise that he would never see. In this way, his university was a sacred place, doing three things simultaneously: expressing his adoration of nature, adapting history, and awaiting history. To most of his correspondents, Jefferson preferred to communicate his purpose in these strains, emphasizing his own mortality. To a Virginia jurist, the year before his death, he wrote: "Withdrawn by age from all other public services and attentions to public things, I am closing the last scenes of my life by fashioning and fostering an establishment for the instruction of those who are to come after us."[48] To a controversial congressman who was, as he was, acutely aware of the dangers of seeking publicity of any kind: "Seven years ago indeed, I embarked in an enterprise, the establishment of an University, which placed and still keeps me under the public eye. The call was imperious, the necessity most urgent, and the hazard of titubation [stumbling] less, by those seven years, than it now is. The institution is at length happily advanced to completion. . . . But assuredly it is the last object for which I shall obtrude myself on the public observation."[49]

He felt the threat to his personal felicity inherent in the political battle he accepted when he stuck his neck out and petitioned an assemblage of stingy state legislators to allow him to realize his educational vision.[50] Perhaps the most compelling comment on this subject was one he made to a kindred spirit, the Portuguese diplomat and botanist Correa da Serra, a frequent guest at Monticello during Jefferson's retirement years: "Mine, after all may be an Utopian dream, but being innocent, I have thought I might indulge in it until I go to the land of dreams, and sleep there with the dreamers of all past and future times." Here was Jefferson acknowledging himself a dreamer, taken by emotions and desires, and awake to the therapeutic function of the imagination.[51]

It is implicit in his work as a designer that Jefferson recognized imagination as a form of uniqueness that deserved to be praised and protected, so long as it did not become, in his linguistic construction, "sickly," or unbalanced. For him, imagination always served a practical vision—either scientific knowledge or economy and comfort. Curiously, in others of his letters, when he acknowledged the power of imagination within himself, Jefferson identified it not as a constant attribute but as a momentary reverie. In 1815, Lafayette informed him of the deaths of a couple whom he had socialized with in Paris decades before, and the Virginian replied: "They made an interesting part in the idle reveries in which I have sometimes indulged myself, of seeing all my friends of Paris once more, for a month or two; a thing impossible, which, however, I never permitted myself to despair of." Similarly, to President Monroe in 1823, he compared the value of his "off-hand specul[atio]ns" on European politics to the impetus that dreaming sometimes supplied toward conceiving a new idea or developing an existing one: "I thot that I would hazard a copy [of his "speculations"] to you on the bare possibility that out of them as we sometimes do from dreams, you might pick up some hint worth improving by your own reflection. At any rate, the whole reverie will lose to you only the few minutes required for it's perusal."[52] Jefferson was using the words *dream* and *reverie* to convey the humble character of his advice giving; but he was just as decisively indicating that the realm of the imagination could lead to usable, even practical, solutions. The University of Virginia was the perfect marriage of Jeffersonian realism and reverie.

Like the favorite novelist of his younger years, Laurence Sterne, Jefferson saw the imagination as a means of committing one's heart. In the same way that he believed science could not do without generosity, he wondered aloud to Dr. Wistar whether his grandson and namesake possessed "that lively imagination, usually called genius."[53] (He must have sensed Jeff's limitations.) He was, in essence, asking Wistar to confirm for him that charitable dreams, even if termed "idle reveries," were to be lauded.

Who did he know that could identify with his compulsion to imagine, build, re-imagine, and rebuild? Jefferson scanned the republic of letters for colleagues, in government or out, to confer with on such a plane. He heartily approved of the course taken by New York's governor DeWitt Clinton, "father" of the Erie Canal, who had marshaled support for his bold commercial enterprise at just about the same time that Jefferson's university broke ground. "While you get millions to employ so usefully," he wrote to Clinton out of frustration in 1822, "I am laboring for a few thousands to save my fellow-citizens from the Gothic barbarism into which they are sinking for want of the means of education."[54]

And so, until he died, the creative utopian retained his singular position as "father" of the university. He wished to *direct* the imaginations of those who were taught there—he was simply not about to let them loose in this place of classical enchantment. The younger generation, whom he saw, with some exceptions, as irresolute and uninformed, would blunder if they were not given the appropriate guidance.

What would be the value of a democratic republic, he asked, if it existed in an intellectual stupor caused by inattention? So he fretted. He was convinced he was right to feel this way—the politicians of his state had behaved so tentatively, so uncertainly, when they should have jumped at the chance to fund his university. In his final years, the imaginative ex-president was concerned that without his efforts to assemble a cadre of inspiring professors, Virginians would cease to evolve.

And yet, all is lost

It was all to come apart. Not the university, but everything else he cared about. At the end of his life, Jefferson found himself in a desperate situation, obliged to justify taking the unusual step of authorizing a lottery to resolve his personal debt crisis and prevent the loss of Monticello. In 1808, contemplating the end of his second term as president, largely an absentee from his lands, he had written to his daughter Martha of "the gloomy prospect of retiring from office loaded with serious debts," a state that would "materially affect the tranquility of my retirement."[55] (Note again how Jefferson envisions felicity as "tranquility.")

Just how many of the details did he really understand at that point? He knew enough to be concerned with the long term. Part of him calculated on improved productivity to release him from debt. Part of him just hoped for a reprieve. Meanwhile, he thought of ways to show his creditors that he was not neglecting the problem. From the immediate post-Revolutionary years, Jefferson had been beset with financial woes that were common to ever-borrowing Virginia planters. Though shrewder than some, and able to trade on his position in government, he was not in significantly better shape than his miserable son-in-law.

He adopted measures to stave off the financial ruin that finally swallowed up everything, starting with his greatest treasures. The books Jefferson had collected all his life were stacked along the walls of Monticello and painstakingly catalogued. In 1814, recognizing the state of his finances, he offered his library to the young Library of Congress, meant to replenish what was lost when the British burned Washington during the War of 1812. In spite of the bitterness of Federalists who would do nothing to help their old enemy, Congress voted to acquire the books, and in 1815 crates containing nearly 6,500 volumes were delivered. Jefferson used a significant portion of the $23,950 he received in compensation to repay outstanding debts to old friends William Short and the Polish patriot Thaddeus Kosciusko. He wrote to the latter: "The abuse of the institution of banks in this country by . . . the immense amount of paper they have thrown into circulation beyond the competent amount, has brought on a great depreciation of their paper, and imminent danger that all will blow up and end in universal bankruptcy. . . . I thought I owed it to your friendship & confidence to attend to the danger in time."[56]

The sale of his books halved Jefferson's debt, but he continued to struggle financially. He had owed money to a bank in Amsterdam since the 1790s, the interest on which grew and grew. His reputation for integrity secured short-term loans while he waited for good weather and better crops to help him out from under. Then Wilson Cary Nicholas, Jefferson Randolph's father-in-law, a former governor of Virginia, and, ironically, president of the Richmond branch of the Bank of the United States, asked Jefferson to endorse a note on his behalf. When the Panic of 1819 struck, and Nicholas's fortune was wiped out, Jefferson was left owing an additional $20,000, worth many times that today. Under a debilitating attack of rheumatism, his health was suffering, as we have seen, compounding his concerns.

Jefferson seemed to know what was coming, yet he did not see it with sufficient clarity to forestall his own failure. In 1816, he complained that "our deluded citizens are clamoring for more banks, more banks," and he prophesied: "Two hundred millions of paper in the hands of the people. . . . The debt which purchased our independence was but of eighty millions, of which twenty years of taxation had in 1809 paid but the one half. And what have we purchased with this tax of two hundred millions which we are to pay by wholesale but usury, swindling, and new forms of demoralization. . . . Confidence is already on the totter."[57] The crisis he anticipated resulted in the "calling in of paper" and tightening of credit. Specie-poor, over-borrowed Americans suffered en masse.

He temporized. As land values declined, his greatest asset turned out to be human labor—his slaves. In 1820, his remarried son-in-law Jack Eppes, who had been husband to Jefferson's delicate younger daughter Maria, exchanged bank stock for some of the Poplar Forest slaves, whom Jefferson sold with the understanding that they would remain within the extended family.

As he strove to make the University of Virginia a reality, a sound establishment designed to cultivate liberal minds, Jefferson's domestic establishment was anything but sound. Yet he knew only one way: His compulsion was, once again, to imagine, build, re-imagine, and rebuild. He could not stop himself from using up precious funds to upgrade Monticello and finish Poplar Forest. After selling his library, he began immediately to buy books and fashion a new library. *That* was Jefferson.

The Enlightenment burned brightly within him. He lived to promote learning, but he could not avert his own ruin. He finally started to think about selling some of his lands, but even that would not be enough. In 1824, Virginian

George Tucker, who was soon to be appointed professor of moral philosophy at the university, published a novel titled *The Valley of the Shenandoah*. It told the story of a once prosperous planter family wrecked by the death of its debt-ridden patriarch who, just like Jefferson, had unwisely endorsed a friend's promissory note. Adding to the remarkable irony (or perhaps complete predictability) of Tucker's standing at the end of Jefferson's life, the professor would go on to publish a "dispassionate"—as the author described it—biography of Jefferson in 1830.[58]

There is, then, a quality of desperation, an unavoidable melancholy, in the story of Jefferson's last years. In spite of monumental construction activities, both on the mountaintop and below at the site of the university, the 1820s for him were a race against fiscal reality. He had successfully eluded creditors for decades, but they were due to catch up to him. If we were to fashion him as a literary figure (more universal than Tucker's Colonel Grayson), he would be a nobler and quite affable version of Washington Irving's downhearted pedant, Ichabod Crane. He would shed light wherever he went, alternately doling out medical advice and accounts of manners among the French or Anglo-Saxons, spouting rules of rhetoric and the metric pattern of English prosody, repeating the philosophy of the ancients, reviving Palladian architecture, and regaling citizens with upbeat stories of Revolutionary days. But he would not be all that distant from Irving's Ichabod, whom Americans were now beginning to read about in the haunting tale of *Sleepy Hollow*, published in 1819. Straining to get astride Eagle, the Virginia equestrian was still exercising up to eight or ten miles in a day; but he was rapidly losing his lead. It was his own pleasing imagination, not Ichabod's ghostly vision, that sometimes got the better of old Thomas Jefferson. As he contested with fiscal reality, the highly creative highs melted into lows, as his correspondence shows, and he focused all over again on the limitations he faced amid the physical signs of aging.

On February 8, 1826, the ailing, indebted octogenarian wrote this to his grandson: "I should not care were life to end with the line I am writing." He extended the thought by saying he would try to hang on to life for as long as he "may be of some avail to the family." And he meant equally what came next: He would resolve to hang on, if only because of his family's "affectionate devotion" toward him.[59] His education, work, and study would have been less consequential to him had it failed to claim his family's close attention and add to their happiness. He had opened their minds so that they would love what he loved. And so he always needed to feel that his family needed him.

Daughter Martha, who had toughened her soul and then sacrificed her personal comfort (and, perhaps, intellectual ambition) on behalf of her father and her husband both, raised her children and embraced the fate of a southern woman. For her, that included being left, a woman in her middle fifties, without sufficient means. Her unexceptional son Jefferson was not destined for power or greatness, but only for the quasi-maternal role of guardian. He was a conscientious worker for the family interest, but not an initiator or designer, certainly not while his grandfather lived. Had Ellen been a man, she would no doubt have been allowed to achieve what her agile mind had prepared her for; but she, too, like her mother, became a wife. They were all, in that sense, keepers of the flame, more properly considered appendages—not inheritors—of Thomas Jefferson's designing mind.

4

Reading with Women

Reading when I can be indulged in it, is the elysium of my present life.

THOMAS JEFFERSON TO
FRANÇOIS ADRIAN VAN DER KEMP,
FEBRUARY 9, 1818

Where would nineteenth-century literature be without death, foreshadowed by sensational distress and heart-arresting anguish? A minor novel of 1826, *Yorktown: An Historical Romance,* takes its patriotic theme, the decisive battle in securing U.S. independence, and inserts into the contest a wild-eyed, cross-dressing Continental soldier named Maude. She is all the more desperate because she is a fallen woman who abandons her prescribed gender role. In battle, Maude is stabbed by the same man who stole her innocence, a conniving loyalist commander, and she lives just long enough to learn of the American victory. Yet it is not the villain's sword that kills her. Out of control emotions finally lead Maude to take an overdose of the opiate laudanum. Her death is a reminder that a woman who fails to heed society's principal warning to her sex can never be reestablished. In the literature of Jefferson's late years, suicide was generally the only way out for a woman who did not qualify for a life of quiet domesticity.[1]

Thomas Jefferson espoused liberal sentiments that have been the cause of frequent celebratory speech among modern humanists: He defended the rights of ordinary citizens against the disproportionate exercise of power by society's rich and powerful; he believed in extending education to all so as to rouse the general public and stimulate democracy. But he stood in the way of women's rise; he refused to link intellectual capacity to public visibility; he wanted women protected from all coarseness and competition. He could not imagine female talent in the marketplace, or in government.

It could have been otherwise. The intellectual resilience of Abigail Adams is perhaps too prominent an example, and she, seemingly, so confident a thinker that she cannot serve as a singular contrast to Jefferson's sense of the ideal feminine style. But his controversial vice president, Aaron Burr, loved and wed Theodosia Prevost because of her discernment, sturdy wit, and public versatility and fearlessness; she was several years older than he. Previously married to a British officer, who died overseas in the midst of the Revolutionary War, she succeeded, through her unabashed politicking ability, in maintaining good relations with prominent patriots—the respectable equivalent of the fictional Maude's story. The Burrs' subsequent correspondence contains a literary showiness that reveals both playfulness and his respect for the subtle turns of Theodosia's mind. After his wife's untimely death, Burr raised his daughter (named after her mother) to be similarly adept and unafraid, a woman who enjoyed the writings of the English feminist Mary Wollstonecraft (1759–1797). Dolley Madison, who appears to have been introduced to James Madison by Aaron Burr, is another who impressed men by her knowledge of the conduct of politics, no less than by her refined and reassuring manner.[2]

Jefferson, on the other hand, held fast to rather conventional notions of a woman's role at home and in society. In spite of the obvious talents of his own daughter and granddaughters, he subscribed to the medical opinion that men were naturally more firm and made to exercise their reason, women more supple and made to emote—and that sex roles were immutable. He thought that a healthy republic was one in which every inherently passionate female was transformed into a dutiful wife and nurturing mother. He feared the tensions and what he imagined would be anarchic results if well-bred women were too exposed, that is, if they should enter the naturally bold and aggressive man's world (constituting "promiscuous assemblies," in the language of the time). He wrote with foreboding to his secretary of the treasury, Albert Gallatin, in 1807: "The appointment of a woman to office is an innovation for which the public is not prepared, nor am I."[3]

It would seem from this that Jefferson was simply afraid of a society in which women actively went about acquiring the tools to compete with men. But nothing is ever so simple. He was not prescribing cultural uniformity. He did not revolt, as much as the Adamses did, upon witnessing how brazen French women could be. His granddaughter Ellen remarked that his expectations from the female intellect were great: "I have known him to lay down for a young lady a course of reading which might have startled a University student."[4] In later years, Ellen expressed her own faith in the abilities of women. When she visited London and saw young Queen Victoria riding in an open carriage, she wrote in her diary that "it is surprising what a feeling of *loyalty* women of all nations seem to have towards this sovereign of their own sex." She then added: "We are so seldom called to fill high places that our hearts are stirred at once with pride

& love when we see the destinies of a great people even nominally committed to hands like our own."[5] Ellen had learned in her grandfather's house to set her sights high, but also to accept variations among the women of the world without rejecting the healthfulness of the model that he had imagined right (or felicitous) for his own immediate surroundings.

Demonstrating the range of acceptable thinking on this subject, Dr. Benjamin Rush wrote conventionally to a young woman about to be wed: "From the day you marry you must have no will of your own. The subordination of your sex to ours is enforced by nature, by reason, and by revelation." Yet the same Dr. Rush had published a few years earlier his *Thoughts upon Female Education*, a work proposing that young women should be liberated intellectually, and, as citizens, fully encouraged to pass judgment on the subject of politics. The ambitious *Thoughts* would be reprinted many times.[6]

As a medical school lecturer, Dr. Rush based his teaching on the belief that the nerves of women were "more susceptible of impressions of mind and body" than those of men, thus "more subject to nervous diseases." If their natural softness made them neurologically fragile, it also extended their lives (explaining why there were more aged women than aged men). Thus destined to live alone for more years, and "precluded by custom, or perhaps nature [!], from making a choice in matrimony," women were possessed of "more acute" moral faculties and "fitted for their solitary situation by a more exquisite *sense of Deity*." Naturally devout, women were endowed with more "fortitude," if less "courage"—though the latter "attaches no dishonor to their characters, as it does to those of men."[7]

Gender considerations were political, whether or not publicly expressed as such. Believing as Rush did that a woman's chief influence ought to be by way of love, natural perceptiveness, and superior taste, rather than through direct argument, Jefferson, reared among the colonial gentry, found it culturally near impossible to speak or write to a woman in the same way that he spoke or wrote to a man. Though his literary persona exhibited the softened disposition of an eighteenth-century Man of Feeling, and almost transcendently sympathetic when he wanted to be, Jefferson knew the difference between the "male" and "female" forms of "prudence": One was clearly proactive, the other passive. He would not have described his manner as "feminine" in the way certain (friendly as well as unfriendly) commentators did, because his effort to balance sincere masculine sentiment with reliable masculine prudence or rationality was a well-developed matter of style, the manner of a bookish man, and a means of putting people at ease, rather than unconscious behavior one might superficially situate on a spectrum of femininity/masculinity.

The community of men to which Jefferson belonged used a particular vocabulary to secure reputations for decorum and propriety. In being taught to exercise "prudence," they were also taught to shun its opposites: "extravagance" and "frivolity." This is why, when Jefferson's political detractors wished to insult the wide-ranging scholar, they accused him of having his head in the clouds, and of being taken with extravagant or frivolous ideas. He did not respond visibly to provocation, however, reserving his ire for private letters and conversation with trusted friends, especially alter-ego James Madison; his outward behavior was so mild and accommodating that enemies could only condemn him by insisting that his mildness hid his "intrigue," "fraud," and "dissimulation."

The opposite masculine type to Jefferson was, in the language of the time, "the man of furious resentment," whose passions sometimes got the better of him. An example of this unattractive type would have to be the blunt, peevish, yet astonishingly successful Alexander Hamilton, Jefferson's political nemesis in the 1790s. Hamilton's sense of his own masculinity was expressed with far less subtlety: He craved military distinction; he charmed women. His temperament played a role in his sensational death.

As part of both the reserved and the bold masculine behavioral norm, no less than in the more narrowly circumscribed female behavioral norm, one was taught to behave as though one were being watched. Jefferson dealt differently with women in different spaces: In Parisian salons, in the 1780s, he adapted to a place where eager, outgoing female conversationalists were not sexually protected, nor felt they needed to be.[8] But he did not envision America as such a place. He was too easily reminded that the women of Europe were also adept at what Jefferson knew as "female intrigue": Court politics included artful maneuvering by ambitious women, and Jefferson abhorred court politics. He wanted to preserve his nation from anything remotely resembling aristocratic-monarchical maneuverings. His political rise depended upon his ability to sniff out and eradicate that effete style of politics and replace it with the mannerly republican dialogue he considered the singular test of masculine prowess.

Mannerly republican dialogue and decorum sound desirable, but they are not, of course, a convincing rationale for insisting on female submissiveness. It is a lasting bit of curiosity for us that Jefferson could exhibit a modern liberal conscience in very visible ways—promoting public education, opening up political franchise to ordinary men, securing freedom of conscience—and yet be socially conservative, even for his time, in matters of race (as we shall see below) and gender.

Just as there were progressive individuals in his generation who agitated against slavery, there were those who, like Mary Wollstonecraft, insisted that the distinctions drawn between men and women on the basis of sensations, the nervous system, and "natural" affections, were false; aside from that which required brute physicality, women could accomplish whatever men could.[9] Yet it remained hard for a majority of nineteenth-century Americans, of either sex, to understand that female delicacy was a cultural construction and not a natural distinction. Popular writing, North as well as South, reinforced the notion that women needed to make themselves amiable and unassuming, as well as level-headed; as "ladies," they were to conform to the male image of what a woman ought to be, changing men's minds passively by setting a moral example, and not by voicing criticism too openly.

Jefferson could not countenance female participation in politics, or in public office holding, as he indicated to the Swiss-born Gallatin, whose socially prominent New York–reared wife Hannah (née Nicholson) was, even when young, in her husband's words, "a pretty good democrat." But Jefferson sensed no threat from the women who wrote history, such as Bostonian Mercy Otis Warren; for history was a moral enterprise, and within his ideology women were meant to be guardians of virtue. For Jefferson, society was moving in an egalitarian direction, but not so fast that it should overturn gendered rules of conduct, or eliminate gendered spaces, in the process. Europe would do as it wished; New England would do as it wished. But Virginia must remain Virginia, wherein women were understood to be the special agents of sentiment and affection, and men were given the outward authority that enabled them to tap their inner strength and display vigor in all they did, while exhibiting sympathy and magnanimity in appropriate doses, at appropriate times.[10]

This is not to suggest that Jefferson disapproved of wit in a woman. Once again, his granddaughter Ellen, whose letters abound in wit, recorded that Jefferson especially prized the wit of his older sister Jane, who died before the Revolution.[11] Women could wield a sense of humor, provided it was neither loud nor ribald.[12] Ellen accepted the compromise of her generation: She grew up better equipped to deal with men in a variety of settings, because as America expanded and people moved about more and more, society could not always protect a woman. But this did not mean that women had to stop shedding tears—indeed they were still expected to, just as they were expected to place the highest value on love and motherhood.

Jefferson liked to encounter examples of traditional womanhood. When in 1816 he wrote a letter in support of a financially depressed Quaker acquaintance, the friend's daughter struggled over how to write a gracious thank you that would be understood as sincere and not excessive. She tested the letter on her father first: "Though I deny having made any efforts at the sublime," she addressed him, "I fear too thou wilt think some parts extravagant—do not, my father, for it is not *half* I feel—I cannot think of him [the ex-president] with moderation. Great and excellent man!" The father repeated to Jefferson what his tender daughter had written. Acknowledging both father's and daughter's letters, Jefferson remarked of the latter that it was "acceptable . . . the sensibility expressed in hers for services so moderate shews a heart of great susceptibility, and which under your care and instruction promises to make happy parents and friends." Here he represented the sincere and sober male protector of a woman who embraced her subordinate role. The entire exchange could just as easily have come from the tear-filled pages of a novel of sensibility.[13]

Throughout his life, Jefferson's immediate family was chiefly made up of women. He produced no legitimate sons. Except for his eldest grandson and namesake, the males were rather young and, therefore, the recipients of less crucial communication (and consideration) from the patriarch. As an eldest son himself, Jefferson was fourteen when he lost his father, and he was closest to his elder sister as he was growing up. His mother survived until he was thirty-three, and though no evidence exists to enlighten us with respect to the emotional character of their relationship, she no doubt remained a presence in his domestic world. Because Jefferson's wife died young and he did not remarry, he was especially concerned with the upbringing and education of their daughters in the 1780s and 1790s; the pattern would repeat when Martha produced daughters, and only the one son, Jeff, until a second and third came along toward the end of Jefferson's presidency.

Martha had given him eight healthy grandchildren by then. The eldest of the girls, Anne, appears to have helped extensively with the domestic routine; details of household purchases over a period of several years appear in her handwriting in an account book that has been preserved. It was Ellen, of course, who most excelled intellectually, and it was she who ended up farthest from home. She was able to defend herself in "the world" as an adult, whereas Anne could not even defend herself against the brutality of her alcoholic husband.

Jefferson took a steady interest in his grandchildren, constantly giving gifts of books and posing questions at mealtime. Because there were more female than male Jefferson-Randolphs, Grandpapa, without intending on a national scale to implement a program for female education, could not help but undertake one at home. He could see in his own family that women in American society were growing sturdier, by and large, and that moral endangerment, the watchword of an eighteenth-century female's rite of passage, was gradually becoming a less menacing phenomenon in the nineteenth century. But it was hard for one of his years, when it was so personal, to let go of old habits.

"Miss Edgeworth's works. They are all good."

In March 1818, protesting that his daughter Martha, as the mother of six girls, was a better judge than he of the practical means of educating daughters, Jefferson replied to a query from Nathaniel Burwell, scion of a powerful Virginia planter family, with "a catalogue of books" designed especially for young women. He prefaced his remarks by showing how deliberately he had planned ahead when, as a young father, he recognized that his own two girls were bound to be placed "in a country situation," and remote from public schooling. Jefferson had directed his girls' education so that they might in turn direct the course of study of their own daughters—and even sons, "should their fathers be lost, or incapable, or inattentive." He was acknowledging that fathers often tended to be absent, both physically and emotionally.[14]

He praised dancing, drawing, and music. The first, he said, was "healthy exercise, elegant and very attractive for young people," but not to be pursued by a woman after her marriage (he called this "the French rule"). His reasoning was twofold: Dancing was not physically "safe" for one who was meant to spend her years either pregnant or nursing; nor was it "innocent" after sexual activity had commenced. Drawing, he assured, was both "innocent and engaging," and would serve a mother in her role as educator. Music, finally, "furnishes a delightful recreation for the hours of respite from the cares of the day." In his own home, Martha and Maria had played harpsichord and pianoforte, and he had long before learned violin. As president, he occasionally sent sheet music home to his granddaughters.

Jefferson devoted much of the letter to Burwell warning of dangers. He fussed about the threat to young women's minds and morals posed by novel reading, which was already a popular pastime. This was by no means Jefferson's singular concern, but rather a standard complaint among well-educated men of his generation. In describing novel reading as an "inordinate passion," and a "poison" that turns an impressionable mind against "wholesome reading," he was merely echoing the words of ultra-conservative Noah Webster back in the 1790s: Webster had decried the "false and artificial sensibility" that "tickles the nerve and floats in the fancy, without leaving any impressions on the heart, or influence on the conduct." Webster wanted men of distinction to oversee the dissemination of properly moral novels, so as to prevent easily influenced young women from obtaining a "discolored view of the affairs of the world." For female physiology—a complex of unstable and dangerous energies—a "discolored view" meant that the nerves and associated sympathies would be misdirected and misapplied.[15]

Thus Jefferson could be patriarchal and undemocratic in his perception of literary authority, rationalizing his attitude, as Webster did, as an outgrowth of medical concerns. His greatest worry was that novel-reading young women would become romantically excited when they were supposed to remain calm and chaste. Given the professed delicacy of their nerves, he feared the mesmerizing effect of "figments of fancy," as he put it to Burwell. Jefferson took the conservative line that a woman's natural sensibility rendered her best suited for a life devoid of passion. The wrong kind of stimulation led to a debilitating nervous excitement or, in extreme cases, female hysteria or irreversible madness. This female addiction to novel reading corresponded to Dr. Tissot's relentless warnings to men addicted to "the evil" of masturbation: "All the bodily senses, and all the faculties of the soul, weakened," he wrote, occasioning "the loss of imagination and memory." That is why imagination had to be moderated.[16]

The common denominator in medical and literary studies was acceptance that life was an adventure with consequences—a dangerous adventure often thrown off course or put out of balance. But it was invariably an adventure aimed at improvement, and it demanded resolve. Imagination was about temperament; it had to be monitored by the most rational of beings, just as scientific experiment had to be conducted methodically by those with the most training. But imagination always defined genius, and so it should not be stripped of its spontaneous quality, either.

Then why so much fear? Jefferson believed (as many others did) that among those most vulnerable, reading was a process that allowed sensations to circumvent the will and course through the nerves independent of judgment—indeed, sensations were capable of adversely affecting judgment. When one reads the wrong novels, as he told Burwell, "the result is a bloated imagination, sickly judgment"—*again, note Jefferson's medical referent*[17]—"and disgust towards all the real businesses of life." Strong language.

But then he toned down his comments. Though relatively few, there were novels he wholeheartedly approved. Narratives that highlighted "incidents of real life" redeemed the novel form from what he called "this mass of trash." Again, strong words. Our task is to establish, when it came to the content of fiction, where Jefferson drew a line for female readers and what his choices tell us about *his* imagination.

Under suitable novels, the first on his list was: "Evenings at home by Mrs Barbault." Anna Letitia Barbauld, born the same year as Jefferson (he spelled her name "Barbault"), was most noted as a British poet. She was a dear friend of Jefferson's dear friend, the dissenter and scientist Joseph Priestley, whom the Virginian had welcomed to America as a refugee from political violence in the 1790s. Barbauld shared Jefferson's critique of English arrogance, composing verse in 1811 that anticipated haughty Britain's gradual diminution on the world scene: "Yes, thou must droop; thy Midas dream is o'er." It was presumably her political posture as well as her moral posture that suited Thomas Jefferson.[18]

Evenings at Home is something like *Aesop's Fables* in character, and directed toward the very young. Some of the readings are moral lessons, set in dialogue; others are akin to encyclopedia entries, and designed to impart knowledge. One de-

> *Novels.*
>
> *Evenings at home by mrs Barbault*
>
> *Miss Edgeworth's works. they are all good.*
>
> *Lettres sur l'education* ⎫
> *Theatre d'education* ⎬ *by Madame*
> *Theatre de societé* ⎬ *Genlis.*
> *Veillées du chateau* ⎭
>
> *Godwin's Caleb Williams....*

An assortment of novels Jefferson found suitable for young women, which he included in a letter to Nathaniel Burwell, March 14, 1818. Anna Letitia Barbauld published acclaimed poetry as well as juvenile fiction; Maria Edgeworth was, perhaps, the most influential female English novelist of the 1810s; the Comtesse de Genlis wrote her French stories for children in the 1780s, around the time Jefferson and his daughters were in Paris; William Godwin was a radical political thinker as well as a celebrated novelist. Library of Congress.

scribes the processing of paper from rags; another identifies bird species; all convey the values of kindness and frugality. The dialogue "between Mama and Kitty" teaches patience: "I hope you will allow, that mammas know better what is proper for their little girls to learn, than they do themselves." The same tutorial also recognized that social classes exist, as determined by male authority: "It is usual to call all well educated women, who have no occasion to work for livelihood, *ladies;* but if you will think a little, you must see that they live very differently from each other, for their fathers and husbands are in very different ranks and situations in the world, you know." *Evenings at Home* exalts female domesticity.[19]

Jefferson's selection of Barbauld is followed by a notation: "Miss Edgeworth's works. They are all good." Maria Edgeworth (1767–1849) was by this time the author of seven novels and various essays and short stories. Born in England, removed to Ireland in her teens, she marveled at the color and charm of Irish habits and speech, and wrote of them with a mixture of appreciation and good humor. More to the point, she captured the mischievous ways of people from all social classes. Her wealthy, sophisticated father, Richard, introduced her to

Maria Edgeworth, from a mid-nineteenth-century engraving.

the world of country houses that she wrote about—often in collaboration with him—though her reputation as a singular wit was entirely deserved.

Her first and most influential novel, *Castle Rackrent* (1800), is really a novella, narrated by an old servant named Thady Quirk ("honest Thady"), whose deadpan helps her poke fun at Irish aristocratic life and manners. The men tend to be well liked, rakish, inebriated, and debt-ridden; when they are not imprisoned in bedrooms by husbands or fathers, the women remove themselves from the action. Silly, outlandish, and perfectly brutal goes the novel as it chronicles the slow disintegration of a landed gentry family. Castle Rackrent's lovable Sir Condy serves as a distorted mirror image of Jefferson; an unselfish trust (the value they place on friendship) destroys both men's fortunes.[20]

But that is not the message contained for Jefferson in Maria Edgeworth's prose. Her mobile imagination fit his moral definition of the good female-directed novel. So then, how could the satirical Castle Rackrent correspond with Jefferson's insistence that the female imagination was in need of monitoring? The answer is not immediately obvious. First, although he wanted young women to be reserved in their romantic inclinations, he did not prefer them dull. Convinced that Edgeworth's brand of humor did not awaken repressed desire, but only entertained (with a douse of sympathy to the human condition), he was not worried in the manner Noah Webster's words conveyed.

To critique the fashionable world, to mock even the gentility he himself exhibited, was quite all right with Jefferson, so long as it was life affirming. As a young man, he had adored Laurence Sterne's big and small productions, Tristram Shandy (1759–1767) and A Sentimental Journey (1768), taken together the eighteenth century's most profoundly irreverent examination of the soul. So there was precedent for Jefferson's approving a novelist's unconventional approach to morality. He preferred a string of jesting, wit-laden vignettes to the coldly admonishing manner of an orthodox minister; the former tapped into conscience at least as well as the latter.

In the plot-free Tristram Shandy, conscience reigns, and self-absorption becomes imaginative sympathy as the novel progresses. Satire is rich, but never mean-spirited, and laughter, the most human of human expressions, is expected. Sterne was part of the intellectual set that was most responsive to the new physiology by exploring nerves and sensibility and the action of the brain. He proved himself inventive (and often hilarious) by associating the mysteries of delicate sentiment with the failure of eighteenth-century physicians' abstractions to explain the variability of life.[21]

In Sterne, as in Edgeworth, the warm imagination is turned inward, and wit points outward. Jefferson invited both. Rather than devolving into an austere moralist, he sought to be a good-humored one, à la Benjamin Franklin: He told Jeff Randolph, and others of that generation, that good humor was the first quality of mind to be cultivated.[22] His granddaughter Ellen recalled his outlook: "He enjoyed a jest, provided it were to give pain to no one, and we were always glad to have any pleasant little anecdote for him—when he would laugh as cheerily as we could do ourselves."[23]

Jefferson's ideal of domestic harmony required a female to be poised, not grave. In appreciating humor, she was constrained only from laughing too loudly—uproarious laughter was a sexually suggestive sign at this time. Jefferson would have concurred with the conduct book author who wrote in this vein: "There is still all the difference in the world between the entertainer of an evening, and a partner for life." That is, a woman had to engage a man's sympathetic consideration, and not behave in such a way that she might lose it.[24] In short, Jefferson admired wit in an author, humor when affectionately aimed, and self-possession in women. He appreciated the comic absurd, which, as a high form of critical thinking, did not teach impractical behavior, nor provoke a nervous reaction, nor promote unreal expectations from romance.[25]

Edgeworth left *Castle Rackrent* behind and took up more conventional writing. Her subsequent novels, beginning with *Belinda* (1801), were social commentaries, less idiosyncratic than *Castle Rackrent* and melodramatic in varying degrees, their female characters speaking volubly and grappling with the most human of problems, often brought about by the male vices of drinking, gambling, and dueling.

In *Belinda,* the title character is affable, well educated, possessed of the desired feminine traits of the day, and therefore a suitable match for a trustworthy male. One is found in Oxford-educated Clarence Hervey, chivalrous and humane, but "easily led" and "so dreadfully afraid of passing for a pedant that when he came into the company of the idle and ignorant, he pretended to disdain every species of knowledge."[26] It is a novel that highlights the choices facing a girl as she takes the stage of life. When does a woman accomplish most by remaining "soft"? What dignifies a man's character? Edgeworth is trying to define gender roles and moral boundaries.

But the novel really centers on the manipulations of Belinda's on-again, off-again confidante, the socially adept ("Every thing that her ladyship said was repeated as witty") but inwardly confused Lady Delacour, a woman with a past. In a typical chapter, "The Mysterious Boudoir," the reader is witness to the extravagance of female passions, as induced by delicate nerves. Before "convulsions" take over, and amid "shrieks" and other signs of pain, the supposedly dying Delacour begs for a double dose of the opiate laudanum. The prudent Belinda repeatedly refuses, calling for the clever Dr. X___, who provides the correct prognosis. The patient survives and mends her ways, and the characters are all settled in their lives when the story ends.[27]

At once acknowledging her prescribed femininity and mocking the literary stereotype that extends from it, Jefferson's prized granddaughter Ellen expressed the learned fears and tempered vulnerabilities of a proper woman of sensibility: "I have been suffering from one of those 'maladies de langueur,' so common in our country and climate," she wrote her brother-in-law in 1823. "The disease whatever it is, has for the present settled upon my nerves. . . . I would not have you suppose from this that I am giving myself any fine lady airs, I will assure you that there are no shrieks, nor fits, nor tears, nor tremblings in the case, I have 'executed no elegant outrages' nor excited one spark of 'tender admiration' by my fascinating weaknesses.' No one from common observation would perceive that anything was the matter with me." The key to a young woman's success, as Ellen understands it (her grandfather would agree), is to maintain a "vigorous mind" and "force of character" amid challenges, even those inwardly generated.[28]

In Edgeworth's *The Absentee* (1812), the stakes are slightly different—life under a financial cloud—but maintaining friendships and making sound choices remain key elements. The young and deserving Lord Colambre consistently refuses to yield to caprice, and is rewarded for it. As in all such novels, deception abounds. An ambitious woman has designs on the unsuspecting hero: Her "whole figure . . . suddenly metamorphosed; instead of the soft, gentle, amiable female, all sweet charity and tender sympathy, formed to love and be loved, he beheld one possessed and convulsed by an evil spirit—her beauty, if beauty it could be called, the beauty of a fiend."[29] Where human feeling is being defined, "convulsions" are transparent markers, as useful to the plot as the moral peril that tests the hero or heroine.

Edgeworth places women at the heart of her novels, but she as clearly requires the social order to be sustained by a benevolent patriarchy. In *The Absentee,* perhaps the most outstanding example of this, the garrulous, well-intentioned Lady Clonbrony is completely irrational for most of the book. Her practical-minded son Colambre must demonstrate over and over how her erratic behavior threatens the happiness of the whole family. Colambre's love interest, Grace, possesses just the right degree of "pride" (dignity) that he wishes his mother owned, as well as "affectionate tenderness," "indefatigable patience," and "strong attachment." Edgeworth's women give up a certain amount of autonomy in return for what one scholar calls "new-style patriarchy," in which "children learn to respect authority when that authority wears a benevolent and disinterested countenance." One can see a Jeffersonian domestic order in this.[30]

Maria Edgeworth never married. She is often compared to her contemporary, the better-known (at least to later generations) Jane Austen. But Edgeworth's writing is generally considered less pious, less judgmental, and Jefferson's family must have been quite comfortable with female characters who recognized temptation and were yet dutiful to Jefferson's call for mental and moral balance. Jefferson himself refrained from taking high-handed control over his granddaughters' marital prospects; he was content to instruct with loving concern. Picturing the Jefferson-Randolph women as well read yet appropriately modest, competent hostesses and superior conversationalists, he could associate Edgeworth's moderate tone with home life at Monticello.

He was proud of how loyal Martha turned out, and now hopeful about his granddaughters' future, too. He had overseen his elder daughter's education from the time of her mother's death in 1782, when she was ten; in a similar way, Maria Edgeworth had lost her mother at the age of five, and her equally larger-than-life father, a patriarchal moralist, came to share (if not dominate) her literary voice. What is interesting, then, is the question of subliminal control.

Thomas Jefferson and Richard Edgeworth were publicly prominent men who seem to have given primary shape to their daughters' intellectual and emotional lives. Martha Jefferson Randolph had early on internalized the command that she find her proper place in society as wife and daughter, and that she simultaneously fulfill her father's need for a partner to oversee the domestic routine and comfort him whenever he emerged from his embattled position in the political realm.

Granddaughter Ellen, living at Monticello from 1809, replayed this role. She grew so enamored with Maria Edgeworth's imagination that she analogized her own experiences accordingly. Years afterward, married, and accommodating herself to her Boston surroundings, she learned—"this gossip came to me doubly distilled through the mouths of two servant girls; Mrs L__'s and my own"—that a matron in the vicinity had no patience for small children. Ellen, now a mother, wrote in her private journal: "I have a worse opinion of servants than Miss Edgeworth herself, & have freely expressed my disapprobation of those ladies who listen to their tattling." Even her style of writing has an Edgeworthian ring to it. Though domesticated, Mrs. Joseph Coolidge retained her sharp powers of observation and presence of mind, as her grandfather most certainly would have advised—and as Richard Edgeworth would have advised his daughter, too.[31]

In *Belinda*, Maria Edgeworth originally intended Lady Delacour to sink under the weight of her own recklessness and die, and for Belinda to be pursued by the dissipated Lord Delacour before coming into an inheritance and landing on her feet. Revealingly, it was Maria's strong-willed father and collaborator on the novel who tampered with his daughter's art. Though she later wrote that "there was no danger of offending or of disappointing him by not using what he offered," it seems clear that he wanted to replace her simpler, more calamitous narrative solution with his own pedagogy. It was he who had spirited her away from her sympathetic comedy of manners, *Castle Rackrent*, and directed her to a heavier-textured appraisal of virtue and vice. And so we must seriously ask, with which perspective did Jefferson identify more readily? Maria Edgeworth's or Richard Edgeworth's?[32]

There is another way to approach this question: Did he identify with the female novelist from a patronizing perspective or from a genuinely admiring one? There was no question about it for Sir Walter Scott, the most celebrated male novelist of the decade of the 1810s, who proclaimed himself in Maria Edgeworth's debt. It is difficult to draw a sure conclusion about Jefferson, because he read less and less fiction as he aged; it is just possible that his daughter Martha and her brood prompted his statement "Miss Edgeworth's works. They are all good." The two younger generations were not fans of the author merely because of Grandpapa, but rather because Edgeworth wrote of a society that resonated for them—and they had no doubt read more of her works than he had. At least we can say that they would not have helped tailor such a list if it did not entirely coincide with Jefferson's tastes.[33]

A Fictionalized Jefferson?

In her preface to *Castle Rackrent,* Edgeworth wrote: "That the great are not as happy as they seem, that the external circumstances of fortune and rank do not constitute felicity, is asserted by every moralist."[34] Think now about the felicity-seeking Jefferson, protective of domestic life, peering out from his pastoral retreat with general satisfaction. How knowable is this man? He entertained regularly but he plainly cherished his privacy. He set his private quarters apart from the rest of the downstairs at Monticello, and he enclosed this space behind louvered shutters. Venetian blinds allowed him to regulate incoming light while controlling access—even visual access—to his physical person. In the dining area across the large hall from these quarters, especially at the 3:30 P.M. main meal, he gave himself over to company.[35]

As a man with a well-defined domestic routine, the engaging, multifaceted Jefferson held a unique position in his community. He might be considered a Virginia version of Maria Edgeworth's Irish landowners, distinguished from the English plantation model, yet still influenced by it. She calls her tale a "biography." Does it somehow encompass him? After all, we must already feel his life at Monticello describable in storied terms.

Perhaps the most intriguing possibility is this: that Jefferson was introspective enough to see his own life as one an inventive writer might be inspired to fictionalize. Here he was, the workaholic patriarch, cataloguing and tabulating his life, busy amid his gadgets and drawings, communicating eagerly with distant friends, clamoring to know what new ideas had emerged in the wider intellectual world, yet just as busily focusing on the immediate, and taking notes on the efficiency of his plantation labor force. We can envision him as he must have been from time to time: gazing at the skies, charting changes in the weather and in the growth of plants, all the while conceiving a university in the neighborhood, quantifying its needs, preparing an inventory of required books, and a means to attract promising students and a superior faculty. Was his creative empathy sufficient to restrain him from feeling "greater" than the more typical men with whom he daily interacted? Is not such a man tempted to consider himself a human phenomenon, one who is even more than a political icon?

He left a tidy collection of letters, copies of those he had written and originals he had received, totaling some 16,000 of the former and 26,000 of the latter.[36] His life was already a book-in-the-raw. The creative possibilities within language seemed endless to the thinking revolutionary—one can almost hear him speak at supper words he wrote in 1821: "Science must be stationary unless language advances pari passu" (at the same pace). He seemed to spend his days playing with forms of words, as much as he was adapting technology: "Judicious neology can alone give strength & copiousness to language and enable it to be the vehicle of new ideas."[37] Of course, such a public figure—holding court at his legendary dinner table—would have been an object of immense curiosity.

Ellen presumed that other Virginians looked upon his French style of dining with "good-humoured indulgence."[38] Did he acknowledge himself this way, as outsiders saw him? Could he at all imagine himself, a graceful yet set-in-his-ways ex-president in his seventies, as the subject of anecdotes, gently spoofed in an Edgeworth-type tale? In 1823, the Marquis de Lafayette wrote to Jefferson asking whether he had seen a "moral novel," titled *Oriele*, in which the hero is traveling in America and "has the pleasure to converse with Mr. Jefferson."[39] Was he conscious that he was a *character*?

One thing Jefferson, as letter writer, regarded with intense interest and concern was emotional hurt and how the human mind dealt with disappointment. So perhaps the appeal of Edgeworth had something to do as well with a literary penchant to ruminate about human imperfection, grief, and misery. The tenor of his letters in the middle years of his retirement indicates that Jefferson felt himself in decline; he was contending with physical limitations, concerned that his intelligence and fortitude would not be enough to enable him to prevail over pain and weakness. Certainly his letters to John Adams during this period attest to that. He wrote straightforwardly of human frailty, of mortality, here criticizing Napoleon for his cold-bloodedness, there nostalgic for the eighteenth century: "While the world is thus turned up side down, on which side of it are we?" he asked preciously.[40]

It would be absurd to claim that he had a death wish, even at the end. Yet faced with uncertainty, he was many times tempted to withdraw, wanting not to engage, not to be seen. That was one reason why, toward the end of his presidency, he began to build himself a second retreat, on property three days distant by carriage in the southwestern part of Virginia—his charming, octagon-shaped Poplar Forest home. He went there two or three times a year in the mid-1810s, as construction proceeded. He went, usually for months at a time, to escape the bustle of Monticello. "I have fixed myself comfortably, keep some books here," he wrote to Benjamin Rush in 1811, "am in the solitude of a hermit, and quite at leisure to attend to my absent friends" by letter.[41]

A half year before he wrote the letter to Nathaniel Burwell, he visited Poplar Forest and took two granddaughters with him, twenty-year-old Ellen and eighteen-year-old Cornelia. His favorite servant, Burwell Colbert, rode on horseback alongside their carriage. The little family took walks and occasional rides, sat together and read regularly at times set by Grandpapa; sometimes Jefferson read aloud to them. Here his mind was generally undisturbed, his eye focused. When he complained to the architect Robert Mills about his weakened faculties, he had to qualify: "sight excepted." He wore glasses only for small print, and he did not consider his distance vision impaired. At Monticello, when not entertaining guests, Jefferson spent his evening hours in retirement reading as much as possible. "Doctr. Franklin used to say," he wrote Abigail Adams, "that when he was young, and had time to read, he had not books; and now when he had become old and had books, he had no time." Jefferson made time. As his slave Isaac put it, "Old Master had abundance of books; sometimes would have twenty of 'em down on the floor at once—read fust one, then tother."[42]

At Poplar Forest, he kept a stock of British, French, Italian, Greek, and Latin poetry, more than one hundred volumes, to share with his granddaughters; then there were the latest books acquired at Monticello, which he carried down for extended visits. He made sure, at Poplar Forest, that he was rarely distracted, so that he had more spare time for his favorite amusement: "Reading when I can be indulged in it, is the elysium of my present life," he wrote to a Dutch intellectual in 1818. Not only did he discuss books in letters to his friends, he leaned on his bookbinder to supply wanted books in exquisite leather: "[I] am impatient in being so long out of the use of my books," he wrote in the spring of 1819. Finally receiving shipment—"I am so well satisfied with your bindings"—he instantly issued a new order and named the one boat he trusted to carry his next precious cargo: "Bind them all in your best manner, gilt and letter according to the labels, & above all solidly pressed." His country neighbors gaily referred to Jefferson as "squire."[43]

Approving Maria Edgeworth's fascination with the domestic activities of country squires does not mean that Thomas Jefferson found felicity in the publicity of his own domestic affairs. Far from it. It was something he endured. Long before his retirement began, the literate world already knew a great deal about the master of Monticello. The Marquis de Chastellux visited Jefferson in 1782, and famously described the gentleman architect as "the first American who has consulted the Fine Arts to know how he should shelter

himself from the weather." In his *Travels in North America*, the French aristocrat accorded the Virginia planter the high praise that first established his reputation as a worldly provincial: "No object has escaped Mr. Jefferson; and it
seems indeed as though, ever since his youth, he had placed his mind, like his
house, on a lofty height, whence he might contemplate the whole universe."
This was well before most of his countrymen even knew that he had authored
the Declaration of Independence.[44]

Another French writer, the duc de la Rochefoucauld-Liancourt, visited Jefferson at home in the mid-1790s, and published an English account of his travels in 1799. He discussed Jefferson's methods of cultivating land, noted how
much each bushel of corn earned him, gave Jefferson's thoughts on apportion-
ing the energies of his field slaves, revealed how the master directed his other
slaves ("He animates them by rewards and distinctions"), and alluded to the
domestic lives of Jefferson's (then) two daughters. The duc could not resist the
subject of miscegenation on Virginia plantations, for which white employees,
rather than employers, were assigned paternal responsibility.[45]

Whatever the Sage of Monticello, as the entertainer of many travelers, illustrious and ordinary, thought of these published accounts, he often pondered
what it would take to keep his private life private. In spite of the remoteness of
his situation, the restless political environment drew attention to him. Did he
anticipate that not all visitors' observations would be favorable? The most impertinent instance of intrusive journalism was, of course, the scandal over Jefferson's suspected involvement with his house servant Sally Hemings, which
erupted in 1802.

Jefferson the builder and dreamer shopped for works of science and philosophy. Yet he also apparently developed a taste, or at least a tolerance, for the
kind of literature that in fictional form dwelt upon house and locality, and private foibles. Perhaps he approved of Maria Edgeworth because she consistently
defended his world of caring gentility. Certainly she gave voice to bookish, spirited, industrious women. Above all, she symbolized clarity, prudent reflection,
and female common sense.

Jefferson and his female progeny appreciated the novelist's self-confidence as
well as the compassion she felt as a creator. As in his earlier reading of Sterne,
Jefferson must have responded to Edgeworth's conviction that good fiction
caused the human spirit to surface in artistic glimpses of a noteworthy person's
domestic life and uncensored thoughts; and that these glimpses, properly understood, contributed to moral improvement.[46] Exposed as his celebrity made
him, our nearly fictional Squire Jefferson had his large and growing brood of
grandchildren to educate in the Edgeworthian mode, and this no doubt
grounded him.

"wicked and tyrannical men": Godwin's Caleb Williams

Standing apart on Jefferson's list of prescribed female reading is William Godwin's 1794 novel *Things as They Are; Or, the Adventures of Caleb Williams.*[47] Among the few contemporary novels recommended, it is the only one written by a male. The story is one that mixes lessons about the desire for heightened human sympathy with a critique of the arbitrary power inherent under a rigid class system.

In the early nineteenth century, everyone had heard of Godwin (1756–1836). His name was as recognized internationally as Jefferson's, and he was no less controversial. He had begun life in England as a dissenting minister, and he espoused a radical view of politics that Jefferson thoroughly approved. Godwin was one of a few robust British writers who embraced the tumultuous French Revolution. He disputed the reactionary sentiment of Edmund Burke's *Reflections on the Revolution in France* (1790), which famously upheld the values of the conservative state. Godwin's *Enquiry Concerning Political Justice* (1793) was a bold endorsement for individual self-affirmation, rich in the vocabulary of natural rights. Only the emigrant Thomas Paine, whose *Common Sense* prompted Americans to declare their independence in 1776, was a half-step ahead of Godwin, having answered Burke with his resounding *Rights of Man* (1791–1792). Paine openly attacked the perversions of Christian religion, and he scoffed at monarchy and aristocratic pretense, which he claimed to be archaic forms due to be cast into oblivion in the enlightened, modern world that the political radicals wished to bring about.

As with Barbauld and Edgeworth, there is no doubt, once again, that Jefferson's selection of Godwin's novel was influenced by more than literary method. Jefferson was the American-born counterpart to Paine and Godwin. At the time that his political personality was permanently refashioned into this more radical set of values, he was serving as George Washington's secretary of state. He led the political faction that saw events in France hopefully. The radical intellectuals, idealists all, aimed to upset the elite monopoly of power; they caused conservatives to shudder at the prospect of the anarchy and atheism that "democracy" might bring with it.

It is worth noting, too, in this context, that Jefferson's 1818 letter to Burwell highlighted the value of teaching young women the French language and making the best French literature available to them. "The French language," he wrote, "become that of the general intercourse of nations, and, from their extraordinary advances, now the depository of all science is an indispensable part of education for both sexes." The juvenile guide *Evenings at Home*, by Barbauld, explained to young girls that though they might never visit France, learning the language remained important: "There are a great many books written in French that are very well worth reading; and it may every now and then happen that you may be in company with foreigners who cannot speak English, and as they almost all talk French, you may be able to converse with them." His selection of the instructive stories of the Comtesse de Genlis, aimed at young girls, shows that Jefferson believed that a mastery of French was important at an early age. Jefferson was America's best-known Francophile; he rejected the exaggerated English style of class privilege and wished his countrymen and women would escape the British cultural as well as political orbit.[48]

Godwin's controversial ideas played out in the conflict of the 1790s between Jeffersonian Republicans and the Anglophile Federalist party of George Washington and John Adams. British domestic repression was matched in the United States by passage of the Alien and Sedition Acts in Congress on the eve of Jefferson's successful bid for the presidency. The Federalists' outright suppression of First Amendment speech led to show trials and the imprisonment of writers, of any nationality or background, who criticized government policy. Jefferson decried this "reign of witches" and held out the hope of realizable political equality for common men.

Here, then, was the crystallization of Jefferson's cause, where all doubt in his mind disappeared. Either America would follow the road back to monarchy and tyranny, or it would continue on the path to popular sovereignty that he saw embodied in the spirit of 1776 and tenuously pursued in Revolutionary France. There was no more boldly drawn line charting direction.

The question, then, is why a novel containing an overtly political message belonged so prominently on Jefferson's short list of novels for young females. The answer, at least in part, is that Jefferson believed that as one facet of their education, without encouraging them to take the political stage, women should be taught to distinguish in a man between a soft, sympathizing republican temperament and a hard, unfeeling aristocratic temperament. He may have desired that women remain politically harmless, but he did not want them politically uninformed.

The story of *Caleb Williams* is a meandering one. The hero of the opening volume (of three) is the levelheaded Mr. Falkland, a prosperous landowner who, in volume two, will employ the socially unexceptional Caleb. Falkland is cast against the acerbic Squire Barnabas Tyrrel, whose "diseased imagination" makes him obsessively jealous and controlling.

Every reader attuned to the prevailing culture of sensibility would have instantly recognized Godwin's purpose in constructing these two characters: One was beyond reproach, the other heartless. The novel of sentiment put its characters on trial for their moral lives. One character's sensibility defined tenderness—male reformation—and the other was entirely unable to resist taking advantage of the female state of delicacy.[49]

Squire Tyrrel is to the novel what King George III is to Jefferson's Declaration: an unfeeling tyrant. The "diseased imagination" Godwin attributes to him is, once again, a medical characterization; it describes a person who has allowed his or her nervous system to overwhelm the capacity to reason. Tyrrel turns his attention to fragile, hopeful Emily Melville, his orphaned cousin, whom he torments and drives to an early grave, in part because she becomes enchanted with the upright Falkland. Emily sees no evil, believing virtue an invincible shield. Only Mrs. Jakeman, the elderly housekeeper whom she has adopted as a surrogate mother, is able to detect that Tyrrel is set on conquering the virgin's will. Mrs. Jakeman counsels: "There are very wicked and tyrannical men in the world." Every victim in the novel is given melodramatic parting lines; before she breathes her last, Emily forgives her brutal oppressor.[50]

Before volume one concludes, Falkland's fate, too, must be sealed. In avenging those whom Tyrrel has destroyed, he kills Tyrrel, but allows two innocent farmers to be executed for the murder. Knowing what he has done causes Falkland to wish for "insensibility;" the murderer becomes a "rigid recluse." He becomes a different person.[51]

Enter Caleb Williams, a curious, intelligent young man who has (as he himself narrates) yet to discover "the world and its passions." He enters into Falkland's service, and almost immediately begins prying into his past, looking to uncover secrets. "To do what is forbidden always has its charms," Caleb admits, cooing: "To be a spy upon Mr Falkland!" The recluse grows suspicious that his hired man is out to solve Tyrrel's murder.[52]

In his mounting psychological struggle with Falkland, Caleb remains caught up in the hazardous world of sensations. He confesses that each recollection of the danger he was generating for himself "gave a kind of tingling sensation not altogether unallied to enjoyment." He elaborates: "The further I advanced, the more the sensation was irresistible."[53] Finally, Falkland owns up to everything. He had planted the bloody knife that sealed the innocent farmers' fate and so preserved his own social station. "This it is to be a gentleman! a man of honour!" Falkland exclaims. "I was the fool of fame."[54]

The two men's destinies are joined. It is a fight to the finish; one or the other will lose everything. For much of the final two volumes, the underdog Caleb is pursued by Falkland's personal police force—the arm of privilege. For accusing "the master," Caleb must suffer a series of unspeakable torments as he runs, hides, is captured, escapes, trusts, is betrayed, and along the way develops the self-preserving weapon of disguise (here an Irishman, there a Jew) to avoid recapture. Through it all, the formerly mild and generous Falkland exhibits a powerful obsession: the need to destroy Caleb just as the vindictive Tyrrel had once needed to destroy those whom Falkland had befriended. "It was a million of men in arms against me," Caleb expostulates at the height of the pursuit.[55]

Falkland retains the advantage, because in a society such as theirs, his "truth" will always outweigh Caleb's.

Which emotion will win out: sympathy or the desire for vengeance? This is what lies at the core of Godwin's drama. The hunter and hunted feel the same conflicting emotions at various times in the novel. But when Falkland is left "convulsed" with "fury," his passion unchecked, Caleb persists in his journey of self-discovery; he emerges the stronger man by learning the value of openness.

At the end of his tale, standing before a magistrate, Caleb is able to unburden his heart with self-effacing innocence. In doing so, he overawes Falkland. Although armed with his truth, he refuses to brand his tormentor a murderer, calling him instead "a man worthy of affection and kindness." As he lets his resentments go, he finds absolution: Sympathy and sincerity conquer Falkland, who rises to confess his crimes. As Caleb tells it, "He saw my sincerity; he was penetrated with my grief and compunction. He rose from his seat, supported by the attendants, and—to my infinite astonishment—threw himself into my arms!" Something in Caleb's conciliatory voice had cleared the fog of old society privilege and obliged Falkland to surrender to emotional democracy.[56]

This is an essentially Jeffersonian ending, for Jefferson had predicated his career on the ideal of fashioning social harmony: "We are all republicans, we are all federalists," he pronounced in the Senate chamber in his most heralded attempt to leave behind the "throes and convulsions of the ancient world," and bind the nation. The first inaugural address was meant to embrace those among the political opposition whom Jefferson called "candid" Federalists, men still strongly identifying with the old regime of wealth and privilege, but equally responsive to the appeal of republican sensibility. Jefferson, like Godwin, believed that there were Falklands to be converted, melted by the language of enlightened republicanism; Jefferson and Godwin each wanted to believe that class tyranny would be crushed in the natural course of human events.

It is intentional in the novel that Falkland, unlike the deviant Tyrrel, is "a man of the acutest sensibility" throughout. In a subsequent novel, *Fleetwood: Or, the New Man of Feeling* (1805), Godwin refinished the sentimental man, the real Jeffersonian: humane, susceptible (sometimes acutely so), and aided by the moral imagination. Years later, Ellen Coolidge referred to her father, Thomas Mann Randolph, as "a near resemblance" to Fleetwood, an intense man with a heightened sense of honor, undone by his passions and jealousies and violent outbursts. Though decidedly flawed, at times torn by contradictory emotions, the Fleetwood type was always able to express friendship by attending to his natural feelings, and he had a palpable sense of social justice.[57]

The Godwinian hero is a natural republican, typically stripped of a father figure when young and obliged to take charge; he is aggressive without wanting to appear so, unaware that he can be weakened by his need to control—by his own occasionally despotic tendencies. He is, indeed, very much like Jefferson himself.

Nothing deters the Godwinian hero from perceiving justice in sublime terms. Caleb speaks Godwin's mind:

> I was born free: I was born healthy, vigorous, and active, complete in all the lineaments and members of a human body. I was not born indeed to the possession of hereditary wealth; but I had a better inheritance, an enterprising mind, an inquisitive spirit, a liberal ambition.[58]

In his last public letter, on June 24, 1826, Jefferson wrote similarly, with his thoughts on the upcoming fiftieth Fourth of July:

> The general spread of the light of science has already laid open to every view the palpable truth, that the mass of mankind has not been born with saddles on their backs, nor a favored few booted and spurred, ready to ride them legitimately, by the grace of God.[59]

Yet even *Caleb Williams* does not progress beyond eighteenth-century literary conventions in its depiction of women, though Godwin himself unquestionably admired the female intellect. He loved the feminist Mary Wollstonecraft, author of the powerful *Vindication of the Rights of Women* (1792); their daughter, Mary Shelley, was the very public author of the classic *Frankenstein* (1818), which she dedicated to her father. It is curious that both *Caleb Williams* and *Frankenstein* were confessional in nature, and dealt with extremes of curiosity, the penalty for selfishness, and the conscience under attack.[60]

Were Jefferson to apply the lessons of Godwin's life, he might have reconsidered the arbitrary power that American men, and Virginians in particular, exercised over domesticated women. But such sentiments were not within Jefferson's reach. He had enjoyed warm friendships with strong-willed women, but he did not desire to import outside gender roles into Virginia. He preferred that women master the household economy first, and learn to be interesting and charming second. Their only ambition should be artistic—in other words, nothing that might lure their imaginations to desire a level of public distinction beyond what their industrious husbands could generate. He wished to insure harmony by confining females' stimulation to moral pursuits such as drawing and uplifting reading.

Jefferson undoubtedly liked Godwin's novel best for its embrace of the sentimental individual whose decent yearning for private felicity placed him in opposition to the oppressions of society. He most likely saw in this book the same things the friendly critics in 1794 admired: It set forth "a first principle that virtue consists in justice," showing that what is commonly considered honor is not necessarily so. It also caused the reader to regret that a "mad passion for reputation should suppress every feeling of humanity"; and it exposed "oppression which is often practiced under the form of law."

We can see how the novel remained Jeffersonian in 1818 by reading the words of a critic of that year, prominently reviewing a later edition. William Hazlitt noted that Godwin's writing successfully bridged the ideal and the real: "By an intense and patient study of the heart . . . the author launches into the ideal world, and must sustain himself and the reader there, by the mere force of imagination." Hazlitt, a well-known British essayist, concluded: "This novel is . . . one of the most original as well as powerful productions in the English language."[61]

Jefferson saw *Caleb Williams* as fiction suited for young women because a) it taught that the end of life was to foster inner contentment; and b) it did not challenge gender barriers in place. Self-monitoring, which led to self-improvement, all but guaranteed the repose that Jefferson coveted. Everyone, house servants and overseer included, remarked on his unexcitable temperament. This traditionally feminine quality found expression in the subtle demands he placed upon the young women in his family.

Just as viewing the results of his inspired building projects leads us to marvel at the balance in Jefferson's mind between order and liberation, a glimpse of his literary imagination helps us to better appreciate his campaigning psyche. We have come to know him as a great doer. When we think of him as a reader (which he was for hours each day, several volumes propped up at a time on the revolving bookstand in his cabinet), we imagine him absorbing new knowledge and ancient ethics from across the ocean, and it seems that his heart was as pure as a man's could be for one so politically driven.

But there were flaws in his judgment. We know that. He could not deny that he owned other human beings, and that his loftiest words—"All men are created equal"—were a lie, even if by "men" he meant only enfranchised men, white men with independent public roles. And no matter how well he studied or how many letters he wrote in a salute to the Enlightenment, at the end he could not escape one grim fact of life. It came to him as he was sinking physically: He was unable to pay any longer for his dreams.

In the pursuit of "tranquil permanent felicity," a tyrant spirit was lurking. Indeed, just as in Maria Edgeworth's Irish sagas, Death stalked the restless patriarch.

Taking Liberties

5

The Continuing Debate:
Jefferson and Slavery

Where the disease is most deeply seated, there it will be slowest in eradication. In the northern States it was merely superficial, and easily corrected. In the southern it is incorporated with the whole system, and requires time, patience, and perseverance in the curative process.

THOMAS JEFFERSON TO
DAVID BARROW, MAY 1, 1815[1]

The slave who went by the name of Israel Jefferson was in his late twenties when Thomas Jefferson died. From a young age, he had served as a waiter at Monticello and generally lit the fire in his master's bedroom. Anticipating his own fate after July 4, 1826, Israel later recalled: "His death was an affair of great moment and uncertainty to us slaves." Israel was sold from the auction block, as were at least 150 others. Although his siblings were forcibly taken in various directions, he was relatively fortunate in that he was purchased by Thomas Walker Gilmer, of a family dear to his deceased master; about ten years later, after Israel's wife, also a slave, died, he married a free, biracial woman, who purchased his freedom. Preparing to leave Virginia for Ohio with his "free papers," Israel was asked by a clerk at the Albemarle County Courthouse whether he wanted to keep his original surname, Gillette. Convinced by the clerk that it would give him "more dignity to be called after so eminent a man," he "consented to adopt" the name of Jefferson.

Israel, who attained literacy after beginning life as a free man, also recalled having been present when the aging Revolutionary War hero Marquis de Lafayette visited Jefferson at Monticello in 1824. The Frenchman had often decried the continuation of slavery in the land he had helped in the fight for liberation from colonial status, and Israel took pride in having been at the reins of their carriage on one occasion when Lafayette apparently took up the matter of freedom and bondage with his distinguished host. In this and other ways, Israel said, Jefferson's private life, "till the day of his death, was very familiar to me." He asserted that one particular story going back to 1802 was indeed true, and that Thomas Jefferson had been "on the most intimate terms" with his chambermaid.[2]

Most Americans now believe that slave-owning Thomas Jefferson was the father of biracial children, and that he possibly had a warm, if not loving, relationship with one of those slaves, Sally Hemings. This belief is, for some, a simple way to dismiss Jefferson as a hypocrite for treasuring and owning a woman at the same time. For others, it is an effort to show that the contentious president did not necessarily belittle all blacks. For others still, it is an unconscious desire to endow Jefferson with bourgeois values and emotions. And there are many more possible scenarios.

It has been Thomas Jefferson's unsought historic role to invite controversy. With his medical understandings and literary imagination as prelude, this and the following chapter combine to reexamine the nature of his racism and to clarify the limits of his emotional connection to Sally Hemings. Once again, it turns out that the most revealing texts date to his understudied retirement years.

I begin this discussion with a brief personal preface. Since the publication of the DNA test results of 1998,[3] establishing that "a Jefferson" fathered at least one biracial child at Monticello, it now seems that I took an unacceptable shortcut in *The Inner Jefferson,* which was a book about Jefferson's literary self-construction and touched only briefly on the issue of slavery. Because there was little to go on in the public record, I allowed conventional notions of sexual propriety to describe the mind of Jefferson. Absence of information does not equal celibacy, of course; yet, without other textual evidence, Jefferson's implicit denial (and his family's *explicit* denial) of sexual activity in the decades after the death of his wife seemed plausible.

I did take note of the oral history passed down through generations of once enslaved families in Monticello's neighborhood. This history, widely accepted by the African American community, challenged the Jefferson family denial. I recognized that this alternative picture had to be taken seriously, but it was not "hard" evidence either; and indeed, DNA has so far discredited critical portions of that oral history.[4] That said, even in questioning the oral history, I remained troubled by the apparent failure of Martha Jefferson Randolph to clarify for her family a truth she must have known—the paternity of domestic servant Sally Hemings's children. Hemings never became pregnant when Jefferson was away from home—and he frequently was.

Yet the crux of the problem, for me, was contending with Hemings's conceptions of 1805 and 1808, the births of sons Madison and Eston. Thomas Jefferson was in his second term as president at that time, sixty-five years old when Eston was born.* The troublesome allegations of his connection to Sally Hemings had been published earlier, in 1802, when he was nearly sixty. He was a popular president who had pestering political enemies and remained under close scrutiny. What could explain the readiness of a man who was a grandfather many times over to father two more children with a woman he owned? Love was one possible answer, sexual desire another, egoistic impulse a third. Yet Jefferson's intimates consistently described him as undemonstrative and, at least publicly, restrained; contraceptive knowledge existed if he was inclined to hide his extramarital sex life from inquiring minds. As an eighteenth-century man, why would he want additional descendants who were not heirs?

Such ruminations had led me to consider the traditional explanation credible: that a white man or men close to Jefferson, who routinely visited Monticello but only when Jefferson was there, fathered Sally Hemings's children. The DNA match, however, verifies a genetic relationship between Sally's youngest son and a Jefferson, that is, a male descendant of Field Jefferson, who was the third president's uncle.

For most, Thomas Jefferson's paternity of Sally Hemings's children has now been convincingly established, yet there are those who insist on reminding us that it has not been *absolutely* established. The president's grandson Thomas Jefferson Randolph confided to biographer Henry S. Randall in the mid-1850s that Jefferson's favorite nephew Peter Carr (who died in 1814) was the father of Sally Hemings's children—this was the explanation most historians believed until 1998. Now, the grandson's explanation seems impossible. In matching Jefferson's genetic type, DNA *eliminated* the Carr family.

But even the paternity of Sally Hemings's last child, Eston, has been contested by those close to the investigation who would prefer to believe that Thomas's historically unimpressive younger brother, Randolph Jefferson, an occasional visitor to Monticello who played his fiddle in the slave quarters, or his sons, were at least as "likely" candidates. Randolph was widowed in 1796 and did not remarry until 1808, by a curious coincidence the same year that Sally Hemings last gave birth.[5] The problem with this scenario, however, is that no one—no white Jefferson descendant, no historian—ever suggested Randolph's name until a defense of Thomas Jefferson's celibacy was mounted immediately after the DNA findings were publicized. A new candidate suddenly had to be found.

Nor, technically, is it yet proven that all the Hemings children had the same father, although Madison Hemings, the most authoritative source of the Hemings

---

*It was the DNA of Eston Hemings's descendant that was later matched to Jefferson's.

family tradition, reported in 1873 that he heard this in no uncertain terms from his mother's lips. He stated: (1) as a teenager in Paris, his mother "became Mr. Jefferson's concubine"; (2) "We [Madison and his siblings] were the only children of his by a slave woman"; (3) although "uniformly kind to all," Jefferson "was not in the habit of showing partiality or fatherly affection to us children"; (4) "We were all permitted to be with our mother, who was well used" and given only moderate tasks to perform within "the great house"; and (5) "I learned to read by inducing the white children," that is, Jefferson's grandchildren.[6]

That a key portion of Madison's testimony is now widely accepted as true, owing to the DNA results, strongly supports the pre-DNA argument of the law professor Annette Gordon-Reed that Madison Hemings was a man of veracity and sound memory.[7] His testimony, given to an Ohio newspaperman, tells us what his mother told him. And she had less reason to lie about a relationship than the publicly scrutinized Thomas Jefferson did.

By the terms of Jefferson's March 1826 will, along with their uncle, the carpenter Johnny Hemings, Madison and Eston Hemings were freed (after ostensibly serving as Johnny's apprentice until they attained their majority). At Jefferson's extraordinary request, the brothers were given permission by the Virginia legislature in 1826 to remain in the state after winning freedom—an 1806 law had decreed that emancipated slaves otherwise had to leave Virginia within a year.

In 1835, after the death of their mother, Madison and Eston separately migrated to Ohio. Both brothers married biracial women. As a freeman, Madison retained the Hemings name, but Eston eventually took the Jefferson name and, in Madison, Wisconsin, passed for white. Their older brother and sister, Beverley (born 1798) and Harriet (born 1801), had earlier been permitted by Jefferson to "run away," in 1822, after attaining their majority. Both passed for white (Harriet was called "nearly as white as anybody"), and subsequently married whites.[8]

We must go back 196 years before the DNA test for the earliest publicity given to the Hemings children's paternity—to an account that has been written about often. James T. Callender was a disreputable, hard-drinking, but frequently truth-telling independent columnist, and an utter foe of miscegenation. He was acting out of political spite when he sensationally announced in a Richmond, Virginia, newspaper in the autumn of 1802 that President Thomas Jefferson kept a "concubine" named Sally Hemings, who was his slave. "Dusky Sally," "the African Venus," had borne Jefferson several children, he said. Jefferson haters seized on the characterization and mocked their president with great glee.

As part of the same campaign, another potentially damaging charge emerged. This one questioned Jefferson's sexual restraint. More than thirty years earlier—indeed, before he was married—the young lawyer had made advances toward

Betsey Walker, a neighbor's wife. When confronted, Jefferson settled the matter privately with the offended husband; later, he wrote to his attorney general and his secretary of the navy: "I plead guilty to one of their [his political enemies'] charges, that when young and single I offered love to a handsome lady. . . . It is the only one founded in truth among all their allegations against me."[9]

All their allegations? Depending upon how one interprets Jefferson's statement, he might have been denying the Sally Hemings charge. In 1824, a former associate of Callender's sent Jefferson a flattering letter that chastised the long-dead columnist for "unwarrantable indiscretions" begun amid "paroxysms of inebriety." In his reply, the eighty-one-year-old Jefferson grumbled: "He was a poor creature, sensible [i.e., oversensitive], hypocondriac, drunken, pennyless & unprincipled."[10] Recalling the eighteenth-century meaning of *hypocondriac*, Jefferson is claiming that Callender was "disordered in the imagination," clinically disturbed or hysterical, as well as unethical. These remarks constitute the closest the historical record has to a response from Jefferson. Otherwise, we possess no information to suggest that he ever discussed the details of Callender's accusation.[11]

The problem before us now remains one of will and imagination. How did Jefferson assess his options? That question lies at the heart of this and the next chapter. To reframe the cultural environment in which Jefferson moved requires new information with regard to Jefferson's feelings about race and sex—it requires unearthing sources that historians (myself included) have missed. Finally, I have undertaken this more exhaustive study of the Jefferson-Hemings matter because I believe it is essential for students of history to understand how one who presented a sexually repressed persona (as that which emerges from Jefferson's correspondence) could have acted in a sexually forward manner. In my earlier scholarship, while able to locate an aggressive political partisan hidden within his harmonizing prose, I did not go far enough beyond Jefferson's portrait of himself as a sexless widower. I was guided as well by the remarks of others among his contemporaries, who interacted with Jefferson and who alike saw him as self-possessed, moralistic, and (compared to most of his peers) even prudish. He was consistently described as soft and gracious in his demeanor. But demeanor, or appearance, we know, is not always essence. There is always more to know about human motivation. What follows is an attempt to explore all of the possibilities with critical detachment.[12]

"turmoil of sensations"

Though largely silent on Callender's allegations, Jefferson did, on many occasions, discuss race and slavery in terms as sensual as they were political. His most renowned and most unpalatable professions of black inferiority issue from the only book he authored, *Notes on the State of Virginia.* It first appeared in Europe in 1785 and in the United States two years later, but the bulk of the writing was done in 1780–1781. It was early in Jefferson's career, therefore, when he ventured his opinions. The Revolution was in its final phase, and the young legislator not yet the focus of controversy, when he suggested that the races could not live together permanently, and that the colonization abroad of African Americans—free and enslaved alike—was necessary to avert large-scale racial violence. What conditions was he responding to when he wrote at once fearfully, and, one is to suppose, sympathetically about blacks?

Let us examine Thomas Jefferson's "real world" as he, with a rich mind for detail and with philosophic intent, set out to characterize a hopeful yet turbulent society. Prior to the American Revolution, patriots like himself repeatedly employed what strikes us today as a curious vocabulary in protesting British tyranny: In newspapers North and South they complained that their erstwhile political parent aimed to "fix the shackles of Slavery upon us." (These happen to be the words of the Virginian George Washington in 1774.) The slavery metaphor suggested a dreaded destiny that Whig leaders wished to avoid. Yet as they played up their figurative slavery in prose, these same patriots could not entirely ignore their own complicity in the enslavement of blacks.

What, then, did the word *slavery* mean? In the abstract, it conjured a loss of respect, power, and property—precisely what the American colonists felt in their dealings with Parliament. But using the despised term as revolutionary political capital ended up calling attention to the gothic possibilities of the South's fractured society. *Actual* slavery could not be ignored, and, in the words of one recent scholar, "this policing of linguistic boundaries failed." Jefferson used the nonracial variant of *slavery* in his 1774 *Summary View of the Rights of British America,* to decry Parliament's "systematical plan" of political oppression; and when he got around to drafting the Declaration of Independence, he directly blamed King George III for encumbering his colonies with an African slave trade they would have preferred to abolish on their own. He and his fellows wished to imagine that their antislavery statements moderated their actual failure as emancipators of African Americans.[13]

But Jefferson's "real world" was involved in more than a linguistic battle over the future of slavery. About the time that Boston was the focus of Revolutionary agitation, and in months between Lexington and Concord and the Declaration of Independence, white assemblies across the South broadcast bulletins calling for action to combat "instigated insurrections," the common expression for slave rebellions that they expected the British to engineer. During that season of heated conflict, the last royal governor of Virginia, Lord Dunmore, removed the colony's store of gunpowder to a waiting warship. He left open the possibility, as one local physician recorded, that slaves would "reduce . . . to ashes" the colonial capital of Williamsburg. As impassioned words were exchanged, the patriot-run *Virginia Gazette* began to satirize the royal governor, a noted philanderer, for his supposed taste for African ladies. A quarter-century later, Jefferson would read similar poetic productions aimed at his taste for an "African Venus."

In the autumn of 1775, operating from offshore, Lord Dunmore made good on his threat to proclaim freedom for patriots' slaves who joined his army. Scores did, and the erstwhile governor contemplated adding Ohio Indians to his racially mixed company. Some of the blacks under Dunmore defeated a white militia contingent near Norfolk; the commander was captured by his own former slaves. Planters continued to publicize incidents of "impertinent behaviour," loss of property, and of whites suffering bodily harm. Jefferson took these panicky reports with him to the Continental Congress in Philadelphia. Diseases and a lack of resources eventually sank Dunmore's bold plan. For a time, Virginia was spared.

Later in the war, when Jefferson was Virginia's governor, the traitor Benedict Arnold invaded the state along its interior waterways. Virginia then contained more than 50 percent of America's black population. As a mobilized force, Virginia's slaves could easily have threatened the plantation community. So from the beginning to the end of the war, whites were afraid of the devastation that was likely to ensue if the British were to call for liberation. During Arnold's invasion, stories spread among slave communities that this was what might soon happen. As British forces neared, more and more slaves became aggressive, determined to flee their plantations and join the invader. Violence would have escalated had the British not become ambivalent about the potential of this slave army: In certain instances, it welcomed slave fugitives; at other times, it turned them away, or even returned them to their owners. In 1781, whites patrolled the rivers as best they could, trembling at the prospect of what might happen if the British suddenly resolved to let chaos reign. This historic moment of uncertainty had to have been on Jefferson's mind as he was laying out his notions about race relations, that year, in *Notes on Virginia*. He lost thirty slaves of his own to the British.[14]

Notes on Virginia was also an effort to compile a scientific catalogue of Virginia's geographic features, climate, natural resources, plant and animal life, a history of its Indian settlements, and rational efforts to extend liberty. It was intended as an enlightened, encyclopedic study of an emerging polity, a taxonomy providing America with an idealized national identity, though the subject was Virginia alone. Knowing how comprehensive Jefferson's aims were helps us understand the vital ambition underlying his textual performance.[15]

Jefferson went through life classifying the world's peoples according to a moral anthropology that is foreign to us. This explains why subsequent generations have found it increasingly difficult to pin him down on the question of race. Can he be called a liberal and a racist at once? Are such terms at all useful to us in chronicling the range of views among his generation? Though they help us to frame his general sentiments, it is best said that there are other, more accurate measures of Jefferson's thought, because the ideology we know as racial tolerance (within a pluralistic, largely middle-class society) did not exist until the twentieth century.

As a humanist, Jefferson abhorred the very idea of slavery, but he practiced it all his life; his mentor and "most affectionate friend," the gentle, broadminded legal scholar George Wythe, taught slaves to read and write and later freed them. Wythe did not believe in the natural inferiority of the African, but Jefferson held that blacks did not equal whites in mind *or* body.[16] Thus, class background or regional identity was not the only determinant of Jefferson's racism; his attachment to the books in his library mattered, too, for they—especially natural history and medical science—led him to his characterizations and conclusions as much as economic self-interest did.

His liberalism was overturned, his racism promoted, by sensations, especially. Jefferson's personal reaction to black bodies generated his most pronounced racist vocabulary. In the *Notes,* wary of the influx of unwholesome ideas occasioned by America's continuing population from abroad (meaning Europe), he wrote generally: "It is for the happiness of those united in society to harmonize as much as possible in matters which they must of necessity transact together." He could write of harmony when variations of "white" were in his mind. But on the subject of American blacks, he more famously decreed why it was that closer interaction was improbable and undesirable: the deficiencies he found in Africans' physical, if not moral, constitution.

He thought, for one, that he was proving "a difference of race" in physiology. Blacks, he wrote, "secrete less by the kidneys, and more by the glands of the skin, which gives them a very strong and disagreeable odor"; "In imagination they are dull, tasteless and anomalous"; "They are more ardent after their female; but love seems with them to be more an eager desire, than a tender delicate mixture of sentiment and sensation. Their griefs are transient"; their men appreciated the white woman's beauty, just as "uniformly" as, in Africa, "the Oranootan" preferred "the black women over those of his own species."

It should be no surprise, by now, that Jefferson established differences within his racial science on the basis of physiological categories, sensations, and sexual inclinations. In an effort to show the depth of his involvement in the study of human variation, he went beyond the assumptions of most of his peers—at least in his use of vivid language. But the orangutan example was not Jefferson's invention: It had been bandied about by others for at least a century. His friend Dr. Benjamin Rush of Philadelphia, though an opponent of slavery, would not long after publish a piece surmising that Africans' skin pigmentation was the result of widespread leprosy. In a liberal moment, and with a rhetorical bow to the scientific method, Jefferson allowed that his notions of black inferiority were merely tentative and would have to be proved through submission to "the Anatomical knife." The metaphor means less than it suggests, however, because we know that Jefferson lacked real faith in eighteenth-century surgery.[17]

A no less pertinent corollary to Jefferson's impressions about race involves the prevailing "science" of physiognomy, that which presumed moral inclinations to be detectable in facial features. To adherents of physiognomic science, a person with "a nose curved at the root" was "born to command;" a long neck was "declaratory of gentleness;" blue eyes were "generally more significant of weakness, effeminacy, and yielding than brown and black," and so forth.

These kinds of suppositions were commonly expressed throughout Jefferson's life, but the most celebrated and oft-quoted interpreter of human characteristics was the Swiss physiognomist Johann Casper Lavater (1741–1801), whose work remained influential in America from the 1790s through Jefferson's last years. Lavater's theory held that most children inherited their firm bones and muscles from their fathers, and their nerves from their mothers. "It is undeniable," Lavater wrote, "that there is a national physiognomy, as well as national character. . . . All English women whom I have known . . . are inclined to be tall, slender, soft, and as distant from all that is harsh, rigorous, or stubborn, as heaven is from earth." According to Lavater, such cultural characteristics were indelible.

In fiction especially, but in society generally, animation of countenance was thought to betray sensations of the heart. It was easy, for one so inclined, to reach the same conclusions about blacks as Jefferson had. As Lavater noted: "If the lips are thick and fleshy, this is a sign of sensuality and of slothfulness"; and, "When the sides of the nose are flexible . . . it betrays a proneness to sensuality." In his 1807 *Essay on the Truth of Physiognomy*, Charles Caldwell, a medical student of Dr. Caspar Wistar's and Dr. Rush's (whose odd racial science we have just alluded to), thought it striking how Desdemona justified her choice of the "swarthy" Othello; it was a rare instance in which the power of physiognomy actually transcended one's natural color preference: "I was insensible of his dark complexion," she says, "so wholly were my senses absorbed in the manly and noble expression of his countenance."

A later correspondent of Jefferson's (while serving as editor of a literary magazine, on his way to becoming a famous medical thinker), the opinionated

Caldwell continued speculating on white superiority into the 1830s. Proud of America's temperate situation, he declared: "Caucasian natives of the United States are superior in natural endowments to their European ancestors. . . . Those Negroes born and reared in this country are, in both body and mind, very strikingly superior to their African progenitors." Thus, in the mind of the solicitous Jefferson and comparably resourceful people, credible cultural indices close at hand made it easy to find Caucasian attributes "rising and ripening," as Caldwell put it, and the African countenance comparatively uninviting; and this is what led otherwise generous-spirited citizens to concur with the view that racial separation was for the good of all. Liberal scientists were, by our standards, profoundly racist.[18]

We have returned, then, to the vocabulary of medicine. It is not without reason that, in his *Notes,* Jefferson chose to evaluate the relationship between African Americans and European Americans according to glandular secretions, nervous responsiveness, and a capacity for sympathy; or that he differentiated between city dwellers and farmers according to the effect of the air they breathed. With the environment as stimulant, human interaction consisted in "a perpetual turmoil of sensations," as the mid-eighteenth-century French medical theorist Théophile de Bordeu put it. Eroticizing the disastrously unequal relationship he perceived between master and slave, Jefferson in essence used Bordeu's language: The "commerce" between white and black was "a perpetual exercise of the most boisterous passions . . . unremitting despotism . . . degrading submissions."

He knew well at this time of the interracial sex (and rape) that occurred on Virginia plantations. In neurophysiological terms, Jefferson associated slavery's "boisterous passions" with male urges; one could not think of sexual relations initiated by despotic masters and unregulated overseers without identifying the male sex organ as the irritable body part responsible for the spasm, the convulsive reaction, the provocation. As Bordeu put it, "the convulsions and tremors that precede this [seminal] excretion" were an irresistible force shared by all animal life.

The destructive impulse engendered by the institution of slavery was being passed down from white father to white son, Jefferson mourned, in secondhand sympathy for the enslaved. Amid that "intemperance of passion . . . the parent storms, the child looks on, catches the lineaments of wrath, puts on the same airs in the circle of smaller slaves, gives a loose to his worst of passions, and thus nursed, educated, and daily exercised in tyranny, cannot but be stamped by it with odious peculiarities." Jefferson's titillating prose tells all: Allusions to sensations, irritability, and excessive stimulation indicate that he fully knows what slavery is. He would know even better, after his years in France among medical reformers and liberal philosophers, why slavery should be stopped. But that was not the same as knowing how to emancipate without sending the white majority into a panic.[19]

Crude Assumptions

Southern society provided Jefferson with plenty of evidence of race hatred. Others of his generation, less intellectually rooted in their racism, commonly regarded slave owning as a standard of success, a mark of their assiduous attention to an agricultural livelihood. Theirs was not simply an economically, but also an emotionally, self-sustaining way of thinking. They turned slaveholding into a virtue while adopting the legal means to limit opportunities for the free blacks who continued to live among them. In 1796, for example, the exceedingly wealthy Robert Carter, a Virginia slaveholder who was perhaps even more powerful within his state than Jefferson was, found himself roundly criticized by a neighbor for considering the manumission of his slaves. He was told that "a man has almost as much right to set fire to his own building though his neighbor's is to be destroyed by it, as to free his slaves."[20] No matter one's social status, or how liberal one's impulses might be, the neighbor's opinion was not easily ignored.

Although in Philadelphia in the 1790s Jefferson witnessed a thriving free black population that generated little racist hostility, it was also true that prominent members of the New York Manumission Society at that time still owned slaves. In fact, between the American Revolution and the Civil War, racist ideology hardened and hysterical stories about interracial sex multiplied, as assumptions became cruder and more exaggerated. For the majority of whites, racial subordination was understood as normal, one of the "immutable laws of nature." In the northern states, even as slavery disappeared through legislation, free blacks were artificially held back in restrictive apprenticeships and even subtler forms of degradation and segregation. As abolition grew into a national issue, northern critics of race mixing or "amalgamation" would as vociferously as southern whites pronounce on the simian features of the African skull and the ridiculous prospects accompanying black attempts at gentility in a racially integrated society. Many assumed that the female abolitionists were prompted in their advocacy by a perverse desire for sex with a black man. And so, white supremacy (triggered in part by sexual anxieties) was alive and well, North *and* South, and would remain so. Blacks were not trusted. They were discouraged from seeking the advantages that whites aggressively reserved for themselves. A climate had long existed in which blacks or Mexicans or Jews could always be imagined stupid or lazy or sneaky or treacherous.

It is much easier to see Jefferson as well-meaning in the context of his time and place when we record the impulsive racist utterances that were commonplace, both before and after his lifetime. One example is religious symbolism. It was not unusual to hear southerners rattle on about black inferiority *in the eyes of God.* Not to be deprived of their voice, slaves and free blacks alike insisted, in return, that they were equal to whites *in the eyes of God.* In 1810, the ex-slave and minister Daniel Coker published "Dialogue Between a Virginian and an African Minister," and demonstrated skill in using the Bible as an antislavery text. But white preachers for the most part heeded the warnings of white planters as to the danger of giving blacks "ideas." Pro-slavery advocates' efforts to indoctrinate slaves, to make them more docile by manipulating the Christian message, did not succeed. Whites' fears rose accordingly.

It is in the nature of the individual to accommodate oneself to a less than ideal situation, to seek a supportable level of comfort with imperfection. For this reason, slavery ground down some whites who at one time might have preferred to speak out. There were, of course, prominent examples of southern slave owners who sacrificed financial comfort to advance abolition. Others, for a variety of motives, agreed to free their slaves upon their deaths. But must we judge Thomas Jefferson entirely on whether he was, ultimately, as munificent as the most susceptible, most compassionate southerner? Must he be all racist or all liberator? That seems too dismissive. His pseudoscience mirrored that of others, equally well educated, who measured skulls to determine the relationship between race and intelligence. And why should we expect him to be any less likely to dismiss black prospects for social equality than the apparent majority of northerners? Lest we regard progress as a strictly chronological phenomenon, the pre-Revolutionary period was probably less fixated on the desire to whiten North America than was the early nineteenth century.

Pressures existed. Slaveholders sought to maintain a standard of living in an uncertain market. This is what made them especially concerned with the monetary value of their human property; and, as unpalatable as it is to us, this is also what made them interested in slaves as "breeders." Many slave owners became speculators in slave fertility, and they felt no moral qualms about this added dimension to the problem of slave ownership. "Negro raising" caused white planter families to focus attention on issues of profitability instead of issues of humanity. In this vein, one naturally questions the motive behind many masters' concern for their slaves' health. The less frugal managers among the planter set regularly sold slaves to pay bills. Even the kinder, gentler masters were occasionally put in this position.

The Virginia Republican elite was convinced, by and large, that slavery was "an evil of great magnitude," to quote a representative statement. But the same

Virginian would say that slavery was less pernicious than abolition would be if imposed upon the state without consideration for the social disruption it would cause. And Jefferson agreed. Convinced that slaves enjoyed more comfortable conditions than most poor whites and free people of color, and knew incomparably better circumstances than "their savage ancestors, naked and starved, roaming through the wilds of Africa like the wild beasts," self-satisfied slave owners insisted that they were making the best of an inheritance. They were not, they insisted, accountable for a system of labor introduced by the British during colonial rule. In time, as they continued to maintain a sense of "duty" toward the enslaved, masters figured they would find a suitable place for the emancipated— but they would do this on their own terms, not by compulsion.[21]

"I tremble for my country when I reflect that God is just; that his justice cannot sleep forever," Jefferson wrote with regard to race enslavement.[22] *Notes on Virginia* was hailed as bold in the mid-1780s, not because of its racial science, but rather because it embarrassed his white brethren; it did not shy from irritating those southern leaders who refused to recognize a God that would not rest until slavery was eliminated. Jefferson did, after all, say, in no uncertain terms, that slavery was "unremitting despotism." The justice-seeking on both sides of the Atlantic prodded Jefferson to work harder at finding a humane solution, but they did not question his motives. John Adams wrote admiringly to the author in 1785: "The Passages upon slavery, are worth Diamonds."[23]

That said, Jefferson's objectionable pseudoscience rightly diminishes him in the eyes of history for one inescapable reason: He did not grow over time. We can see that in spite of moral protestations—in adjudging slavery a crime against humanity—a thinker who conveyed the views he did in *Notes* was unlikely to take meaningful steps toward enacting racial justice, even on a scale within the reach of his generation, unless he questioned his original assumptions with respect to blacks' physical attributes or their capacity to acquire taste and express love. But Jefferson did not doubt himself on this score, nor on the impossibility of an integrated society, indicating to one correspondent in 1815 that he had yet to see a more "sound," a more "practicable" plan for a resolution to the race issue than the removal plan he had proposed three decades earlier in *Notes*.[24]

During his presidency, he joyfully presided over the termination of the ocean-going slave trade, sealing off U.S. ports from further imports of Africans. But he did nothing to arrest the course of the domestic slave trade. His most heralded foreign policy achievement, the Louisiana Purchase, added greatly to the slave economy. Jefferson cannot alone be blamed for this, but neither did he exercise moral leadership when an opportunity presented itself. Instead of seeing an independent black republic in Haiti as a prospective home for American blacks, he refused to consider diplomatic recognition to the slaves who overturned French colonialism, and even encouraged France to re-invade. Taken together, these constitute damning evidence of moral ambivalence.[25]

As a young, activist politician in the 1780s, he had championed the states' cession of territory west of the Ohio River to the national government, for which he helped to legislate a ban on slavery. But in retirement, the social reformer reversed himself. His reading of the 1819 Missouri controversy is perhaps his most nearsighted and least flexible political reaction during these years. As Congress debated whether to bar slavery from new states formed from the Louisiana Purchase (Missouri, in this case), Jefferson construed the measure in two ways: first, as an effort among northern members of his own Republican Party to shift power away from the "Virginia Dynasty" that had allowed Jefferson's neighbors James Madison and James Monroe to succeed him as president; and second, as an imposition upon the southern states' right to eradicate slavery on their own terms, and in their own time. Additional pressures contributed to the problem. After a short burst of prosperity following the War of 1812, Virginians were now witness to a declining state economy; it hit planters and other personally invested local leaders hard. Even without the Missouri issue, they felt burdened and ill at ease.[26]

Jefferson was worried about freedom, the freedom of white citizens from intrusive big government. Even Madison, usually more expansive in his liberalism, agreed with Jefferson at this moment that the North was engineering a power play, not a humane policy for the sake of African Americans. The "uncontrolled dispersion" of slaves westward would do more, Madison told Monroe, to advance their eventual emancipation. For Jefferson, too, only a union of the states in which each state was equal to the others—a union without jealousies, a union in which cumulative power was harmoniously configured—only a union with conciliatory objectives could influence and abide a state-by-state remedy for the evil of slavery.[27]

We wonder, having in mind the course of events that led to the Civil War, how Jefferson could adopt this dilatory posture. After all, he was asking the politically impossible in desiring a union without jealousies as the precondition for an end to slavery. But we must again consider the larger context. Jefferson could not know that there would be a war between the states, nor how bloody and costly it would be. Nor did he consider the slavery problem a singular problem, the way we do as students of history. Though it makes little sense to us, he was unable to separate slavery from the larger threat he perceived of an externally imposed tyranny and the restricting of white southerners' ability to maneuver, migrate, and grow.

In Jefferson's view, there were indignities more exceptional, more encompassing, than those routinely suffered by the underclass of black Americans. As a white man accustomed to the exercise of power, one who looked up at the weather vane to predict the nation's political direction, he perceived other threats to tranquil felicity that took precedence. The relevant vocabulary is already present in an 1811 letter, in which Jefferson complained of a British despotism that was slow to recede from the Atlantic world:

> What in short, is the whole system of Europe towards America but an atrocious and insulting tyranny? One hemisphere of the earth, separated from the other by wide seas on both sides, having a different system of interests flowing from different climates, different soils, different productions, different modes of existence, and its own local relations and duties, is made subservient to all the petty interests of the other, to *their* laws, *their* regulations, *their* passions and wars, and interdicted from social intercourse, from the interchange of mutual duties and comforts with their neighbors, enjoined on all men by the laws of nature. Happily these abuses of human rights are drawing to a close on both our continents.[28]

This was his model. For Jefferson, white-on-white political tyranny had not yet disappeared, and had to be—and would be—overcome first. The world would be right when London reviewed its conduct. The world would be right when northern politicians ceased to promote a powerful central government that aimed to squash southern culture by imposing a national standard based on dominant northern economic interests and urban sensibilities. The world would be right when localities were free to nurture themselves in accord with their native climate and social environment and generous impulses.

James Madison joined his friend in explaining to the world that colonial-era slavery was far more pernicious than it had become in the years since independence. The lives of slaves had much improved, and would continue to improve, until a proper solution was found. Nationalists such as Robert Walsh, a Philadelphian who *opposed* the extension of slavery into Missouri, nonetheless drew upon Madison's perspective and countered British newspaper attacks upon the institution: The U.S. slave population was now doubling every twenty-six years, Walsh observed, arguing that healthy post-Revolutionary conditions explained the phenomenon. It was better to live as an American slave than as a British laborer. The fact remained, he and others proclaimed, that the American republic embodied a quality of freedom that England did not; oligarchic rule within Britain made the common people free in a technical sense only. Add to that London's aggressive commercial policies and maritime dominance. Where was there mercy shown in the halls of power in Britain? Americans' intense hatred of political tyranny presented a hopeful model of government to the world, separate and apart from the nagging (inherited) problem of race enslavement.[29]

Whether it was England or the northern states of his own country that impinged, Jefferson was adamant in desiring to ward off all outside "tyranny." His white yeoman constituency, his agrarian ideal, appeared to be under attack. It was apparent after 1800 that agriculture no longer paid the same dividends for his social class, but that did not dissuade Jefferson from embracing the past. Bolstered by justifications he devised as a result of his extensive reading in medical science and natural history, fed by his personal revulsion toward "blackness," he was able to apply his long-cultivated pastoralism to his politically fashioned racism. For him, the South defined its wealth in a sprawling countryside, resisting the unhygienic ways of the increasingly populous northern cities: The South would remain closer to nature; the North, modeling its growth after cities such as London, would descend into "luxury" and inactivity. What Jefferson did not see as clearly, of course, was northerners' fears that the "Virginia Dynasty" of presidents insured southern dominance. As the years went by, the lives of black Americans ceased to take precedence in Jefferson's mind because (or at least in part because) comparative sociological conditions in the North and South unnerved him. Retrograde slavery, like it or not, empowered the South.

The seeds of national self-destruction were already present, but a timely compromise in Congress slowed the march toward civil war. In a bizarre twist, Missouri achieved statehood in 1820 as a slave protectorate, and so preserved a mythological pastoral republic, sheltered from the threat of the combined North, which, as Jefferson saw it, disguised its commercial avarice (almost British in character), and paid mere lip service to the interests of southern slaves.

And then there was the lurid imagination. For years after Jefferson's *Notes* examined racial difference, the mere existence of free blacks and runaways constantly "threatened" whites' sense of security. In 1822, a free black leader in his mid-fifties, Denmark Vesey, conceived a slave uprising in Charleston, South Carolina, meant to carry the oppressed to freedom in Haiti, which had won its struggle for independence from France two decades before. When word of Vesey's plan leaked, the local authority rounded up the conspirators. There followed impassioned trials, court-sanctioned hangings, and surgical mutilations. Relations among white families and the slaves they owned turned ever more fearful. Though Vesey had plotted not race war but a mass exodus, it was the extreme thought of black men bent on indiscriminate murder and, worse, wild sexual desire for aristocratic white women, that haunted the South.[30]

Jefferson's clear dilemma in confronting the race issue was tied to his identification with a class of men. These were the neighbors he grew up admiring, the friends he made in college and afterward, and the political allies who could acknowledge, along with him, the South's distinctive character. His description of northern and southern qualities to the French Marquis de Chastellux in 1785 remained essentially unchanged in later years: He credited northerners with independence and industry, but called them a "chicaning" and "hypocritical" people; southerners were at once "fiery" and "indolent," but he loved them for their "generous" and "candid" personality. Morally, he felt perfectly comfortable in the South, and distrusted the North.[31]

"a suspicion only"

Jefferson's political identity could not be separated from his desire to protect and sustain the cultural and economic power of the South. Just as he could not extinguish his personal debt, he could not extricate himself from slave owning without abandoning Virginia, as he knew it. Though he read and corresponded widely, his core values were as provincial as they were cosmopolitan.

Jefferson submitted in his *Notes* that the humane remedy, the only nonviolent solution to America's race problem, was to re-colonize blacks elsewhere. They were, he felt, a people without a country, because they had been kidnapped and taken from their homeland—unlike the European Americans, they had not come voluntarily. As Peter S. Onuf has demonstrated in his exemplary study of Jefferson's racially sensitive concept of nationhood, a coaxing of all Americans into aesthetically desirable and politically healthy breeding conduct would alone prevent a catastrophic race war. Subordinated blacks had built up too much legitimate hostility over the generations, whereas whites' supposedly higher reasoning faculty should have made them, as well, loath to accept the evolutionary debasement that racial "amalgamation" implied. These are rather stark terms, but they decisively sum up Jefferson's theory. In Onuf's words, "Jefferson's sustained assault on the physical attributes and mental abilities of enslaved Africans helps illuminate his conception of white Virginians as a distinct 'people.' The presence of two peoples in one country, and their conspicuous tendency to mix, jeopardized the integrity of both."[32]

From as early as 1798, because he was so much in the public eye, Jefferson the white supremacist was subject to lampooning from northern critics. In that year, readers of the *Connecticut Courant* were treated to a satirical poem examining his musings in *Notes on Virginia*. The Federalist newspaper questioned his tepid embrace of the black mathematician Benjamin Banneker, who in 1791 had sent on an almanac based on his own complex computations in an effort to prompt Jefferson to readjust his theory of racial inequality. In the course of his spirited burlesque, the Connecticut versifier mocked the Virginian's bizarre evolutionary thinking in figuring the slaves "a race beneath the whites":

So far beneath, he thinks it good,
To exile all their brotherhood,
Lest blood *be* stained *in love's embraces,*
And beauty fade *from Southern faces:*
Yet traces not their lineage back,
To Adam white, nor Adam black
But thinks, perhaps, Eve's hand-maid had 'em
By some strange oran-outang Adam.[33]

White Connecticut lacked Virginia's racial anxiety, and so the *Courant* could painlessly point to Jefferson's ultimate fear, never far from the surface of debate: the fear of mixed race Americans darkening and sullying the continent. Though he equivocated in a letter to Banneker—"No body wishes more than I do to see such proofs as you exhibit, that nature has given to our black brethren, talents equal to those of the other colors of men"—Jefferson wanted, again in Professor Onuf's words, "to secure the sexual frontier between two nations."[34]

Jefferson was not open to Banneker's evidence, nor did he give credit to the prodigy Phillis Wheatley, a slave who learned English in mere months and published ingenious, if imitative, poetry in her teens.[35] Of the ex-slave Ignatius Sancho, a sentimental correspondent of the novelist Laurence Sterne, Jefferson found only incoherence, extravagance, and a lack of restraint in his published letters; he refused to believe blacks capable of reflective literature. Yet Sancho was a veritable ambassador of enlightened sensibility: "May you know no pains but of sensibility!" he wrote to a young female, quintessentially. "And may you be ever able to relieve where you wish!—May the wise and good esteem you more than I do—and the object of your heart love you—as well as you love a good and kind action!"[36] Jefferson made it clear that he thought it impossible for blacks ever to approach love in the same tasteful, elevated spirit of romance that well-bred whites enjoyed. He surveyed the sexual frontier between the races, and wished it to be fixed and walled off.

In the autumn of 1809, as he was settling in to his retirement, Jefferson critiqued a book that highlighted the literary accomplishments of blacks around the world. He asserted that anyone so credulous as to believe blacks capable of good writing could be easily dismissed: The author had thrown together "every story he could find of men of color," not distinguishing "degree of mixture" among the various authors. A true black could not rise to the level of a mulatto. Banneker, Jefferson went on, may have had a bit of spherical trigonometry, but otherwise he must have had help from a white mathematician to complete his almanac. And yet, Jefferson smugly insisted, "it was impossible for doubt to have been more tenderly or hesitatingly expressed than that was in the *Notes of*

Virginia." Doubt? Here Jefferson looks entirely deceitful. He meant that he had written: "I advance it therefore *as a suspicion only,* that the blacks . . . are inferior to whites in the endowments of both body and mind" (italics supplied). But, of course, Jefferson's "suspicion" is not healthy skepticism; in reading the least self-censored of his correspondence one is hard pressed to avoid the conclusion that his only doubt on the subject of race relations was that anyone could teach him anything new.[37]

There is no way to mince words: Jefferson considered blacks ill suited to live free among whites. He frequently used the word *harmony* in his political prescriptions for national union; but racial harmony was impossible for him to project, or to embrace as a political ideal. Jefferson's distaste for blacks ran deep, though he did not consider it personal. He regarded the "problem" philosophically. Yet he held views that comported with those of most of his white neighbors and other proper Virginia gentlemen who could anticipate, as he did, the terror that a hostile slave population might someday unleash.

For Jefferson, an insider's view of slavery limited his range of responses. He understood slavery as only one who had adapted to it could. He viscerally understood what most white liberals did not: the physical impulses and vulgar assumptions associated with slavery. Large numbers of white men figured they could do whatever they wanted with *anyone's* slaves; and in these circumstances, black men and women, politically ineffectual as they were, could only look on in utter disgust. The novelist James Baldwin told of this kind of racist brutality, through the eyes of a pretty young Harlem woman, as she came to grips with an inheritance of emotional imprisonment and assumptions about her sexuality:

> How I hated them, the way they looked, and the things they'd say, all dressed up in their damn white skin, and their clothes just so, and their weak, white pricks jumping in their drawers. You could do any damn thing with them if you just led them along, because they wanted to do something dirty and they knew that you knew how.[38]

Racism in Jefferson's world, as in Baldwin's two centuries later, was about differently pigmented people who had become permanently distrustful people. A bold line separated white and black realities, rival understandings (agonizing, potentially violent understandings) of power and humanity.

During Jefferson's retirement years, the colonization of blacks abroad came to represent a noble dream in the minds of many whites. The American Colonization Society was founded in 1816. A spirit of philanthropy distinguished the vision of northern clergy who thought of ennobling American blacks by returning them to Africa to build a black republic; many southern leaders embraced the same philanthropy, perhaps with genuine thoughts of African Americans' welfare, but always figuring at the same time that colonization would rid society of dangerous elements.[39]

The spirit of beneficent paternalism that strengthened colonization as an idea also sustained the slave owner's positive self-image. Self-congratulatory remarks about the comparative "mildness" of American slavery easily grew to encompass the presumption that democracy flourished perfectly well among whites who practiced slavery. Jefferson invoked that "mildness" rationale when it suited his purposes. Before 1826, while Jefferson survived, slavery's apologists blatantly targeted oppressed free laborers in the North and the English underclass as proof that the system was "good" for blacks, and the motives of slave owners unselfish.

It is entirely appropriate for us to weigh the moral burden we ought to put on Jefferson for having embraced the role of master. We do not like his attitude and no one can defend slavery, but that does not mean we should automatically affirm that the intelligence and wherewithal to create a just biracial or multiracial society existed in, say, 1809, when Jefferson retired to private life, and that he could have formulated such a society as efficiently as he went about conceiving his university. Though select individuals did emancipate their slaves, no one in a position of power was articulating a large-scale plan for a healthy postemancipation society. That is why Jefferson's myopic choice—to accommodate mild, benevolent slavery or to work for mass deportation and colonization—continued to strike him as the most "practicable" plan.

If, privately, he took to heart his own dictum that each generation should be independent of the preceding, and able to fashion progress on its own terms, he might have examined slavery in a different way. He wrote in 1816: "Laws and institutions must go hand and hand with the progress of the human mind. As that becomes more developed, more enlightened, as new discoveries are made, new truths disclosed, and manners and opinions change with the change of circumstances, institutions must advance also, and keep pace with the times." Good theory, but not put into practice. Thomas Jefferson could have approached the institution of slavery as he had the laws of Virginia immediately after his return from Philadelphia in 1776, when he worked to replace English edicts with republican principles. But when it came to racial justice, "manners and opinions" had not changed sufficiently—including his own.[40]

Did Jefferson have options from which he turned away? Certainly, but the debt-laden planter was nowhere near daring enough to free his slaves and make a symbolic personal sacrifice, such as would set a standard for future times. Still, we must recognize that the problem of slavery was much bigger than any one man. The political realists of America could not carry sympathy far enough to integrate society, nor were they willing to take their radical Revolutionary language beyond where they had already taken it. As important, the patriarchal family remained the model of social relations in most places. All of these are mitigating factors, suggesting that we should not damn Jefferson and leave it at that. There was effusive sentiment but no agreement within religious circles— let alone between North and South—on how to proceed. The slavery stalemate had to be worked out on a massive scale—a cross-sectional consensus needed to form—and it was not in Thomas Jefferson's constitution to build this kind of consensus.

He appreciated life as a perfectly natural mix of sensations (feelings) and intellect. From this starting point, he made moral sense of his world. "Moral sense of his world" may sound a bit jarring when we classify him as a slave owner: Even a well-intentioned one is hard for history to love. This is why we need to recognize that as deficient as he was, Jefferson never set out wanting to represent, above all others in his generation, the common white belief in black inferiority. We magnify his limits as a political actor by forcing his racism to define him. We would probably contextualize his racism better if racial injustice did not still blatantly manifest itself in our lifetime.

Though he made many unfortunate concessions to unattractive, unenlightened, and long since discredited social views, Jefferson behaved as he did because his world allowed it. The shrill sound of racism carried far and wide; and the notion that black-white unions were an aberration of nature extended well beyond his designing mind.

Useless Iron

Jefferson was, the written record strongly suggests, a dutiful master, though his concern for artisans and house servants is more apparent in the historic record than his concern for field workers. According to his granddaughter Ellen, during his financially desperate retirement years, Jefferson preferred to limit the productivity of his farms rather than permit his overseers to drive the slaves hard. He was particularly moved by the deaths of enslaved children for whose well-being he was responsible. In February 1826, under the heavy pressure of convincing the Virginia legislature to permit a lottery to rescue his finances and save Monticello, Jefferson wrote to his grandson: "I hope the negro clothing is on it's way."[41]

At Monticello and Poplar Forest, he concerned himself with the distribution of food, clothing, shelter, and other necessary supplies. During his retirement years, he routinely asked his overseers to confirm for him that his slaves had blankets and beds sufficient for their comfort. He might show disappointment with a slave who did not possess the work habits he expected, but, if physiognomy accounts for anything, he did not terrify anyone. He thought kindness and reciprocity—and incentives—succeeded better than a menacing temper. Jefferson preferred a show of politeness in lieu of interracial equality.

Here are two brief sketches of the master's mindset: In 1818, when his rheumatism prevented a planned visit to Poplar Forest, Jefferson wrote to his overseer Joel Yancey in urgent tones, and gave clear instructions that he was to insure adequate supplies: "What your home-spun [cotton, wool, flax, and hemp] falls short of clothing for the people must be supplied by mr Robertson. I will state below who are to have [new] blankets, and who beds this year." Adding pork distribution, Jefferson demonstrated that he took a personal interest in the slaves who lived at this distance from Monticello when he listed by name twenty-one recipients of blankets, and separately instructed Yancey: "Maria's having now a child, I promised her a house to be built this winter. Be so good as to have it done. Place it along the garden fence on the road Eastward from Hanah's house." It was that very week that Han[n]ah learned, apparently from overseer Yancey, of her master's indisposition. "I am sorry to hear you was so unwell you could not come[.] It greive me many time."

The following year, while Jefferson remained at Monticello, Johnny Hemings, his talented, ever-trusted carpenter—and his eyes and ears—was securing the windows at Poplar Forest and keeping him abreast of slaves' activities. Jefferson relied on Hemings's reports as much to prevent disruption of production, and arrest poor work habits and poor supervision, as to guarantee contentment among the enslaved population. "Write to me every Wednesday," Jefferson instructed Hemings.[42]

These were not exactly what we might call fond communications, but they were certainly considerate. In 1825, he closed a letter to his bound but largely self-regulated carpenter: "Your friends here [at Monticello] are well, and I wish you well."[43] It is worth noting, too, that Jefferson recorded his correspondence with John Hemings in his *Summary Journal of Letters*, an official log ordinarily reserved for his most significant correspondence with respectable gentlemen.

Jefferson saw to the training of many of his slaves by specialists: He was responsible for creating skilled cabinetmakers, blacksmiths, brewers, bricklayers, spinners, and weavers—artisans who spent little time laboring in the fields, though they might help at harvest time. The Monticello artisans were able to earn extra money doing occasional jobs for local free artisans.

Yet Jefferson was capable of insensitive behavior on occasion. He could be demanding, and even cruel, in his paternalistic manipulations. To prevent his slaves from proposing marriage to slaves living on other plantations, which might have yielded complications, he offered material incentives to all who found love at Monticello. As president, he brought slave Fanny Gillette, who was trained in the French style of cooking, to Washington; her husband, wagon driver Davy Hern, was left behind at Monticello. Long-distance marriage proved a strain, and Davy feared what his wife was up to. On one of Davy's rare visits to the President's House, Davy and Fanny fell to arguing; and as their marital problems escalated, Jefferson ordered his overseer to Washington expressly to take the Herns to Alexandria's slave market to be sold. He may never have intended to separate the couple—we cannot know the full story—but he succeeded in quieting their feud by the use of a threat: Davy and Fanny "wept, and begged, and made good promises," before Jefferson agreed to rescind his order.[44]

Jefferson also found it easy to participate in slave trading, though he preferred to keep it familial, or at least, among friends. When he first retired from public life in the mid-1790s, for a brief three years before assuming the vice presidency, he gave his energy to rebuilding his mountain estate and restoring domestic manufacture there. His younger sister Anna's husband, Hastings Marks, living to the east in Louisa County, expressed a desire to sell thirty-four-year-old Nance, a weaver, a Hemings, and Sally's older half-sister, who had been given to Mrs. Marks upon marriage. Writing to a planter, neighbor to the Markses, who had done favors for him in the past, Jefferson "presumed to sollicit" this gentleman to act as intermediary and to purchase Nance for Jefferson "at whatever price you shall think her really worth." In describing Nance, Jefferson assigned a value in terms we would find crude: "I believe [she] has ceased to breed." As a decent man of his time and place (if such activity can be put in relative terms at all), Jefferson allowed that he would be willing to purchase, along with Nance, her teenage daughter, "if she insists on it, and my sister desires it." But, for reasons of economy, presumably, he refused to purchase Nance's teenage son, and keep the family intact.[45]

Jefferson's daughter Martha expressed her perspective in a letter to her daughter Ellen in 1825, when the family's finances necessitated the sale of some slaves on the Edgehill property (near Monticello), and made the broader sale of slaves first appear inevitable:

> The negroes may be disposed of to people that we know, in many instances friends, and neighbours. . . . My mind is greatly relieved by this arrangement. The discomfort of slavery I have borne all my life, but it's sorrows in all their bitterness I had never before conceived. The sale of Susan [her daughter Virginia's maid] was only a prelude in my imagination to the scenes which the 8th [date of proposed public sale] would exhibit in the Negro buyers, and the advertisement would have been the signal to have collected them from every part of the state.

How much trouble and distress y[ou] have been spared my beloved Ellen by
your removal, for nothing can prosper under such a system of injustice.[46]

Devoted as she was to her father, it is hard to conceive that Martha Randolph
would have expressed herself this way had she not been reflecting, as well,
Thomas Jefferson's view. Indeed, Ellen happened to write her grandfather from
Boston the day after her mother composed the letter to her; and Ellen put the
sentiment most succinctly: "[New England] has given me an idea of prosperity
and improvement, such as I fear our Southern States cannot hope for, whilst the
canker of slavery eats into their hearts, and diseases the whole body by this ulcer
at the core." The medical metaphors should sound familiar, too, given her
grandfather's preferences.[47]

He may have been a race separatist, but Jefferson was frequently directed by
an unselfish impulse, as when he wrote in 1815: "The mind of the master is to
be apprised by reflection, and strengthened by the energies of conscience,
against the obstacles of self interest to an acquiescence in the rights of others;
that of the slave is to be prepared by instruction and habit for self-government
and for the honest pursuits of industry and social duty." Who is to say that Jefferson did not feel a sincere obligation to oppressed individuals? It appears to
have been his honest hope that conscience should prevail over self-interest, and
that separation would not occur before self-sufficiency was taught and dignity
restored to the slave.[48]

Though a flawed philosopher, Jefferson correctly saw the institution of slavery as a dehumanizing and morally, as well as politically, corrosive system. As a
"physician," he wished to treat the festering sore, but his tools were little better
than the instruments of medicine of his time. And so he rationalized—if perhaps too easily. As a member of the ruling race, he fretted over economic conditions under slavery, but he expected far worse for America if abolition were to
occur without provision for the happiness of the whites who owned the land. In
the end, of course, he did little more to end slavery than agree to discuss the
subject in reasoned, rather than emotionally charged, language. It is somewhat
ironic, then, that abolitionists in the years before the Civil War could claim Jefferson as a "prime mover" behind their crusade, for it was he whose decisive
language introduced many of them to the truism that slavery was evil and in-
defensible—he knew precisely what to say, though he turned out to be the most
timid of abolitionists.[49]

We still want to ask why a man so immersed in scientific knowledge, and
bent on questioning established rules of conduct, should have been so comfortable with racial stereotypes. After all, as a general rule with him, problems
required dispassionate study. They were addressed by testing principles, as in a

scientific examination. He wrote to Dr. Hosea Humphrey in 1816 of the ideal circumstance: "The freer the enquiry, the more favorable to truth." To a progressive mind, there can be no better watchword. Yet Jefferson's very next sentence marked the shame of his refusal to re-encounter race relations: "But when a whole system is proposed to be reformed, the undertaking is for the young, not for the old."[50]

Here lies the key to our criticism of Thomas Jefferson, the uncertain slavery opponent. In retirement, he was unwilling to devote his foremost energies to public causes beyond the university he was to see rising in his view from Monticello. At a certain point in his life he was able, to his own satisfaction and for his own sense of peace, to transfer responsibility to the rising generation. Should we fault him for retiring from that issue which, from our tortured modern perspective, we see as the most crucial and unresolved moral dilemma that still links our American society to his? Yes, but a qualified yes. We should fault him for missing the opportunity to prove—and improve—himself.

The most famous example of Jefferson's mixed message on the subject of slavery in his retirement years is the 1814 exchange with his Albemarle County neighbor, Edward Coles. He was President Madison's private secretary and a remarkable young man of insight and action, justice and humanity, who not only emancipated his slaves, but also brought them to freedom by establishing them on land in Illinois, where he later became governor. In 1814, as he conceived the effort, Coles thought he could count on Jefferson to lend support, because Jefferson was, of course, a reasonable man.

Jefferson had been an idealist at Coles's age, but now he was more cautious than encouraging. "The love of justice and the love of country plead equally the cause of these people," he opened his letter to Coles, but before long he was qualifying that miscegenation was a real and present danger: "Their amalgamation with the other color produces a degradation to which no lover of his country, no lover of excellence in the human character can innocently consent." The sexual frontier again comes to the forefront of his mind.

To Coles, Jefferson rationalized his inaction not in plain English but in Latin: "*Trementibus œquo humeris et inutile ferrum cingi*," or "Shoulders trembling from old age, he put on useless iron." The phrase is an abbreviated line from Vergil's *Aeneid* recalling the fall of Troy. It excludes the always evocative word *convulsaque* ("convulsed") of the previous clause in the original, and therefore requires a full translation to retrieve Jefferson's context: "As he viewed the reduction of the taken city, and the convulsed thresholds of the buildings, and the middle of the enemy within its structures, the older man in vain put long unused weapons upon his *shoulders; trembling from old age, putting on useless iron* and about to die, he was carried into the crowded enemy."[51]

Proud Priam, king of Troy, was killed as his city burned and his family help-lessly looked on. Jefferson, alarmed by the convulsive potential of the slavery issue, may have been aging, like the Trojan, but there was no burning city around him.[52] It is questionable whether Jefferson would ever have been per-ceived as a ridiculous relic in useless armor if he had bravely tried to raise a hand against slavery. But he found the issue too delicate, too fraught with polit-ical danger. He had retired. "This enterprise is for the young," he told Coles. "It shall have all my prayers & these are the only weapons of an old man."

It needs to be said that of all the species of letters Jefferson received and replied to during his retirement years, a large proportion of them found him ra-tionalizing his inaction. It was not just slavery that he resisted committing to; literally hundreds of petitioning correspondents who sympathized with him in political or moral principle and asked his support were met with the same kind of ambivalence.

"The only exact testimony of a man is his actions," Jefferson pronounced in 1815, on a subject other than slavery. Yet he easily, perhaps too easily, justified his inaction by recollecting a time in his career when he did speak out. Only months before the exchange with Edward Coles, he explained to his protégé Joseph Carrington Cabell that he did not want his thoughts on public affairs to be known, except when it came to advancing public education: "I frankly con-fide to yourself these opinions, or rather no-opinions, of mine, but would not wish to have them go any further. I want to be quiet: and altho' some circum-stances now and then excite me to notice them, I feel safe, and happier in leav-ing every thing to those whose turn it is to take care of them." This would be his policy, he said, "as long as I breathe."[53]

Jefferson continued to see himself as appropriately sensitive, and practical, if quieter in his advocacies. As Cabell lobbied the Virginia legislature in support of Jefferson's plan for a university, the shadowy presence thanked the younger man for honoring his wishes: "I am much indebted to you for keeping me in the back-ground." Excepting the period of debate over Missouri (1819–1820), when he launched into a flurry of private correspondence defending his sec-tion's pro-slavery stand, Jefferson approached southern slavery as he did most other thorny issues: If his generation had failed to arrive at a workable solution, it should step aside and allow others to take the lead. He drew upon a medical metaphor in 1815 to explain slavery's persistence: "Where the disease is most deeply seated, there it will be slowest in eradication. In the northern States it was merely superficial, and easily corrected. In the southern it is incorporated with the whole system, and requires time, patience, and perseverance in the cu-rative process." The curative or therapeutic process, he is saying, needed more energy than his remaining years allotted him.[54]

Jefferson's 1821 memoir, sometimes referred to as his *Autobiography,* consists of pages written in anticipation of a friendly biographer. It is a text that Jefferson undertook not for self-publication, but as a more modest and indirect means of declaring himself to history. In the middle of this carefully constructed work, Jefferson unhesitatingly inserted a line that rang out with respect for the enslaved people of his country: "Nothing is more certainly written in the book of fate than that these people are to be free." It could have been stretched in large letters across a banner at the head of a compassionate parade. The man who wrote this was seven years older than the one who had been lukewarm in his support of Coles, and perhaps in the justness of its tone he was consciously seeking history's praise. But it is interesting, too, how on this subject he could segue so easily from charitable and humanistic to more arbitrary language, for the very next two lines are just as meaningful: "Nor is it less certain that the two races, equally free, cannot live in the same government. Nature, habit, opinion has drawn indelible lines of distinction between them." He believed what he was writing. From Revolutionary times to old age, he consistently judged that emancipation without a permanent separation of the races was contrary to the republic's interest.[55]

We must appreciate the full weight of the historic irony encompassed in Jefferson's language: His scientific racism, his cool calculation, were employed as part of a strategy that would allow him to bide his time when he refused to do more to end slavery. In fact, though, in aiming to avoid pain, he caused pain. In conserving his energy, he undermined his own cause of tranquil felicity across American society. Even as he compiled such sublime statements as the "book of fate" passage above, he could not escape the potential of violence emanating from his own more damaging rhetoric.

What caused the liberal thinker to give up on the critical questioning that constituted proof of enlightenment? What made him so inflexible on this one subject?

It was, in fine, the mixed message of eighteenth-century science and medicine. He was a Revolutionary when in his prime, perhaps an abolitionist at heart, who forecast a freedom that he was too afraid to envision fully once he had embarked upon a more thorough study of medicine, physiology, and natural history. The medical Enlightenment actually supported the growth of a racist ideology in America: The books Jefferson read, distinguishing male and female traits, urban and pastoral conditions, brain activity and controlled sentiment, supplied him with a more racist vocabulary than he might otherwise have developed. His intense reading on these subjects made him a bolder amateur anatomist (he was not a true cultural anthropologist); he reached conclusions based on stark determinations within the Linnaean taxonomy. He classified by way of mere surface appearance, and ignorantly speculated on deficiencies within. With the illusory character of Jefferson's naturalism, blacks became a lower, less reflective order of humanity.[56]

He misapplied science to politics because he craved certainty in politics. He appeared to be trying to retrieve through a philosophical exercise that happy state of nature where pastoral peace and contentment might remove America from the ravages of time, and where politics could be managed (through a massive colonization program) so as to eliminate the threat of race war.[57] In service to his ideal, and reticent to abandon his fellows, his white slave-holding brethren, Jefferson allowed his aesthetic judgments about skin color combinations and his bleak observations about degraded slaves' behavior to overwhelm his humane impulses.

Practically speaking, Jefferson's attitude was, in fact, not far from that of Abraham Lincoln. Lincoln did not wish to interfere with slavery where it already existed, though he wished that slavery would be ended as soon as possible. Lincoln, like Jefferson, did not propose radical action, nor did he envision blacks and whites as political equals. That is why context is so important. History does not always provide the gratifying antecedents we seek.

Lafayette's Companion

In 1824, as the fiftieth anniversary of American independence drew near, Congress expressed the people's wish once again to set their eyes on the sole surviving general to have commanded the troops of the Continental Army—the man who had helped save Virginia from ruin after Thomas Jefferson's shaky tenure as wartime governor in 1780. Thus, in the last two years of his life, Jefferson was fortunate to have the chance to rekindle his friendship with Major General Marie Joseph Paul Yves Roch Gilbert de Motier, Marquis de Lafayette, who had been absent from America for all of forty years.

Though they had corresponded regularly, Jefferson had not seen Lafayette since the outbreak of the French Revolution in 1789. In the American imagination, Lafayette still represented battlefield courage, honest patriotism, and the liberal spirit. After a letter from President Monroe reached France, a nostalgic drama got underway, one that would bring "the nation's guest" across the ocean, to set foot in each of the twenty-four states and express his undying affection for his adopted country. Among the nationally featured stories of Lafayette's eighteen-month-long tour would be his warm embrace of Thomas Jefferson at Monticello's portico in November 1824, and the next day's banquet at the University of Virginia. Less celebrated was the challenge to Jefferson's unsatisfying theory of race posed by Lafayette's companion, the ardent antislavery agitator Frances Wright.[58]

Wright was the young British author of the highly complimentary *Views of Society and Manners in America* (1821), which Jefferson had read. "You and I," Lafayette wrote to Jefferson a month before their momentous reunion, "are the two Men in the World the Esteem of whom she values the Most." Wright had shown in her book that she was, at least at that juncture, sensitive to Jefferson's argument in the *Notes on Virginia* that blacks and whites had a long history of ill will to overcome, an antagonism that was perhaps ineradicable. She expressed sympathy with the principle of colonization—returning educated ex-slaves to Africa to establish their own republic—and even defended southerners by pointing to the way foreigners visiting America (far more than American-born whites) displayed an "absolute disgust at being served by black hands." Uncomfortable with slavery, she was nonetheless convinced, as Jefferson was, that "there must inevitably exist a barrier between the American and the negro," because even whites' wholesale "repentance" could not "obliterate in a moment the wrongs of years," or transform slaves into the political equals of whites.[59]

But on this, her second visit to America, Fanny Wright resolved to take action personally. By the time she reached Monticello, she was already starting to revise her mild critique. Though unfailingly polite to Jefferson, she would, in 1827, publicly endorse interracial sex as the appropriate solution to America's race problem, and thereby damn herself in the eyes of more and more who found her extravagance in speech rash and reckless. She helped found the biracial utopian community of Nashoba, in western Tennessee, and infamously rejected the unequal institution of marriage. Ellen Randolph (not yet Coolidge), who met the nearly six-foot-tall Fanny at Monticello in 1824, reviled her a few years later as "this unsexed thing who dares to scorn her God. . . . I feel mortified, as a woman, as having formerly been a personal acquaintance." Even in 1824, Fanny Wright must have been, for Jefferson, an extreme symbol: She was Ellen carried too far, a woman of impressive stature and intellectual attainments, who lacked the domestic detachment of the Virginia lady. Ellen knew how to show reserve in a man's world; Fanny felt differently, and refused to be held back by her sex.[60]

The devotion of Frances Wright to the Marquis de Lafayette was unusual enough. In 1822–1823, she lavished praise and affection on the old warrior in a barrage of letters: "My paternal friend whom I love better than friend ever loved friend or daughter father"; "You are my teacher, my conscience"; "I am alone without you"; "I am only half alive when away from you." By then, she was widely believed to be his mistress, which incensed his family, and caused *her* to suggest that he either adopt her or marry her. As they prepared to embark for America in 1824 (along with her sister Camilla, for the sake of propriety), Fanny wrote without restraint that she wished she and the marquis might remain in the United States permanently, to avoid the recriminations of Lafayette's French family. It appears that as he set out on his triumphal return to America, the marquis was as unconcerned with possible damage to his own reputation as Miss Wright was to hers.[61]

Jefferson had long since shed his prudery, and had found what was for him a satisfactory means of dealing with Callender's revelations about his private life, but the rumors about the venerable Lafayette and the irrepressible Miss Wright must have affected him in some way when he encountered them together. Lafayette was sixty-six (virtually the age Jefferson was when Eston Hemings was born), and Fanny was twenty-nine—almost the same distance in years as that separating Jefferson and Sally Hemings. The Frenchman and the Virginian spoke of bougies and catheters—of caring for the prostate gland. How deep did their confidences go? Did they allude in any way to sex and much younger women?

Unfortunately, there exists no transcript of what was said over supper at Monticello when, in Fanny Wright's presence, Lafayette and Jefferson revisited the slavery question. They had been discussing it—Lafayette passionately so—for several years. "All know that permitting the slaves of the South to spread into the West will not add one being to that unfortunate condition," Jefferson had assured, amid the heat of the Missouri crisis in 1820. "The boisterous sea of liberty indeed is never without a wave." He optimistically reported that the spread of slavery westward was a dilution of the problem, not an intensification of it, and would actually "increase the happiness" of human property. Lafayette, unmoved, replied: "Are You Sure, My dear friend, that Extending the principle of Slavery to the New Raised States is a Method to facilitate the Means of Getting Rid of it? I would Have thought that by Spreading the prejudices, Habits, and Calculations of planters over a larger Surface You Rather Encrease the difficulties of final liberation."[62]

A year later, Lafayette was still stuck on Jefferson's awkward logic: "Let me Confess, my dear friend, I Have Not Been Convinced, and the less as I think More of it, By Your Argument in favor of dissemination." Suggesting that his geographical distance gave him a clearer perspective, the Frenchman added candidly that when called upon to defend the moral superiority of America's government among critical Europeans, he never quite knew how to counter this one charge: "This wide Blot on American Philant[h]ropy is ever thrown in My face when I indulge my Patriotism in Encomiums, otherwise Undisputable. To see that plague Cured, while I live, is Next to impossibility, But I would like, Before I die, to Be assured that progressive and earnest Measures Have Been adopted to attain, in due time, So desirable So necessary an object." But again, Jefferson sought to convince his old friend that the spread of slavery west was not really about slavery; rather, he persisted, northern politicians had used "the trick of hypocrisy" to invent an issue while surreptitiously moving to consolidate the national government and destroy states' rights and constitutional protections, "which must immediately generate monarchy." In Jefferson's troubled mind, "the people of the North went blindfold into the snare . . . until they became sensible they were injuring instead of aiding the real interests of the slaves."[63]

Lafayette's aide, Auguste Levasseur, remarked upon the "good appearance and gaiety" of the Monticello work force, but the visitors, as a group, were undeterred in their thorough condemnation of slavery. In preparing an address to be delivered at the banquet honoring Lafayette, Jefferson curiously altered one line as he went over his draft. Recalling the visiting general's Revolutionary exploits, he changed the phrase "releasing us from foreign dominion" to "freeing us from foreign bondage." Was this done with Lafayette's sensibility in mind? Perhaps.[64]

Not long after making the acquaintance of the Jefferson-Randolph clan, Fanny Wright wrote from Washington to her late hostess, Martha Randolph, that "the days passed at Monticello will ever be treasured up in my memory as in that of my sister as among the most interesting of our lives." Afterward, as she headed west to demonstrate the extent of her commitment to social justice, she and Jefferson continued their conversation. Knowing "how deeply" her moral objective engaged his attention, she wished for him to evaluate the Nashoba plan, her personal crusade to defeat "that one great national evil" threatening "this proud citadel of human liberty." She expressed concern that he might consider her "presumptuous," but still she entreated him to authorize what she was already doing. The Memphis area settlement was an even bolder proposal than that of Edward Coles in 1814, which Jefferson had only lukewarmly cheered on.[65]

Jefferson adopted an apologetic tone in his reply to the feminist adventurer. He opened by protesting that his health was "very low." Her letter had found him too preoccupied with failing health—"at the age of 82. with one foot in the grave and the other uplifted to follow"—to address what he acknowledged had been "thro' life" that enterprise for bettering the human condition which had caused him the "greatest anxieties." Now housebound, he insisted that he was an "inefficient counselor, one scarcely able to think or to write."

Nevertheless, he summoned as much liberality as he was able to muster at this stage of life: "The abolition of the evil is not impossible: it ought never therefore to be despaired of. Every plan should be adopted, every experiment tried." Once again, while professing his own neutrality as a scientist, he returned to the style he had adopted in his *Notes* so many years before:

An opinion is hazarded by some, but proved by none, that moral urgencies are not sufficient to induce [the man of colour] to labor; that nothing can do this

but physical coercion. But this is a solecism to suppose a race of animals created, without sufficient foresight and energy to preserve their own existence. . . . We are not sufficiently acquainted with all the nations of Africa to say
that there may not be some, in which habits of industry are established, and the
arts practiced which are necessary to render life comfortable.[66]

He was yet to be convinced that blacks could uplift themselves.

For the rest of the time that remained to him, Jefferson would be pricked by
creative and morally assertive members of the next generation who expected a
bit more of him than he was prepared to give. Edward Everett was more subtle
and understanding of Jefferson's views than some others. A noted Greek
scholar and a new member of Congress from Massachusetts who had become a
regular correspondent, Everett wrote in April 1826 that he was wrestling with
the concept of consent: whether "the kind and merciful master, who feeds &
clothes and from birth till death supports his slave, has not the right to his obedience, in a State of Society, where a General Emancipation is allowed to be impracticable." He surmised that the comments Jefferson made in *Notes on Virginia* expressing sympathy for the plight of slaves could no longer be voiced in
parts of the South.[67]

The Ohioan James Heaton wrote the same week as Everett; he introduced
himself thus: "a plain man, a native Virginian, an admirer of your character,
who feels an interest in your fame." Heaton hoped for a final testament in
Jefferson's hand, to be directed to a nation eager for moral guidance from
him:

> It has for many years been conjectured, that you would favor the world, at some
> period, with a political treatise, having for one object *the abolition of slavery*. If
> Heaven, in mercy to the blacks, and safety to the whites, and unfading honor to
> your already great name and fame, should so *move* you, to leave but *one single
> page* to that effect; many of your devoted friends, and political disciples firmly
> believe, it would have a more certain, calm, permanent, and irresistible effect
> than any, and all things, said, and written thereon.

Jefferson's reply to the Ohioan was predictably weak: "A good cause is often
injured more by ill-timed efforts of it's friends than by the arguments of it's enemies. . . . The revolution in public opinion which this case requires, is not to
be expected in a day, or perhaps in an age. But time, which outlives all things,
will outlive this evil also." On this one question, it appears, Jefferson met the expectations of too few of his contemporaries, just as he fails to measure up to the
retrospective wishes of modern Americans.[68]

At rustic Nashoba, Fanny Wright gave her all. "Her whole heart and soul were occupied by the hope of raising the African to the level of European intellect," wrote the proper Englishwoman Frances Trollope, who was there at the end of 1827. Fanny was an eloquent speaker, her "rich and thrilling" voice an unexpected force at a time when women were ordinarily proscribed from public speaking. As time passed, the charismatic radical would draw crowds from Cincinnati to Boston.[69]

Meanwhile, in France, Lafayette wrote Jefferson the last letter the Virginian would receive from him. Mentioning with pleasure the ongoing efforts of his young companion at Nashoba, the French nobleman once more prodded: "My dear Jefferson, the more I see, I Hear, I think, and I feel on the subject the greater Appears to me, for the white still more if possible than the Colored population of the Southern States, the importance and Urgency of Measures pointing towards the Gradual Emancipation of Slavery." Lafayette could not have been clearer.[70]

Jefferson read this letter on June 9, 1826,[71] just three weeks before his death. We can fairly predict what his response would have been—and how it would have fallen short of expectations.

The Importance of Skin

There is yet another reason why Jefferson's conclusions perplex us. When we think historically about the body, we do not always acknowledge the problem inherent in explaining what is "natural" and what is "cultural." It is quite clear that Jefferson treated the body as the site of a discourse about passions—whether it was his own contesting Head and Heart or an African American's capacity relative to whites. The natural body he observed (which was, in fact, the body as culturally constructed) became his text for developing a narrative of America's racial choices—and his own sexual choices.

We can surmise that physical contact was important to Jefferson. For instance, when his wife, Patty, died amid his production of Notes on Virginia, he cut and preserved a lock of her hair, and lovingly placed it in the drawer beside his bed at Monticello, where it was found upon his own death more than four decades later. This physical token was a tactile reminder of a life that had brought life—that brought him children—and that palpably assisted him in feeling his humanity. Patty's hair was a connection to her spiritual self, and to his. Skin held that which made her soft and real and inviting to him.

Jefferson focused significantly on skin as the permeable boundary that distinguished inner and outer blackness and inner and outer whiteness. The relationship between physical and psychical was a meaningful part of how he defined a human being's "nature." He imagined selfhood by way of interior organs, nerves, mind, emotions, and the soul. He wanted to make better sense out of their functions, and he speculated on the meaning of the body's components to racial uniqueness.

He used the body to reach conclusions of tremendous cultural weight, basing the superiority and privilege of his own race, as we have seen, on an imagined insight into physical nature. Jefferson's racism made dark pigmentation into something repellent. Though he did not invent these categories of racial conceit, and would surely not be the last to employ them in terms of loathing, he revealed that in ordering his life, and America's, he was more interested in hygienic concerns (consistent with his reading of the French medical Enlightenment or his decrying Williamsburg's polluted environment) than in experiencing the exotic "other" through intimate contact. At least, as far as we can tell.[72]

In one of the most revealing passages in *Notes*, Jefferson expressed his fear of "the extermination of the one or the other race." He explained that when the "deep-rooted prejudices" held by whites came face-to-face with the "ten thousand recollections" held by viciously exploited blacks, it was—what word did Jefferson choose?—*convulsions*, that would provoke the catastrophic race war he foresaw sometime in America's future, if a solution to the problem was not found. But what was it that triggered his use of "convulsions" here? His next thought informs us: color of the skin, color of the blood, color of the bile, "or some other secretion." In this critically important discussion, he was drawn to consider bodily fluids, racial comparisons of beauty, and "mixtures [producing] expressions of every passion."[73]

The outwardly mild Jefferson's inwardly pronounced emotions were again cast in the language of philosophical medicine. Coupling mind and body, he showed that he did not just believe blacks' minds undeveloped, but their features unappealing and bodies defective. And he raised the uncomfortable notion that blacks would never warrant equality with whites in either political society or the private sphere. Because of their colored bodies. He was preoccupied with the physical body.

This tells us that if Sally Hemings became his sexual partner at some point during the decade after he wrote his *Notes*, and gave birth to his children, she must *not* have represented blackness (in his words "eternal monotony") to Jefferson. When he chose to speculate on race, he was clear in his mind that "cleaning the issue of Negro blood," as he put it, occurred when a quadroon (one-fourth black, like Sally) bore a white man's child; and that the emancipation of slaves ought to be accompanied by a gradual but certain "deportation" beyond U.S. borders of those whose blood remained African.[74]

Blood relations loomed large in the thinking of Jefferson's generation, as in the potent reference to "consanguinity" in the Declaration of Independence:

$$\tfrac{q}{2} + \tfrac{C}{2} = \tfrac{a}{8} + \tfrac{A}{8} + \tfrac{B}{4} + \tfrac{C}{2}.$$ call this e. (eighth) who having less than $\tfrac{1}{8}$ of a. or of pure negro

blood, to wit $\tfrac{1}{8}$ only, is no longer a mulatto. so that a 3.^{d} cross clears the blood.

from these elements let us examine other compounds.

for example, let h. and q. cohabit. their issue will be

$$\tfrac{h}{2} + \tfrac{q}{2} = \tfrac{a}{4} + \tfrac{A}{4} + \tfrac{a}{8} + \tfrac{A}{8} + \tfrac{B}{4} = \tfrac{3a}{8} + \tfrac{3A}{8} + \tfrac{B}{4}$$ wherein we find $\tfrac{3}{8}$ of a. or of negro blood.

let h. and e. cohabit. their issue will be

$$\tfrac{h}{2} + \tfrac{e}{2} = \tfrac{a}{4} + \tfrac{A}{4} + \tfrac{a}{16} + \tfrac{A}{16} + \tfrac{B}{8} + \tfrac{C}{2} = \tfrac{5a}{16} + \tfrac{5A}{16} + \tfrac{B}{8} + \tfrac{C}{2}$$ wherein $\tfrac{5}{16}$ a. makes still a mulatto.

let q. and e. cohabit. the half of the blood of each will be

$$\tfrac{q}{2} + \tfrac{e}{2} = \tfrac{a}{8} + \tfrac{A}{8} + \tfrac{B}{4} + \tfrac{a}{16} + \tfrac{A}{16} + \tfrac{B}{8} + \tfrac{C}{2} = \tfrac{3a}{16} + \tfrac{3A}{16} + \tfrac{3B}{8} + \tfrac{C}{2}$$ wherein $\tfrac{3}{16}$ of a is no longer mulatto.

Excerpt from Jefferson's letter to attorney Francis Gray, March 4, 1815, explaining how Virginians understood the "cleaning," or removal, of negro blood over the course of generations. Answering a query concerning the legal definition of "mulatto," Jefferson determined that 3/16 black was no longer mulatto, indicating that Sally Hemings had produced, in his mind, white sons and daughters. "This does not reestablish freedom," Jefferson went on to state. "But if e [a person with less than 1/4 'pure negro blood'] be emancipated, he becomes a free *white* man." Library of Congress.

The British had somehow betrayed their consanguineous colonial blood-brothers. Blood was easily spilled in war, and blood was easily "corrupted" through interracial sex; in both instances, blood symbolized power. As Michel Foucault has explained, modern thinking has substituted sex for blood (as the biological instrument of production) in symbolizing this kind of power. Sex became "the stamp of individuality" in the nineteenth century, as it marked "the life of the body and the life of the species." Sex became more crucial to society's measure of itself, and continues to be so, linked as it is to larger issues of health, vitality, and domination. But for Jefferson, the moral implications of sexual behavior were still less of a concern than the fantasy and symbolism of the bequest of blood.[75]

It was Virginia's law, as well, that made the problem of blood mixing so intractable. Boundaries separating the races in the South were *supposed* to be clearly demarcated, and all for the comfort of the ruling whites. The system was meant, at least in part, to maintain the "purity" of white women, that is, to keep them from intimate relations with nonwhites. At the same time, the nature of power in the South made it impossible to prevent white men—of varying social standing—from having sexual relations with black and mulatto women. Long before Jefferson pronounced on the issue, familiar stereotypes (race-specific biological determinism) rationalized white male reactive behavior: African women were endowed with an unusually passionate, sexually aggressive nature;

African men were virile, potent, and dangerous. The expansion of free black communities in Virginia and elsewhere in the years following the Revolution only intensified perceptions of the threat to racial distinctiveness.[76]

In Jefferson's Virginia, enslaved women of varying shades found themselves the object of their masters' lust, and many eventually consented, often in exchange for material or other benefits, to becoming a mistress or a concubine. But there were other, equally pervasive, reasons for white anxiety. Keeping white women "pure" proved elusive, if not impossible. The courts heard a great variety of cases relative to honor, virtue, and whiteness—cases of adultery across the color line: a white husband who found his wife in bed with a free man of color, a white wife who felt degraded when her husband treated his enslaved mistress and children as family members. Because of the frequency of these cases, laws prohibiting fornication and interracial marriage were categorical, and 17.6 percent of all divorces granted by Virginia's legislature concerned adultery across the color line.[77]

Perhaps the extent of sexual exploitation, like the persistence of racial prejudice, is to be read as an indictment of Jefferson, and of everyone else who knew as much as he knew about southern culture and let it go on. But it should be clear by now that this discussion is not intended to indict Jefferson alone, or above all. To protect the existing power structure and reduce anxiety, the courts litigated whiteness; Jefferson, fully understanding the law, insulated himself from this debate, as best as he could, on his mountain. There he imagined his freedom to be unbounded. Sally Hemings was a house servant, her social status and that of her brothers and sisters fixed, and her color, in this environment, in the eye of the beholder.

In purely genealogical terms, Sally Hemings was almost certainly, as is often noted, the half-sister of Jefferson's late wife. Patty Jefferson's father, John Wayles, had taken Sally's mother, Elizabeth (Betty) Hemings, as his acknowledged mistress or unacknowledged concubine, after having outlived two white wives. Patty was born to Wayles and his first wife, Martha Eppes, in 1748; Sally was born to Wayles and the half-black, half-white Betty Hemings in 1773 and was nine, a prepubescent, when Patty died at Monticello. She was only months younger than Martha, the Jeffersons' eldest. Sally Hemings was thirty years younger than Thomas Jefferson.

We can more or less deduce her skin tone. All the Hemingses were described, in memoirs and newspaper stories over the years, as variations of "near white." The slave Isaac Jefferson, born at Monticello, referred to Sally as "mighty near white . . . , very handsome, long straight hair down her back." Her older brothers James and Robert he called "bright mulattos." "Bright" meant light-skinned. Their mother, Betty, was also "bright mulatto."[78]

We have to ignore the northern satirists who, in 1802–1803, spoofed the sitting president. The dominant image of their bawdy songs about "Monticellian Sally" was the biracial slave's essential blackness. "Black is love's proper hue," is how the cruelly imaginative versifier put words in Jefferson's mouth. "Her skin is sable," lips thick, and Jefferson will not be embarrassed though "My virgin daughters—see! they weep—Their mother's place supply." Part of the reason that history came to depict Sally Hemings in African tones was that the only publicity she received (after Callender's initial report) was fictionalized. Jefferson's emotion was construed in such a way as to mock him; to achieve their effect, antimiscegenation scandalmongers had to invent Sally's color as well as her position as Jefferson's substitute wife.[79]

Did Jefferson imagine Sally Hemings as one-quarter black or three-quarters white, that is, "mighty near white," as Isaac Jefferson remarked in his as-told-to memoir? Given Thomas Jefferson's hygienically sensitive view of the body, the answer is, I contend, the latter. He put Sally Hemings's racial traits in an entirely different category from those attributes (including "color of the blood . . . or other secretion," and "strong and disagreeable odor") that sickened him in the *Notes*. This assumes, of course, that Jefferson's *stated* aversion to blackness was what he *really* felt, and did not merely constitute a rhetorical argument designed for political purposes, or to convince the medically enlightened of Europe as to the scientific underpinnings of his thesis.[80]

If we take him at his word, in this instance, and accept as fact that black skin repelled him, Sally Hemings was not a register of skin pigmentation but something else. She may have been "dusky" to the satirists who had never seen her, but to Jefferson, who had known her from her early years, she was anything but an anthropological stereotype. Her presence may have caused him to feel his own privilege, but it did not make him imagine Africa.

6

The New Debate: Sex with a Servant

The world must be peopled by marriage, or peopled without it.

SAMUEL JOHNSON, IN *RASSELAS* (1759)

We have established that Jefferson's psychology was fundamentally different from ours, and that we cannot simply expect to understand his impulses by engaging with terms and concepts comfortable to the twenty-first century. Neither race nor sex was thought of precisely as we imagine; nor equality, nor virility. Race and social justice occupied a place within a "natural order" we no longer recognize, and sex occupied a place within a therapeutic vocabulary of health, moderation, and harmony from which we are detached. But that did not make racial science, for all its rigidity, less anxious; or sexual desire, for all its ambiguity, less lustful.

There was greater tolerance for sexual activity in Jefferson's time than the modern mind generally attributes. Most today are unaware, for example, that prostitution was the full-time occupation of perhaps one in twenty-five women in America's principal towns. In part, our misapprehension occurs because a language of virtue dominated the republic of letters. America's founding texts herald republican manners that exalt reason and govern human passions. But this is an idealization of the Enlightenment only. It does not mean that James Madison, who married the vivacious Dolley Todd when he was past forty, was necessarily sexually innocent up to that point; or that Jefferson's disparagement of Europeans' behavior (a lack of conjugal fidelity, the wider availability of prostitution) meant that he never found sexual outlets for himself in the years after Patty died, before a maturing Sally Hemings came to his attention.[1]

We know enough about Jefferson's worldview to state that his marriage to Patty, from January 1, 1772, to September 6, 1782, was a match made between social equals that was sustained by mutual commitment and real affection. His intimacy with educated and accomplished white women during his five years in Europe (most notably his "flirtation" with the Anglo-Italian painter Maria

Cosway) may or may not have involved sexual relations. The veiled language he and his female correspondents used keeps us guessing. Most of these letters subsist on conventional warmth; a few hint at ardor. Before the DNA "solution," there was as much to suggest sublimation and celibacy as sexual activity on Jefferson's part.[2]

For Jefferson's generation, women's bodies were mysteriously formed and capable of dangerous disturbances. Female flesh, for this reason, was frequently used in exaggerated depictions of social upheaval and threats to civility (especially as drawn in caricature).[3] The latent power associated with men's sexual sensations was still to a large degree self-monitored. No external control arrested the activities of a man of Jefferson's social status.

A moral man—such as the widower Jefferson was constructed—honored womanhood by burying sexual activity that threatened to complicate his relationship with his immediate family. His closest affections were meant to be reserved for them. Yet male desire was just as "real" to the people of his time and place as female self-control. So the bookish elder Jefferson, weighed down by a demanding schedule of intellectual work while writing to his learned friends around the world, presumably made it appear that he had had little time to develop emotional connections beyond those that bound him to his daughter and her children, his nephews and visiting cousins, and select young men of Albemarle County—the corps of protégés who were helping him establish the university. As far as this circle of friends and relatives could tell, he was the most physical when he exercised on horseback, a daily ritual he undertook after morning letter writing was behind him. He convinced his family that he was not a sexual being.

The published *Family Letters of Thomas Jefferson* captures the closeness of father and daughters and grandchildren—the Enlightenment family. The young ones made claims on his time. They were educated with tenderness; they studied hard; they enjoyed toys and pets, and read for pleasure, and felt indulged.[4] Thomas Jefferson loved and honored that family with "pure affection," as he said often. To Martha, in 1793, craving a retirement from the hostile politics inside George Washington's cabinet, he expressed his intention to spend the rest of his days with her: "When I see you it will be never to part again." In the months leading up to his final retirement, in 1808–1809, he signed off a letter to his eldest grandson with unusual solemnity: "God bless you, and prosper your pursuits." And to Ellen, always with special sentiment: "To yourself I am all love." Similarly, to Cornelia: "Kiss Ellen and all the children for me."[5]

At this meaningful time in his life, the strength of family ties promoted health and well-being. Encouraged as his administration wound down, Martha wrote to her father, the president: "As the *period* of your labours draws near, My heart beats with inexpressible anxiety and impatience. Adieu again My ever Dear and honoured Parent. That the evening of your life may pass in serene and unclouded tranquility is the daily prayer . . . [and] the dearest and most sacred duty of your devoted child." After this, her father restated: "I look with infinite joy to the moment when I shall be ultimately moored in the midst of my affections." He signed off, "My love to the children and most of all to yourself."[6]

Nothing in his life compared with the emotions he felt for this family.

Securing the Sexual Frontier I: Jefferson's Options

The Hemingses were house servants with particular skills: Sally's brothers James and Peter were trained in the culinary arts; her half-brother John was a master carpenter. Sally was the personal maid to Jefferson's younger daughter Maria from the late 1780s, and may have looked after her master's private quarters during her middle (childbearing) years. She also sewed for the family, as her son Madison testified.

As much as we may want to view the Jefferson-Hemings matter as one that stands to open potential new directions in understanding the country's confused history on the subject of race relations and secret love, it may reveal something else: Sex and class privilege. Whereas the combination of race and sex in the South routinely caused serious social dysfunction, the particular relationship of Thomas Jefferson and Sally Hemings was very likely something different. Legally a slave—his property—she was, to him, not a black woman but part of a socially subordinate netherworld of parallel family, related through John Wayles to Thomas Jefferson's white descendants. She lacked a public identity, that is, she lacked any publicly construed "honor"; in the private sphere of the extended, largely self-sufficient family at Monticello, her rights and feelings carried an indeterminate but not inconsequential weight.

For a useful comparison, and to demonstrate that Jefferson's situation was replicated in many places in the South, consider the relationship between Martha Washington and her enslaved half-sister, Ann Dandridge, who, quite curiously, is not mentioned in any of the first president's household records. Ann's mother was apparently part Cherokee, as well as black; and though she retained the surname Dandridge (Martha's maiden name), Ann was in fact owned by the Washingtons, and was only freed in 1802, after George and Martha had died. As Henry Wiencek, the historian who pieced together this information, observed: "Martha had the mental steel to hold a half-sister as a slave. Martha's act reveals the capacity of the masters and mistresses to tolerate profound psychological dislocation, the conversion of kin into property." Implicit denials and evasive behavior were ordinary. We can surmise that one such as Martha Washington justified this demeanor according to an eighteenth-century Virginian's sense of "duty" to protect those subordinate relatives who existed in legal limbo. She provided for her half-sister without being seen publicly at her side. Underlying feelings are always harder to assess.[7]

Given the custodial nature of the work she did, Sally Hemings had to be one of the most visible persons inside the walls of Monticello in all seasons, a servant who understood her role. This being so, she could never have risen to be Jefferson's "substitute wife," as the most hopeful egalitarians wish to believe. Wives are not instructed to masquerade as domestics. Though middle-class wives of this period performed tiring household chores, southern plantation wives had servants. Jefferson's feelings toward Sally Hemings, no matter the duration of their physical intimacy, cannot be analogous to marital affection, first because of the work she did, and second, because Jefferson was not open about the relationship. There were eighteenth-century men who loved, had children with, and went on to marry their servants, but Jefferson does not belong in this category.

How Sally Hemings was dressed was only one of many visual status reminders dictating feelings of subordination. Presumably her time, as well as the space she occupied, was not her own. Jefferson appears not even to have taught her to read and write; otherwise Madison Hemings and his siblings would not have been compelled to "induce" (Madison's characterization) Jefferson's white grandchildren to impart these basic skills. If these factors demonstrate that Jefferson did not "love" Sally Hemings in the conventional sense, then what more plausibly might have been his feelings? The best available evidence suggests two things: If Jefferson was having sexual relations with his servant, they were undertaken to satisfy his personal appetite and, as a result of his medical conditioning, to preserve his health.

Some historians wish to credit Sally, even at a young age, with greater agency. As evidence, they cite Madison Hemings's statement that his mother initially refused to return with Jefferson to Virginia, as he was preparing to leave France in 1789. "To induce her to do so," he recounted, Jefferson "promised her extraordinary privileges." These are not spelled out, other than the "treaty" by which Sally's children would be freed at age twenty-one.

She and her older brother James, who was trained in Paris as a chef, knew that they could have successfully sued for their freedom in France, and that by returning to Virginia, they would remain, legally, enslaved. Jefferson's motives in convincing James, twenty-four, and Sally, sixteen, to return with him are unclear: Whose welfare did he have in mind? James was an accomplished cook and would prepare his brother Peter to succeed him in Monticello's kitchen. Offering him a regular salary, Jefferson found a way to retain James until 1796—just months after Sally bore her first (recorded) child—which means that James saw fit to wait a good number of years, until after this momentous event, before earning his freedom.[8]

Sally did not negotiate her freedom at any time. At sixteen, and having lived in France as maidservant to the Jefferson daughters for only eighteen months, it was already a considerable coup to exact Jefferson's promise to allow the children they might have together to enjoy independent adult lives. What other tangible reward did she obtain? She did only light work, and may have held a special place in the hearts of the white grandchildren who helped Madison and his siblings become literate. But in the end, there was no place for her in the Monticello economy other than as a maidservant. Jefferson does not mention her in any extant letters to his daughter Martha—if he did, or if he wrote to Sally directly, these letters were all destroyed. Nothing in evidence even remotely suggests Jefferson's warmth toward her. He evidently got what he wanted at little cost to his comfort when he "negotiated" with James and Sally in Paris—he retained their continued services.

He apparently was not given to explain his action, either. He was protected by his daughter Martha, who had to have recoiled whenever her father the president was attacked in the press. His grandchildren, too, persisted in denying the possibility of an alternate family. Either they refused to face the Hemingses' truth or they could not imagine the reality of it. But Martha, who knew Sally Hemings from birth and remained in close contact, had to know who the father or fathers of her several children were.[9] ("Father" makes more sense than "fathers": As Madison Hemings testified, his mother informed him that Jefferson did not have children with any other woman he owned.) As an adept household manager, Martha would have been a person devoid of curiosity had she not possessed the answer to the paternity question.[10]

Now let us discuss the factors governing Jefferson's behavior. We know that he labored for the sustenance and the success of family members, and denied himself comparable feelings of emotional attachment to Sally Hemings and her children. In accepting that he did not transcend his historical moment, we must explain his relative lack of affection for the Hemingses according to cultural assumptions as unfamiliar to us as his recurrence to a vocabulary drawn from eighteenth-century neurophysiology. Without giving them his name, he took care of Sally's children in his own way, and thought it sufficient. In anticipating their emancipation after his death, he gave no more of himself than it took to provide for their general comfort and independence.

Another strain of thinking every bit as much a part of Jefferson's world held that women were subject to strong sexual urges and might be thought of, without censure, as men's playthings.[11] In his clinical study *Nymphomania,* for instance, Dr. Bienville wrote:

It rarely happens that a girl reaches the age of puberty, without soon acquiring such intelligence as is capable of leading her to the means of penetrating into the mysteries of love. Her imagination induces her to improve every occasion of gratifying her curiosity . . . and in the end [she] becomes a victim to the fierceness of desire.

Treating sexual knowledge among young women as a poison, Bienville added that girls were routinely corrupted by servants or "false friends."[12] It was for this reason that the medical literature in Jefferson's library (as well as the works of novelists such as Maria Edgeworth) recommended attempts to monitor and restrain female sexuality: If elite women had the presence of mind to ward off sexual thoughts, they could preserve their virtue until marriage, and then enter the maternal stage of life. As Dr. Rush adjudged, women could capitalize on their nature-given "delicacy and modesty," which made them more keenly aware, instinctively, of the "dishonor" caused by "want of chastity."[13]

The sexual fidelity of wives insured predictability of descent and inheritance. On the other hand, lower-class women had less space in which to display modesty—it was less expected—and their bastard children did not as automatically upset society. In the words of one analyst of the sexual order, "What needed to be suppressed was fertility and poverty, not sexuality." This is key to our understanding.[14]

Jefferson the Francophile was exposed to flexible French notions in matters of sex, though for some time historians have assumed he was not entirely pleased by them (that is, if we confine our evidence to his pose in letters from France during the 1780s). Yet we already know that when he formed ideas and shaped language he based many of his conclusions on a medical sensibility; so why should his sexual imagination have profited any less from that sensibility? Medical theorists, though for the most part clinically ineffective, studied every conceivable human disease and nervous condition. They cared about melancholy, psychosomatic manifestations, and excess eroticism as much as they cared about smallpox, gout, and consumption. Despite (or perhaps because of) people's vulnerability to mortal diseases, families heeded medical reports with the same diligence as people do today.

Sexual curiosity is certainly not a new phenomenon. Though we do not know the actual extent to which Jefferson was influenced by those who wrote about sexual energy and (for lack of a better term) the aesthetic involved in selecting a sexual partner, we know enough to pay attention to something else: "the nervous origins of imagination" (a definitive phrase of his time). That imagination was either "healthy" or "diseased," of course, and well-read individuals such as Jefferson found in the works of Dr. Tissot, and those of Tissot's school of thought, descriptions of people of their social class whose energies were drained by some combination of poor diet, sedentary habits, external environment, and physiological defect. Middle age was a time of anxious prevention, and standard advice books might recommend, for example, that "there is nothing in the world more refreshing to those that are bilious than the caresses of women."[15]

As a reader of medical treatises who corresponded frequently with medical professionals, Jefferson would be familiar with the role of sex in maintaining a healthy balance to the body's internal forces. Sex was seen much as diet was, part of a regimen of self-control, and important to understand if one was to enjoy a productive life. Sexual intercourse was good if practiced in moderation, bad if abstained from completely or experienced too frequently. Alternately known, in Dr. Tissot's works, as "the genital liquor," "the Essential Oil," and "most perfect and important of all the animal liquors," semen was thought to support one's nervous constitution. The suddenness of ejaculation—the loss of this vital fluid at a moment of excitement—caused a change within that required replenishment. For this reason, too, masturbation ("onanism," as it was known), or immoderate sexual activity, weakened the nerves over time and led to melancholy.[16]

Jefferson's taking of Sally Hemings as a concubine would have offered him a nearby sexual outlet, fulfilling Tissot's urgent call for accomplished, intellectual men to forego the wasteful activity of masturbation. The Swiss physician even asserted—allowing Jefferson to justify further the correctness of his course—that spermatic fluid was as healthy for the female who received it as it was unhealthy for the man who wasted it through masturbation. His servant's exclusive attention to him would also have protected him against venereal disease, which was then quite prevalent. Thus, their monogamy did not have to represent a loving commitment, but rather her implicit agreement to safeguard his sexual health. If this picture is accurate, Jefferson would have been able to resist having intimate contact with married women after his return from Europe in 1790, which attraction had been "an issue" for him in France in the 1780s, and in Virginia in the 1760s, before his marriage.[17]

Lust may be absent from Jefferson's preserved correspondence, and confined largely to literary satire and the suitably serious medical treatises he owned and read, but as a post-Revolutionary widower seeking to avoid the melancholy and attendant ills that the medical theorists projected, he unquestionably understood the options available to him outside of remarriage. It is reasonable to think that Jefferson took care to locate a solution to his sexual idleness through forms of exercise and comfort. We know that he regularly followed the dictates of philosophic medicine when he limited his consumption of meat and alcohol.

Let us, then, adjust our expectations from Jefferson to coincide with the mental processes common to sexually active intellectuals of his day. If he accepted that the sedentary life was destructive of health, and that all seminal emission was, as Tissot described, "a very violent action, which borders upon convulsion, and which thereby surprisingly weakens, and prejudices the whole nervous system," he would also have seen masturbation as the most "pernicious," as well as embarrassing, form of sexual gratification. In contrast, sex with a healthy and attractive female was productive of "joy," which "aids digestion, animates circulation," and "restores strength." It seems pertinent to add that Sally Hemings was considered physically attractive, and Tissot and his colleagues judged that sexual relations with a beautiful woman did not "exhaust so much as with an ugly woman."[18]

The Jefferson-Hemings puzzle may boil down to something quite conventional. Assuming that Jefferson was persuaded by the respected physiologists whose work he owned, he would have looked upon his servant much as an English aristocrat who sought pleasure with a young, fertile, white, technically free but utterly dependent servant in his household. Power, in both situations, was very real. Sally's condition of servitude relative to other slaves, like that of all the Hemings family generally, was mitigated by light skin and the genetic connection to Jefferson's father-in-law. But only a tabloid fascination with amorous drama should lead us to conceive of the Jefferson-Hemings relationship as a great love story, long hidden from the general public and now suddenly revealed by forensic detectives.[19]

There was a significant amount of sexual experimentation by well-to-do men in the eighteenth and early nineteenth centuries, apart from prostitution. In England especially, maidservants were subject to the advances of men much older than themselves; when these women became pregnant, so long as their bastard children were properly cared for, the morals of the unacknowledged fathers were not publicly questioned. Sterne, the young Jefferson's favorite author, constantly taunted his readers with sexual innuendo, and concludes *A Sentimental Journey* with a famous nonending, in which sex may or may not be the result of a fortuitous encounter with a maidservant, in a shared bedroom, in total darkness: "So that when I stretch'd out my hand, I caught hold of the Fille de Chambre's—"[20]

Though he frowned on prostitution and extramarital sex that was flaunted, Jefferson did not, in his ample correspondence, construe liaisons that were kept discreet as morally objectionable. For him, everything seemed to hinge on discretion. In the society in which he traveled, well-bred women who were not taken unfair advantage of were fair game. Admittedly, we know less of how he felt about socially unequal pairings.

We do know, at least, that the female body was constructed as an inferior body. It was easily stimulated and sexualized. "Normal" femininity was, in essence, victimhood, and "normal" masculinity, if not tempered by conscience, was marked by sexual aggressiveness. Plots in literature featured young girls away from home and without their parents' guiding influence, helpless before the empty promises of deceitful men who taunted them with the prospect of stability. In these tales, and in the minds of men in need of sex, sexual and economic vulnerability were joined. The poor were dependent, and sex was typically negotiated.[21]

This, then, is really a story about sexual urges and the treatment of the unacknowledged children of secret unions. We must cast the net wide if we are to encompass the boundaries of sexual knowledge in Jefferson's America. The United States, even in its early years, was part of an interconnected world. Patriotic writers and orators declared America's uniqueness and moral superiority and were slow to acknowledge what the country borrowed from other cultures. But their newspapers and the legal training that elite men received say otherwise. Educated Americans knew, for instance, that in England, a bastard was a bastard for life, and that the common law was generally meant to protect traditions of inheritance. But in colonial Latin America (including Florida and Louisiana) at the end of the eighteenth century, legitimacy and illegitimacy, and racial definitions themselves, were fairly fluid.

For political as well as commercial reasons, Americans, especially in the South, were intensely interested in what was occurring in the Spanish possessions on their doorstep. There, individuals could be known as illegitimate in private *(privado)* and at the same time considered legitimate in public *(publico);* women could be privately pregnant and publicly virgins. There, too, Africans brought over in chains were living free in proportionately greater numbers than in Jefferson's Virginia; and the native population, long in decline, was beginning to reestablish itself. Spanish-Indian unions produced what were described as "totally white" offspring, though they were not permitted to be called "Spanish" until the fourth generation. These racial permutations demanded that government adopt a flexible approach to the granting of *gracias al sacar,* or decrees of legitimation.

Hispanic Americans did not adhere to the taboos of their northern neighbors. Birth status was not indelible. Illegitimate offspring could claim honor, recognition, and political standing if publicly acknowledged by their elite birth parent, and even a bastard who was not accorded public recognition might enjoy the free exhibition of affection by the elite parent without that parent's being made to feel morally suspect. Widowers frequently produced illegitimate offspring, and notably with mixed-race women. By the end of the eighteenth century, mobility for the racially mixed was made legally easier, though the purchase price for "whiteness" rose.

Thus color mattered in colonial Latin America, but it bore less emotional weight than civic condition. A popular saying, "Rather the mistress of a white man than the wife of a negro," indicated a desire to lighten the next generation. But "passing," in the Latin American sense, was not strictly a matter of looking "white enough" to cross into white society; it was more about attaining public acceptance—honor.[22]

Did Americans completely reject these "foreign" qualities? The common term for a person of mixed race in Virginia was a Spanish word, *mulatto*. And, of course, the importance of honor that prevailed in Hispanic America was not lost on the South.[23] Jefferson's culture was not in all ways as insular as later, dreamier depictions of the South suggest, nor were the late eighteenth and early nineteenth centuries precisely as virtue-bound as authorized publications and mainstream fiction proclaimed.

Public reputation built up over many years of service must have made it not just possible but extremely tempting for a gentleman with sexual secrets to walk that fine line between ignoring evidence others saw and actively managing an ever-expanding lie. Jefferson's rural circumstances made it possible for him to suppose that his private world could be protected. Gentlemen—even his northern visitors—would have considered it in bad taste to publicize, let alone eroticize, what they may have suspected was going on between Jefferson and his house servant. That is how James Callender's onetime collaborator could write in 1824 of his falling out with the discredited columnist who had resorted to "unwarrantable indiscretions" begun amid "paroxysms of inebriety." Dr. Dunglison refused to give the Sally Hemings story credence. Straight-laced John Adams shook his head over the extent of interracial sex on southern plantations, but reportedly did not believe Callender's charge, either.[24] And the vulgar Callender never visited Monticello to see with his own eyes. Jefferson was protected, though not, of course, completely protected. The rumors were "out there."

Securing the Sexual Frontier II: Jefferson the Greek

Before sex was a voyeuristic fantasy celebrating fun and daring and cheating spouses, inviting graphic self-help books, and driving the practice of modern psychiatry, insights about it were part of a broader scientific discourse about nervous sensations. From the time of the Greeks, in fact, sex was not so much a way to characterize someone's interior life as it was a means for a man to control his social universe. Again, with respect to fertility, family organization, and the future of society, sex was meant for men to direct and control.

No precise date can be put on the moment, occurring as it did during Jefferson's lifetime, when the relationship between sex and social stability took a turn. But desire was being redirected. It was, therefore, Jefferson's generation that we may count as the last in America's history to partake significantly of the less prohibitive sexual codes that preceded the Victorians' far-reaching concern with purity, male as well as female. Jefferson's was the age of combating unproductive onanism, the age of inculcating virtue among modest and genteel young women in search of restrained, respectful, honorable young men of the governing class; but it was not yet the age of pervasive, obsessive sexual sinfulness, when aggressive men came to be seen as beasts who needed to be controlled.[25]

In this respect, Jefferson's Greek studies may provide further clues to his sexual imagination. In a pathbreaking book, *Thomas Jefferson, American Humanist*, written more than a half-century ago, Karl Lehmann explored the power that Greek literature and philosophy held over its greatest early American devotee. The teacher with the most influence over young Jefferson, lawyer-humanist George Wythe, shared his lifelong adoration of the Greek language. And when he was finally able to devote less time to political matters, Jefferson read in Greek throughout his retirement: Homer, Plato (whose work he openly disparaged), the biographer Diogenes Laertius, the playwright Euripides, a host of lyric poets. He studied the teachings of Jesus in Greek. Over and over, he recommended Xenophon, whose *Memorabilia* contained, he said, the only "genuine" account of Socrates. That text happened also to stress men's physical conditioning and natural desires, along with character of mind: "When he was asked what he thought was the best occupation for a man [Socrates] replied, 'Effective action.'"[26]

The Greeks understood intellectual freedom in a way that had never ceased to impress Jefferson. They wrote of human beings in a world of trial and setbacks, who somehow rose above; they taught a man his proper temperament. In Jefferson's time, because of how the Greeks contested fate, and the Romans described republican simplicity, men invoked the lessons of antiquity to bolster their authority in an argument, or to display their philosophical enthusiasm, or to reinforce their virility in a written performance. For those who moved in Jefferson's intellectual circle, self-confidence, authenticity, moral assertiveness, and taste all had classical definitions. Here, too, Jefferson found candor and truth telling. Lehmann wrote that Jefferson saw the Greeks "driven by a spontaneous, deep-rooted emotional belief in the perfectibility of man."[27]

It is hard to overestimate the influence of the Greeks on Jefferson's sense of what it meant to be human. Writing to a commentator on Greek pronunciation in 1819, he remarked that the languages of classical antiquity were such "mod-

els of pure taste in writing" that he considered it a luxury to be able to read
them:

> I think myself more indebted to my father for this, than for all the other luxu-
> ries his cares and affections have placed within my reach: and more now than
> when younger, and more susceptible of delights from other sources. When the
> decays of age have enfeebled the useful energies of the mind, the classic pages
> fill up the vacuum of ennui, and become sweet composers to that rest of the
> grave into which we are all, sooner or later, to descend.[28]

Modern medicine, ethics, and government, he said, owed a great debt to
Greek and Roman thought. His staunch opposition to religious indoctrination
was grounded in his reading of the ancients, as well.

In the same letter, Jefferson spoke with a kind of nostalgia for Greek, that
"finest of human languages." He viewed his late years' reading as part of a
search, the guiding spirit in a final journey to the grave. (His almost maudlin
tone in the letter accompanies a rare mention of his father, who died when Jefferson was only fourteen.) Rejoicing to find a correspondent sharing in his enthusiasm for the recovery of something so tenuous as the "antient pronunciation" of Greek, Jefferson exhibited a fervor he was never ashamed to own up to.
He praised "the Luxury of reading the Greek & Roman authors in all the beau-
ties of their originals." Latin he read devotedly, but the "remains" of Greek were
his measure of beauty.

Allowing for a certain hyperbole as part of his epistolary art, Jefferson could
hardly discuss ancient Greece without being sentimental. Offering tribute to
the sensuous Greeks was one of the ways he reached out to elite women. When
he wrote to Maria Cosway, he likened himself to Aeneas, and described his European travel as "a peep into Elysium." As Lehmann emphasized, Jefferson
adored Greek as the source of greatness in poetry. Its elegance and richness of
sound, its seductive euphony, never ceased to draw him in.[29]

He composed his wife's epitaph in Greek. He sealed their life together with
a quote from Homer's *Iliad*, pronouncing that their flame of friendship would
"burn on through death."[30] To the Greeks, as he fully knew, marriage came
with conjugal responsibilities. The wife was meant to bear a man's "legitimate"
children and to remain faithful. But marriage did not restrict a man sexually to
one woman. (This is not to suggest that Jefferson was unfaithful to his wife
during their ten-year marriage.) In words attributed to Demosthenes, concubines were kept "for the daily care of our persons." Men were reared to exercise
command over their selves and their land, to train their bodies, and to exhibit
a hospitable spirit toward the citizens of the region. It all sounds very Jeffer-

sonian. Women, given bodies less resistant to the elements, were to contribute to the household economy from within; men concentrated their energies on the outdoors. Men took risks and expended, domesticated women received and preserved what men created. That was the governing balance initiated by the Greeks.

Did Jefferson, without a wife, make adjustments, in more or less the Greek mode, when he reconstituted his life at Monticello in the 1790s, after returning with his two daughters, and Sally Hemings, from his five years in Europe? According to Xenophon's *Œconomicus,* the husband was duty-bound to uphold the preeminence of the wife, as Jefferson did, even after Patty's death, in symbolically retaining her deathbed adieu and a lock of her hair to remind him of his commitment. Madison Hemings refers to his mother quite plainly as Jefferson's "concubine." Sally Hemings, if this is true, did nothing to challenge the Greek marital order.

The Greeks prided themselves on raising girls to be chaste and sheltered, protected from the male gaze, yet their writers and artists avowed sex to be a frolicking entertainment for well-to-do men. Masturbation, erections, and a variety of sexual acts, heterosexual and homosexual, were made light of openly. But even as lust was acknowledged, it was not anarchically embraced: The Greeks had rules governing their sexuality. For one, prostitution gave their men a sexual outlet other than adulterous relationships with other men's wives (which might be punished by death). Houses of prostitution were regulated by committee, set fees established, and taxes paid by brothel owners. The prostitutes themselves were slaves.[31]

In brothels depicted on Greek vases, unengaged sex workers are shown immersed in domestic production. Sally Hemings sewed at Monticello, and housebound Greek sex workers spun wool, because their owners did not wish them to remain idle and unproductive as they awaited their assignations. (The difference, of course, is that Sally Hemings appears to have had only the singular sexual obligation of accommodating her master on occasion.) The common denominator is that domestic labor meant restriction, and sex was potentially just another chore for the unfree.

It is critical to remember that the "treaty" of Paris between Thomas Jefferson and Sally Hemings, as Madison Hemings termed it, was a treaty of sexual commerce: Jefferson promised lenient, indulgent treatment in return for sexual favors. Surely, if Jefferson's biracial son thought that his parents' relationship had a love component, he would have used words other than "treaty" and "concubine" to describe it. Indeed, there was no pretense of love in Madison's statement, no declaration of love when Jefferson asked Sally Hemings to return, with her brother the chef, to Virginia.[32]

In ancient Greece, what apparently intrigued men of ordinary privilege was not so much the thought of a wife's propriety and virtue but the vision of an available sex object, sitting at the spinning wheel. In search of gratification and amusement, they wandered across class lines. The same kind of temptation existed for young Virginian males. On the other hand, we must note that though extramarital sex was undisguised, success in resisting its attraction was also an attribute of the ideal Greek male.[33]

Equally important for our consideration, men in Greek culture were taught not to consider women as their moral equals. Rather, women were a kind of property, and marriage a transfer of goods from one family to another. Female infanticide was not unknown. The Greeks also supposed, as the eighteenth-century did, that women, though "weaker," possessed a kind of mystique. Women were believed to reap greater pleasure from sex than men were able to; they were seen as slaves of their desire. Oversexed wives were to be feared. For reasons related to these prejudices, Aristotle wrote: "Young women are more wanton, once they have experience with sex." He recommended that men marry, at thirty-seven, to women of eighteen.[34]

Jefferson knew of Greek life in all its detail. He admired the Greeks better perhaps than did anyone else of his time and place. Of course, he did not abandon his own culture to live like an ancient Greek, but he justified his political and religious doctrines by referring to Athenian values. So it is not unthinkable that the Greeks gave *some* shape to his unrevealed sexual views as well.

In the Greek mode, concubinage was an understandable action on the part of a widower, though statistically a concubine was more often an enslaved woman purchased by a man who was not yet married. Yet Aristotle himself was a prominent example of a widower with a concubine, Herpyllis. She bore him a boy and a girl, all three of whom were named in his will; Herpyllis was therein praised by Aristotle for the "steady affection" she gave him, and was permitted to marry after his death "if she desire[d]." Among the Greeks, a concubine who was kept for the production of free children was thought to be assuming a positive social role. Might Jefferson have felt the same, given that so many of his peers looked eagerly to antiquity for masculine models?[35]

Bastardy *(notheia)* was well documented in ancient Greece. Children conceived outside of wedlock, whether through adultery, concubinage, or by unmarried couples, were not entitled to citizenship, unless as children of concubines their fathers treated them as members of the household *(oikos),* which meant qualitatively more than merely living on the father's property. It involved a ritual of acceptance.[36]

The implication regarding the emotionally excluded children of Sally Hemings is obvious. Jefferson had no intention of going public with regard to the

Hemings children. The bastard child of a Greek man and his concubine did not receive his patronym; the Hemingses similarly retained their mother's surname, although Eston took the name "Jefferson" years after Jefferson's death. At the same time, a *nothos* (bastard), under Solon's law, though the son of a man and his long-time concubine, had no obligation to his father; so in all respects, the bond between the two was of little consequence. When Beverley and Harriet Hemings left Monticello in 1822 and melted into white society, they apparently stopped communicating with the white Jeffersons.[37]

Jefferson was a persistent stylist of language, a neologist and etymologist. It was Socrates who first imagined the connection between language, nature, and the body, noting that *anthropôs* (man) was derived from a phrase indicating upright posture.[38] Jefferson's exactness, his studies of historical authenticity, his love of architecture, are all Greek qualities. His avid interest in acquiring fine wines, balancing elements of a moderate, healthy diet with exquisite taste and exceptional variety (he grew thirty-nine types of peas), suggests that food was more than necessity; it seduced his palate.

"I too am an Epicurean," he wrote in 1819 to William Short. "I consider the genuine (not the imputed) doctrines of Epicurus as containing every thing rational in moral philosophy which Greece and Rome have left us."[39] Epicureanism was not about selfish pleasure seeking, though it was (and still is) often so presented. Dr. Tissot wrote, meaningfully: "Epicurus, that respectable man, who knew better than any one that man could be happy only by pleasure, but who at the same time limited this pleasure by such a rule as a Christian hero would not disapprove of . . . has been shockingly distorted and blackened." The way of Epicurus was unobtrusive living, cultivation of friendship, and a total dismissal of those superstitious beliefs that mystified instead of enlightening the human mind. As he was described by Diogenes Laertius, Epicurus retired to a garden outside Athens and entertained guests in a democratic fashion.[40]

Epicurus preceded Jefferson in conceptualizing happiness in terms of sensations. Reason itself was responsive to sensation *(aisthesis)* and feeling *(pathé)*, which led to a cultivated serenity and peace of mind ("tranquil permanent felicity"). In simple terms, sensation helped human beings appreciate the art of living. Among the Greeks, Epicurus was the philosopher most concerned with human emotions and unconscious motivations, and the social implications of these things. The Epicurean was, meaningfully for us, a diagnostician, immersed in the pursuit of bodily health and removal of bodily pain. Indeed, Epicurus charged: "Empty is that philosopher's argument by which no human suffering is therapeutically treated."[41]

Epicurus was not, however, an advocate of free love. Most of what he wrote on human sexuality was lost, and what remains clearly shows that he privileged the pleasure in friendship over the pleasure in sexual contact. He was concerned, too, lest passion remove peace of mind; the simpler the enjoyment of life, the better. Withdrawal from public competition—so critical a component of Jefferson's retirement persona—was one step in that direction.[42]

Whether it was Epicurus, Aristotle, or a composite of philosophers and trained physicians, ancient and modern, who spoke most convincingly to Jefferson in his concern with human desires, the Greek example regarding concubinage, bastardy, and the *oikos* may have helped persuade him to separate emotionally from Sally Hemings's children. But the principal appeal of Epicureanism was something greater: the ennobling of sensual pleasures, of right passions, and the notion that inner peace was attained through enjoyment of the world rather than an ascetic withdrawal from it. (Withdrawal from public competition was not the same as ascetic withdrawal.)

As a lawgiver, philosophically inclined, Jefferson must not for a moment have doubted the propriety of his sex life (whatever it was) on the mountaintop. His anxieties were not the same as ours. As a lawgiver, too, he had interests that related to sex and procreation, but which appear obscure to us. In ancient Greece and in Jefferson's Virginia, the legal code was primarily concerned with the protection of bloodlines, for fear of social disorder. As we shall soon see, this fact of early American society and economy could not but have been on Jefferson's mind when he gave his love to his white children and grandchildren, and did only his honorable duty with respect to the Hemingses.

"the fortuitous concourse of breeders"

If what Jefferson read and responded to matters, then we should not reject the historical possibility that among his salutary (and guilt-free) options was the Greek option: procreative sex with his attractive servant. He does not openly embrace this argument in any of his letters—he certainly would not have done so after the Callender embarrassment of 1802–1803. But he does, in an unexpected way, lead us back to the possibility in a letter to John Adams posted in 1813, when he had just turned seventy, and Sally Hemings's youngest child, Eston, was five.

In several letters, over several months, Jefferson and Adams had been tossing about observations on languages, ancient religion, political reputation, the nature of aristocracy—all peppered with Greek references. Jefferson tried to keep up with the chatty New Englander, explaining his disengagement: "The summum bonum with me is now truly Epicurean, ease of body and tranquility of mind; and to these I wish to consign my remaining days." Then, capping a flurry of unanswered letters, Adams returned to the subject of natural aristocracy, crediting the Greek poet Theognis with a spirited knowledge: "When We want to purchace, Horses, Asses, or Rams, We inquire for the Wellborn. And every one wishes to procure, from the good breeds. A good Man, does not care to marry a Shrew, the Daughter of a Shrew; unless They give him, a great deal of Money with her." Adams's point in quoting Theognis was that the notion of a "Wellborn" did not really amount to anything of substance—the only nobility was nobility of mind.[43]

A few weeks later, the New Englander followed up with a deeper reading of Theognis, asking: "Now, my Friend, who are the ἄριστοι [aristocrats]? Philosophy may Answer 'The Wise and Good.' But the World, Mankind, have by their practice always answered, 'the rich the beautiful and well born.' And Philosophers themselves in marrying their Children prefer the rich the handsome and the well descended to the wise and good."[44]

Adams was not delving into sex here, but in his response Jefferson did. He had already written Adams that in his view aristocracy was an ingredient in an unstable political stew: "The same political parties which now agitate the U.S. have existed thro' all time. Whether the power of the people, or that of the ἄριστοι should prevail, were questions which kept the states of Greece and Rome in eternal convulsions." But the "convulsions" he now had in mind were not strictly political:

> The passage you quote from Theognis, I think has an ethical rather than a political object. The whole piece is a moral *exhortation,* . . . a reproof to man, who, while with his domestic animals he is curious to improve the race by employing always the finest male, pays no attention to the improvement of his own race, but intermarries with the vicious, the ugly, or the old, for considerations of wealth or ambition.[45]

To Jefferson, social chaos was abetted by undesirable (but seemingly inevitable) pairings. Human nature had to be accommodated. He saw in Theognis that erotic sensations predominated: The recklessness of the human spirit was manifest in an unpredictable world governed by men whose aims were not always clear but whose responsiveness to the ambiguous god Eros was.[46]

Jefferson went deeper into his Greek to advance the ethic laid down by Theognis. He translated from the little known Pythagorean philosopher Ocellus Lucanus[47] that "interprocreation" *ought to be* done according to right principles: "We do not commix for the sake of pleasure, but of the procreation of children. For the powers, the organs and desires for coition have not been given by god to man for the sake of pleasure, but for the procreation of the race." *Was the desire to procreate how he characterized his own intent in having sex with his concubine?* It is hard to tell, because Jefferson's next words undercut that suggestion: Nature, "not trusting to this moral and abstract motive, seems to have provided more securely for the perpetuation of the species by making it the effect of the oestrum [continual state of sexual excitability][48] implanted in the constitution of both sexes." *Lustful sex, he is saying, rules human behavior whether we like it or not.*

Let us also underscore what Jefferson, stating his facts with detachment, is conceding: He is (or, at least, affects being) unconcerned that his society will become dangerously corrupted as the result of a natural process of degeneration. He has answered Adams's appeal to Theognis with his certainty that "the commerce of love," an "unhallowed impulse," cannot be resisted. Sex happens. The privileged in society may persist in orchestrating reproduction in line with their selfish preferences; but even so, neither "healthiness" nor "virtue" ultimately matters in human breeding practices.

Nor does Jefferson show surprise that this should be so. "Natural" sex comes guilt-free in a male-dominated, Greek-influenced culture. The male seed is all-powerful. In his discussion of Epicurean pleasure, Dr. Tissot wrote that Epicurus "looked upon the seed as part of the soul and body." There was no guilt here, for the Greeks or for Thomas Jefferson.[49]

Jefferson is untroubled that the procreative fantasies of Theognis and Ocellus remained unfulfilled. It would be naïve to expect men and women to approach sex rationally. This was the way the world had always been and, he presumed, the way the world would always be. Theognis wished to breed the best male with the best females of the "Haram" so as to "produce a race of veritable ἄριστοι." Jefferson agrees in theory, because according to his eugenic science, "the moral and physical qualities of man" are passed on "in a certain degree" from father to son. But he is also guided by nature as he understands it, and nature is defined by the ungovernable inclinations of human attraction that would never allow Theognis's ideal to be realized; and so, Jefferson concludes, it is necessary to "continue acquiescence" to the degeneration of the race that so long ago troubled Theognis, "and to content ourselves with the accidental aristoi produced by the fortuitous concourse of breeders."[50]

His procreative activity with Sally Hemings tells us that Jefferson was "content" with the "fortuitous" result of his private sexual behavior. To answer the puzzling question of how he could have fathered two children with his concubine *after* the Callender revelations, we can suggest that he did so, in part, because he saw nothing immoral in *following nature.* In addition, he presumed he would be able to return in his postpresidential years to the splendid seclusion he had enjoyed on his mountain before Callender. No doubt Jefferson had feelings for Sally Hemings, but these were not so deep that he was prompted to im-

> the selecting the best male for a Haram of well chosen females also, which Theognis
> seems to recommend from the example of our sheep and asses, would doubtless im
> prove the human, as it does the brute animal, and produce a race of veritable
> aristoi. for experience proves that the moral and physical qualities of man.
> whether good or evil, are transmissible in a certain degree from father to son.
> but I suspect that the equal rights of men will rise up against this privileged Solomon, and his Haram,
> and oblige us to continue acquiescence under the 'Ἀφαυροτατος γενος αστων' which
> Theognis complains of, and to content ourselves with the accidental aristoi
> produced of by the fortuitous concourse of breeders. for I agree with you that there
> is a natural aristocracy among men. the grounds of this are virtue & talents.
> formerly bodily powers gave place among the aristoi. but since the invention of
> gunpowder has armed the weak as well as the strong with missile death, the bodily
> strength, like beauty good humor. politeness and other accomplishments, has become
> but an auxiliary ground of distinction. there is also an artificial aristocracy founded
> on wealth. and birth, without either virtue or talents; for with these it would belong to
> the first-class. the natural aristocracy I consider as the most precious gift of nature,
> for the instruction, the trusts and government of society. and indeed it would have
> in creation

Excerpt from letter of Thomas Jefferson to John Adams, October 28, 1813, on a man's natural inclination to mate with someone other than his socially ideal partner. Referencing the Greek poet Theognis, Jefferson acquiesced, under the principle of "degeneration of the race of men," to "the fortuitous concourse of breeders." Library of Congress.

prove her social position. Many modern Americans want to reject this idea and instead be persuaded that Jefferson and Hemings loved one another—they do so because the Greek model (or the Latin American model) accepts sexuality beyond marriage and gives institutional form to a kind of procreation that our society has taught us to find distasteful.

"proof, defence & a substantial corpus delecti"

Aside from the language of nervous sensibility used by physicians and novelists, aside from his Greek affinity, what is there to suggest Jefferson's mature thoughts on human sexuality? There are few distinct indicators in his voluminous correspondence, published and unpublished. The case of Stephen Cathalan, a longtime U.S. consul in Marseilles, France, demonstrates Jefferson's sense of male prerogative in sexual matters.

Jefferson visited Marseilles once, in 1787, and was entertained by Cathalan, his wife, and grown daughter. The American minister agreed to send a copy of his then newly published *Notes on Virginia.*[51] Though the two men did not see one another after Jefferson's departure from France, over the years they carried on a rather considerable—and rather comfortable—correspondence relating mainly to commercial matters. Jefferson, who continued to purchase French wine through the able consul, professed a warm regard for the Frenchman. In Jefferson's view, Cathalan had always discharged his professional obligations honorably.

In 1817, however, toward the end of his career, Cathalan's reputation came under a dark cloud. His morals were called into question by an American named Fitch, who was living in France and who, in Jefferson's well-chosen words, "began to gape after his office." Rumors that focused on an alleged sexual indiscretion reached the U.S. ambassador in Paris, and were then conveyed to President James Monroe. Monroe consulted Jefferson, not wishing to remove Cathalan unless the former president concurred that removal was warranted.

Letters sailed across the Atlantic for months. Monroe was troubled by statements that "impute to him a scandalous life, as to women." Jefferson investigated the charges and determined them to be mere "insinuations," "loose and general, . . . no fact being specified which can be laid hold of and brought to the test of proof." He addressed the moral question in plain terms, learning about Cathalan's domestic situation while comparing American with French views on the subject:

> The charge of passion for women is a very equivocal one in that country. After the loss of his wife, his only daughter & her husband continued to live with him till 2. or 3. years ago, when he married a 2d wife. . . . It is possible that, before his 2d marriage, he may have indulged himself with women: perhaps, since that, he may not have withstood the gallantries of the country. Of this I know nothing. But you know how little is thought of it there, while to Americans generally, it does appear scandalous; and especially, may be with the commentaries, the exaggerations, and industrious circulation of matter by his friend mr Fitch. I do not think however the wisdom of our government will add to it's other cares that of making themselves guardians of the chastity of all their officers, at home and abroad; or of erecting themselves into a court Christian, to take cognizance of the amours imputed to them truly or falsely. Rumors of this kind may furnish sufficient cause for refusing an office; but to take it away requires, in the forum of justice, particular specifications, proof, defence & a substantial corpus delecti.[52]

It is necessary to quote at length, because several issues are being addressed, and a complete context is helpful. First, the Cathalan matter arose a good many years after Jefferson's private life was made the subject of political lampoon; we cannot know for certain just how sensitized he had become as a result of that scandal. It is worth noting that a few years before the Sally Hemings allegations, James Madison had shared his glee with Jefferson over Alexander Hamilton's "ingenious folly"—a public confession to "an irregular and indelicate amour." Their Federalist adversary, while married, had seen fit to admit to an affair with another man's wife. He published a long and convoluted pamphlet in which he asserted his public morality and declared that he had used his own funds—not the government's—in paying hush money to the offended husband. In that instance, Madison had written: "Next to the error of publishing at all, is that of forgetting that simplicity and candour are the only dress which prudence would put on innocence."[53] Jefferson makes clear in his letter to President Monroe (concerning Cathalan) that the sexual activities of a public official, as a rule, are best spoken of quietly and not raised as a political issue.

Second, Jefferson is able to relate to Cathalan's situation as a widower. During the period between his marriages, the consul had quite possibly taken advantage of the less restrictive ways of French society and, to use Jefferson's phrase, "indulged himself." Jefferson understands temptation. He also understands that masculine behavior is culturally influenced. As much as interracial sex occurred routinely on Virginia plantations, and among free blacks and whites throughout the South in spite of legal and moral strictures, Cathalan "may not have withstood" French "gallantries."

Third, Jefferson is exhibiting impatience with the aggressive judgments of a certain breed of American—holier than thou, one might say, given Jefferson's reference to "a court Christian" that some would establish in order to "take cognizance of" alleged sexual transgressions. In writing to Monroe in 1818, he adopts a very different posture from that of the mid-1780s when, in France, the widower Jefferson cautioned young men against coming to Europe and losing that certain moral purity he attributed to American tastes and conditions. Jefferson had invented a generic traveler for his purpose: "He is led by the strongest of all the human passions into a spirit for female intrigue destructive of his own and others happiness, or a passion for whores destructive of his health."[54] Jefferson in retirement writes rather differently. He shows no sign of wishing to judge other men's sexual mores when no one is being hurt.

His recommendation to President Monroe is meant to convey discretion. It is a reasoned allegiance stopping just short of blind loyalty to his old friend Cathalan. Do not court fate by appointing a man with a questionable history to a consular post, he advises the president, but neither should the government take on the role of moral policeman. Sex that takes place in private is not the public's business.[55] In the end, Jefferson was happy to inform Cathalan: "You are safe in your office during my life, & the continuance of the present administration, if you chuse to hold it." Cathalan died a short time later.

The Cathalan scandal, minor in the scheme of things, was kept from the American public. As it was, personal attacks, intentional insults, and politically charged rumors never came as a surprise to the ex-president. Jefferson had been forced to endure them time and again, which explains his readiness to respond to the accusation against Cathalan. When the miscegenation charge initiated by Callender made the rounds in 1802–1803, Jefferson had done his best to ignore it. More personal mockery than political challenge, it eventually disappeared from the press. But Jefferson's refusal to address an inquiry into his sex life does not mean his family completely escaped the hurt of it.

Ellen's Sally

Ellen was so close in mind and spirit to her grandfather that in August 1819, she wrote from Poplar Forest to her sister Virginia, describing how she did not need to steal a few extra gulps of wine to taste the pleasures of life: "I am too much of a *real* Epicurean, to be prodigal of my means of enjoyment; and this 'care killing nostrum, this fountain of pleasure' has so far, been used with a moderation which philosophers might admire." This was two months before the moderation-upholding Jefferson wrote William Short, "I too am an Epicurean."[56]

Once again, granddaughter Ellen serves as a guide to the emotional life of her grandfather in his retirement years. She takes us into the world of Monticello, this time by raising additional possibilities and concerns with respect to the Jefferson-Hemings issue. Ellen had a personal maid named Sally from 1809 to 1825. She may have been Sally Hemings's niece or she may have been a slave belonging to the household of Ellen's father—we do not know for certain. Ellen's extraordinary comments about Sally belong, at any rate, to the ongoing debate over who knew what, or more particularly, who hid what.

Over the years many have asked why Jefferson, in his will, freed the two Hemings children who remained at Monticello, Madison and Eston, and did not free their mother. At her age, Sally Hemings's monetary value was insignificant. In wanting to keep her name out of his will, did the master of Monticello consign her to a longer term of bondage? She was effectively freed sometime between 1827 and 1830. Something was going on behind the scenes, and possibly in circumvention of the law.

Ellen's maid was given a choice in 1825. A state law passed while Jefferson was president stipulated that a manumitted slave had to leave Virginia within one year; she could either accept formal emancipation and find a home in a northern state, or she could remain in Virginia as a slave. But Ellen's maid re-

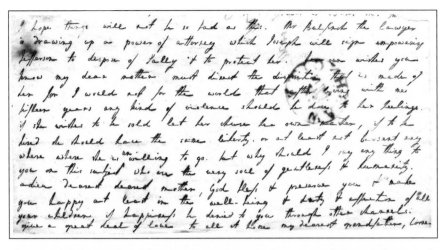

Excerpt from 1825 letter of Ellen Wayles Coolidge to her mother, Martha Jefferson Randolph, in which Ellen expressed her fondness for her maid Sally. Special Collections, University of Virginia Library.

fused to agree to one or the other option; she wanted both freedom and the right to remain in Virginia. And so she seems to have remained a slave until her protectors at Monticello worked out a plan that satisfied her.

The evidence exists in a series of letters. The first is a remarkable appeal from Washington, D.C., that Ellen wrote to her mother in June 1825 while en route to Boston with her new husband, Joseph Coolidge. Ellen writes of the apparently quiet effort underway in Washington to sell Sally:

> Mr [George] Bulfinch the lawyer [a relative of Joseph Coolidge] is drawing up a power of attorney which Joseph will sign empowering Jefferson [i.e., Jeff Randolph] to dispose of Sally & to protect her. Her own wishes you know my dear mother must direct the disposition that is made of her for I would not for the world that after living with me fifteen years any kind of violence should be done to her feelings. If she wishes to be sold let her chuse her own master, if to be hired she should have the same liberty, or at least not be sent any where where she is unwilling to go. but why should I say any thing to you on this subject who are the very soul of gentleness & humanity.[57]

We learn from this, of course, that Ellen was deeply attached to Sally, and that Sally's happiness was closely considered by the family. Ellen was entrusting her brother Jeff to find a proper home for her personal attendant.

To the outside world, the plantation elite generally displayed a remote, aloof posture with regard to their slaves' desire for freedom and public standing, as we shall see momentarily in the case of Ellen; but within the immediate family a different emotional picture emerges, marked by sincere, humane, and ongoing efforts—heartfelt concern. In the year leading up to Jefferson's death, then, prompted by Ellen's departure for the North, a committee was deciding her maidservant's fate. Sally was apparently not interested in joining Ellen's new household as a free woman, an employee of the house—or else the Jefferson-Randolph clan never seriously considered this option. If Ellen Coolidge, in traditionally anti-Jefferson Boston, employed a biracial maidservant named Sally (quite possibly a Hemings), no matter what her age, might this prompt a new round of sexual satire? Meanwhile, as her youngest sons approached the age of twenty-one, the elder Sally Hemings was not to remain at Monticello much longer either.

In 1827, Ellen's Sally served as nurse to the infant child of a University of Virginia professor of mathematics, Thomas Key, an Englishman. When the Keys packed up and left the country a short time later, Mary Jefferson Randolph updated her sister Ellen:

> Sally is going into Dr. Emmets service when he returns from New York with his bride. I do not know what grounds she counts upon remaining in the State for the law forbidding it, was expressly explained to her when she had her choice between freedom and continuing to belong to you [Ellen]. The price given for her is considered a very good one in these times.[58]

John P. Emmet was a professor of natural history at the university, an American citizen whose father had been an Irish patriot. Professor Key apparently intended to free Sally, but his sudden departure, and ambiguity surrounding the implementation of state law, left her fate unresolved; entering Professor Emmet's "service" as his new wife's maid, Ellen's Sally would, once again, be employed in one of the pavilions on the lawn of the university. But with what legal status?

This uncertainty is implied in Mary Randolph's letter, in the statement, "what grounds she counts upon remaining in the State for the law forbidding it, was expressly explained to her." That recognition of the legal requirement that an emancipated slave had to leave Virginia within one year means that Sally was continuing to exist in limbo. Most likely, Emmet had purchased her services with the understanding (obligation?) that he would free her after her term of service was completed. A year later, she was earning an independent living making clothes.[59]

In 1825, Sally Hemings was fifty-two, and would, like Ellen's Sally, remain in Virginia. In 1826, when Madison and Eston were granted the unusual right by the state legislature to remain in Virginia after becoming free, nothing was done by Sally Hemings's owners to call public attention to her. By 1830, according to that year's census, she was living as a free woman in a house in Charlottesville, with her sons, where she remained until her death in 1835. But it is just as possible that the most talked about and least understood not-quite-white slave woman, whose image was never captured, was left unfree according to law at the end of her life. Like Ellen's Sally, she may have lacked the requisite paper but was recognized locally as a free woman, and not bothered.[60]

No one unrelated to the Hemingses was freed upon Jefferson's death. Why would Ellen's Sally have expected to be freed by the Jefferson-Randolph clan? If she were a Hemings, her bloodline would have made it reasonable for her to presume such a "right"—in which case she may indeed have been the youngest daughter of Sally Hemings's sister Thenia, who died in 1795. The fact that Sally did not become Ellen's maid until 1809, the year Ellen moved permanently to Monticello to live with her grandfather, lends circumstantial support to such a conclusion.

We do know that Jefferson's prized granddaughter, Ellen Wayles Randolph, remained concerned with her maidservant's fate after moving to Boston, and indeed, continued to inquire about her, at least through 1835, according to existing records, when she wondered whether her former maid would consider accompanying her on an ocean voyage. We can only conclude that Ellen's emotional connection to the servants and servant children living at Monticello was deep and sincere. And most remarkably, thirty years after Ellen moved north, Madison Hemings, now in Ohio, named his youngest daughter "Ellen Wayles Hemings." It was the only one of his children whose name bore any connection to his former master's white family. That simple fact speaks volumes. And, like the third president, she had red hair.[61]

Now the mystery deepens. In 1858, as Henry Randall's highly sympathetic three-volume biography of Jefferson was published in New York (a biography written in close cooperation with Thomas Jefferson Randolph and Ellen Randolph Coolidge), Ellen visited her brother in Virginia. From Edgehill, Jeff's home just down the road from Monticello, she wrote to her husband, Joseph, in Boston, a rather bewildering letter—bewildering because it seems contrived—and because a portion of it is, by Ellen's reckoning, contrived.

The first section of Ellen's letter deals with the rumor that Thomas Jefferson sold into slavery his own biracial children:

> I have been talking freely with my brother Jefferson on the subject of the "yellow children" and will give you the substance of our conversation, with my subsequent reflections. It is difficult to prove a negative. It is impossible to prove

that Mr. Jefferson never had a coloured mistress or coloured children and that these children were never sold as slaves. The latter part of the charge however is disposed by it's atrocity, and it's utter disagreement with the general character and conduct of Mr. Jefferson, acknowledged to be a humane man and eminently a kind master. . . . It was his principle (I know that of my own knowledge) to allow such of his slaves as were sufficiently white to pass for white men, to withdraw quietly from the plantation; it was called running away, but they were never reclaimed. I remember four instances of this, three young men and one girl, who walked away and staid away—their whereabouts was perfectly known but they were left to themselves—for they were white enough to pass for white.

Ellen establishes her credibility by making these points. She was referring, at least, to Beverley and Harriet Hemings, who left in 1822.

So she acknowledges a familiarity with the kind of sexual activity that took place at Monticello, but she goes on to explain that the white fathers came from among the Irish workmen who were constantly present and from "dissipated young men in the neighborhood who sought the society of the mulatresses"—though the women they got pregnant "were much better pleased to have it supposed that such children were their master's." One ex-Monticello slave, "black as a crow," was sold after Jefferson's death, took his late master's surname, and gave the impression that Thomas Jefferson was his father. There were also, of course, those with political motives—"Mr. Jefferson's traducers"—who could be counted on to make up lies. Ellen, over the years, had thought up a host of explanations in defense of her grandfather's good name. Recall that the same explanation for mulattos on the mountaintop had been given to the duc de la Rochefoucauld-Liancourt, and put in his published account of a 1796 visit.

Ellen raises the key question for us: "How comes it that his immoralities were never suspected by his own family?" To answer, she supplies evidence that it was improbable if not impossible that her grandfather was having sex:

His apartments [section of the house where his bedroom was] had no private entrance not perfectly accessible and visible to all the household. No female domestic ever entered his chambers except at hours when he was known not to be there and none could have entered without being exposed to the public gaze.

Reared to consider sex with a servant as "immoralities," Ellen insisted that the grandpapa she knew so well and whose style she imitated, a man so "tender, considerate, refined," would be the least likely person driven "to rear a race of

half-breeds," to "carry on his low amours," while so closely watched by an ador-
ing family.

Next she mentions Sally Hemings by name—but not familiarly, as she
should have. She refers instead to "one woman known . . . as 'dusky Sally,'"
whom Ellen now comfortably identifies as "pretty notoriously the mistress of a
married man, a near relation of Mr. Jefferson's." Sally, she adds, was "lady's
maid" to both Martha and Maria Jefferson in Paris in 1787–1789—once again
ignoring the opportunity to indicate her own very special relationship with the
Hemings family. And she concludes the thought with these words: "Again I ask
is it likely that so fond so anxious a father . . . [should] have selected the female
attendant of his own pure children to become his paramour! The thing will not
bear telling. There are things, after all, as moral impossibilities."

Reading the above, one ought to find it quite improbable that the moralizing
Ellen knew anything about her widower grandfather's sexual activities. She is
repeating what her mother's pose indicated, what her older brother told her directly. And it seems to coincide with what she herself saw growing up. As to the
alleged culprit—the unnamed "near relation"—she ends one page of her letter
and begins another with a parenthetical whisper to her husband:

> I have written thus far thinking you might chuse to communicate my letter to
> Mr. Bulfinch. Now I will tell you in confidence what Jefferson [her brother]
> told me under the like condition. Mr. Southall and himself being young men
> together, heard Mr. Peter Carr say with a laugh, that "the old gentleman
> [Thomas Jefferson] had to bear the blame of his and Sam's [Peter's brother's]
> misdeeds." There is a general impression that the four children of Sally Hem-
> mings [sic] were all the children of Col. [Sam] Carr, the most notorious
> good-natured Turk that ever was master of a black seraglio kept at other
> men's expence.

Thus, Peter and Samuel Carr, sons of Thomas Jefferson's sister, were, until
the DNA findings, presumed by most historians to have been—one or the
other of the brothers, at any rate—father of Sally Hemings's several children.
Jeff Randolph repeated the same "secret" to biographer Henry Randall, singling out Peter.

Ellen's language throughout the letter is strong, insistent, and what we would
now call insensitive, with racially and sexually charged epithets: "a notorious
villain," "master of a black seraglio" ("a house of women kept for debauchery,"
according to Johnson's *Dictionary*), "a race of half-breeds," "low amours." Her
defense is based on a morality she had learned growing up at Monticello. So if
Sally Hemings was in fact the sexual partner of Thomas Jefferson, Ellen did not

know—or else she would not have used such moralistic language to paint a picture of a "moral impossibility."

What Lies Within?

Yet Ellen also tells us that her letter to Joseph is contrived, because it is designed for wider distribution. Only the final page, directed to her husband alone, reveals names (the Carrs). Lest we forget, Ellen denies that the Hemingses meant anything to her, when her husband knows otherwise. She writes of Sally Hemings with uncharacteristic condescension. If she can deny, for posterity, a relationship to Madison and Eston's mother, perhaps she is at the same time denying what she actually knows about Sally Hemings's relationship to her grandfather. How can we be sure?

We already know from Madison Hemings that the white grandchildren (most likely led by the erudite Ellen) taught him and his siblings to read and write.[62] We know that Madison named a daughter after Ellen: Ellen Wayles Hemings was not born until 1856. Thus we can only assume that Ellen and Madison corresponded warmly from time to time during the intervening decades after she moved to Boston and he left Charlottesville. How else would the memory of Ellen's kindness have weighed so heavily on Madison when he selected his daughter's name? Why would Ellen, who must have genuinely cared for Madison and Eston, appear so cold in the contrived letter, unless that letter was *completely* contrived, even its moralizing language?

So what seems fairly certain at first—her combined innocence and moral outrage—all of a sudden looks questionable. There is yet another possibility: What if Ellen adored Madison, and perhaps even adored Sally, without knowing her grandfather's true relationship to them? What if Ellen and her siblings truly believed that the Carr boys, mixed up in interracial sex on the mountaintop, were indeed the likeliest suspects in Sally's conceptions? The possibilities— the convolutions—read like the pages of William Faulkner's novel of family, race, secrets, and consequences, *Absalom, Absalom!* The very existence of the octoroon children as a "threatful portent," to borrow Faulkner's phrase, suggests to him that the white planter family would be able to go through life at once knowing and not knowing; and the octoroon children would never have spoken of themselves as slaves. So much about their position in the social order was not referred to directly.[63]

The historian Jan Lewis has published the most interesting, most informed conjecture in this regard. She examines the statements of Ellen and Jeff and finds it revealing that Ellen's story about the Carr brothers has Peter laughing about their supposed sexual behavior, yet Jeff's has Peter shamefacedly crying.

"The lies are elaborate," Lewis observes, rightly fascinated that the Carr connection was a secret kept inside the Jefferson-Randolph family until modern times, functioning as their own special mantra for maintaining a believable fiction. Laughing or crying, the Carr boys convey an essential meaning with regard to the southern white imagination: *That* kind of sex, whoever practiced it, made the Jefferson-Randolph clan agitated and uncomfortable.

They kept their Jefferson on his godlike pedestal. The family could not permit itself to abandon a moral narrative, their common memory of the dignified forebear who was, in Ellen's words, incapable of "insulting the sanctity of home." Yet the DNA findings have led us to draw a different conclusion: Grandpapa lied to them. In "protecting" his grandchildren from the knowledge of something they might find unpleasant, in refusing to reveal his sexual past, he led his sensitive grandson and granddaughter to define him as "pure" and, as adults, to smooth out the historic record by every means at their disposal. Their misdirection to Henry Randall was set in motion by Jefferson himself—he, by omission, had done most of the doctoring. Is it possible, Lewis momentously asks, that the Hemingses knew who their father was, and the white grandchildren did not?[64]

What did Ellen know? This is a hard question to answer. It does appear, though, that in distancing Sally Hemings's brood from the truly meaningful activities of the household, while his white grandchildren took notice of them on their own and unofficially taught Madison and Eston to read and write, Jefferson did not give Ellen or her siblings clear reason to suspect that Grandpapa was the slave children's father. We may find it difficult to imagine that one as astute as Ellen asked no questions and heard no offhand comments about the Hemings children's paternity. But the way of life on the mountaintop may have created such a condition. Bearing in mind that she was merely a toddler at the time of Callender, we just cannot know for certain at this point whether she knew more than she said.

Of course, there is another puzzling question: What did Ellen's mother say or not say? There is less of a chance that Martha Jefferson Randolph was unaware of intimacy between her father and Sally Hemings. Having been born within months of each other, Martha and Sally had known each other since childhood. They were in France together, and spent weeks onboard a sailing vessel returning to America, a harrowing voyage none could forget. They were both at Monticello most of the time when Jefferson was there during his presidency; and Martha and her children had moved back permanently upon Jefferson's retirement in 1809.

If Jefferson lied to his family, Martha appears to have been complicit in her father's lie. She would have helped him lie (by omission) to her children for the greater good of preserving in them a certain kind of innocence, while pre-serving his reputation as a man who traveled farthest when he traveled in his mind, who lived amid books, planted flowers, designed a university; he was, for them, a soulful, endearing older man who lived beyond physical urges. Perhaps he justified his actions based on male privilege, Enlightenment medical think-ing, his reading of the Greek ethos, plantation norms, and other cultural fac-tors, but he did not think he could incorporate these ideas into the emotional world of his grandchildren—Maria Edgeworth's ideal community. Still, moth-erless Martha, his trusted companion for so many of his widowed years, under-stood how he had suffered, publicly and privately, and rationalized along with him.

According to Jeff Randolph, his mother made no reference to the Callender charges until a short time before her death (which came only months after Sally's death). And she made that reference only as an effort to demonstrate to her sons how to exonerate their grandfather before the bar of history. She cited evidence (unfortunately, it was not specified in Jeff's statement) of one partic-ular Hemings child whose conception ostensibly did not coincide with Jeffer-son's time at Monticello. What is interesting here, if Jeff is to be believed, is that Martha went so many years without addressing the scandal in the presence of her children.[65]

That Jefferson paid little direct attention to the Hemings children may have been one factor in allowing him to invite guests to the mountaintop without disrupting his studied effort to achieve "tranquil permanent felicity." If we judge by the anecdotal evidence presented by those who knew him, no man was more discreet in his behavior. In his retirement, Jefferson tried his best to stay out of the public eye and the opposition press. As long as he succeeded in doing this, he would remain too absorbed in good deeds to be any longer thought of in such terms as the late scandalmonger James T. Callender had once exploited for a vengeful purpose. But one wealthy Virginia planter, John Hartwell Cocke, an original member of the university's Board of Visitors, apparently knew some-thing, and could not forget.

Cocke was in his mid-forties during Jefferson's last years, when he helped to oversee construction of the university's dominating structure, the Rotunda. Since his first wife's death in 1816, he had adopted a zealous, evangelical Pres-byterian worldview. He held stern expectations from other men, and stood far from the religious liberalism of the Enlightenment-bred Jefferson. Believing that his conduct in life would inspire imitation, Cocke had put himself forward as a God-fearing messenger of moral reform, and became deeply engaged in the transformation of the institution of slavery. Some of his emotional energy was channeled into the African Education Society and American Colonization Society, whose plans for the resettlement of blacks in Liberia had grown, in a way, from Jefferson's early proposition in *Notes on Virginia*.[66] But Cocke's association with particular Jeffersonian projects did not make him "Jeffersonian" in the Epicurean sense. This committed Christian, an effusive diary writer, twice noted with despondence that Jefferson had failed to set a moral example for other planters.

In 1853, hearing of a pair of North Carolinian planters who had sent away "illegitimate spawns" of the institution of slavery, Cocke was reminded of the many similar occurrences in his "beloved" Virginia: "Nor is it to be wonderd at," he wrote, "when Mr Jeffersons notorious example is considered." To the apologists who continued to find good points in the institution of slavery, Cocke added that he thought men with recognizable names who had fathered mulatto children "must be confronted with undeniable facts—however disgusting the exhibit." In the second such diary entry, six years later, Cocke again bemoaned the consequences of slavery: "The defenders of the Institution—omit to look at the feature—that all Batchelors—or a large majority at least—keep as a substitute for a wife—some individual of their own Slaves. In Virginia—this damnable practice—prevails as much as any where—and probably more—as Mr Jeffersons example can be pleaded for its defence."[67]

This would appear to be strong contemporaneous evidence, a foretaste of the DNA evidence (if less objective). In the diaries, Cocke's persona is emotional, at times fanatical, and often brutal in tone. He does not indicate how he knows firsthand of Jefferson's complicity in race mixing—whether he had even seen Sally Hemings or the Hemings children. Certainly he knew the content of the Callender articles, as a young adult, out of college and newly married when they were published.

Cocke's diaries of the mid-1850s are no less unforgiving in his accusatory language toward other sinners. As a temperance advocate, he jotted to himself ten days before his first notation about Jefferson: "The pastor who is a wine bibber will henceforth gather few Sheep into the fold of the great shepherd." This devout Presbyterian felt antagonistic toward Jefferson's undemanding Unitarianism, a feeling that had built over decades. The week of Jefferson's death in 1826, knowing Cocke's strong religious views, a friend wrote to him suggesting that they might want to lobby for a replacement for Jefferson on the university's Board of Visitors who better satisfied the "friends of Religion."[68]

Jefferson's alleged "atheism" caused perhaps as many Americans of his time to think ill of him as his liberal political philosophy did. So we cannot, without pause, consider Cocke an unimpeachable observer on the subject of Thomas Jefferson's private conduct. His involvement with the university, his proximity to Jefferson, strongly suggests his veracity; but we cannot be 100 percent certain that he *knew* and did not merely *assume.* Certainties are hard to come by. At any rate, Cocke is the only elite Virginian with direct ties to Jefferson who committed to writing his convictions with regard to Jefferson's sex life.

Some Inferences

Since 1998, the burden of proof has most definitely shifted. Perhaps the DNA findings have not absolutely made Thomas Jefferson the father of his house servant's children, but mounting circumstantial evidence makes him by far the most plausible father of these children, as most would now agree. It matters more now that Ohioans who personally knew Eston H. Jefferson in his mature years recorded that he was a dead ringer for the president whose bust they had seen on display in the nation's capital; he was, like Jefferson, more than six feet in height, he stood erect, and he had nearly straight auburn hair. Only the emotional character of the relationship between Thomas Jefferson and Sally Hemings remains at issue.[69]

Here is a recap of the evidence presented: (1) Jefferson's medicalized sensibility directed him to behave in accordance with the regimen recommended to men of letters, which included a semi-vegetarian diet, physical exercise, and regular sexual activity; (2) Jefferson's taxonomic work on race and his aversion to blackness suggests that he thought of the "nearly white" Sally Hemings more in accordance with her class identity; her racial background, though undeniable, was sufficiently suppressed so as to enable feelings of attraction to develop; (3) Jefferson's fascination with the Greek way—its language, literature, and morals—may have contributed to his acceptance of extramarital sex that was not adultery (as a widower taking a young concubine), especially in combination with the relative isolation of his mountaintop estate and the sexual freedom southern planters had reserved to themselves across generations.

Jefferson may not have been the rigid moralist that the majority of his preserved correspondence and public addresses tends to show. That said, the study of history is an imperfect enterprise. The best historians can do in a case like this is to suggest ways in which the historic memory may have been corrupted.

Questions will persist. Even if we think we now know something about Jefferson's sense of male prerogative, we can do no more than speculate about the real moral boundaries within which he considered his feelings toward this particular servant. It still seems odd that as president, when he was, in a sense, the nation's most visible citizen, he would have risked further embarrassment by continuing to father children by his servant. Did he feel protected from further outside intrusions upon his private life? Did he think he would never have to explain to his grandchildren, over whom he doted? The explanations given do not cover every contingency. And it is important to add that no human being behaves rationally all the time. We can try to make Thomas Jefferson make sense; but in suiting *our* needs, we may unknowingly detour from historical truth.

To understand an alien psychology is a daunting challenge. We may imagine him capable of it, but Thomas Jefferson exhibited no particular signs of a guilty conscience. Why should we think that he personalized every moral concern and moral responsibility in the same way our society expects of us? He exercised his mental faculties in ways we no longer relate to. We would probably never have occasion to regard ancient Greek notions of bloodlines and procreative choices as meaningful; but he and his peers did.

What about telling truths and telling lies? Was the ethical line in Jefferson's day drawn just where it is today? Presumably it was, but perhaps not quite as we imagine. It is more than a little curious that he deliberately hid his chronic diarrhea from his immediate family for many years.[70] If he was embarrassed to talk about diarrhea, how, then, did he handle his sexual relationship with Sally Hemings, if he had one and it was longstanding? As a skilled and committed household manager, could his daughter Martha have failed to inquire, when Sally Hemings became pregnant, who was responsible? It is beyond comprehension that she could have remained oblivious. The best we can do is to presume that however her father rationalized his behavior to her, he and she together, perhaps with her son Jefferson as a willing co-conspirator, led her younger children to accept the Carr brothers scenario.

Relations across color and class lines were not constant. It is unlikely that we will ever be able to discover the whole emotional truth. But there are contingent matters worth our relating to Jefferson's private history, to wit: If he and Sally Hemings were having sexual relations for decades, can consent remain at issue? Here again, we need to examine southern prejudices as Jefferson knew them, and to take note of the adjudication of sex-related cases in the courts as a symptom of prevailing attitudes.

Southern white women were generally seen as having sexual desires—it was in the North that the feminine ideal of "passionlessness" found more ready acceptance. Although in the South an unmarried white woman's chastity was assumed and expected, it was also understood that the actions of an "unsullied" woman could not be compared to the actions of one who was no longer a virgin and might, therefore, be inviting a sexual encounter. A woman who had succumbed to sexual desire once might do so again.

The race, as well as class, of an individual charged with rape or attempted rape was decisive in southern courts, as was the race and class of the victim. The rape of a black woman was not a capital offense; the rape of a white woman was. A white woman of low social status was more likely seen as prone to indulge in unconventional or interracial sex. Furthermore, if the race (white, black, or mixed) of the alleged female victim was not immediately apparent and came into dispute, an indictment might not stand up.

Forcible sex was ill defined, and typically linked to the character of the alleged victim. Rules often changed. Even male slaves' rape convictions were overturned in significant numbers, owing in part (incredibly, to us) to the court's recognition that the defendant had a meaningful economic value to his owner. At the same time, southern jurists were careful to maintain strict courtroom procedures, because they wished to portray the institution of slavery as humane. But the uncertain guidelines we are describing could only have added to the intensity of that racially based sexual anxiety southern whites felt.[71]

Thomas Jefferson's Monticello was part of a culture that feared "disorder," a world unto itself in which the plantation owner made his own rules. Law and society almost always protected the planter if he chose to have sex, wanted or unwanted, with a woman he legally owned. Largely for their own purposes, whites stereotyped slaves, male and female, as promiscuous. And because slaves did not enjoy the legal rights or share in the obligations that marriage brought, a slave owner had the final say about the partnering of his slaves. Jefferson's universally attested mildness makes it appear unlikely that he would physically overpower a woman, yet subtle psychological pressure is impossible to estimate. The point is that we cannot know the extent to which he pursued intimacy with Sally Hemings—or whether she gave signals indicating a willingness to satisfy his sexual and/or emotional needs.[72]

What could their attachment have been like? As one scholar of the eighteenth-century French mode has written, "The deeper bond between master and servant was forged within the household. It is in the hallways, the antechambers, the bedrooms and kitchens . . . that we must go looking for the roots of *fidelité*." The shrewd master used rewards and punishments, as well as affection and authority, to win cooperation or devotion. Was it like that here? In dealing with Sally Hemings, thirty years his junior, Jefferson must have acted with premeditation—but to what effect, precisely? Attitudes and gestures spoke a language, unavailable to us, that the two of them understood. In France, technically free female servants, "hoarded" by their masters, lived in a kind of sexual limbo; some stayed aloof when they went beyond the master's property, adopting a self-protective method to ward off insult from those who would imagine them as quasi-prostitutes. We simply do not know what kind of mobility Sally Hemings had, in Charlottesville or beyond. Except for her time in France, she has never been pictured away from the mountaintop.[73]

It is entirely possible that Jefferson convinced young Sally Hemings—or she concluded on her own—that, as her grandmother had been the concubine of a sea captain named Hemings, and her mother Betty had been the mulatto concubine of Jefferson's father-in-law John Wayles, that she, too, could enjoy a decent life as concubine of the master of Monticello. However she may have expressed her needs and desires in 1789, as a teenager, there is no reason not to believe that she continued to display a lively commitment to her own best interests in later years.

The Hemingses were favored at Monticello. But to what degree were they made to feel black or white? This, again, is a hard question to answer with any confidence. To be sure, they were enslaved, and thoroughly understood the legal difference between free persons of color and themselves. Presumably, they were very much conscious at the same time of the advantage that their light skin and relation to the Wayles and Jefferson lineages afforded them. To the master, they were, above all, privileged and trusted servants, and they were defined at Monticello by the contributions they made. Some possessed the wherewithal to sustain themselves economically and were eventually (but not easily) given their freedom. Yet, Jefferson apparently did not care to educate Sally, and he planned for her to remain in servitude for as long as he lived; her children were given vocational training and a practical education meant to serve them as free artisans. But Sally was never more than a servant. Though three-quarters white, she would never have a public identity, never rise beyond caring for her master's bedchamber and linens.

Without knowing more about Sally Hemings's real personality and the nature of the privacy she and Thomas Jefferson shared, it warrants repeating that no evidence exists on which to conjure a loving intimacy. The word Madison Hemings uses is "concubine," a word that, in this period, implied not only low status but also a relationship based on the man's sexual need and nothing more emotionally meaningful. It is only the imaginations of modern champions of interracial harmony that attribute to Jefferson a progressive ideology and, in turn, his acceptance of Sally Hemings as a putative social equal.[74]

That sounds fairly definitive, but we must recognize that key aspects of the Jefferson-Hemings relationship were known only to the parties themselves. If Jefferson withheld essential (factual) truth from history, how much more (emotional) truth did he withhold? As in the ambiguity expressed in the French example of master-servant relations above, he may indeed have treated Sally Hemings with respect and affectionate concern during their private moments, away from the white family; the apparent fact that she bore not just one but several of his children over a period of at least thirteen years indicates that he may have enjoyed the knowledge that he was fathering children who would produce descendants. Even if he did not give outward signs, he may have privately felt a special bond with these children—and with their mother. In this sense, Annette Gordon-Reed is encompassing the full range of possibilities when she reminds us that Sally Hemings's father was the father of Jefferson's lamented wife as well. The long-term emotional impact of this connection on Thomas Jefferson cannot be summarily denied. As a child, Sally even had a sufficient amount of time to bond with Patty Jefferson before the latter's death in 1782.[75]

These caveats aside, the most reasonable cultural explanation still appears to be that Jefferson found a healthy, fruitful female to bear children for him, whom he supported just as an ancient Greek man of honor, or a colonial Latin American man of honor, would have done. What in modern times appears as the selfish pursuit of physical gratification was easily rationalized by the medical literature of Jefferson's age. Sally Hemings helped him to preserve his body's health, even as he approached an energetic old age.

Ultimately, the taboo of interracial sex meant less in this relationship, because the strict racial boundaries that Jefferson prescribed in his *Notes on Virginia* were for America at large, and not for Jefferson in his private world. The protected plantation population was "family"—his personal records consistently denoted all in his care, black and white alike, as family. Within this family, there were degrees of attachment and degrees of practical power and opportunity, all of which were implicitly understood. The emotional connections, whatever they were, were very real. But this does not help us fathom whether the Hemingses felt more comfortable among the white Jeffersons or with the black field hands. In whose company did they break into smiles or reveal private concerns with greater ease? In their subordinate role on Jefferson's plantation, what sense of prospect did they grow up with?

It is quite conceivable that in Jefferson's private world, race meant something different than what it meant to him in theory. The all too easy indictment of Jefferson as a hypocrite for advocating racial separation while keeping a concubine who was one-quarter black becomes as careless a statement as calling him a hypocrite for writing "All men are created equal." We cannot expect the eighteenth-century liberal to speak the language we speak, to envision racial equality, or to have put an immediate and absolute end to slavery, when others could not, and when in practical terms American society has yet to become colorblind two centuries later.

To say these things is by no means to be an apologist for Jefferson's behavior. We can certainly ask—and ought to—why he did not do more to advance the cause of justice for blacks, free and enslaved. It was certainly within the realm, within the reach, of his everyday world that he could have championed black Americans *for real.* He made contradictory statements, and refused to clear them up. We must accept that no one statement attributed to Jefferson can encompass the full range of his beliefs. We can criticize him for his indecision, or expose his limited skills in interpreting the human potential, but we should at the same time say that he aimed to be practical.

Then why did Thomas Jefferson not remarry? That would have been a practical step for him. Family tradition alleges that he promised Patty on her deathbed that her girls would not have a stepmother. Had he done otherwise, he would have married a woman who brought wealth and could have rescued him from his later pecuniary embarrassments. But it seems entirely possible that Jefferson was a man increasingly fixed in his habits who found self-sufficiency preferable to having a partner whom he would feel obliged to consult. In his world, such a choice did not have to result in celibacy.

The highly symbolic letter to Charles Bellini in which Jefferson used the phrase "tranquil permanent felicity" was sent from France in September 1785, shortly after the third anniversary of Patty's death. In it, Jefferson was eloquent in his praise of American society because, he believed, marriage was revered there. He contrasted what he was witnessing in Paris:

> Conjugal love having no existence among [the French], domestic happiness . . .
> is utterly unknown. In lieu of this are substituted pursuits which nourish and
> invigorate all our bad passions, and which offer only moments of extasy amidst
> days and months of restlessness and torment. Much, very much inferior this to
> the tranquil permanent felicity with which domestic society in America blesses
> most of it's inhabitants.[76]

Apparently, Jefferson found a means of enjoying a kind of "domestic happiness" without re-experiencing "conjugal love." But he also does not deny knowing what "bad passions" feel like. The Betsey Walker incident, dating back to 1768, informs us that he knew lust and, at least on the one occasion, had propositioned the wife of a friend. That he initially concocted a story about an argument over money to explain to his inquiring daughters in the early 1790s why he had stopped being cordial toward Betsey's husband shows once again that he was reticent to talk about his sex life.[77] But the sanctity of marriage was something he held dear, or so he repeatedly professed after his years of "unchequered happiness," the words he chose in his 1821 *Autobiography* to describe his ten-year marriage.

Patty's loss was more than he could bear. By all accounts, his commitment to her was real and heartfelt. Taking Sally as a sexual partner rather than looking for a second wife might have resolved, or at least tempered, his fear of loss; his emotional tie to the lover would now presumably be weaker, owing to her enslaved condition. One rationale for taking a concubine would be to have less invested emotionally in the survival of his partner and their children.[78]

So, then, even if the bondwoman's life was somehow made better by being Jefferson's concubine, was her happiness really considered? There is nothing to dispute Jeff Randolph's statement that Sally Hemings was dressed no better than the other house servants; this fact becomes even more interesting when we consider that Martha Randolph was generally responsible for requisitioning the servants' clothing. Was appearance reality here?

To suggest, as some have, that Sally Hemings was a "liberator" of sorts seems doubtful. A more typical development is the kind reported by another former slave (not one of Jefferson's), who recalled that in her teen years she successfully turned down her master's sexual advances, out of a sense of self-respect, only to agree to a similar arrangement with another white man sometime later. It was, she explained, "less degrading to give one's self, than to submit to compulsion."[79] In other words, "arrangements" between the races, or between classes, in which powerful men sought to exert authority over vulnerable, unequal young women, involved a certain amount of coercion—even as affection grew. No amount of discretion or patient negotiation could change that. The relationship may have had compensatory elements, but it was not really liberating.

Except for the leering publicity that maverick journalist James T. Callender gave his private life, Thomas Jefferson, a man of privilege who lived in splendid isolation, apparently indulged his desire for physical intimacy without upsetting the social order. Though politically he opened himself to potential risk, from the perspective of philosophical medicine his actions did nothing to violate the principle of moderate, healthful living that he clearly sought to enjoy.

Active Memories

7

Administering (Political) Medicine

I wish to avoid all collisions of opinion with all mankind.

JEFFERSON TO CHARLES YANCEY,

JANUARY 6, 1816[1]

I s this unintended irony? "Collisions of opinion," after all, perfectly character-
izes Thomas Jefferson's four decades as a public office holder. He not only applied his principled, sentimentally charged pen to the cause of American independence, he also gave birth to a political party that dismissed the Federalist Party
of George Washington as an alliance of the privileged few, leaving his Democra-
tic-Republicans to reconstitute the nation's "true" values. He lived in a time of
great intellects and as great contentions—indeed, he stood in the middle of them.
That the ingenious democrat, seven years into his retirement, would insist on his
repugnance for "collisions of opinion," instructs us that he was exhausted from
the years of political struggle, and, just as important, that he was trying to convince himself, along with his correspondents, that he was capable of change.[2]

In his prime, he had entered into debate with his enemies fully aware of the
consequences of doing so, for they were just as determined as he was. From the
beginning, Jefferson had fought against what was in his mind the exercise of
unjust authority, the center's usurpation (or threatened usurpation) of representative right. From 1769, when he entered Virginia's House of Burgesses, until
1809, when he retired from the presidency, he held fast to one vision of a hearty,
healthy American polity, liberated from aristocratic pride and greed. The epit-
ome of that vision was the unity forged in 1776, which Jefferson remembered as
a democratic upsurge, and as a consensus among states that each was free, and
each committed to its embattled sister states.

His principles did not soften. In post-Revolutionary America, he regarded as
the greatest threat to public order a concentration of power among a self-se-
lected elite of vain characters who considered themselves fit rulers in a republic,
and who would restrict power and wealth to their own narrow circle. (*They*

191

were the government; *they* were the people's ideal advocates.) Jefferson recoiled from such a proto-aristocracy, whose dubious claim meant constricting the definition of "leading citizens" to monied citizens. He preferred instead to open government to those who embraced the energy and spirit of ordinary people. His definition of respectability was not oligarchic; he stood for small independent landownership rather than wealth that was questionably tied to one's personal connections with those at the pinnacle of national power. In Philadelphia, the nation's capital through most of the 1790s, men of humble origins became politically active—among them printers, tradesmen, and small-scale manufacturers. These people embodied the Jeffersonian movement.

In retirement, Jefferson held deeply to the values of his political youth. He kept alive a particular dream: a government that refused to encroach on people's lives, and especially on their pocketbooks. He feared that this quality of liberty had yet to be fully secured. But how easy would it be for the retired president to keep his opinion to himself? Though a man who conventionally denied that he was ambitious, he had nevertheless directed an immense amount of unholy political combat: from 1791 to 1793, he strenuously opposed Alexander Hamilton's centralizing economic program; in 1794–1796, he agitated against the news-dominating Jay Treaty, which Republicans believed would shackle America to a British-led commercial empire; in 1798, he secretly authored the Kentucky Resolution, in which he asserted a state's right to resist unjust laws passed by Congress. By the time he became president in 1801, he was notorious for his behind-the-scenes cunning.

The Enlightenment values that conditioned so much of Jefferson's political creed described knowledge as a means to enjoyment, medicine as a category of improvement, and politics as a game of absolutes. Jefferson played that game masterfully. Seeking the presidency in 1800, he suggested that political "medicine . . . must be very mild and secretly administered."[3] He acquired his reputation for sneakiness by meticulously avoiding direct confrontation, resorting instead to private ministrations when he sought to eliminate his enemies and empower his friends; but all the while he presented a courteous and thoughtful outward image.

Politics could be a shock to his system, even so. As president, he suffered "periodical" headaches of several weeks' duration because of it. He sensed what he needed to do to secure his health; but how could such a battler ever give up politics completely? Even in his long-deferred retirement, and even as he limited his newspaper reading to one publication (Thomas Ritchie's Richmond *Enquirer*), and even as he professed the desire for "tranquil permanent felicity," Jefferson could not sit idly by as others twisted the meaning of the two revolutions with which his name was prominently associated: the War for Independence (1775–1783) and the "Revolution of 1800."

As to the first, consider the disturbance caused by Timothy Pickering. The arch-Federalist had served as secretary of state under John Adams, and in 1803–1804 led a movement to separate Federalist New England from a "union" with Jefferson at its head. In 1823, this particularly inflammatory politician gave a Fourth of July address in Salem, Massachusetts. In it, he reported on a letter he had received from old Adams only the year before, attesting that Jefferson's Declaration of Independence was unoriginal and undistinguished, and was as much Adams's work as the Virginian's. Presumably, Adams had not intended to challenge his friend's intellect, though Pickering did all he could to drive a wedge between the retired presidents.

Writing to the ever-trusted, always sympathetic James Madison, Jefferson expressed no surprise at Pickering's incurable hostility toward him; and though he faulted Adams, it was only for his imperfect recollection:

> Mr. Adams' memory has led him into unquestionable error. At the age of 88., and 47. years after the transactions of Independence, this is not wonderful [i.e., extra-ordinary]. Nor should I, at the age of 80., on the small advantage of that difference only, venture to oppose my memory to his, were it not supported by written notes, taken by myself at the moment and on the spot.

He knew what he had, right there at Monticello: all the texts he needed to prove the extent of his personal contribution to the birth of a nation.[4]

It is not important, for the moment, to consider who was right as to the distinctiveness of Jefferson's original draft.[5] The point worth making here is that Jefferson's remarkable lifelong penchant for record keeping, his compulsion to build a history of his role in the founding moment, was done as if he were prosecuting a legal case. He compiled what he considered irresistible evidence to privilege his interpretation of events over that of others. If no one could compete with his own detailed written record, then ultimately none of the other founders could substitute their history for Jefferson's.

He tried the same method in the touchier matter of the struggle for civil liberties leading up to his "Revolution of 1800." This was a historical controversy much closer to the present and, unlike his knowledge of the provenance of the Declaration, a question still capable of producing deep resentment because it spoke to his motives as a political organizer. Thus Jefferson was moved in 1818 to compile his *Anas,* a patchwork collection of his personal on-the-spot notes from the Washington administration.* It told the tale of Federalist vanities, tricks and hidden designs, dangerous financial speculation, abuses of power—all to assert

---

*The Latin term *ana* is defined as "anecdotes or sayings" of a person, in Randall 2:26–27.

the legitimacy of the popular discontent that ensued, and that awarded Jefferson the presidency.

In the simplest terms, the 1790s marked out America's political destiny. The politicians of Jefferson's day universally acknowledged that. Depending on one's interpretation (even at that time), Jefferson was either an underhanded opportunist or the man chiefly responsible for the success of representative democracy. He meant for his detailed and anecdotal *Anas* to be used by sympathetic political writers to justify his every public act from 1790 forward; it was as if his recorded conversations were verbatim transcripts, impartial and incontestable.

He expected his personal notes to expose the Federalists' nearly successful attempt to hoodwink the electorate, and to deprive citizens of their constitutional remedy for fraudulent representation. By his own analysis, Jefferson's presidency brought an end to Federalists' seizure of the cause of 1776—that was the finding his *Anas* hoped to generate. Whether it was the shining moment of 1776 or the highly divisive 1790s, the guiding principle in Jefferson's thinking, the root cause of his anxiety, was the same: *History might be unfriendly to him without critical help from his personal records.*

By the time he had retired, the Federalists had been crushed. They were no longer a significant force in Congress. But they were prodigious in their writing, and not about to permit a Jeffersonian narrative to become America's way of memorializing the Revolution and its aftermath. Men of social grace and social distinction were to be the focus of their "proper" narrative.

And not men with a social conscience? What, Jefferson inquired, was the rationale for the Revolution, if not that? In the 1790s, he and Madison, with the help of many others, had had the foresight and courage to rescue republicanism from a Federalist plot to "monarchize" America. That rescue was nothing short of a second revolution to them. In 1800, Jefferson was obliged to abandon the tranquil felicity of Monticello and accept executive responsibility because, if he was to defend a principle, he had to. Or so his story goes.

Declaring Authorship, Defining His Revolutions

Once he retired, Jefferson genuinely tried to stay out of politics. Correspondents invited—some pleaded for, others demanded—his comment. He protested that he should not have to weigh in any longer. But as time passed, the temptations became greater.

Eloquent assertions to the contrary, Thomas Jefferson could not resist politics. In his mind, the integrity of the American Revolution would be at stake for the foreseeable future. That was why he remained consumed with the historic record, and why, in 1819, he first characterized his election as the "Revolution of 1800," a bloodless revolution to inaugurate the new century. Modern historians have routinely adopted Jefferson's phrase for it.

The "Revolution of 1800" might also be called the "civil revolution of 1801." For, as we shall see shortly, he labeled it that, too. Defeating John Adams in the fall of 1800 had not secured Jefferson's election, in that a few more uncomfortable months of politicking were needed to break the unplanned electoral tie between Jefferson and his erstwhile vice-presidential ally, Aaron Burr of New York. To break their tie, the House of Representatives had to decide between the two men, each state's delegation possessing a single vote. Federalists wondered aloud whether Burr might be less antagonistic toward them than Jefferson, and so they separately sought promises from both. Suspicions were shared and the Constitution ever so slightly bent, before Jefferson was declared victor. The governor of Pennsylvania, friendly to Jefferson, strongly hinted that an army was waiting in the wings. The civil revolution was not exactly courteous.[6]

How he won ultimately matters less to our narrative than that his Republican partisans had displaced cynical, high-toned Federalism. It was a "civil" revolution because bloodshed was averted; but, more meaningfully to Jefferson, it announced a new social framework, one that privileged the many over the few. Polemics continued, of course, along with whispering campaigns at both ends of the political spectrum; the administration moved to solidify its claim to civility at home and abroad by promoting a virtuous and less grasping commerce, and prosperity more diffuse among the populace. In his first inaugural address, Jefferson promised "a wise and frugal government, which shall restrain men from injuring one another, which shall leave them otherwise free to regulate their own pursuits of industry and improvement, and shall not take from the mouth of labor the bread it has earned."[7] It sounded little different from the crisp definitions of liberty that had prevailed in the year 1776. Jefferson handily won reelection in 1804.

So the question repeats: Why did Jefferson need to anoint his age? Again, we look to the later years of his retirement for telling pronouncements. As an old man, he only *pretended* that the second, or "civil," revolution was secure, because deep down he did not really believe that it was. Opposition Federalists had, so far, outpaced the Republicans in writing of the founding. Where were Republican historians to come from? How was posterity to receive the truth, and so avoid surrendering their liberties to resurfacing Federalists?

Jefferson increasingly felt that his personal retrospective could be a means to right wrongs. And so he sought to deliver his words into helpful hands. Quotable letters, one to the Virginia jurist Spencer Roane, and one to the Virginia-born Kentuckian William T. Barry, tell of Jefferson's state of mind as he began bequeathing what to him was reliable history, and to us must be, less prejudicially, historic validation.

It was in writing to Judge Roane from his Poplar Forest retreat, in September 1819 (not long after the *Anas* was compiled), that Jefferson first referred to his election as the "Revolution of 1800." Though the slogan stuck, the rest of the sentence should be included: The "Revolution of 1800" was, Jefferson explained, "as real a revolution in the principles of our government as that of 1776. was in it's forms; not effected indeed by the sword, as that, but by the rational and peaceable instrument of reform." He was being careful to differentiate between the two: 1776 as an outline, a plan conceived at a moment of invasion and excitement, and 1800 as a revolution of real and enduring value—as though there might actually have been more at stake for the American way of life in the second revolution.[8]

On July 2, 1822, Jefferson wrote the letter to Barry, who had migrated west to Lexington, Kentucky. Barry served under General William Henry Harrison during the War of 1812 and briefly served as a U.S. senator afterward. He would go on to be a not-too-popular postmaster general during the presidency of Andrew Jackson, but in 1822, Barry was involved in Kentucky state politics and interested in funding public education. He had sent Jefferson a deferential letter not long before this—"to express my admiration of your character"—and enclosed a questionnaire concerning state educational needs.

Jefferson rejected Barry's flattery in words that he repeated time and again in the correspondence of his retirement years: "I was only one of a band devoted to the cause of independance [*sic*], all of whom exerted equally their best endeavors for it's success." Of consequence, he added, "so also in the civil revolution of 1801," when "very many and very meritorious were the worthy partners who assisted in bringing back our government to it's republican tack."

But Jefferson did not stop after praising the collective effort. In the letter to Barry, coming three years after that to Judge Roane, and as he neared his eightieth birthday, he betrayed mounting concern. He felt impelled to remind his correspondent (as he would others over ensuing months and years) that the same threat to the republic he had seen in the years leading to 1801 was present once again, and building. Though rhetorically denying himself the right to claim more credit than others for the historical transformation taking place in America, what he said between the lines was most instructive: Jefferson felt he possessed a singular insight, a sleuthing ability, when it came to the secret motives of his traditional enemies. He was moved to tell Barry of his fear that the combined republican visions of 1776 and 1800–1801 remained in danger of being suffocated by undemocratic interests in 1822! He urged "unremitting vigilance."[9]

Jefferson was fighting a battle on two fronts: the present and the future. On the one hand, he felt that the "Revolution of 1800" might not withstand the shocks delivered by revisionist historians; on the other, he had to deal, from time to time, with detractors who hated him enough that they would not even allow him to retain full authorship of the Declaration of Independence. Prior to his presidency, the Fourth of July was celebrated and the Declaration was anonymously honored, its particular penman left unmentioned. Jefferson had not been widely known as the author until 1800, when his now renowned role in America's formal birth as a nation was used for overtly partisan purposes.[10]

He felt he needed to secure his claim to 1776 if he was to legitimize his subsequent political activism. He considered himself no mere accidental draftsman of what was already sacred text. And, to prove it, he had kept—for eventual publication—a documentary history certifying his central role at Independence Hall. He would go to lengths to insure his immortality as author, knowing that there was nothing momentous, unique, or especially clever in putting together a rough draft, particularly one so uninspired that it required upgrading by his betters in Congress before they would inscribe their names to it. What was at stake for him was historical reputation.

The trials of Jefferson in attempting to secure his authorship for posterity began three years after he had sold his private library to the Library of Congress. In 1818, John Trumbull's majestic portrait of the Declaratory moment was exhibited in several cities, and would be, in 1826, the first of his four patriotic tableaux mounted in the Capitol Rotunda. Though the centerpiece of Trumbull's "Declaration of Independence" was the Committee of Five (Jefferson stands with John Adams, Benjamin Franklin, Robert Livingston, and Roger Sherman), it is Jefferson whose hands grasp the precious parchment; it is Jefferson who delivers the Declaration to the president of the Continental Congress. It is not surprising that the scene is presented with this bias, because the artist embarked on his work while he was staying under Jefferson's roof in Paris, in 1786, and he was fed details by the then–American minister.

Though estranged during the partisan warfare of the 1790s, the artist and the statesman were restored to a relationship of mutual respect when the painting was revealed in the period of heightened nationalism following the War of 1812. Trumbull wrote graciously to Jefferson in the fall of 1823, announcing that an engraving of the painting "has been finished with great beauty" and printed with "uncommon success." Shipping two framed prints from New York to Virginia, he wrote: "It is delightful to me that after the lapse of so many years, this work which I meditated, & which you assisted me to arrange at Chaillot in 1786, is at last completed—rarely does it occur that two Individuals, advanced as we then were on the Road of Life, remain to see the completion of a favorite project at the end of 37 years." He was sure to add, "The Event was great in its consequences beyond all others in human history.

The Actors in it . . . deserve to live in the grateful memory of mankind to the end of time."[11]

In 1819, the year following the Trumbull exhibitions, a Raleigh, North Carolina, newspaper published what purported to be the Mecklenberg County Declaration of Independence. This dramatic paper was said to have been pronounced by the people of Charlotte in May 1775, more than a year before Jefferson's. Although neither Jefferson nor John Adams had ever heard of such a document, its sudden appearance served as a reminder that Jefferson's position in Revolutionary history was still not safe. Within a short time, Jefferson and Adams pronounced the Mecklenberg text "spurious," "fiction," "a fabrication"; and so the always direct Adams revealed their common sensitivity with respect to historical reputation when he reminded Jefferson of the existing danger: "But who can be the Demon to invent such a machine after five and forty years, and what could be his motive? Was it to bring a charge of Plagiarism against the Congress in 76, or against you, the undoubted, acknowledged draughtsman of the Declaration of Independence?" There it was: Adams had confirmed his knowledge of the truth, at least to Jefferson's satisfaction.[12]

Jefferson regarded such issues as the Mecklenberg claim—and Timothy Pickering's 1823 Fourth of July oration—in the larger context of his concern with the direction of national politics. No one was quite so worried about the durability of Revolutionary principles, and the possible appearance of a home-grown monarchy, as he was. When his close friends Madison and Monroe succeeded him in the President's House, and while they served the nation in that capacity for sixteen years, Jefferson gazed uneasily at the political horizon. For him, the Federalists remained a force to be reckoned with: He underscored in the 1822 letter to William Barry that crypto-Federalists had assumed the name "National Republican," discarding their party identity without actually changing their political opinions. There could be no doubt about it: Either they had truly surrendered and entered "our camp," or they were surreptitiously contriving to "weaken the genuine principles of republicanism."

Singling out the Supreme Court under the Virginia Federalist Chief Justice John Marshall, Jefferson expressed alarm at "the power, installed for life, responsible to no authority (for impeachment is not even a scare-crow) advancing with a noiseless and steady pace to the great object of consolidation"—"consolidation" being the operative term at this time for the placement of power in the hands of a federal elite, one that would go on to steal constitutional rights from states and individuals. Then Jefferson amplified: "If ever this vast country is brought under a single government, it will be one of the most extensive corruption, indifferent, and incapable of a wholesome care over so wide a spread of surface."[13]

He was not simply exaggerating to achieve a literary effect. Jefferson was deeply alarmed. Popular government, he said, depended on "wholesome care" exercised by elected leaders; healthy governance required that human liberty be maintained as the ultimate political value. The worst imaginable scenario, in his view, was what would follow the cataclysmic loss of the Revolutionary spirit. Jefferson lived in fear that resurgent Federalists would (to repeat one colorful catechism of the banner year of 1776) "usurp dominion over others, and reduce them to a state of dependence on absolute will, . . . high treason against the *majesty of human nature.*"[14]

A majestic struggle persisted in the aging Revolutionary's mind: Anti-republican Federalists plotted, disguised as National Republicans, and would ultimately reintroduce arbitrary government. Jefferson was mechanically transposing an old dynamic to the politically fluid 1820s. Had he conflated past and present? Or were his fears justified? And how had this terrified political imagination evolved?

"nervous persons" with "languid fibres" oppose the republic of felicity

Jefferson knew he would be remembered. He knew it years before the political histories that appeared in his later years were being compiled. He tried from an early period to manage the life of his legacy, enlisting those contemporaries who would be among his immediate posterity, and on whom he felt he could best rely to promote his causes. And so we need to take our cue from his political prime.

In 1795, with party disputes intensifying in character and consequence, Jefferson was momentarily retired to Monticello. Federalists (the party in power) as well as upstart Jeffersonian Republicans were trying to get the word out that their side alone embodied just principles of government. That is when Jefferson, the standard-bearer of the party out of power, heard from Christoph Daniel Ebeling (1741–1817), a historian-geographer in Hamburg, Germany. Ebeling had begun to publish a comprehensive treatment of America's Revolutionary history that would inevitably have to describe the state of post-Revolutionary politics. The German scholar was directed to Jefferson by two highly regarded New Englanders: Harvard-educated Jeremy Belknap, whose well-received *History of New Hampshire* considered the relationship between geography and political settlement; and Ezra Stiles, a minister and the president of Yale College, whom Jefferson had met during his only visit to New England, in 1784, before he sailed to Europe. Ebeling appealed to Jefferson with fairly conventional words of admiration: "A man of your celebrity, of such patriotism and public spirit . . . is certainly a benevolent man." He was preparing a history of North America, he said, after twenty years' research, and he informed Jefferson up front who his other American correspondents were.[15]

The scope of Ebeling's history was broad. Concerned with the character of republican government, he meant only to praise America as a "free and happy country." Two volumes of a planned four-volume set (it would eventually extend to seven) had been published in German, and the author intended his work to be translated into French. In attempting to produce "a faithfull picture of your Constitution, Laws, and Government," Ebeling was interested in receiving from Jefferson materials relating specifically to Virginia. Jefferson, however, was more interested in educating his correspondent about personalities and prejudices. It was not enough for him that Ebeling had received considerable advice from the nationalistic poet Joel Barlow of Connecticut, a tried and true Jeffersonian who, the German explained, "lived more than a year in my neighbourhood"; there were also northern correspondents such as Jedidiah Morse and Noah Webster, who Jefferson feared would convey a hostile political perspective.

Demonstrating just how consumed he could become with the historical record, Jefferson drafted a careful response, and showed his "Notes on Professor Ebeling's letter of July 30, '95" to a Virginia ally in Congress, William Branch Giles, and no doubt to others as well. Amid what can only be called a rant against his opposition, Jefferson divided Ebeling's American correspondents into categories of competence: Yale's Ezra Stiles, though "an excellent man, of very great learning," was easily deceived. Morse and Webster were "good authorities for whatever relates to the Eastern states," but south of Delaware "their information is worse than none at all." Jefferson reveals his irritation with Federalists Morse and Webster:

> They both I believe took a single journey through the Southern parts, merely to acquire the right of being considered eye-witnesses. But to pass once along a public road thro' a country, & in one direction only, to put up at it's taverns, and get into conversation with the idle, drunken individuals who pass their time lounging in these taverns, is not the way to know a country, it's inhabitants or manners. To generalise a whole nation from these specimens is not the sort of information which Professor Ebeling would wish to compose his work from.[16]

The insult was complete.

As he continued his unusually long-winded statement, Jefferson outlined an interpretation of the American Revolution. Prior to the outcry for independence, the people of the colonies, "being attached to England, had taken up, without examination, the English ideas of superiority of their constitution over every thing of the kind." The Revolution had converted Americans from worshippers of the English model to genuine Whig republicans; those who saw differently "either left us, & were called Refugees, or staid with us under the name of tories." After 1789, when the federal Constitution was adopted, republicanism appeared to be in triumph, but did not totally displace the pro-British stance: Returned "Refugees," "old tories," and "timid whigs who prefer tranquility [here attesting to a fear of change] to freedom" expressed a common purpose, "hoping monarchy might be the remedy if a state of complete anarchy could be brought on."[17] At least this was how Jefferson saw things. He called this faction "monocrats," and described their nefarious aim as a strengthening of consolidated national government at the expense of the states.

In his notes for Professor Ebeling, Jefferson avowed that the republican element was using the Constitution to undermine the monocrats' scheme and would "defeat the plan of sliding us into monarchy." At this point in the text, Jefferson shifted from "monocrats" to "Anti-republicans" in describing the domestic opposition. He found it easy to characterize "the Republican part of our Union": They were "the entire body of landholders" and "the body of labourers." But for the anti-republicans, his definition was rather more involved: They were the "old refugees & tories," "British merchants residing among us," "American merchants trading on British capital," "speculators" in bank stock, many officers of the federal government, "office-hunters," who would eagerly trade their principles for lucrative appointment; and, finally, "nervous persons, whose languid fibres have more analogy with a passive than active state of things."

This last, most curious, and most unambiguous invocation of the medical metaphor for political purposes instructs us that Jefferson either convinced himself that hardened Federalists could only believe as they did if suffering from damaged nervous systems and diseased minds, or else he found pleasure in vicariously associating them with these symptoms. Their nerve-induced passivity denoted a pathological resistance to growth or healthy progress. Jefferson wants to suggest here that no intelligent person would shrink from enacting social justice on his terms, unless in a diseased state.

He could rationalize in this way because he perceived the majority as healthy in their political choices. He was preaching to the converted (Representative Giles) and assuring Ebeling, by means of an outlandish statistic, that Republicans outnumbered anti-republicans by "500 to one." What made the latter faction appear stronger than they really were was merely a function of geography: "Trifling as are the numbers of the Anti-republican party . . . , they all live in cities, together, & can act in a body readily & at all times; they give chief employment to the newspapers, & therefore have most of them under their command." Jefferson's supporters would remedy the problem over the next years and decades by rapidly expanding their own network of partisan newspapers, eventually drowning out the Federalists' voice.[18]

- *aripitions of persons*
The Anti-republicans consist of
1. The old refugees & tories.
2. British merchants residing among us & comprising the main body of merchants;
3. American merchants trading on British capital. another great portion.
4. Speculators & Holders in the banks & public funds.
5. Officers of the federal government with some exceptions.
6. Office-hunters, willing to give up principles for places, a numerous & noisy tribe.
7. Nervous persons, whose languid fibres have more analogy with a passive
    than active state of things.
The Republican part of our Union comprehends
1. the entire body of landholders throughout the United States
2 the body of labourers, not being landholders, whether in husbandry or the arts
The latter is to the aggregate of the former party probably as 500
to one; but their wealth is not as disproportionate, tho' it is also great

Excerpt from Jefferson's highly volatile "Notes" to Professor Christoph Daniel Ebeling, 1795, identifying the "Anti-republican party" as "nervous persons" with "languid fibres." His remarks were so stinging that he apparently chose not to put his name to them in any communication with the German historian. Library of Congress.

Nonetheless, some mystery remains in trying to assess what might have happened to Jefferson's strongly worded notes to Ebeling. There is no record of Jefferson's directly dispatching a letter to Ebeling, either in 1795 or in later years. This is strange: Jefferson's records are nearly complete with regard to his major public correspondence, and so it would *appear* that he ignored Ebeling's request. But this cannot be. It is strikingly odd that he would not respond to a letter from so distinguished and well intentioned a foreign scholar, or that he would allow the manuscript to sit in a drawer, eventually to be forgotten. It makes more sense to conclude that Jefferson's notes were transcribed by someone else, to distance Jefferson from their polemical content, and reached Ebeling by indirect means.[19]

The Virginia volume, the final volume, of Ebeling's *Erdbeschreibung und Geschichte von Amerika* (Geographic Description and History of America) was finally published in 1816, during Jefferson's retirement. The author sent an inscribed copy to Jefferson at Monticello. More interesting is Jefferson's reply to a letter he received from William Bentley of Salem, Massachusetts, in the autumn of 1815, which had announced the imminent publication of Ebeling's book in German and French.

Bentley, a scholar and linguist whose library rivaled Jefferson's, reported that he and Ebeling had been in touch often over the years, and he quoted Ebeling: "I have a mind to dedicate this Volume to Mr. Jefferson" (though he ultimately did not). Jefferson was feeling effusive when he replied to Bentley, in a letter bitterly decrying Napoleonic despotism and the bloody price Europe had to pay before its ultimate deliverance to "rational government"; for he had long desired to insulate new America from what he saw as Old World depravity. As to the German author, Jefferson showed that he had not forgotten the expansive, seemingly unanswered letter of 1795: "I had many years ago understood that Professor Ebeling was engaged in a geographical work which would comprehend the US. and indeed I expected it was finished and published. I am glad to learn that his candor and discrimination have been sufficient to guard against trusting the likes of Dr. Morse on this state."

He had not forgotten the Ebeling project, indeed, not after twenty years; and he recalled distinctly that he had endeavored to counteract the Federalist prejudice against Virginia that he expected Ebeling to receive from geographer Jedidiah Morse, the target of Jefferson's earlier insult. Knowing that Ebeling had profited from his reading of Jefferson's *Notes on Virginia,* the satisfied Jefferson concluded: "I wish the part of the work which gives the geography of this country may be translated and published, that ourselves and the world may at length have something like a dispassionate account of these states."[20]

In Jefferson's name-calling political script, the only condition more potent and destructive than nerve-induced lethargy was the looming threat of a violent "convulsion," or, events that might spin out of control. He wrote fearfully to George Washington in 1792, with regard to Alexander Hamilton's policies, that "convulsion" would result if the North came to dominate the South economically. Three days before his inauguration in 1801, he wrote to Lafayette about the impact of European strife on America's prospects for domestic peace: "We have passed through an awful scene in this country. The convulsion in Europe shook us even to our centre." His accession to the presidency led him to believe, and to assert, that the Federalist Party, though it might continue to pester, would never again command the power it had in the 1790s. The popular tide had turned against that covetous minority, and fear of political convulsion ceased—at least for a while.

Yet within his own party, Jefferson saw a different kind of convulsion, which he as often called "schism." He became riled over the popular support Aaron Burr attained through his links to hardy, impassioned western Americans, in 1805–1806, when his first-term vice president, now displaced politically, sought to conquer Spanish lands in the Southwest and establish a republic that might be unresponsive to Washington. In the aftermath of Burr's treason trial, Jefferson repeated the language he had used in writing to Lafayette: "The Union itself would have been convulsed to it's center, had that conspiracy succeeded." In medico-political terms, armed conspiracy was a case of nervous agitation that threatened even greater "convulsion."[21]

Jefferson drew his fundamental optimism about America's prospects from an extensive continent, and pessimism from his consideration that divisive or aggressive forces existed and might deter an otherwise bright destiny across that fruitful landscape. In essence counterposing the successful conclusion to the Lewis and Clark expedition against the unsuccessful Burr conspiracy, he wrote: "It seems that the smaller the society the bitterer the dissensions into which it breaks. . . . I believe [our republic] is to owe it's permanence to it's great extent, and the smaller portion comparatively, which can never be convulsed at any time by local passions."[22]

Never be convulsed. America's natural expanse provided a kind of immunity, so that locally generated convulsive episodes could never take over the whole body politic. Nevertheless, dangers loomed that required medico-political intervention: It was not the "languid fibres" of effete, city-bound Federalists, but visionary passions and cunning machinations that might steal a portion of the widely dispersed "Agricultural interest" from Jefferson and thus sicken the republic of felicity.

Looking at Jefferson's political vocabulary during the time of his active years in the federal government, 1790–1809, certain other key words crop up. Beyond the lethargy-convulsion dichotomy, there were two additional, psychologically significant conditions that Jefferson invoked in seeking to explain how opposition principles could possibly attract adherents: They were "intrigue" and "delusions." Both suggested moral perversion, irrationality, imbalance, and disharmony.

In Washington's administration, the emotional aspect of Jefferson's quarrel with Hamilton centered on name calling. Each branded the other an "intriguer," Hamilton in a pseudonymous newspaper attack, Jefferson in an indignant letter to Washington. I am not an intriguer, declared Jefferson outright, using some form of the word three times in the one letter. "No cabals or intrigues of mine have produced those in the legislature," he railed. He also came out against "mysteries," another synonym for intrigue. At his most irritable, Jefferson labeled Hamilton "a tissue of machinations" against the good of his country. And he used the word *perverted* to characterize both Hamilton and Burr, the first "perverted by the British example," the second a "perverted machine." Jefferson held himself blameless, writing before he left the presidency: "I never did them [the Federalists] an act of injustice nor failed in any duty to them imposed by my office."[23]

As he entered that office in 1801, Jefferson had described the recently weath-ered Federalist age as a time of "delusion." The following year, he set forth one of the principles of faith of his "Revolution of 1800" in a letter to Thomas Cooper, whom he admired as a man of great learning and would subsequently go to lengths to attract to the University of Virginia: "As men become better in-formed," he opined, "their rulers must respect them the more. . . . Our citizens are fast returning from the panic into which they were artfully thrown to the dictates of their own reason; and I believe the delusion they have seen them-selves hurried into will be useful as a lesson . . . in the future."[24]

He maintained this vocabulary. As the seemingly purposeless War of 1812 came to an end, Jefferson wrote Lafayette of tendencies in British domestic pol-icy. London, he said, "will not make peace as long as by any delusions they can keep the temper of the nation up to the war point." As Jefferson aged, his faith in the average American's ability to recognize the "delusions" perpetrated by artful anti-republicans at times wavered, though in the majority of his public communications he was loath to admit such fears. He preferred to be known for his optimism.[25]

The "afflicting atrocities" of Politics

It should surprise no one that such a man, possessed of the need to reshape po-litical language, hoped to have an effect on posterity's understanding of his gen-eration. As the Jeffersonian Republicans had triumphed over the Federalists, Jefferson thought it his right to tell the story. But he wanted to commission oth-ers to write it. It would be authoritative if it relied on *his* memory, and *his* per-sonal notes. Yet he repeatedly resisted all appeals that he write it himself.

It is easier for us to comprehend why Jefferson refused to rest than why he believed that monarchy, so thoroughly discredited in America, might be resur-rected. The Federalists were becoming more of a minority in Congress. But as he looked at the composition of the judiciary, he perceived a bitter irony. The Supreme Court's largely conservative members were elected for life, and he imagined that the succeeding generation, if not sufficiently warned, might sim-ply stand by as "consolidated government" (national authority limiting states' rights) led America to "monarchise." "Young men are more easily seduced into this principle," he fretted as the election of 1824 approached, in a letter to Samuel Harrison Smith.

Smith was an old friend whose Washington, D.C., newspaper, the *National Intelligencer*, had demonstrably supported Jefferson during two administra-tions. The ex-president surveyed the political scene. Among the Republicans, many appeared to be asleep. He doubted the wisdom of acting as though harmony existed, when it did not. He recalled 1814, when in Hartford, Connecticut, some diehard Federalists had aired secessionist views. Moderates had called the Hartford Convention, but Jefferson dwelled on the extreme expressions of discontent that had emerged. To Smith he complained: "The federalists, baffled in their schemes to monarchise us, have given up their name, which the Hartford Convention had made odious, and have taken shelter among us under our name. But . . . the same men rally together." These consolidationists needed to be isolated and exposed, he warned.

In the letter to Smith, Jefferson claimed, with false modesty, that he was unqualified to judge the upcoming presidential contest; but he promptly revealed his general suspicion of former Federalist John Quincy Adams and his general comfort with Georgia's William H. Crawford. The turbulent seas provided the metaphor for his tired protest that younger Republicans (perhaps Smith would spread the word?) should take his place in active politicking: "I ought not to quit the port in which I am quietly moored to commit myself again to the stormy ocean of political or party contest, to kindle new enmities, and lose old friends. No, my dear sir, tranquility is the *summum bonum* of old age, and there is a time when it is a duty to leave the government of the world to the existing generation."

Significantly, after Smith wrote back suggesting that he wanted to show Jefferson's letter to sympathetic others, his skittish correspondent forbade it: "Do not for the world, my dear Sir, suffer my letter of Aug. 2. to get before the public, nor to go out of your hands or to be copied. I am always averse to the publication of my letters because I wish to be at rest, retired & unnoticed. But most especially this letter." He might have worried that his apparent insult to the Adams family would spoil his restored friendship with John Quincy's father, or more generally that his identification with Crawford would place him, at the age of eighty, in the political crosshairs, where he had dodged attackers for years. All that Jefferson was comfortable saying publicly came in generic terms, and he said what the interested parties could already assume: that he preferred "a real republican" in the presidential chair. He definitely wanted to inspire; he just wanted his name kept out of the press.[26]

The mood of his letters in retirement shows him keenly aware that his reputation lay at the center of political controversy, and that he would remain for an indeterminate number of years, in some symbolic form, at or near the center of historical argument. Twenty years after the high tide of Federalism had passed, his devastating language reveals the depth of his hatred for the old enemy. He professed in 1818 that the *Anas* was reconstructed as a "calm revisal" of his original rough notes, "when the passions of the times are passed away." But that statement is utterly disingenuous. Federalism lived on in an activist Supreme

Court whose admired and seductive head, Chief Justice John Marshall, despised Thomas Jefferson.

Excusing his recovered Federalist friend Adams, whom he saw as a victim of worse Federalists, Jefferson wrote alliteratively in the introductory section of the *Anas,* before the unvarnished text began: "In the fervor of the fury and follies of those who made him their stalking horse, no man who did not witness it can form an idea of their unbridled madness, and the terrorism with which they surrounded themselves. The horrors of the French revolution, then raging, aided them mainly, and using that as the raw head and bloody bones, they were able . . . to spread alarm in all but the firmest breasts." He used the same tone and similar words in a letter written that same month to Joseph C. Cabell, a trusted member of the younger generation and his chief political coordinator in the drive to win support for the university: "There are fanatics both in religion and politics, who, without knowing me personally, have long been taught to consider me as a raw head and bloody bones."[27] The emotional content of Jefferson's vocabulary—insisting that the Federalists were out for blood—absolutely belied his calm and retiring manner.

Of course, a rational, detached response is not the easiest pose to maintain. Without reconsidering his resolution to stay out of public debate, Jefferson elaborated on his political views, at different moments during his retirement, and to many of his known supporters, as well as to some whose character he knew little about, and he somehow expected word not to get out. This was an important source of anxiety that he could have minimized if he had been more circumspect. But the ex-president, the energetic founder, found it hard to remain completely quiet when an issue arose that he could not but take personally.[28]

To George Logan, a Quaker friend, he wrote quintessentially in the spring of 1816: "As to federal [i.e., Federalist] slanders, I never wished them to be answered, but by the tenor of my life, half a century of which has been on a theatre at which the public has been spectators, and competent judges of it's merit." Expressing his desire to steer clear of further partisan disagreement, Jefferson added: "I should have fancied myself half guilty had I condescended to put pen to paper in refutation of their falsehoods, or drawn to them respect by any notice from myself." He wanted Logan to know—and he would inform many others many times over—of his "repugnance to take part in public discussions."[29] He tried not to worry and not to care; but when he cared, and emoted with pen in hand, he begged not to be quoted. In his experience, whether his opinions were accurately or inaccurately put forth, he generally suffered for the publicity.

In the spring of 1816, he heard from William Short, too, the onetime protégé whom he had instructed in the law in 1780, while wartime governor of Virginia, and who had served as his private secretary in France a few years later. As an intimate during some of the most emotionally trying years of Jefferson's life, when he lost his wife, accepted assignment to France, and finally found overseas an aesthetic kinship and intellectual community to lift his spirits, Short communicated with little self-censoring. Indeed, though their years of active collaboration were far fewer, it is arguable that Short knew Jefferson as well as his political alter ego James Madison did.

"There is one thing that I have long wished to know," Short prodded,

> I mean the writing of your memoirs. It seems to me that when a man has passed a great part of his life in public & important situations, & retires like the gladiator alluded to by Horace; it is clapping the climax, to employ himself for the advantage of his country, during his retirement, to trace over & leave behind him a map of his navigation as a guide to future explorers. It is thus that human knowledge becomes advanced. You have I know a most valuable collection of papers. I do not doubt they will be left in good hands. But be assured that no one can utilize them in the manner that you can.[30]

Jefferson answered Short's letter the day after he returned from Poplar Forest and found it waiting for him.

> You express a wish and a hope that I may have been writing memoirs of myself. While in public life, my whole time has been absorbed by the duties that laid me under; and now, when the world imagines I have nothing to do, I am in a state of heavy drudgery as any office in my life ever subjected me to. From sunrise till noon I am chained to the writing table, at that hour I ride of necessity for health as well as recreation, and even after dinner I must often return to the writing table. . . . It precludes me entirely from the course of studies and reading which would make my hours pass lightly and pleasantly away.

Jefferson went on to describe his stiffened wrist, a condition that Short well knew had arisen in France, when Jefferson vaulted a fence during an outing with Maria Cosway and fractured his writing hand. In retirement, the wrist, because it was not properly set in Paris, gave the famed penman occasional intense pain.

But Jefferson could not entirely avoid providing Short with a proper explanation for why he was not writing his own history for publication. Acknowledging that copies of his letters from crucial years past were available to right-minded commentators in the present who wished to use them, and fully intending that his official papers would eventually "furnish something to the historian," he confessed that he did not want to engage in any writing that marked his reentry into the political arena:

> But you propose a more Quixotic task in the reformation of what may be deemed defective in our constitution. No, my dear friend, nothing could allure me again into the furnace of politics. While engaged in the various functions of government, duty required me to go straight forward, regardless of the enmities and execrations it excited. I felt and deplored them as a man; but scouted them as a public functionary. Still I wished that in retiring from my duties, I might retire also from their afflicting atrocities. To volunteer again into these scenes and sufferings would be to forget what I have undergone, to be insensible of what I feel of the moral and physical decline which the laws of our structure have ordained. I submit to these with entire contentment. Tranquility is the softest pillow for the head of old age.[31]

Remonstration with political life formed the subtext of a majority of Jefferson's letters to friends and family. Here politics was a "furnace" that produced "enmities and execrations" and "afflicting atrocities"—the medical metaphor of "affliction" being, by now, almost automatic. Jefferson never once described politics as an enjoyable profession. In the defining decade of the 1790s, he had complained of "scenes of constant torment, malice and obloquy"; of the temporary national capital in Philadelphia, he protested "the dreariness of this scene, where not a single occurrence is calculated to produce pleasing sensations." (Again, life was felt elementally when "sensations" were invoked.) To Dr. Caspar Wistar, toward the end of his second term as president, he painted affairs of state as a bleak landscape, contrasting "the dry & dreary waste of politics" to "the rich fields of nature" in which he would rather indulge himself.[32]

By invoking for Short his proverbial quest for a time of "tranquility" (now the "softest pillow" for his hoary head), Jefferson closed his practiced argument by pointing to his acceptance of life's end. He professed that he would let history judge his life and political accomplishments: "I leave with satisfaction and confidence to those who are to come after me, the pursuit of what is right, & rectification of what is wrong." There is friendly banter here, but his explanation still sounds a bit too rehearsed. Even to Short, who he could assume would not release their correspondence, Jefferson maintained the pose of the imperturbable Virginia gentleman, and did not tell all.[33]

No matter how many implored him, the answer was always the same. When a grandnephew, the Kentuckian Dabney Carr Terrell, wrote in 1825 requesting that Jefferson go on record with a politically supportive opinion, for local use, the sage of Monticello replied: "I have at different times recieved [sic] many letters from thence making the same request. I have never answered a single one of them to now however. . . . for why, dear Sir, should I, at the age of 82. thrust myself into a controversy which divides a nation?" Slyly, he directed Terrell to the historical record: "If anything I have heretofore written on other questions can be brought to bear on this . . . I can only say with Pilate 'what I have written I have written'[;] all are free to test it's meaning by the common rules of construction. But for me to give further explanations in order to make it applicable to this case would be to take a side in it, which I wish not to do." He returned to a standard refrain, cited above in an 1823 letter to Samuel H. Smith: "At my time of life, tranquility is it's *summum bonum,* the peace and good will of mankind it's nourishment and solace."[34]

With a certain amount of disguise, Jefferson wrote to another regular correspondent, François Adrian Van der Kemp, early in 1825, to say that he had no set plan for the publication of his writings. He claimed, in the vaguest terms, to have retained decades of correspondence merely in order to indulge in "reflections on the things which have been passing. Some of them . . . may give a moment's amusement to a reader, and from the voluminous mass when I am dead, a selection may perhaps be made of a few which may have interest enough to bear a single reading." Allowing for the epistolary style that presented a refined gentleman with less than obvious self-love or self-indulgence, Jefferson is still withholding that information which his correspondent has requested.[35]

There is a rather curious, but rather understandable, inconsistency here. Jefferson frequently declared that he wished to contribute nothing to political controversy. Yet he could not mask his frustration with the way America's political history (especially his role in it) was being presented while he lived. When in 1816 he wrote to fellow Virginian Charles Yancey, "I wish to avoid all collisions of opinion with all mankind," he was being coy. His statement was, at best, wishful thinking.

8

Writing (His Own) History

*Though never captious or petulant, [Jefferson] was sufficiently
prone to resentment for intended injury.*

— GEORGE TUCKER, IN

THE LIFE OF THOMAS JEFFERSON (1837)[1]

Historians had so far disappointed him. The unanswered work of history
that confounded Jefferson most was that which painted him as peevish,
misguided, and disloyal. It was proudly authored by no less a personage than
the sitting chief justice of the Supreme Court, John Marshall. This was the only
history, then completed, that was based upon the unimpeachable writings of
George Washington. It credited the Federalist Party for wise, reasonable, and
even-tempered leadership, rendering it the just inheritor of the American Revolution. It made Jefferson's party grasping and unreasoning.

The thorn Jefferson needed to remove from the historical record, that which
truly demeaned his "Revolution of 1800," was Washington's personal enmity. As
the eighteenth century ended and the nineteenth was about to open, the father
of the country had died. He died hating Jefferson and all he stood for. Jefferson
needed to reclaim Washington, without whom political legitimacy would be
hard to argue. Over and over, as he professed the desire to absent himself from
political controversy, he knew he could not pretend that nothing was wrong. He
could not allow the Federalist view of history to predominate, as it had despite
three successive two-term Republican administrations. How could he simply
rely on posterity—on unnamed future biographers—to use his papers to *his*
best advantage, and consign Federalism, like monarchism, to the dust heap?

The Chief Justice Pierces Jefferson's Skin

John Marshall symbolized "perversion" to Jefferson. First, Hamilton had been
"perverted by the British example," until Burr's well-aimed pistol removed him

as a threat; then Burr had been a "perverted machine," until Jefferson pronounced him a traitor, and he became a political pariah. Now Marshall had perverted history.

It is by examining the threat Marshall posed that we can relate Jefferson's obsessive warnings about Federalists in Republicans' clothing, in the 1820s, to his compulsion to manage the history of the founding generation. At the time he left office in 1809, Jefferson was already stewing about the fifth and final volume of the chief justice's *Life of George Washington*, which was published in 1807. Volume five was the portion that dealt with Washington's last decade, when two distinct political parties formed.

Well before Marshall took up his pen, though, he and Jefferson had begun to record a history of mounting hostility, ever worsening, over the motives each assigned to the other. Almost without conscious intent, they began to needle, until political divisions widened beyond the point where conversation could have relaxed their fixed suspicions. It could have been different. They were both Virginians, Jefferson a dozen years older. Marshall's early school chum was James Monroe, the model Jefferson protégé. The two young men had collected similar experiences while fighting in the Revolution—their paths crossed at Valley Forge—and they continued to maintain respect for one another. Yet they were poles apart in how they stood on the subject of Jefferson's personality and political legacy. Marshall's grandmother was a Randolph, as was Jefferson's mother, so the two were distant cousins. Marshall married the daughter of a woman whom Jefferson had wooed unsuccessfully in the 1760s.

The two statesmen's lives and careers were uncomfortably connected fairly early on, and remained that way throughout Jefferson's lifetime. First, Marshall became an intimate of Patrick Henry, the modestly read but oratorically magnificent courtroom pleader who became Jefferson's political enemy when Jefferson succeeded Henry as governor of Virginia in 1779. Wherever Governor Jefferson turned, it seemed that Henry was trying to undo his initiatives. Marshall and Henry were co-counsel for the defense in a famous case of 1792 concerning adultery, infanticide, and Randolph family honor, in which Jefferson's daughter Martha was called as a prominent witness: The accused woman had sent to her for abortion-inducing medicine.

But it was not until the mid-1790s that Marshall began causing Jefferson real concern. That was when Jefferson's chief tormentor, Hamilton, beseeched John Marshall to convince Patrick Henry to stand for vice president in 1796. They were hoping to produce a Federalist ticket that would bar Jefferson from national office. Marshall did as asked, an ailing Henry refused to run, and Jefferson, without relish, assumed the vice presidency under John Adams. As a state legislator, Marshall seemed to Jefferson to wear a "mask" of republicanism, while adhering, like Hamilton, to "English principles." It was just a matter of time, Jefferson figured, before Virginians would see through the deception. He was wrong. Instead, as Jefferson's relationship with George Washington soured, the national father called Marshall to his Mount Vernon estate and urged his favorite young Federalist to devote himself more visibly to public service. Thus anointed, Marshall saw his career take off, which plainly irritated Jefferson.

In 1798, amid talk of war with France, Marshall traveled to Paris as an envoy of the Adams administration. He appeared to stand up to French insults, and returned home a hero. In Philadelphia, Vice President Jefferson witnessed the triumphal parade, sourly writing to James Madison of the carriages and cavalry, and the immense crowds that had turned out. Promptly elected to Congress, Marshall was not long after tapped for a cabinet position. He served as Adams's last secretary of state. Upon news of Washington's death in December 1799, Marshall delivered a heartfelt eulogy. Then, on the eve of Jefferson's presidency, before a Federalist-dominated Congress yielded to a Republican one, the lame duck President Adams appointed John Marshall chief justice. It was Marshall who swore in Jefferson on March 4, 1801, and who would swear in his successors through Andrew Jackson. He would not retire from the national scene. Short of impeachment, he would never have to.

When Jefferson was inaugurated, in fact, the Supreme Court was made up entirely of Federalists. During Jefferson's two terms, Marshall asserted the constitutional power of the judiciary whenever an opportunity presented itself. Jefferson sought to rein in the political speech of judges: He clashed with the chief justice over the impeachment trial of an outspoken Federalist justice; they clashed again during the Burr conspiracy trial, when Jefferson's first-term vice president was found not guilty as a result of Marshall's restricted definition of treason. Such judicial spectacles only heightened the tension and mutual suspicion. Overall, Marshall considered Jefferson's political temperament unpredictable, his mind subject to wild speculations; and Jefferson considered Marshall's court the hiding place for retrograde monarchists. They saw each other as men of cunning, capable of defrauding the populace in their efforts to secure personal popularity. They held their doubts so strongly that each believed the other was conspiring to humble him at every chance.[2]

As soon as he learned that John Marshall was compiling a history, Jefferson devised a strategy to contest him. Always wishing to avoid the appearance of involvement in a campaign of self-promotion, especially when he held national office, Jefferson attempted to find some persuasive pen, equal to his own, to contest the power of the Federalists in documenting America's political history. In 1802, with James Madison's concurrence, Jefferson turned to the politically friendly poet-diplomat Joel Barlow, then in Paris, for assistance.

Barlow (1754–1812) was a colorful, once widely known figure in the early years of the American republic who has unfortunately been marginalized in most modern narratives of the period. If he is known at all it is as one of the "Connecticut wits" who wrote a pretentious epic poem in 1807, "The Columbiad," now quite hard to digest, which heralded America's rise on the world stage. Born to yeoman farming life in southern New England, Barlow was modestly educated until he found his way to Yale on the eve of the Revolution. The college had the habit of graduating social conservatives, future Federalists, such as Barlow's classmate Noah Webster; but the financially strapped Barlow, navigating the war as a hapless militiaman and later as a chaplain, turned to the law. He sailed off to Europe in 1786, where he imbibed a liberal spirit and befriended the Marquis de Lafayette and the American minister to France, Thomas Jefferson.

Jefferson returned to America in 1789, just after the French Revolution began, but Barlow stayed on to witness the first years of hope, and then endured the subsequent years of the Terror. His wife, Ruth, safe in London, associated with the feminist writer Mary Wollstonecraft as her husband grew in stature as a political activist. He teamed up in Revolutionary Paris with the always-controversial Tom Paine, writing pamphlets, and he narrowly averted imprisonment after Lafayette, and then Paine, were taken away. Like Jefferson, Barlow mourned a republican movement gone awry, and he removed to Hamburg. There he advised the sympathetic Professor Ebeling on the character of American republicanism. As a friend to France, however, he alienated the Connecticut Federalists who had once touted his promise. Still, President Washington thought well enough of Barlow to appoint him to a diplomatic mission to Algiers, as the U.S. negotiator to the piratical Barbary states. He crossed the Mediterranean to northern Africa, and served his country nobly.

As partisan politics heated up in the United States, Joel Barlow anchored himself in France once again, though the country was now beset by capricious government, and eventually yielded to Bonaparte. He planned on writing a history of the French Revolution upon his return to America. But as relations between France and the Adams administration soured, Barlow thought his continued presence in Paris might serve the cause of peace. When John Marshall and a team of Federalists arrived, and misunderstandings enlarged, Barlow kept in touch with Jefferson, conveying his perspective on the exchange of diplomatic insults. After Federalist warmongers were replaced, communications improved, and war fever died down. When Jefferson became president, Barlow again contemplated a return to America. He finally sailed home in 1803, after seventeen years abroad.[3]

In 1802, then, when Jefferson wrote to Barlow concerning John Marshall's forthcoming political history, his administration was ascendant. The "candid federalists," he pronounced, were ready to acknowledge "that their party can never more raise it's head." It was Jefferson's thinking, nonetheless, that there would always be "the division between whig and tory" in one form or another, because human nature dictated it. Elaborating on the imagery of "nervous persons" with "languid fibres" that he had found useful seven years before, he redefined the two parties as the "weakly and nerveless, the rich and the corrupt seeing more safety and accessibility in a strong executive; the healthy, firm and virtuous feeling confidence in their physical and moral resources." The Federalist was perfectly comfortable with monarchical tendencies in government; the Republican, of sound minds and bodies, "willing to part with only so much power as is necessary for their good government."[4]

From here, Jefferson got right to the point. He wanted Barlow to return to Washington, D.C., right away to undertake a crucial mission:

> Mr. Madison and myself have cut out a piece of work for you, which is to write the history of the United States, from the close of the War downwards. We are rich ourselves in materials, and can open all the public archives to you; but your residence here is essential, because a great deal of the knoledge of things is not on paper, but only within ourselves for verbal communication.

Jefferson wanted to write his own political history, using Barlow's pen and Barlow's name. He and Madison would provide firsthand information, and lay out the full narrative they wanted printed. Utter confidentiality was required. Why the urgency of Jefferson's appeal? In 1802, he already knew the meaning of Marshall's having complete and sole access to the papers of George Washington, who was just two and a half years in his grave. Jefferson told Barlow directly:

> John Marshall is writing the Life of Gen. Washington from his papers. It is intended to come out just in time to influence the next presidential election. It is written therefore, principally with the view to electioneering purposes.

Jefferson had his own, very clear-cut purpose. Barlow could be relied on to cast the post-Revolutionary story in Republican relief. If it was meant to be Barlow vs. Marshall, it was also, inevitably, on some level, going to be Jefferson vs. Washington. As Jefferson notably recorded in his *Anas* later on: "We are not to suppose that everything found among Gen. Washington's papers is to be taken as gospel truth."[5]

To Jefferson's dismay, Barlow was not prepared to undertake this massive project, at least not right away; but neither did Marshall's multivolume work appear in time to hurt Jefferson's reelection prospects. Barlow now turned his creative attention to the "Columbiad," which would prove, at length, a critical flop. He did, at least, accept several boxes of historical documents from the president, and he did come to Washington to champion the idea of founding a national university.

Jefferson was more afraid of Marshall than he was of other Federalists, because Marshall was a Virginian. He shared Jefferson's modest appearance, his body language, his informal dress, his ability to identify with a variety of people beyond the well-heeled northern Federalist elite. Marshall was hard to equate with those of "languid nerves" whom Jefferson found so easy to dismiss. In closing his 1802 letter to Barlow with the forceful "Think of this, and agree to it," he had squeezed a P.S. into the bottom left corner of the last page of the letter, promising the poet and would-be historian access to a hilltop residence with "a most extensive view of the Potomac." The property featured fine gardens and thirty to forty acres of surrounding property, which he predicted Barlow could purchase for a song. Barlow did so finally, in 1807, the same year that Marshall's formidable volume five appeared.

That same year, Barlow's epic poem was published. In it, the Republican poet echoed Jefferson's anxiety about the health of political liberty, with this caution: "Think not, my friends, the patriot's task is done, / Or freedom safe, because the battle's won." When his second term as president came to an end in 1809, Jefferson once again sought to interest Barlow in countering the chief justice's work. "I have taken up Marshall's fifth volume," the ex-president wrote to the poet, "and mean to read it carefully, to correct what is wrong in it, and commit to writing such facts and annotations as the reading of that work will bring into my recollection, and which has not yet been put on paper; in this I shall be much aided by my memorandums and letters, and will send you both the old and the new."[6] Appointed by President Madison to a diplomatic mission, Barlow died in Poland in 1812, without having written a history.

What was it in Marshall's history that Jefferson could not leave alone, and that caused him so much concern throughout retirement? Most important, as a jurist, an intimate of Washington's, and a veteran who was well acquainted with the main players of the Revolution, Marshall had enduring credibility. He also presented a plausible argument showing that Jefferson had attempted to steer the government away from the path that Washington had chosen. Writing about the moment in 1795, when Washington resolved not to run for a third term, Marshall observed: "The suspense produced in the public opinion . . . seemed to redouble the efforts of those who laboured to rob him of the affections of the people, and to attach odium to the political system which he had pursued." This low blow made the Jeffersonians seem vicious. Defending Washington's foreign policy, Marshall charged the Republican opposition with an all too instinctive hatred for England and an equally unreasoning love for France. In Marshall's script, the Federalists had devised a more rational approach to international relations. And the Republicans were passionate in their longing to "eradicate" Americans' "love [of] Washington."[7]

After 1815, when he shipped his private library in eleven wagonloads to the Library of Congress, Jefferson gradually replenished his stock at Monticello. But he could not wait even one month before ordering Marshall's five volumes from his preferred Washington, D.C., bookseller, Joseph Milligan.[8] Toward the end of that year, during one of his regular visits to Monticello, Jefferson's nephew Dabney Carr brought up a factual error in the second volume that, for good reason, rankled him. The chief justice accorded Massachusetts full credit for having conceived committees of correspondence, which had aided communication among the colonial legislatures in 1773, and had doubtless brought the Revolution closer. But it was Jefferson's clear recollection that Virginia and Massachusetts had each "acted about the same time" to form the committees, and moreover, that it was Dabney Carr (father of the present instigator) who had introduced the bold resolution in the Virginia Assembly.

The elder Carr, the husband of Jefferson's younger sister, was also Jefferson's best friend. His career had been cut short when he contracted a fever and died shortly after his debut in the legislature. He was the first to be interred in the Monticello cemetery, and the education of his three sons—Peter, Samuel, and Dabney—was carefully monitored by their soon-to-be-famous uncle. (Peter and Samuel, of course, would eventually assume roles in the modern Jefferson-Hemings controversy.)

The youngest of the Carr boys felt little hesitation about pursuing the matter of the committees of correspondence, because family honor was at stake, as much as getting history right. So Dabney wrote a letter to his uncle Jefferson in December 1815 to remind him of his promise to consult documents and draft a reliable corrective to Marshall's statement. Unlike the ex-president, who had failed with Barlow, Dabney Carr knew precisely what vehicle to use to see Marshall's history repaired, at least on this one point: His own best friend, the attorney William Wirt, another Jefferson protégé, was nearing completion of his much-awaited biography of Patrick Henry, who, along with Dabney Carr senior and Jefferson, was a member of the Virginia committee of correspondence. Carr would have Wirt insert in the text, above a long explanatory footnote, the reconstructed episode. To do so made perfect sense: In the nineteenth century, historical controversies were often fought out in footnotes.

Wirt complied. He accepted Jefferson's revisions from Carr and faithfully called attention to the ingenuity of Carr's father back in 1773, while pointing to

the late Revolutionary's estimable character—"spotless integrity, sound judgment, handsome imagination, enriched by education and reading"—words
adapted from Jefferson's tribute to him. "We ought not to suffer the Old Dominion to be robbed of her fame, & made to follow in the wake of Massachusetts," wrote the son, aggressively. When Wirt's *Life of Patrick Henry* went to
press in 1817, a lively public argument between stalwart New Englanders and
Virginia revisionists ensued, all because of the Jefferson-Carr retelling.[9]

But it was not Marshall's volume two so much as volume five that pierced
Jefferson's thin political skin. With Barlow gone and no one else to take up his
cause in a competitive format, Jefferson, in 1818, countered Marshall's claim to
Washington's spirit in his own way when he fashioned his introduction to the
Anas. He had collected and maintained notes on a series of combustible conversations within the Washington administration, and now he patched them all
together in three notebooks. There can be no doubt that he expected someone
to draw upon his raw history as religiously as he did.

But how to reclaim Washington, after the job Marshall had done? Jefferson's
explanation for the incontrovertible fact that Washington in the end had grown
personally to despise him was that Washington was senile, or, as Jefferson put it,
he had lost "the firm tone of mind for which he had been remarkable." Jefferson
used the word *firm* to praise Republicans for their fortitude, just as he associated
Federalists with the qualitative opposite, "languid fibres." Thus, when his mind
"was beginning to relax," President Washington allowed the High Federalists to
manipulate him. As their tool, he abandoned his firm republicanism, but only
half-consciously. His heart had remained uncorrupted. The last sentence of Jefferson's introduction to the *Anas* mourns Washington's "mortal decay."

As a historian, Jefferson was himself a skillful manipulator. When he wanted
to, he made his political enemies into brainwashing goons. In a remarkable letter of 1823, wishing for the day when someone other than "the high priests of
Federalism" would be granted access to Washington's papers, he complained
that, under existing circumstances, "Caesar's notes and memorandums [were]
in the hands of Anthony." He vowed that history would see a less selective use
of texts and so reckon with the true Washington; indeed, posterity would know
the first president as a "candid . . . friend to truth" and, when it mattered most,
a Republican.[10] In reading Jefferson, we are meant to understand that Washington was stolen from the American people for at least the last four years of his
life, when "a desire for tranquility [implying reduced mental energy] had crept
up on him."

To accept Jefferson's reconstruction of the 1790s, from the perspective of
1818 or 1823, one would have to have agreed with five highly ideological statements: (1) that Hamilton was "not only a monarchist, but for a monarchy bot-

tomed on corruption"; (2) that Adams was a Republican who came to be fascinated with "the glare of royalty and nobility"; (3) that Washington lost his ability to resist the monarchists' argument shortly after Jefferson resigned from the cabinet in early 1794; (4) that Marshall used Washington's papers "for the suicide of the cause" of republicanism that Washington, in his prime, subscribed to; and (5) that Jefferson himself symbolized "the steady and rational character of the American people" and their just hopes for self-government.[11]

These were the battle lines of history, for as long as Jefferson survived. To him, Washington's age (mid-sixties) and mental relaxedness had caused the father of the country to turn his back on his natural constituency, the Republican majority. In the mind of Chief Justice Marshall, meanwhile, Jefferson had used tricks of his own to usurp the federal government when he vilified Federalist efforts—Washington's efforts—to achieve political stability and general economic strength.

In linguistic terms, Jefferson and Marshall had taken up incongruent definitions of the word *firmness,* and that made all the difference in their politics. In his volume five, Marshall described Washington as firm in his philosophy, indicating that his principles never changed, even at the end, when Marshall knew him best. "No man ever appeared upon the theatre of public action," the chief justice wrote, "whose integrity was more incorruptible, or whose principles were more perfectly free from the contamination of those selfish or unworthy passions which find their nourishment in the conflicts of party. Having no views which required concealment, his real and avowed motives were the same." To Marshall, Washington had governed with—to use a twenty-first-century term—transparency. It was Jefferson and his party operatives who had intruded upon the steady, solid planning of Washington, and who had sought change that was decidedly uncomfortable to Washington. It was the Jeffersonians whose motives were suspect. Washington's means were "always pure," but the Republicans' were otherwise: "If Washington possessed ambition, that passion was, in his bosom, so regulated by principles . . . that it was neither vicious nor turbulent." What Jefferson had in mind for the nation was, by implication, turbulent.[12]

In his characterization of the Hamilton-Jefferson feud, Marshall feigned objectivity, equalizing the two men's "irreconcilable hostility." But he portrayed Hamilton as sharp, alert to dangers, a man who reasoned that government "should possess in itself sufficient powers and resources to maintain the character, and defend the integrity of the nation." As Federalists, and fearing that local prejudices threatened the growth of a national identity, Hamilton and Marshall were "particularly apprehensive" about the Jeffersonians' favorite topic of states' rights.

The chief justice judged that Jefferson had been influenced by his years in a liberalizing France, just prior to its bloody revolution, and was keenly fixated on "the abuses of monarchy which were perpetually in his view, and he might be led to the opinion that liberty could sustain no danger but from the executive power." Washington had sought to reconcile his two talented cabinet secretaries; but after "earnest endeavours to sooth the angry passions," the president finally admitted that he could not succeed.[13]

This was not how Jefferson wished to see his personal style or political thinking handed to posterity. In binding his *Anas,* he insisted that its contents, these "scraps . . . rugged, rubbed, and scribbled," were genuine artifacts of history, told with "candor," and utterly reliable. Jefferson explains that he had these notes joined together "by a binder . . . doing it under my own eye, and without the opportunity of reading a single paper"—thus, in secrecy—but he does not perceive that his method suggests an obsession. Writing, at the end of the transcription of a conversation with Hamilton, "Th: Jefferson has committed [the foregoing] to writing in the moment of A. Hamilton's leaving the room," Jefferson times and dates his "truth" to let us know just how conscious he is of its historic import. He wants no doubt as to the authenticity of his transcription, no matter how much time passes. There is certainly more to the *Anas* than the "calm revisal" of the past that Jefferson claims.[14]

He wants posterity to believe that only Marshall's effort to twist the truth is "artful." He mocks the chief justice for trying to minimize the democratically inspired spirit behind the American Revolution and for propping up only the undeserving members of a rather exclusive political party, whose leaders, in fact, did far less in the Revolution than Marshall states. When it comes to the real heroes of the war, Marshall is stingy in his praise. Writes Jefferson: "The sufferings inflicted on endeavors to vindicate the rights of humanity are related with all the frigid insensibility with which a monk would have contemplated the victims of an Auto da fe!"[15] The language, again, is revealing: In his momentous 1786 "Head and Heart" letter to Maria Cosway, the "frigid speculations" of a monk symbolized the failure to engage generously with "spasms of the heart"; here, Jefferson invokes the insensible monk (impervious to heartfelt sensation) to brand the chief justice as one who would stand by, devoid of feeling, as judgment of death is passed on a heretic. Insensibility to the Revolutionary republican spirit is as damning an indictment as exists in Jefferson's vocabulary.

Carrying forward his argument, Jefferson asserts that Washington never looked favorably upon monarchy and even "frowned indignantly at the proposition." Then, in the same language he would use until the end of his days, Jefferson straightforwardly identified "the real difference" between the parties as "their different degrees of inclination to monarchy or republicanism. The Federalists wished for every thing which would approach our new government to monarchy: the republicans to preserve it essentially republican. This was the true origin of the division, and remains still the essential principle of difference between the two parties."[16] Later in the *Anas,* exploiting every opportunity to call attention to the Federalists' betrayal of the Revolution and their effort to sway President Washington, Jefferson jots down a conversation with Washington's private secretary, Tobias Lear:

> Conversation with Lear. He expressed the strongest confidence that republicanism was the universal creed of America, except of a very few . . . said that he had seen with extreme regret that a number of gentlemen had for a long time been endeavoring to instil into the President, that the noise against the administration of the government was that of a little faction, which would soon be silent, and which was detested by the people, who were contented and prosperous.[17]

In Jefferson's rendition, the witless king, separated from his people by the machinations of a few conspiring ministers, was being lied to, and led to believe that the thoughtful Republicans were actually the ones out of touch with the popular will. The *Anas* is a moral tale on the order of *King Lear,* replete with irony: Washington's good and bad children clamor for attention, and the deserving child, Jefferson, is his Cordelia.

In Jefferson's view of the 1790s, because Washington was duped, perversity reigned. The "Revolution of 1800" had reinvigorated the republic, yet Marshall's version of events still prevailed. After the death of Joel Barlow in 1812, Jefferson began to drop hints when trustworthy Republicans wrote supportively, that is, when old allies held out the prospect of assisting in translating Jefferson's memoranda into a volume that would supplant Marshall's. John Adams, too, shook his head in disbelief at Marshall's effort to confer sainthood on Washington, whom he knew to be a man with as many mediocre as impressive qualities. But for Jefferson, of course, recasting Marshall's history meant far more.

In 1814, Jefferson thought he might have another chance to right wrongs. That year, a former congressman from Virginia, Walter Jones, asked him for material to help him complete a character sketch of George Washington. Professing a desire to have the history of their times put in "dispassionate" language, Jefferson sounded out Jones on the idea of writing the proper history that Barlow had declined. Jones's Washington would be a Republican, just as Jefferson claimed. Intent on leading Jones to the larger project, Jefferson provided him with a character sketch of Washington; he later added one sentence to it, a sentence of little apparent consequence, but so important in Jefferson's consideration that he wanted Jones to glue it in just where Jefferson indicated it belonged. But after all that effort, Jones made it clear that Jefferson had overinterpreted: He was hoping merely for Jefferson to write his own memoir, and had not meant to suggest that he was inclined to undertake the massive project Jefferson had in mind.[18] And why could Jefferson not see this? Because he passionately believed that his essential truth, well told, would be irresistible to students of America's political tradition; and so, he could scarcely stop himself from pressing on until he had found a willing penman. It had to be one of his political generation, whom he could entrust with his personal records and his well formed reflections and recollections. Barlow would have been perfect. Who of the appropriate stature could he now call upon? He would keep looking.

The entire episode of Jefferson and Marshall has a remarkable literary parallel, if one chooses to see it: In William Godwin's *Caleb Williams,* the title character composes a long and winding narrative that explains and justifies his taking on the powerful Squire Falkland; he constructs his dark memoir because he knows it is the only countertext strong enough—morally sound enough—to bring about the surrender of his prominent accuser. "These papers shall preserve the truth," Caleb avows. "They shall one day be published, and then the world shall do justice on us both. . . . This Falkland [read: Marshall] has invented against me every species of foul accusation. . . . In vain! With this engine, this little pen I defeat all his machinations." At his emotional low point, Caleb seethes: "Didst thou imagine that I was altogether passive, a mere worm, organized to feel sensations of pain, but no emotion of resentment?" One literary critic who focuses on the main character's resentments even sees Caleb from the view of eighteenth-century medical thinking: a man whose nerves have been damaged by his obsession with Falkland's lies about him. As a story about sincerity, vulnerability, the uneasy mind—and obsession—*Caleb Williams* speaks to the personal politics of Thomas Jefferson. This is not to say that Jefferson expected Marshall to admit error, as Falkland did (and notably, in the courtroom). As always, Jefferson's concern lay with the court of public opinion.[19]

Henry Lee's Tissue of Errors

It was not just Marshall. From the time Professor Ebeling set out to write about America's political geography, Jefferson was bothered by his enemies' undiminished authority over the construction and interpretation of political tradition. This extended to their alleged misrepresentation of his personal behavior. In his last years, he made an extraordinary effort to convince the South Carolinian he had named to the Supreme Court, William Johnson, to write an authoritative history of Jeffersonian Republicanism. (Who better than Marshall's colleague on the high court to answer Marshall?) And, as we shall see later, almost with his final breaths, Jefferson sought to convince the son of a Revolutionary War general to undo his father's reproachful historical account of Jefferson's unproductive wartime governorship. Jefferson's behavior in these cases provides irrefutable evidence of his passion to see history done "right"—if not in his own lifetime, then to have some assurance that the job would be done not long after his death.

As the 1802 Callender columns attest, President Jefferson was regularly pursued by allegations about past personal conduct. But, whatever he thought of the Sally Hemings stories (for he did not respond to his accusers), he was openly disturbed by the persistent charge that he was a coward for having fled a British detachment bent on capturing him, near the end of his term as Virginia's governor, in 1780. When the harried state legislature, after itself disbanding, met again once the threat had subsided somewhat, outgoing Governor Jefferson was called to account for his conduct, and was charged with dereliction of duty. A special committee concluded that the charges were baseless, and Jefferson was given his due: A formal resolution called his administration "impartial, upright, and attentive," and left his personal "ability, rectitude and integrity" unchallenged. The rumors dissolved, but they would regenerate over the years whenever partisans looked for new means to attack the popular politician. No impartial investigator would ever call Jefferson a great governor, but it seems equally clear that his bad press was a result of the political infighting that went on amid glory-seeking in a time of war.[20]

The memoirs of Henry ("Light-Horse Harry") Lee, the Revolutionary War general, were published in 1812, and they plainly sought to discredit Jefferson. Lee was a Virginian, educated, as was James Madison, at Princeton before the war, who served with distinction under General Nathanael Greene, and was a favorite of George Washington's. After taking his turn as Virginia's governor in the early 1790s, this Federalist went bankrupt owing to bad land investments and spendthrift ways. He wrote his history of the war largely from his cell, during 1809–1810, as Jefferson began his retirement.

Questions of accuracy aside, Harry Lee produced a very readable book. He had an energetic writing style. In the third person, he told of the battles and events in which he took part. According himself credit for having "completely baffled" Britain's General Sir Henry Clinton in Charleston, in 1776, Lee narrated the March 1781 Battle of Guilford Courthouse to chivalrous effect: "The night succeeding this day of blood was rainy, dark, and cold; the dead unburied, the wounded unsheltered, the groans of the dying and the shrieks of the living, cast a deeper shade over the gloom of nature." He professed humane concerns and wrote with a knowing confidence: "The campaign so far presents the un-dulation common to war." He dispensed patriotic advice, and assured readers of the improvements brought by the Continental Army to the ravaged South. The victory of his force "bestowed the solace of inward satisfaction on our re-view of the past." There was more than a little self-congratulation.[21]

Lee did not, however, confine himself to what he had seen with his own eyes. He embellished in similarly rich language a series of wartime occurrences from which he was hundreds of miles distant, only to exclaim: "What must posterity think of their ancestors, when they read these truths!" Lee's patriotic zeal was magnificent, and so volatile (in print) as to seem nearly combustible. The prob-lem with his memoir, as one might expect, is that Lee himself comes off as dar-ing and decisive, ingenious and inventive, and larger than his commander.[22]

Much as Jefferson was frustrated when Washington's private papers were turned over to Marshall, he could not have been pleased by the acclaim Light-Horse Harry received in 1800, when he eulogized Washington in memorable words: "First in war, first in peace, and first in the hearts of his countrymen." Moreover, Lee had already proved that he had an axe to grind with Jefferson: As a congressman, he had sought to stop Jefferson's election in early 1801 by ele-vating Aaron Burr to the top station. He was no less severe in preparing his book, though Jefferson had just retired to Monticello, where he sought refuge from politics. Lee cunningly portrayed Benedict Arnold's 1780–1781 invasion of Virginia in such a way as to demonstrate Governor Jefferson's culpability and incapacity alike. Arnold had entered the state capital of Richmond with nine hundred men, "untouched," and Jefferson was "driven out of its metropolis." The enemy ranged across the heartland, as Jefferson ran. With Jefferson in charge, Lee infers, "What chance then could exist of stopping Cornwallis by any intermediate force from the country?"[23] Next, Lord Cornwallis's most relied upon associate, the reputedly bloodthirsty Lieutenant Colonel Banastre Tar-leton, led an expedition into Charlottesville, and sent a detachment up Monti-cello's mountain to bring back the governor in handcuffs. But Jefferson had made off, just in time.

Lee's Federalist bias was evident as well in his celebration of Jefferson's most noteworthy political foe. Early in the war, Lee had fought alongside Washing-ton's young aide Alexander Hamilton, whom he went out of his way to make heroic:

> Lieutenant-Colonel Hamilton took possession of a flat-bottomed boat for the purpose of transporting himself and his comrades across the river, should the sudden approach of the enemy render such a retreat necessary. In a little time this precaution manifested his sagacity. . . . Hamilton was committed to the

flood, struggling against a violent current, increased by the recent rains; while Lee put his safety on the speed and soundness of his horse.

In 1781, Hamilton's pride temporarily estranged him from Washington's "family," but at the decisive Battle of Yorktown, "Hamilton, always true to the feelings of honor and independence," stood up, even to "beloved" Washington, and earned himself a lead role in the attack. He rushed forward, "with impetuosity," and helped oust the British. In the same season that the cowardly Jefferson was avoiding the action, his rival was conducting himself gallantly. So, in any event, says Lee's news-making 1812 memoir.[24]

This was how history was being presented—through a Federalist prism. Around the same time as Lee's two-volume work appeared, the Frenchman Louis Girardin moved into Jefferson's neighborhood and began teaching school. He wished to write the final volume of a history of Virginia whose author had died, and he found an eager ally in the squire of Monticello. Jefferson subtly directed Girardin to texts that countered Lee's interpretation. Afterward, Jefferson read over Girardin's manuscript and made suggestions.

Jefferson's personal notes on his behavior as governor became an appendix to the volume. Girardin wrote: "It was Mr. Jefferson's fortune to fill the office of Governor of Virginia, during the most perilous and disastrous period of the revolutionary war. . . . the State was almost disarmed, by the troops it had furnished to the North and to the South." Jefferson, under the circumstances, had done the best job anyone could, acting with dispatch and proper expedience. Yet, Virginia's distressed situation caused passionate people to seek a more militant, dictatorial governor (unnamed by Girardin, but meaning Patrick Henry). Thus, for a time, "the misfortunes of the period were ascribed to" Governor Jefferson, who fell under an "absurd" censure in the Assembly. Later, when the Assembly reconvened and Jefferson was present, his name was completely cleared: "Not a word of censure was whispered," wrote Girardin, "and the impeachment was no more heard of, until revived for the purpose of party and calumny." After the book's 1816 publication, Jefferson took little credit for its contents, but frequently directed his correspondents to Girardin as an infallible source on Virginia from the start of the war through Yorktown.[25]

Also in the mid-1810s, the Philadelphia publisher Joseph Delaplaine embarked on his multivolume biography of the founders, *Repository of the Lives and Portraits of Distinguished Americans.*[26] He wrote to Jefferson frequently over the next several years for information about him and others who had figured in the rising glory of the American republic. In an effort to resist the publicity that Delaplaine's efforts would invariably produce, Jefferson maintained a retiring pose in his replies; but when Delaplaine pressed for reliable material on

Jefferson's role as governor during the Revolution, Jefferson eventually sent him copies of the documents Girardin had seen, papers clearly meant to prove his detractors wrong. These included a 1781 letter to General Washington documenting the British invasion and assailing "the parricide Arnold," which revealed Jefferson's committed effort to contend with the enemy. Extracts from Jefferson's diary at the time showed that he closely followed military matters, assessed threats, and moved to and fro without undue concern for his own safety. He compared what he was doing with what the legislature was doing. And when members of the legislative body questioned his competence, Jefferson answered with irresistible explanations.

Finally, in his extended letter to Delaplaine, Jefferson turned the tables on Henry Lee: "And here it is but proper to notice the parody of these transactions which Genl Lee has given as their history. He was in a distant state at the time, and seems to have made up a random account from the rumors which were afloat where he then was. It is a tissue of errors from beginning to end."

Did Jefferson run when Tarleton approached Monticello?

> The nonsense which has been uttered . . . is really so ridiculous, that it is almost ridiculous seriously to notice it. . . . I ordered a carriage to be used to carry off my family; we breakfasted at leisure with our guests. . . . when a neighbor rode up full speed to inform me that a troop of horse was then ascending the hill to the house, I instantly sent off my family, and, after a short delay for some pressing arrangements, I mounted my horse, and knowing that in the public road I should be liable to fall in with the enemy, I went thro' the woods, and joined my family at the house of a friend where we dined. Would it be believed, were it not known, that this flight from a troop of horse . . . has been the subject, with party [i.e., partisan] writers, of volumes of reproach on me, serious or sarcastic: that it has been sung in verse and said in humble prose that, forgetting the noble example of the hero of La Mancha, and his windmills, I declined a combat, singly against a troop, in which action would have been so glorious? . . . These closet heroes forsooth would have disdained the shelter of a wood, even singly and unarmed, against a legion of armed enemies.

Jefferson's prose is disarming as he cuts Lee to shreds. Providing further testimony of his lack of fear—an 1805 letter from one Virginian to another, asserting that throughout the invasion Jefferson did all he could, and fearlessly— Jefferson proved that he had no reason to flee the history of Henry Lee. Indeed, he faced it down, and decried it as "romance" rather than history. In his cover letter to Delaplaine, he assured the publisher: "I now enclose [the requested documentation], detailed with an exactness on which you may rely, with entire confidence." Exactness, as well as certainty, marked Jefferson's stern self-defense. When in 1817 Delaplaine sent out the volume containing Jefferson's biographical sketch, the subject thanked the publisher—"I find the style and execution entirely good"—and then listed the seven substantive errors he nevertheless had discovered in the text.[27]

Courage and cowardice are not fixed attributes. If he had been cowardly by nature, Jefferson would have exited politics early. It is true, however, that he relied heavily on political allies to dish out dirt, or to answer attacks. He was extremely uncomfortable with confrontational situations that exacerbated personal conflict, and he called dueling "barbaric." If he wanted something done, he spoke quietly or wrote confidentially. When his temperamental son-in-law, Thomas Mann Randolph, openly doubted Jefferson's feelings toward him, Jefferson "adopted the wise plan of seeming ignorance," as granddaughter and witness Ellen put it, maintaining "his unalterable calm," to avoid unfriendly discussions.[28] He adopted a similar tactic in face-to-face politics.

He did not take up arms. He was not a soldier. Jefferson in his mid-retirement years gave his credentials as a man of peace, an advocate of international "friendship and commerce" who believed that Americans were superior to Europeans because they lacked an impulse, centuries-old, to favor war. At the close of Napoleon's time in power, he used wit as well as logic to analyze the human condition: "The world will remain after 25 years of war, and half as many millions of human beings destroyed, pretty much as it was, with only here & there a change of A. for B. as master."[29]

To pursue peace at the expense of being thought cowardly is something other than cowardice. Jefferson implicitly divided men into three essential categories: those like himself who were not fit to fight, those who imagined they were, and those who adapted to soldiering. Referring to the largely unproductive War of 1812, he said: "Our short war was, in it's beginning, unpropitious, from the want of able & faithful officers. The 2d year however began to bring forward those characters which nature had moulded for military purposes, & the tide began with them to turn in our favor." He well knew that he was not one of "those characters" molded for the military.[30]

His temperamental opposite, Alexander Hamilton, who eventually rose to the rank of general, had suggested that Jefferson lacked something masculine when he refused to face the Federalists' principled challenge directly and instead acted stealthily through intrigue and deception. Hamilton even referred to the unmartial pair of Jefferson and Madison as "womanish" in their foreign policy preferences.[31] But Jefferson, at that time, was embittered enough to belittle Hamilton's reputation for courage, telling Madison during the 1793 yellow fever epidemic in Philadelphia that Hamilton was afraid: The New Yorker's machismo did not impress him, and, indeed, Hamilton was not even a competent horseman—at that time a symbol of martial vigor. "A man as timid as he is on the water, as timid on horseback, as timid in sickness, would be a phaenomenon if the courage of which he has the reputation in military occasions were genuine," wrote Jefferson.[32]

Finding a way around danger did not automatically make Jefferson a coward, nor did the methods he used in building a political consensus necessarily make him deceitful. Perhaps he was just a subtler strategist. "When capable, feign incapacity," advised the ancient Chinese military theorist Sun Tzu, with universal application. Relying on aides deflected some of the enemy's barbs and freed Jefferson from wrangling in the newspapers.

When in the final two years of his presidency he acted to embargo all foreign trade, he was not being cowardly. It could be said, whether one approved or disapproved his method, that the embargo was an act of courage, for he invited economic discomfort, even scarcity, knowing he would be blamed for it. His act was meant to test Americans' virtue, in the language of the time. If cowardice springs from fear, uncertainty, a sense of gloom, or anticipation of impending doom, Jefferson was certainly no coward. Indeed, he was a strong-minded executive.

Panic was not in Jefferson's nature, either, as far as we know. He deliberately built, researched, and wrote for public consumption. He was results-oriented. As the head of a party, he incurred a certain amount of risk in pursuing the moral collapse of his adversaries to realize his vision of how the world should be. His was not a rash kind of courage, such as that a charging trooper exhibited in battle. Perhaps it is best termed "craft."

Society tends to define actions in bipolar terms, in this case hero versus coward. It suggests consistency, when in real life few people are entirely consistent. But to be labeled a "coward," even on the strength of one episode over the course of a long life, is a highly threatening prospect. Jefferson felt he had been put in the position of having to explain himself. In the end, what we can know about Jefferson's actions in 1781 is anecdotal and unreliable. Though it does appear in this instance that he behaved prudently, the interesting thing, once again, is not whether Jefferson's version is wholly or partially correct, or wholly or partially wrong, but that Jefferson—without ever admitting it—was prepared to go to lengths to modify the historical record in his favor.[33]

Urging Justice Johnson

In 1822, the year after Jefferson wrote his not-for-self-publication unfinished autobiography, Associate Justice William Johnson authored a large two-volume biography of the Revolutionary War general Nathanael Greene, a Rhode Island Quaker who had acknowledged the necessity of war and saved the South from being overrun. Greene was Henry Lee's commander, and in fact Lee wrote of Greene's "vivid, plastic genius," and called him a man of "vigilance and penetration," a "hero." However, in Lee's rendition of the war, Greene's combination of prudence and resolve is obscured by Lee's own heroism.

Justice Johnson's work, dedicated to "the Venerable Survivors of the Revolution," was based on original materials made available to him by Greene's family in an effort to rescue a reputation sullied by the general's detractors—more or less the same state of affairs Jefferson was unwilling to submit to in the twilight of his own career. "I am not ambitious of the fame of a writer," Johnson wrote in his preface. "I would rather serve mankind by an useful compilation, than fascinate them by the charms of fine writing." Was this a cut at Lee? It was certainly a Jeffersonian bow to moral responsibility. Even if he was risking the wrath of his "most valued friends" by embracing historical controversy, Johnson proclaimed that he was prepared to set the record straight.[34]

When Jefferson received his copy of the Greene biography, he read it "with the greatest satisfaction." It lifted his spirits to encounter at long last "a fair history of the Southern war," one that made it possible "to see the Romance of Lee removed from the shelf of History to that of Fable." In Justice Johnson, Thomas Jefferson had found a man who embraced his pertinacious style of vengeance through historiography.[35]

Johnson countered those who alleged that Greene was a man of "dangerous ambition"—the very charge that the Federalists leveled against the outwardly passive Jefferson. He characterized Greene's pursuit of health and moderation: "Although General Greene never relinquished his early habits of temperance—never indulging himself in more than one full meal, he always retained his full muscular form, and that robust health which indicated a full compliance with the demands of nature." Like Jefferson, Greene was "never known to be, for a moment, thrown off the most absolute equilibrium. . . . In his tent, or in private society, his intercourse with [friends and officers] was on the easiest footing."[36]

Johnson thus fashioned a hard-hitting exposé of recent history. He concluded his biography with a fetching appeal, likening Greene's Quaker spirit to the "political religion of the United States."[37] Though Greene had in fact abandoned the Society of Friends, it did not matter: This was the benevolence Jefferson claimed for his party, and he needed a pen other than his own that was capable of dashing off the emotional strokes he had earned fame for—but felt he could not employ directly, self-servingly, anymore.

And so he asked the jurist-biographer just where he stood: "What do you think of the state of parties at this time?" Tipping his hand, Jefferson prodded:

"An opinion prevails that there is no longer any distinction, that the republicans & Federalists are compleatly amalgamated but it is not so. The amalgamation is of name only, not of principles. . . . [M]onarchy is a desperate wish in this country." He predicted that "the old Federalists" would fail, no matter their disguise under the name "Republicans," and that "the friends of the real constitution and union will prevail against consolidation, as they have done against monarchism." He closed, "I have . . . committed to you thoughts which I would do to few others."[38]

Jefferson was encouraged when the judge honored him with a twenty-one-page letter. William Johnson, it turned out, was just as indignant as he was about the Federalists' resurgence. "The whole Remains of the Federal party is up in Arms against me," Johnson railed. As for writing "the History of Parties," though, he required convincing. "But what Inducement, my dear Sir, can I have to proceed with that undertaking?" The hostile reviews of his Greene biography and unpleasant dealings with publishers and booksellers combined to make him skittish about trying a political subject again. Besides, he noted, word had it that the retired James Madison was to attempt such a work—the only person other than Jefferson whom Johnson considered worthy of the task.

But Madison was not going to write the antidote to Marshall. And so Justice Johnson (like William Short, like Walter Jones) pressed Jefferson to fill the gap: "I regret exceedingly that it has not occupied your Hours of Retirement hitherto, for believe me, we have been all looking up to you for the Vindication of the Purity of our Intentions & Patriotism of our Efforts. . . . We have hoped for a rich Legacy of History from your Pen." He had heard that Jefferson kept a "Journal from the earliest Time of your public Service," as of course Jefferson had. "If so, pray bequeath it to some Friend who will fearlessly do Justice to the Part you have acted, and vindicate us along with you, from the foul Imputations which have already passed into History against us." Johnson had perfectly mimicked the plea inside Jefferson's own head. The problem was, simply put, that Jefferson could find no one to perform this critical task. And who better suited than Justice Johnson to go after Chief Justice Marshall?

He must have read Johnson's aggravated harangue with repeated nods of concurrence. How can it be, the justice brooded, that "we have never turned our Thoughts to the Opinions of Posterity." As his letter raced on, he perceived a larger threat to America's union in the weakening of southern republicanism, and for this he recommended a judicial solution: that the Supreme Court be equally constituted of representatives from the various sections. In the end, it appeared to him that Jefferson's nation-expanding Louisiana Purchase had prevented the powerful Northeast from "establishing a general Monarchy." Justice Johnson made it perfectly plain that he was afraid of the Federalists, for, like Jefferson, he reckoned that they had merely abandoned their name—not their consolidationist agenda.

Jefferson read and absorbed the letter, and wrote to Justice Johnson again a few months later with renewed purpose. "Do not fear therefore these insects," Jefferson wrote, censuring the book reviewers who had frightened Johnson away from undertaking another political work. He was softening up the justice for another attempt at convincing him to weigh in against Marshall's five volumes: "What you write will be far above their grovelling sphere." Jefferson went on to remind the South Carolina Republican of the larger object, and what was at stake: "Let me then implore you, dear Sir, to finish your history of parties. . . . We have been too careless of our future reputation; while our tories will omit nothing to place us in the wrong." Building his argument, Jefferson clarified that former President Madison would leave behind "only particular passages of our history." Hinting at his own record keeping, he added: "My letters (all preserved) will furnish the daily occurrences and views from my return from Europe in 1790. till I retired finally from office."

From this point, Jefferson held back nothing. He made clear that he thought a chronicle of his letters and other papers would not only display his convictions, but also tell historical truth and do the country good. It could not wait for future biographers—it had to be begun right away. Here is how he finally made his case: "No day has passed without a letter to somebody. Written in the moment, and in the warmth and freshness of fact and feeling they will carry internal evidence that what they breathe is genuine. Selections from these after my death, may come out successively as the maturity of circumstances may render their appearance seasonable. But multiplied testimony, multiplied views will be necessary to give solid establishment to truth."

He had prepared the means for posterity to receive, in "seasonable" installments, the story of his political life—that is, in such a way as his family and the executors of his will decided on, so as to protect his reputation. Anything deemed shocking, or too radical, would wait until the country was ready for it. But that did not obviate the need for a book from Justice Johnson; it was crucial for there to be "multiplied testimony" on Jefferson's behalf, if his legacy was to be secured.[39]

Furthermore, it had come to Jefferson's attention in early 1823 that a new, hagiographic Hamilton biography was in the hands of one who represented both "the bitterness of the priest" and "the rancour of the fiercest federalism." Marshall's "five volumed libel" would then have this reinforcement.[40] Time was of the essence. And yet, when in 1824 a Philadelphia newspaper editor, Stephen Simpson, proposed collaboration on a political biography, Jefferson cut the conversation short: "I have uniformly declined any participation in the history of my self," he wrote definitively. This was because he did not really know Simpson, and could not entrust so critical a project to him. Only someone of Johnson's rank and record would do.[41]

Jefferson did not get what he most wanted to see in his final years. Justice William Johnson was to remain on the High Court until 1834, yet the South Carolinian did not consent to supply his Virginia patron—even after Jefferson's death—with the one book only a loyal Republican could write.

"first sympathies"

Though notably self-justifying in his letters concerning political partisanship, in certain rare instances Jefferson was able to acknowledge his own excesses. Edward Livingston, younger brother of Robert Livingston (the latter a fellow signer of the Declaration of Independence), had served in Congress in the 1790s. He was a liberal Republican, an outspoken Jeffersonian, and a friend to both Aaron Burr and Andrew Jackson. But Edward Livingston lost favor with Jefferson at about the same time that Burr did, and he subsequently tangled with the president in court over the ownership of a valuable plot of land outside New Orleans, known as the Batture. It was an at times vicious legal battle that Livingston ultimately won, despite the extraordinary effort Jefferson made in defense of his own position. Diving back into his law books, he prepared a ninety-one-page pamphlet, all to no avail. Meanwhile, he came to view Livingston as a selfish speculator, noting his "assiduities and intrigues."[42]

In 1824, after years of disregard, Jefferson buried the hatchet with Livingston, after the latter, via President Monroe, made an effort to restore communication. Once the overture was made, Jefferson wrote to Monroe and spoke of Livingston with complete magnanimity:

> He may be assured I have not a spark of unfriendly feeling towards him. In all the earlier scenes of life we thought and acted together. We differed in opinion afterwards on a single point. Each maintained his opinion, as he had a right, and acted on it as he ought. But why brood over a single difference, and forget all our previous harmonies? Difference of opinion was never, with me, a motive of separation from a friend. In the trying times of federalism, I never left a friend. Many left me, have since returned, and been recieved [sic] with open arms. Mr. Livingston would now be recieved at Monticello with as hearty a welcome as he would have been in 1800.[43]

The style is virtually identical to Jefferson's explanation for his readiness to repair his long-fractured friendship with John Adams. This was because the decisive spirit of 1776 represented an indissoluble memory, easy for him to latch onto, a defining moment of common resolve. When Adams (again, not Jefferson) made the first move, in January 1812, Jefferson responded to his predecessor as president by declaring that their shared trials, the Revolutionary experience, was all the incentive he needed to act to reconstitute personal harmony:

> A letter from you calls up recollections very dear to my mind. It carries me back to the times when, beset with difficulties and dangers, we were fellow laborers in the same cause, struggling for what is most valuable to man, his right of self-government. Laboring always at the same oar, . . . we rode through the storm with heart and hand, and made a happy port. Still we did not expect to be without rubs and difficulties; and we have had them.[44]

Political conflict understandably created fissures, but one's most critical memories—"our first sympathies," in Jefferson's words to Monroe—could effectively serve, in later years, to restore the historic bond. "The case with Mr. Adams was much stronger," he wrote, comparing the Livingston and Adams ruptures. "Fortune had disjointed our first affections, and placed us in opposition in every point." He concluded the sentiment: "I bear ill will to no human being." It was a corollary of his 1816 quip, "I wish to avoid all collisions of opinion with all mankind."

With Livingston, the historic bond—the formative tie—was not 1776 but the "Revolution of 1800." For Jefferson, the meaning weighed the same: a "revolutionary" political struggle, endured together, was a memory powerful enough to help him to overcome one bitter argument and recover a lost friendship. That is why, when he wrote Livingston in 1824, quick to congratulate him upon election to Congress, Jefferson was just as quick to re-establish their political genealogy. He did so by issuing his familiar warning with regard to the grand subterfuge of their common enemy, former Federalists who in the 1820s called themselves Republicans without really subscribing to the party's principles.

Then came an implicit apology, so infrequent in Jefferson's preserved papers: "I have learnt to be less confident in the conclusions of human reason, and give more credit to the honesty of contrary opinion." Perhaps he was no longer so certain that Livingston's motive in the Batture case was one of vulgar self-interest. In any event, it was a meaningful statement from him. Praising a Livingston speech, Jefferson added: "You have many years yet to come of vigorous activity, and I confidently trust they will be employed in cherishing every measure which may foster our brotherly union."[45]

The next year, Livingston asked Jefferson to read and evaluate a code of laws he had drafted, doubtless aware that Jefferson had undertaken a similar effort in

Virginia during the months immediately following his authorship of the Declaration of Independence. Jefferson declined to venture a legal-constitutional opinion owing to his advanced age ("five and twenty chilling winters" having "rolled over my head and whitened every hair" since they had last seen one another), but he lavishly praised his former adversary nonetheless: "your work . . . will certainly arrange your name with the sages of antiquity." In welcoming Livingston back into the fold, Jefferson was delighted that the congressman was working to restore "original principles," to stymie the consolidationists and protect the states from "usurpation." Moreover, he wrote the Princeton-educated constitutional scholar, "I am pleased with the style and diction of your laws, plain and intelligible as the ordinary workings of common sense."

Nothing could be so Jeffersonian—to Jefferson—as the facility to promote republicanism in language of elegant simplicity. He was now convinced that Edward Livingston embodied that special and necessary talent. The determined Virginian had found compromise and reconciliation possible. As in his estrangement from John Adams, he was ultimately able to set aside differences and appreciate an honest intellect.

The Livingston episode showed how Jefferson could modulate the inner authority of his reactive political memory. He discovered there was no dishonor and no political liability in doing so. He signed off his last letter to Edward Livingston with "unabated friendship and respect," the same expression he often used in writing to his most cherished allies, Madison and Monroe.[46]

Jefferson Dying

9

Disavowing Dogma

Among the sayings & discourses imputed to [Jesus] by his biographers, I find many passages of fine imagination, correct morality, and of the most lovely benevolence: and others again of so much ignorance, so much absurdity, so much untruth, charlatanism, and imposture, as to pronounce it impossible that such contradictions should have proceeded from the same being.

JEFFERSON TO WILLIAM SHORT,
APRIL 13, 1820

For years after his death, Jefferson's family insisted that he never spoke of religious belief with them, either to apprise them of his own or to influence their choices. To certain of his learned contemporaries he pursued rather specific intellectual arguments on subjects ranging from the dubious divinity of Jesus to anti-Calvinism and the rise of Unitarianism; still he had no mission when it came to his own grandchildren, though they grew up in his house and though he paid close attention to their education in other respects. In fact, even as he exercised clear influence over Ellen in many of the essential details of living, she came to embrace an emotionally rich form of Christianity. In a letter to her mother in 1825, for instance, she expressed "confidence in the doctrine of an immediate providence." Her devotion to a god directly involved in human affairs distinguished her from a grandfather who professed little need for conventional expressions of faith.[1]

Thomas Jefferson faced death honestly. In doing so, he remained aloof from a religious system that enshrined stories of miracles, as told by men. For him, the Bible had limited application; it was meant as a criticism of human conduct but could not be taken as divine in any way. He considered such ideas as original sin, election, immaculate conception, and resurrection as absurd. What made matters worse, men of narrow philosophical aims but extraordinary religious zeal refused to acknowledge their limits as moral leaders, disseminating ignorance and inhibiting progress through their preachings. Jefferson had no greater grievance in any area of organized human knowledge.

His temperament remained a revolutionary one. He accepted God in the abstract, as the architect of the universe; but he refuted the notion of an active, omnipresent god, which belief he saw to have been generated solely by historical uncertainties, the most apparent being human anxiety over death. He was content to acknowledge a silent godly majesty, and to separate ethical values from religious authority. He was generally prepared to admit ignorance—owing to incomplete evidence—on the key questions of theology.

Religion, as it still does, found its way into the political process when Jefferson was an official of the government. We have seen that by trusting in the general will, in an educable citizenry, and in popular self-government, he battled the forces of entrenched privilege. This made him a democrat. Stubbornly seeing monarchy and tyranny as the inevitable outgrowth of Federalist principles, he earned the hatred of many born to wealth or given to self-righteous authority, even as he upheld planter power in Virginia. Conservatives considered him a threat to social order. It follows, then, that though he spoke of God in broad terms as "that Infinite Power which rules the destinies of the universe," his vocal political enemies ignored such invocations and found evidence upon which to label him an atheist. Jefferson came to symbolize the breakdown of tradition.[2]

As many as he annoyed with his political liberalism, he probably annoyed even more by his presumed lack of religious faith. In like manner, Jefferson felt he could communicate his real feelings to reasonable people only; and he trusted relatively few (especially northern) church leaders, until given proof of their reasonableness.[3] In 1815, for example, he received a book in the mail, a gift from an admirer named Wendover. The book, authored by a New York Presbyterian, Alexander McLeod, was titled *A Scriptural View of the Character, Causes, and Ends of the Present War*—the War of 1812. Reverend McLeod believed that the war had served to strengthen Americans' piety. Jefferson wrote an appreciative three-page letter to his admirer, nonetheless questioning the author's assertion of "the right of discussing public affairs *in the pulpit.*" After completing the letter, he questioned whether he ought to send it, and wrote a note to himself at the bottom: "On further consideration, this letter was not sent, Mr. Wendover's character & calling being entirely unknown." When the issue involved religion, Jefferson was on his guard lest anything he said might be deliberately used to renew "proof" of his atheism.[4]

He gleaned his philosophy of life from a rich combination of views. He embraced medical thinking on health and morality, and he reflected classical thought, commonsense values, and Christian ideals with different degrees of enthusiasm at different times. With it all, he consistently avowed that institutionalized religion had been inhibiting social progress for centuries. He held in utter contempt those whom he considered selfishly opposed to free inquiry, and incapable of enlightenment.

The unreconstructed New England Federalists who espoused social order and the Trinity were just as certain that the loose-lipped Virginian was an avowed enemy of Christianity, a nonbeliever, a subversive. As early as 1776, in the Continental Congress, Jefferson manifestly scoffed at the proposal of a day of fast and prayer.[5] In *Notes on Virginia,* he went beyond religious toleration to advocate a complete separation of church and state. It revolted him that he had grown up in a Virginia in which a person could not hold public office if he had denied "the being of a God, or the Trinity," or if he refused to acknowledge "the scriptures to be divine authority." Reading his forceful statements on the rights of conscience, the established clergy felt his hostility, as in: "It does me no injury for my neighbor to say there are twenty Gods, or no God. It neither picks my pocket nor breaks my leg."[6] In the election year of 1800, Jefferson rendered that hostility into unmistakable imagery when he wrote to his keen Christian friend Dr. Benjamin Rush: "I have sworn on the altar of God eternal hostility against every form of tyranny over the mind of man."[7] His "altar of God" metaphor was unmistakably meant as a slap in the face of the clergy that opposed his election on moral grounds. To Jefferson, then and throughout his adult life, orthodox religion preached uniformity of opinion. Such a system was mindless dogma at best, tyranny at worst.

Though he confided his most private thoughts about God to a very few friends, Jefferson was prepared to risk his political reputation on the question of religious freedom.[8] In concert with his chief political ally, James Madison, he wrote repeatedly and decisively on the subject. This was quite different from his position on the slavery question, wherein practical considerations always seemed to take precedence over the prompt enactment of a policy aimed at securing justice to the oppressed.

Why did the cause of religious freedom move him? Perhaps because he felt that it would take little more than for American Christians to read the gospels independently to change their minds about essential meanings. Free of outside interference, they would come to appreciate the teachings of Jesus as he had, recognizing a benevolent doctrine in pursuit of human happiness and a clear conscience. No one owed a church anything. Getting people to read around the "mysteries" and to focus instead on the irresistible moral lessons expressed in plain words—encouraging a rational interpretation of Scripture—would be sufficient to discredit Calvinism and its co-conspirators, who had combined to maintain a privileged few in positions of power. By bringing down this despotic system, there would be left only a republican choice: to apply reason, to think for oneself, and, as Jesus said, to love thy neighbor as thyself.

Jefferson embraced Christian life in its simplest form. He was sensitive to a history in which millions had been hypocritically coerced into belief. Who, after all, had burned witches? The best hope for Christianity was a recovery of the actual teachings of Jesus by rejecting centuries of superstitious debasement. "No doctrines of his lead to schism," Jefferson wrote to Ezra Stiles Ely, a young Philadelphia pastor. "It is the speculations of crazy theologists which have made a Babel of a religion the most moral and sublime ever preached to man, and calculated to heal, and not to create differences."[9] There was no mystery about the founder of Christianity, only eloquence and a wonderful humility. Jefferson felt that as Americans became more educated, they would encounter Jesus as he was glimpsed and heard in his own time.

Jefferson's conclusions, in this respect, were not simplistic, but they were rather idealistic. His "enthusiasms," as the historian of religion Paul K. Conkin has written, "were more sentimental than rigorously grounded and much more selective than he ever realized. Such limitations should not conceal the fact that Jefferson was authentically religious."[10] As with slavery, we need to bear in mind that Jefferson was willing to test the waters, to expose himself to scrutiny by hazarding ideas that he knew were controversial. Though he could adopt a cold-hearted approach to his enemies, he could also, pacifistically, search for that place in his moral universe where sentiment, science, and religion happily merged.

We know his attitude toward electoral politics, in which the world was nearly always black or white, progressive or repressive. Yet Jefferson did not try to narrow his definition of Americans' faith. His reformist purpose was to break up the consolidated power of state-supported churches that demanded deference; it was not to win people over to his perspective, at least not in the short term. For this reason, he did not broadcast his beliefs. He admired the simplicity of the Quakers and their tolerant ways, though he did wonder about the persistence of their identification with England. He and Madison enjoyed a longstanding alliance with Methodists and Baptists. Far from subscribing to evangelical doctrine, the two Virginia reformers appreciated, nonetheless, that these fast-growing sects were vocally opposed to what was actually known in some circles as "Federal religion." To Jefferson and his fellow Republicans, the self-directedness and independence of spirit that was manifest among proliferating religious communities strengthened political democracy.[11]

Thomas Jefferson was not what we would call an atheist, but a deist, believing in a Creator who had set the laws of nature in motion but who did not intervene in human affairs. He subscribed to Christianity without supernatural revelation, without miracles or mysteries. For him, the Bible was of primarily mundane character, its structure metaphorical rather than literal. The mortal Jesus brought progress by reforming the faith of the Jews, replacing a wrathful God with a benevolent one. Since the time of Jesus, however, Christianity had been debased. That was the biggest problem for Jefferson's age—convincing a modern, reasoning people to return to the deistic doctrine of the historical Jesus. When Jefferson used the term *deism* with reference to the teachings of Jesus or the religion of the Jews, he understood the word to mean "belief in one God."[12]

As a disciple of the Enlightenment, Jefferson attached himself to the cause of reason as the best way to make sense out of a volatile world. This made enemies of those clergymen who regarded "reason" as a code word for a radical atheism that disrupted "proper" social relations and made a mockery of "holy" matrimony. To Jefferson, stern and self-righteous clerics were perpetuating "unnatural" ideas, which they mislabeled as Christian, ideas that conveniently obliged parishioners to depend on their ministers to continually "explain" things. He aimed to expose all such ill-tempered imposters for subjecting worshippers to a monopolistic punitive power as backward as it was fanatical. If the people were allowed to embark on the path to self-reliance, to exercise their minds without constraint, they would inevitably see through the impious deceptions.

Well before election year 1800, when his ostensible lack of piety became a Federalist rallying cry, Jefferson was already a religious reformer. And so he must not have been entirely surprised by how viciously his anticlericalism was attacked. For their part, the pious Federalists expected that, as president, a God-mocking Jefferson would use his political power to dismantle the Christian church. After his election, responding to the fears generated by New England clerics, some people hid their Bibles lest their good books be outlawed.[13]

His war with the established church would pursue Jefferson all his life. It would even impel him, in retirement, to produce a script that clarified the "pure" teachings of Jesus. He convinced himself that all America would, before long, adopt them—or some form of them.

Priestley's Corruptions of Christianity

One thinker in particular was on the right track, as far as Jefferson was concerned. Joseph Priestley was an early English Unitarian, already famous as the scientist who discovered oxygen, when he turned his analytical mind to the evolution of Christian beliefs. Jefferson read Priestley's *History of the Corruptions of Christianity* (1782) in the early- or mid-1790s, and a short time later had the pleasure of welcoming its author to American shores, as a political refugee. Priestley shared Jefferson's hope for the ultimate success of the French Revolution, and had suffered in his homeland for his unpopular stand, his papers and scientific equipment incinerated at the hands of an angry mob. In exile in Pennsylvania, he so publicly embraced Jefferson's politics that Secretary of State Timothy Pickering, a Federalist diehard, urged Priestley's deportation under the 1799 Alien Act. He was spared, because President Adams esteemed him. As a practical, scientific, liberal republican religious thinker, Joseph Priestley believed himself born into "a most wonderful and important aera in the history of mankind."[14]

He undertook his work on Christianity, he claimed, from a devotion to "the discovery and communication of truth." The Jesus he found in his research did not claim any special powers, and the apostles as well did not consider him more than *"a man approved by God, by signs and wonders which God did by him."* (Acts 2:22.) Priestley was presenting what he had determined to be "rational Christianity": No information from the time of Jesus instructed that Jesus was of a divine nature, or that God was divisible into the Father and the Holy Spirit.[15]

The deification of Christ over time, he wrote, derived from "heresies . . . from men who wished well to the gospels." But Priestley argued that allegory and personification had been taken too far. Exaltation of Jesus Christ was eased into common practice by a flock of philosophers who surmised that if souls had preexisted, then that of Jesus, to be not ordinary, ought to be rendered "a principal *emanation* from the divine mind itself." To make the religion of Christ more "reputable" in a time of philosophical confusion, they gave Jesus greater "dignity."[16]

Though Jesus taught that there was only one God, belief in a separation of the divine nature gradually developed from here. Priestley, furthermore, pointed out that in early writings, there was a pronounced inequality among "the persons in the Trinity";[17] but subordination of the Son to the Father ("having derived his being from him") shifted over time, and eventually "the persons in the Trinity" became "equally eternal and uncaused." Inconsistencies grew increasingly obvious as he examined the texts of the second century: What combination of humanity and divinity did Jesus possess? Did only the "human nature" of Christ suffer on the cross, or could a divine feel pain? As Priestley laid out the actual struggle early Christians went through before accepting the Trinity, the unity of God made more and more sense.[18]

He had had the courage to publish his historical detective work, though it undercut so much of what the modern world of faith rested upon. Inspired by Priestley's groundbreaking book, Jefferson went even beyond it. In his later years especially, he was entirely unsubtle in his critique of the Trinity, noting that "the doctrine of one god, pure and uncompounded was that of the early ages of Christianity, . . . nor was the unity of the supreme being ousted from the Christian creed by the force of reason, but by the sword of civil government. . . . The hocus-pocus phantasm of a god like another Cerberus,[19] with one body and three heads, had it's birth and growth in the blood of thousands and thousands of martyrs." Once reason was returned to its throne, Jefferson assured, once historical inquiry was given its due weight, once freedom of religious opinion was complete in America and all government support of the church ended, then the Trinity would be toppled and "Unitarianism become the general religion of the United States."[20]

Jefferson did not agree with every last one of Priestley's conclusions, however. On the important subject of "the true end and design of the death of Christ," Priestley acknowledged the core Christian faith, that God gave Jesus the special mission of revelation:

> The history of Jesus contains (what cannot be said of any other history in the world) an authentic account of a man like ourselves, invested by almighty God with most extraordinary powers, not only teaching, without the least ambiguity or hesitation, the doctrine of a future life of retribution for all mankind . . . but passing his own life in a voluntary exclusion from all that men call great, and that others pursue with so much assiduity; and in obedience to the will of God, calmly giving up his life, in circumstances of public ignominy and torture, in the fullest persuasion, that he should receive it again with advantage.[21]

As much as he admired the vocation of Jesus, Jefferson was more deistic in his conclusions than Priestley, who accepted the resurrection. Jefferson did not.[22]

No one could convince Jefferson that Jesus of Nazareth was anything but an extraordinary mortal. He praised Jesus for his insight, his perception that Jewish ethics were in a "degraded state," and required reformation. Jesus had clarified the attributes of God. This was his greatness. The problem, as Jefferson saw it after studying Priestley's historical reasoning, was that Jesus himself had not written down his teachings, but left others to preserve them only in a "disfigured" shape, for self-interested reasons.

Like Priestley, Jefferson was not at all impressed by those who followed Jesus. Lifted up alike by the liberal political message they deduced from their reading of Jesus, the scientist-theologian and the philosophic president agreed far more than they disagreed. The furthest Jefferson would go was to state in a letter to Priestley that he believed Jesus had devised a "system of morality" that was "the most benevolent and sublime probably that has ever been taught." After receiving this communication, Priestley wrote to the Reverend Theophilus Lindsey, to whom he had dedicated his *History of the Corruptions of Christianity,* with the message Jefferson in all probability wanted to convey: "He is generally considered an unbeliever; if so, however, he cannot be far from us."[23]

Jefferson composed one of the most profoundly optimistic letters of his entire life to Joseph Priestley. In March 1801, in his third week after being sworn in as president, he was still incensed over the bigotry of the New England clerics who had heaped their scorn on him throughout the election season; yet Jefferson wrote to remind the Unitarian agitator of how important *his* mission was: "Yours is one of the few lives precious to mankind," he praised. "The barbarians really flattered themselves that they should be able to bring back the time of Vandalism, when ignorance put every thing into the hands of power & priestcraft." Turning his thoughts to the moral conditions he saw presented, Jefferson reached a crescendo in the composition:

> As the storm is now subsiding, and the horizon becoming serene, it is pleasant to consider the phenomenon with attention. We can no longer say there is nothing new under the sun. For this whole chapter in the history of man is new. The great extent of our Republic is new. It's sparse habitation is new. The mighty wave of public opinion which has rolled over it is new.[24]

This is a famous letter. But it has not been regarded as the spiritual communiqué that it is. In it, Jefferson is conscious of cadence: He repeats "new" as if narrating a Biblical episode. He treats his accession to the presidency as the genesis of a desirable phase in human history, a new testament for a people who have recently endured solemn struggle, weathered storms, and at length prevailed. The Federalist interlude had been marked by the frenzied rage of misguided men who shunned simple republicans. Jefferson had been the instrument of a humane message. He may not be comparing his morals to those of Jesus directly, but his praise for the ancient teacher's charitable impulse resembles his own hope for real representative government and political harmony. He imagines he turns the other cheek when he says, "We are all republicans: we are all federalists." First of his party to lead the nation, the new president announces a time of awakening; and at least on this day he greets brighter skies.

In 1804, while working on his annotations of the Old and New Testaments, Dr. Joseph Priestley, the best-known advocate of "rational Christianity," died at his home in Northumberland, Pennsylvania. Anticipating the end, Priestley requested of a friend: "Tell Mr. Jefferson that I think myself happy to have lived so long under his excellent administration; and that I have a prospect of dying in it. It is, I am confident, the best on the face of the earth, and yet I hope to rise to some thing more excellent still." The combined diligence and power of conviction that Priestley exhibited throughout his life gave Jefferson a way to feel humble. He considered Priestley a genius, and bore him "affectionate respect," as he put it in a letter to Thomas Cooper, a brilliant thinker and nonbeliever much admired by both Priestley and Jefferson. Priestley had devoted himself to ridding the Christian faith of ignorance without denying its central principles. His efforts to expose religious fallacy emboldened Jefferson to do the same, with vigor and resolve.[25]

"Tyranny over the Mind"

In his *Literary Commonplace Book,* begun in the early 1760s, Thomas Jefferson excerpted more from Henry St. John, Viscount Bolingbroke, an English deist and prominent political critic, than from any other thinker or writer, classical or modern. Lord Bolingbroke questioned the legitimacy of a Christian religion that contained nothing so pronounced as its schisms: "Orthodoxy is a mode," Jefferson copied out. "It is one thing at one time and place. It is something else at another. . . . men have been burned under one reign, for the very same doctrines they were obliged to profess in another. You damn all those who differ from you." Historians generally agree that it was Bolingbroke who set Jefferson on the road to religious skepticism and committed him to exposing clerical deception.[26]

Throughout Jefferson's life, his confidants were men and women of wide-ranging religious convictions with one thing in common: They showed consideration for unorthodox opinions or even unbelief. As they aged, many of them, like Jefferson, returned to this issue with a heightened care and concern stemming from their years of experience. One of these was Charles Thomson of Philadelphia. One day in 1810, the eighty-one-year-old Thomson, former secretary of the Continental Congress, dined with his Revolutionary colleague Dr. Benjamin Rush. He recalled for Rush having lived for several years, as a young scholar, in the home of a dour, ill-humored minister who criticized him for not knowing his catechism. Asked what sect he belonged to, Thomson had replied, "None," adding, "I am a Christian. I believe only in the Scriptures, and in Jesus Christ, my Saviour." For a time a Presbyterian, he abandoned the church because, once again, of the "malignant and unforgiving temper" of the minister.[27]

In later years, Thomson, always a man of philosophic purposes, became a more devout Christian. In 1808, he published a translation of the Bible; in 1815, he followed with *A Synopsis of the Four Evangelists,* which Jefferson owned and read. The two were lifelong friends, having met for the first time in 1764, not long after Jefferson discovered Bolingbroke, when he journeyed to

Philadelphia to receive his smallpox inoculation. He later received aid from Thomson in his preparation of the American edition of *Notes on Virginia.*

In 1816, more than a half-century after their acquaintance commenced, Jefferson wrote to tell the declining Thomson that he, too, had been at work on a "Philosophy of Jesus," calling it a "paradigma" of doctrines "made by cutting the texts out of the book, and arranging them on the pages of a blank book, in a certain order of time or subject." (This was an early, no longer extant version of the more elaborate 1820 production, "The Life and Morals of Jesus.") Most significantly, Jefferson told Thomson that his "Philosophy of Jesus" was

> a document in proof that I am a *real Christian,* that is to say, a disciple of the doctrines of Jesus, very different from the Platonists, who call *me* infidel, and *themselves* Christians and preachers of the gospel, while they draw all their characteristic dogmas from what it's Author never said nor saw. They have compounded from the heathen mysteries a system beyond the comprehension of man.[28]

This "real Christian" took special aim at Plato whenever he reacted against the indoctrinated ministers of his own time. "Platonism," to Jefferson, was another name for the "metaphysicians," who had blended the authentic teachings of Jesus with improbable notions and so concocted a secret "knowledge" that enabled them to confuse churchgoers and the public at large, meanwhile enhancing their own personal power. Jefferson believed that Plato had fraudulently manipulated the moral teachings of Socrates, attributing to him Plato's own reactionary views; the same could be said about Federalist-supporting clergy with respect to Jesus. Jefferson was not shy about saying that his antagonists' professed beliefs amounted in equal parts to superstition and despotism.[29]

Thomson allowed others to read Jefferson's letter, and somehow word circulated far and wide that Jefferson had come to accept the divinity of Jesus. But nothing of the sort had occurred, as he made perfectly clear to Margaret Bayard Smith, a family friend. Yes, he acknowledged, he had written to Thomson "on the subject of the Christian religion." But he had expressed "no adherence to any particular mode of Christianity; nor any change of opinions suggested."

One purpose of telling the story of Thomson and Jefferson, and their exchange of views, is to demonstrate that even as attitudes toward religious knowledge and practice evolved in the two men's minds, no one in America served quite so much as a lightning rod as Jefferson. Many people—friend and foe—wanted him to profess his religion so that they could further pass judgment on him. Retirement did not alter that maddening fact.

One year after his "leaked" letter, having learned how his confidence was forfeited, Jefferson wrote to Thomson again. He knew by now that it was Joseph

Delaplaine (the same biographer who had elicited Jefferson's defense against Henry Lee's insinuations) who had pressed for information about Jefferson's religion, and then took advantage of an opportunity to publicize a letter that had never been intended for the wider world. In corresponding with Thomson this time, Jefferson took greater care. He did not, however, moderate his tone. He reiterated that he was content for God alone to know his religion. Only God, he insisted, could judge whether he had lived a moral life.

Writing in such a way that he could not be harmed if his letter again escaped Thomson's personal control, Jefferson showed he had little patience with those among his critics who seemed only to wish for everyone to think alike. "Would the world be more beautiful were all our faces alike?" he solicited Thomson. "Were our tempers, our talents, our tastes, our forms, our wishes, aversions and pursuits cast exactly in the same mould?" There could be nothing so monotonous as uniformity of thought. Yet, "These are the absurdities into which those run who usurp the throne of god, and dictate to him what he should have done. May they, with all their metaphysical riddles, appear before that tribunal with as clean hands and hearts as you and I shall." Hounded by his detractors, Jefferson fought back with accusatory words.[30]

A virtual lifetime had passed since the early collaboration of the two philosophically inclined Revolutionaries, Thomson and Jefferson. What had remained unchanged was Jefferson's confrontational stance and the war that subsisted between the activist politician and the conservative preachers who would always resent him for conceiving legislation that insured religious freedom by ending state support of the church. In effect, all he had done was to insist that contributions to the church be voluntary. Beyond that, he pronounced that the mind was free, and that all people should choose their faith by exercising reason. Society's leaders—civil and ecclesiastical—were still flawed human beings, he said, and should not be given special preference or advantage over the lives of the mass of citizens in a republic. Disestablishment did not have to sink the fortunes of any church; Jefferson himself gave generously.

His Virginia Statute for Religious Freedom was enacted into law in 1786, while Jefferson was in France. His outspokenness became a political liability when party lines were drawn in the 1790s, and the anti-administration (Republican) interest gained popular support. Jefferson's religion came to be associated with French Revolutionary infidelity, and thus social anarchy. Lumping together his sectarian detractors as "the priesthood," Jefferson charged them with ignorance and absolutism, the first a simple failure to reason, and the second their crazed method of averting a loss of power over their communities—the recourse of bullies everywhere.

During and after the election of 1800, the *"genus irritabile vatum"* (excitable order of prophets), were, in Jefferson's words, "all in arms against me." The priests' irritability, in medicalized vocabulary, presupposed their loss of reason. It was in this context that the incoming president pronounced to his friend Dr. Rush the unrelenting Americanism that today wraps around the inside ring of the Jefferson Memorial dome—his "eternal hostility against every form of tyranny over the mind of man." And this, Jefferson appended, was all that the advocates of religion had to fear from him.[31]

In New England, at least, the election of 1800 centered on Jefferson's alleged atheism. Timothy Dwight, the president of Yale, was among the most vocal in predicting that Jefferson would legislate the incineration of Bibles, turn the nation's churches into "temples of reason," and replace solemn hymns with the popular tunes of the soulless French Revolution. The northern clergy made Jefferson's religious skepticism appear to be no different from sexual liberation. Claiming that Jefferson "insult[ed] his maker and redeemer," the Federalists stirred up opposition to the Republican Party, which somehow professed to understand and represent the needs of the average God-fearing citizen.[32]

If one looks at Jefferson's most notable public addresses, it is clear that he was careful to invoke the name of God, at least generally, in support of patriotic purposes; he was at all times sensitive to the needs of his audience. He safely—cleverly, one might say—invoked the deistic "nature's god" in the Declaration of Independence. He concluded his first inaugural address with a prayer: "And may that Infinite Power which rules the destinies of the universe lead our councils to what is best." More tellingly, in his Bill for Establishing Religious Freedom, presented to the Virginia legislature, he opened with the dictum that "Almighty God hath created the mind free," a mind "insusceptible of restraint." God, "the holy author of our religion . . . chose not to propagate it by coercions."[33]

These few words summarize Jefferson's central presumption about a Creator. God did not force belief, and therefore it was absurd to believe that God could select any one ministry as the most righteous, or deserving of public support. It was simply a corruption of religion for civil authorities to grant "a monopoly of worldly honours and emoluments" to one church, or to connect civil rights to religious opinions at all. That was the tyranny Jefferson worried about. In the words of Priestley, church-state separation underpinned all politics: A civil magistrate should have no concern outside of his duty "to preserve the peace of society," and the church should concentrate on preparing people for "the life to come."[34]

Enemies of indoctrination, Jefferson and Priestley led the liberal effort, in their respective native lands, to banish the state from religious life: "What, then, has the state, or my neighbors, to do in [my religion], any more than with my food or my medicine?" asked Priestley, before he left England.[35] To differing degrees, they monitored the current of corruption that flowed between church and state. It is hard to assess the comparative force of the current, as it existed in their minds. In Jefferson's desire to banish the church from political preference, he seems more worried about the subjugation of the individual conscience, and Priestley, after 1782, seems chiefly concerned with limiting the state.

Jefferson suffered for categorically insisting that "our civil rights have no dependance [sic] on our religious opinions." The latent threat to citizens' independence always loomed large in his mind, which explains why he would not rest when it came to this issue. He refused to allay the concerns of pro-establishment figures, who perceived the threat differently; for them, a church weakened by disestablishment would be ill-equipped to deal with the resulting irreverence, or moral indifference, that conservative pastors imagined developing among the public. Given Jefferson's central role in the cause of religious freedom, they attached their fears to the person of Jefferson himself.

Six weeks before leaving office, President Jefferson wrote to an old friend in Philadelphia, as he would often and to all who queried him, that religion was "a matter between our Maker and ourselves." But he was rarely through with this subject until he had pronounced upon his antipathy toward certain sectarians:

> As to myself, my religious reading has long been confined to the moral branch of religion, which is the same in all religions; while in that branch which consists of dogmas, all differ, all have a different set. The former instructs us how to live well and worthily in society; the latter are made to interest our minds in the support of the teachers who inculcate them.

Now the bitter punch line:

"Hence, for one sermon on a moral subject, you hear ten on the dogmas of the sect."[36]

Eight years later, his perspective was unaltered. To the sympathetic Thomas Cooper: "I believe that a moral lecturer, on Sundays, would be as well attended, and paid, if he would add a rational prayer, as a brawling presbyterian or baptist." Where was the good sense in all that "brawling"?[37]

In retirement, Jefferson could not escape his ecclesiastical critics. As to those who wished him "to be thought Atheist, Deist, or Devil," he steadily maintained that religion was a matter of conscience. He explained to Margaret Bayard Smith in 1816, "I have ever judged of the religion of others by their lives. . . . By the same test the world must judge me." But he understood that he remained a symbol, and for New England's pious he would always be a scapegoat for their diminishing ability to command their communities. The way ahead was lighted when the most conservative state, Connecticut, gave up sponsoring the church in 1817. To Mrs. Smith, he said of the remnant that stood against progress: "They must have a positive, a declared assent to all their interested absurdities." And with his most masterful gibe at organized religion, Jefferson completed the thought: "There would never have been an infidel, if there had never been a priest." Writing to John Adams on the turn of events in Connecticut, he expressed surprise and delight that "this den of the priesthood is at length broken up, and that a protestant popedom is no longer to disgrace American history and character." Knowing that Adams believed as he did on the subject, Jefferson did not withhold: "If, by *religion,* we are to understand *Sectarian dogmas,* in which no two of them agree, then your exclamation on that hypothesis is just, 'that this would be the best of all possible worlds, if there were no religion in it.'" Religion only had value to him if it encouraged free and discriminating minds.[38]

Just as he believed the remnants of Federalism bound and determined to reverse the forward march of American history, he never ceased pursuing those he continued to call the "excitable order," *genus irritabile vatum.* In 1822, Benjamin Waterhouse prodded him with thoughts about the ongoing conflict between conservatives and Unitarians in his own Boston neighborhood. The *"orthodox,"* "high-toned Calvinists" were fretting about recent conversions to the liberal sect, and Dr. Waterhouse feared that these humorless types remained dangerous because they possessed oratorical power and might "soon devour the still, small voice of reason." Jefferson's friend had written before about research into chronic disorders, and with this disorder, as well, he believed a cure possible: "While men are scowling on each other, Heaven continues to smile upon us. Our mountains & vallies, our fields & our gardens bear no tokens of a wrathful God."[39]

These words provoked Jefferson to assume the pulpit. In his reply to Dr. Waterhouse, he called the fabricators who twisted true and simple Christianity "impious dogmatists" and "mythologists," blasphemous, crazy, and full of spite. More than to other recipients of his letters, he was unsparing in the language he used when his thoughts were entrusted to his Massachusetts medical ally. With one minor exception: In Jefferson's draft of the letter, his first impulse and cautious rephrasing are both clearly readable: "Our anti-Christian Maniacs" was altered to "our Platonizing Christians." Otherwise: "Had the doctrines of Jesus been preached always as pure as they came from his lips," Jefferson declared, "the whole civilized world would now have been Christian. . . . [T]he genuine doctrine of one only God is reviving, and I trust that there is not a *young man* now living in the United States who will not die a Unitarian." Drawing on his favorite Latin turn of phrase, he railed at the excitable priesthood, "on whom argument is lost." As with his lukewarm support for racial justice, in trying to steer clear of all public debate he left the decisive work to "younger athletes"; but at least religious reform presented him no difficulty in identifying the enemy as "false branches" grafted onto Christianity that a new, more inspired generation would finally "lop off."[40]

In the spring of 1822, the Reverend Frederick W. Hatch, the Episcopal rector of the church in Charlottesville, informed Jefferson that the diocesan convention was to be held in that town. At first, out of respect, Jefferson agreed to attend the convention; but when given to understand that upwards of 1,000 people from various parts of the country would be arriving in his neighborhood, he admitted that he possessed "neither strength nor spirits to encounter such a stream of strangers." Knowing that Monticello was "among the curiosities of the neighborhood," he opted to head out for Poplar Forest earlier than planned. He did, however, make a generous contribution to help offset Reverend Hatch's expenses.[41]

In his last months, Jefferson thanked one John Fellows for sending him the *Theological Works* of the freethinking Tom Paine, who alone exceeded Jefferson in the degree of his being anathematized by religious conservatives. Paine was an outright deist, and went public with his condemnations of the Christian system as readily as Jefferson sought to keep his religious views quiet. The author of *Common Sense* rejected all "hearsay evidence" in the Old and New Testaments, rejected religious revelation, and regarded as myth the notion that Jesus was the Son of God; the church, Paine insisted, had discarded the study of God through His works for the study of "human fancies concerning God." He wrote of modern Christianity in *The Age of Reason:* "It professes to believe in a man rather than in God. It is a compound made up chiefly of man-ism with but little deism, and is as near to atheism as twilight is to darkness." Thanking Fellows for Paine's *Works,* Jefferson wrote again that the *genus,* the excitable priesthood, was unsparing in its "abuse" and "invective" toward those whose reason they feared.[42] Thus he showed himself, even at the end of his life, to be as restless as he was relentless in his pursuit of religious liberalism. Nothing less than the enemy's destruction would do. Simply put, Jefferson's opposition to the inheritors of New England Calvinism was the theological equivalent of his uncompromising political opposition to European-inspired monarchy.

His "nature's god" of the Declaration was the Creator who brought order and vitality out of chaos. Nature's principles, set in motion by God, did not require God's repeated intervention; physical sensations were more reliable than metaphysical suggestions. Like Paine, Jefferson believed that the most comprehensible way God spoke to mortal men and women was through what was already present—the visible productions of a plentiful nature—and God spoke in no more recognizable a language than that. Jefferson believed, too, that one need not be religious to be moral. Nor were loud professions of religious faith an assurance of personal morality.

As a practical political actor, Jefferson recognized that referencing God was a useful, if conventional, means of mollifying a public steeped in a language of faith. His own moral conviction—his understanding of imaginative sympathy, the impulse to do good—was acquired by reading the Scottish philosophes, such as Adam Smith and Lord Kames, at least as much as it was gleaned from the moral teachings of Jesus. He was impressed by the boldness of the novelist-philosopher William Godwin, the son of a Calvinist minister, who refused to bow to convention, and who recognized in his father's faith a blind dependency on God; human beings should do all within their power to rise above such self-imposed infirmities and translate sensation into social happiness. Jefferson was attracted to eclectic philosophies, that is, to no single overriding philosophy, so much as he recognized philanthropic tendencies in the human heart. A lifetime of liberalism, not his response to a specifically Christian message, had produced his critique of the artificially powerful church authority.[43]

In Jefferson's view, the conservative clergy debased reason and imagination by fearing what imagination could bring: a loss of virtue. He held that the moral faculty did not derive from religion at all, but from the sympathetic imagination. Society would not fall apart without a church. And so it was the clerics' lack of a capacity to imagine what free minds could achieve that caused him to hate the religious order.

Politics (and Little Theology) in "The Life and Morals of Jesus"

In his 1820 rendition of the gospels, "The Life and Morals of Jesus,"[44] Jefferson reconstructed in four parallel columns, that is, in Greek, Latin, French, and English, those sections of Matthew, Luke, Mark, and John (in essentially that order of importance)[45] that he found acceptable—meaning that the gospels had to conform to the physical laws of nature. In this text, Jesus performs no miracles. He does not say, "I am the resurrection, and the life."[46] In an abbreviated eighty-two pages, the anthology of the four evangelists becomes as coherent and rationalistic an account as Jefferson can cut and paste together without losing the vitality of the original.

Hoping to prove he was no atheist, Jefferson warmed to a god who had designed a Newtonian universe. In it, God is omnipotent, all bodies are contained in God, and neither God nor bodies in motion meet resistance from the other.

Newton wrote: "Since every particle of space is *always*, and every indivisible moment of duration is *everywhere*, certainly the Maker and Lord of all things cannot be *never* and *nowhere*."[47] Newtonians understood that humans can have no substantial idea of the way in which an all-wise presence perceives and functions. In the New Testament, Jefferson located a Jesus who brought people closer to that God.

The demystified Jesus, a great reformer, is for the most part a classical humanist hero in Jefferson's hands. In an 1817 letter to John Adams, Jefferson referred to the "deism taught us by Jesus of Nazareth" as "true religion"—and by true religion Jefferson meant the marriage of rationality and humanity.[48] This is, perhaps, an unusual definition of religion for most, but Adams certainly understood him: One did not have to fixate on the supernatural to revere, observe, or think religiously (thus, we get "nature's god"). The inspiration Jefferson found in Jesus lay in the radical moral precepts and humility of the teacher; and in the supplications directed by Jesus toward a god who revealed the entirety of his plan for humanity in the order of all nature, external and internal.

What Jesus did, Jefferson tells us, was to render the singular God ever more precious to the imperfect people of the Earth, by transforming a "cruel, vindictive, capricious, and unjust" Supreme Being into one who expressed "the best qualities of the human head and heart, wisdom, justice, goodness, and adding to them power . . . in infinite perfection." Jefferson extolled Jesus for his "philanthropy and universal charity and benevolence," which was wondrous enough; he did no more than that.[49]

Jefferson re-created the gospel narrative, his "Life and Morals," to establish the originality of thought of the God-loving Jesus. He saw Jesus as a revolutionary in moral philosophy with whom revolutionaries in politics could identify. By concentrating on Jesus as a historic actor who possessed an inspiring wisdom, and as a living guide who aimed at moral perfectibility, Jefferson, in his controversial reworking of the gospels, excluded whatever he felt misrepresented Jesus. Miracles—and anything else Jefferson did not approve—became a "fabrication" that could not have come from a teacher who had, incidentally, never declared himself to be divine.[50]

Nevertheless, depending on how one reads Jefferson's handiwork, his text contains plentiful suggestions of a prophetic, mystical—possibly even a divine—Jesus. We should question why, given Jefferson's clear convictions, he includes them at all, and see how these suggestive passages can be read otherwise.

Jefferson embraces the entirety of Luke 12, in general a discourse on modesty that brings out the perverse and pointless course of covetous behavior. It mocks the rich man for resolving to "take thine ease, eat, drink, *and* be merry." Jesus says: "The life is more than meat, and the body *is more* than raiment." Explaining by parable what true wealth is, and urging right behavior, Jesus builds up to the line: "The Son of Man cometh at an hour when ye think not."

Is not the Son of Man an avenging instrument of God at the time of the final Judgment? Where is Jefferson going with this? There is more clarity a few pages later in the Virginian's patchwork text when, in Matthew 13, Jesus pronounces, "He that soweth the good seed is the Son of Man." It might just as well seem that Jefferson is reading "the Son of Man" as literally a man, doing good. But once again a few lines later: "The Son of Man shall send forth his angels, and they shall gather out of his kingdom all things that offend, and them which do iniquity. . . . Then shall the righteous shine forth."[51]

Does the rational Jefferson not see the "Son of Man" in this passage as a Jesus in Christ-like outline? Or angels as supernatural messengers? Could Jefferson somehow be ignorant of what less suspicious readers of the New Testament perceived?

As Reinhold Niebuhr framed it, a revelatory Jesus combined embodiments of the "suffering servant" and the "Son of Man" in distinguishing his first coming from the kingdom to come. The appearance of the Son of Man, a transcendent, heavenly figure, was meant to herald the reign of justice and peace, replacing human history (to that point, finite and natural) with history's completion or accomplishment. That, in the New Testament, the Son of Man must suffer, as Jesus does on the cross, is to make "vicarious suffering the final revelation of the meaning of history . . . [which] discloses the sovereignty of God over history." We know that Jefferson did not subscribe to either messianic realization described by Niebuhr. So if he includes in his "Life and Morals" passages involving the Son of Man, we must presume he did so without construing the Son of Man as an endowment beyond that of mortal capacity.[52]

What has been, for others, a mystical, holy language is of little significance to Jefferson. He does not dissect and analyze, line by line, seeking meaning. Otherwise, he could have found in the Old Testament that it was Daniel who "saw in the night visions" and reported: "Behold, one like the Son of man came with the clouds of heaven. . . . And there was given him dominion, and glory, and his kingdom that which shall not be destroyed."[53] It does not appear that Jefferson made this connection.

It is still curious that in rewriting the life of Jesus as the narrative of a quest for social justice, Jefferson frequently invokes the visionary Son of Man, who will accompany God when it comes time for Him to "avenge his own elect" (Luke 18:7). But we know that Jefferson does not actually subscribe to such an outcome, nor does he imagine the Son of Man to herald an impending crisis. Thus he includes Luke 18:7 only as part of a parable he likes—the widow and the judge—which, like the Sermon on the Mount that he also favors, registers

Jefferson's concern for those on the margins of society: In this, the determined widow "troubleth" the hardhearted judge until he finally gives in and rules in her interest. Furthermore, the Greek translation of the widow and judge parable reads even more evocatively—she is young, easily victimized, and faces poverty and starvation. Jefferson would have been as sensitive to the Greek meaning as to the English.[54]

Jefferson quite intentionally cuts out the words "till the Son of Man be come" from Matthew 10:23 because they represent a futuristic allusion that can be deleted without sacrificing the flow or essence of the narrative. He excerpts the greater portion of Matthew 10 that concerns Jesus and his disciples, wherein Jesus warns of political persecution and assures that nothing escapes God's notice ("the very hairs of your head are all numbered"); and he deletes supernatural healing as well as Jesus urging: "As ye go, preach, saying, The kingdom of heaven is at hand."[55]

In other respects, too, Jefferson appears to be on the lookout for the irrational. He is willing to allow into his text those prophesies of supernatural interference that are not immediate and miraculous, and that can be used principally to show the difference between true rectitude and false righteousness. The same is true with angels. He includes "The Son of Man shall send forth his angels" (Matthew 13:41) because he wants to preserve the larger parable of the wheat and "tares," or weeds, with the metaphor of the field as the world, in which the righteous are harvested. But he cuts out the line at Luke 2:21, on the birth of Jesus, that declares an angel to have named the baby "before he was conceived in the womb."

Wherever possible, Jefferson removes that which might empower his clerical critics, who condemn him as an unbeliever. He deletes a phrase in Luke 12:46 because it threatens "unbelievers" with a sad fate—recall that in *Notes on Virginia,* he defends a neighbor who would say "there are twenty Gods, or no God." He includes nearly all of Luke 12, but makes a particular point of excising "[The lord] will appoint him his portion with the unbelievers." The only other segment Jefferson does not retain within that long chapter are lines 8–12 and 49–53: The first deals with punishment for blasphemy; in the second, Jesus suggests that he is come to create domestic discord, which makes no sense to Jefferson.[56]

Jefferson made sense of the life of Jesus for himself, convinced by Priestley's *Corruptions of Christianity* that others had transformed it into a hodgepodge of "absurdity . . . charlatanism . . . imposture . . . contradictions," as Jefferson characterized it for William Short around the time he completed his "Life and Morals." Pasting together his multilingual text was a preoccupation akin to pasting together the *Anas.* It was, once again, about selecting credible evidence, while hoping that others would reach the conclusions he did. Based on his selection, we can see that Jefferson saw Jesus as one who had been persecuted for reaching the people, who had been misunderstood when he only sought to extend righteousness. His Jesus linked benevolence to direct action—much as Jefferson himself did—celebrating, with supreme self-assurance, God's implicitly political purpose: preserving the integrity of His creation.

Just as many others did, Jefferson made the teachings of Jesus mean precisely what he wanted them to mean. Thus the historical Jesus, like Jefferson, regarded himself as a servant of the people who simultaneously pursued a life of tranquil felicity; yet his pure and simple philosophy met with skepticism from those of meaner motives who refused to see him for what he was. To put it another way, his Jesus became a Greek, in the way we have already seen Jefferson express admiration for Greek thought; his Jesus was an Epicurean in temperament, to the precise extent that Jefferson himself was: rational, inoffensive, generous in spirit, and enlightened.

A pattern emerges. Just as Jefferson during his young years felt an easy kinship with Lord Bolingbroke, his moral models during his mature years all preferred to conduct themselves in unacceptable ways rather than to yield with unquestioning obedience to established authority. In the heart of Thomas Jefferson, the sensual world of Epicurus, bringing health and peace of mind, melded with the pure compassion of Jesus. Jesus and Epicurus both represented sincerity and candor. They accepted natural human passion as a facet of mind and body alike, and desires as good when fostering balance and harmony. They were realists as well as moralists, and they agreed that needing little was a form of freedom, and that the deity never inspired fear, only serenity. Critically, in Jefferson's construct, Jesus and Epicurus both rejected superstitious belief. Through moderation and toleration, they taught others to think for themselves, while battling pretense and hypocrisy.[57]

In blending parables, Jefferson seems chiefly interested in human weakness and temptation—and turning the teachings of Jesus to political advantage. He does not privilege faith anywhere in his cut-and-paste gospels. Yet in his cutting and pasting, he is plainly not enough bothered by prophetic references so as to delete every last one of them. That is because his first priority is to reconstruct the gospels so that they are compatible with his public purposes; and with a no less consequential sentimental purpose, he retains, as much as possible, such heart-wringing moral reflection as will help to offset remaining tendencies in his world toward social inequality.

So, in spite of errant references to grander possibilities, there is nothing transcendent in Jefferson's message concerning Jesus, beyond its sense of human community. This Christianity is primarily a religion of the political conscience.

In showing sympathy toward "sinners" and the speculating tax collectors, or "publicans," Jesus becomes a political healer, just as Jefferson imagined himself. Jesus "eateth and drinketh with publicans and sinners" (Mark 2:16), a moment in the text that Jefferson undoubtedly associates with his own republican sensibilities: Jesus is the leader who does not fear the people. Here is Jefferson's idealized communion with those who *ought* to be enemies (publicans/"candid" Federalists) and the lowliest residents of the country, whose easily cultivated sense of decency and honesty augurs well for the republic.

Jefferson approves this Jesus, the revolutionary, most of all. In doing so, he recognizes the parables as a progressive literary device, subversive of a staid, old order of contemptuous aristocrats, and a credible device for embracing the meek and honorable. In featuring an activist Jesus, the parables are made to fit Jefferson's vision of the proper means to build an inclusive society enriched through gentle, liberal persuasion and incontrovertible logic.[58]

One more relevant comparison: Jefferson co-opts Jesus the same way he reclaims George Washington. He insists on his infallible understanding of an historical actor whom others might see as antithetical in outlook or earthly purpose to his own view. The posthumous elevation of Washington to the position of supernatural guardian of the American republic makes this connection all the more poignant.[59]

Jefferson did not prepare the "Life and Morals" with an eye toward publication. It was eventually passed on by his family. We see that he looked upon the gospels as a broad devotional tribute, a text without literal certainty. The essential truth he found was that which captured the spirit of Jesus among the people, amid his teaching.

A Future State

Thomas Jefferson also gave considerable thought to what lay beyond, though he did not advance a theory with anything approaching certainty, or, for that matter, anything approaching unease. In his *Commonplace Book*, in the late 1750s or early 1760s, at the beginning of his long career as a scholar, he cited Cicero (in Latin, of course) with regard to the human condition: "What satisfaction can there be in living, when day and night we have to reflect that at this or that moment we must die?" It was followed by the less axiomatic: "If the soul is the heart or blood or brain, then assuredly, since it is material, it will perish with the rest of the body; if it is breath it will perhaps be dispersed in space; if fire it will be quenched."[60]

His imagination led him to wonder about the fate of the essence of personality after death. Because he grew to believe in a benevolent Creator; because he accepted that moral sensations enveloped the individual; because he embraced a world in which justice was to be pursued, then, he considered, death ought to hold some unequivocal plan. What God's plan was, he could not say. He made an attempt to understand, but he apparently felt little anxiety.

Jefferson tended not to use the word *heaven* when he expressed himself in literal terms concerning death and beyond.[61] For that matter, one could not sin against heaven, only against humanity. Earth was secure ground, part of the Creator's sublime purpose; but there was no "nature" to the unknown realm, no sense even of a symbolic sphere. If Jefferson's allusions to the likes of John Adams are instructive, the "future state" (the phrase he generally employed) was a state of being wherein one could hope to meet up with beloved friends and relatives. When Abigail Adams died in 1818, Jefferson commiserated with her husband: The time was "not distant" when they, too, would "ascend in essence to an ecstatic meeting with the friends we have loved and lost and whom we shall still love and never lose again."[62] Whether or not the assurance was meant merely as a measure of comfort to the widower, Jefferson never went so far as to speculate on the form of communication that might be possible in a life beyond—only that loved ones there, having been parted on earth, need never be separated again.

Neither did this language imply that the soul takes flight and, as spirit, lives on. Jefferson's Christianity did not yield to spirit any more than it yielded to miracles and mysticism. "Thought was no proof of the existence of a nonmaterial realm," observed the historian Daniel Boorstin of Jeffersonian naturalism, "for thought itself was nothing but the interaction of material forces." Jefferson called himself a "materialist," disputing the "spiritualism" attributed to Jesus; he believed that a soul had no existence apart from the living person. In the same letter of 1820 in which he told Adams of his watchword, "I feel: therefore I exist," and "When once we quit the basis of sensation, all is in the wind," Jefferson identified with the materialism of three recent philosophers, the English John Locke, the French Destutt de Tracy, and the Scottish Dugald Stewart: "Jesus taught nothing of [immateriality]. He told us indeed that 'God is spirit,' but he has not defined what a spirit is, nor said that it is not *matter.*" Jefferson was aided in his perception—and his lack of absolute certainty—by the Newtonian proposition that matter was not solid, but came together when extremely fine particles were attracted to one another. No one knew for certain the properties of those particles.[63]

How could one be a materialist and at the same time believe in an afterlife? Jefferson is deliberately ambiguous and content just to be scrupulous. The ill-defined material soul might have a postcorporeal existence, in the same way that the Creator had a plan for life in the beginning. It was not through resurrection, but through another, natural process, unknown to science, that an afterlife emerged. Without empirical evidence, Jefferson was at a loss to describe what consciousness (for lack of a better term) delivered a person to rejoin those with whom he or she had acted in life. He believed that the future state, whatever it consisted in, was scientifically classifiable—if not yet scientifically understood.[64]

Priestley expressed his opinion on matter and spirit in his *History of the Corruptions of Christianity.* In the Scriptures, he noted, the state of death was represented as "absolute insensibility," "a state of rest, of silence, and of darkness," and one's ultimate reward was cast as the "resurrection *of the dead*," of the person, and not the "resurrection *of the body*." Moreover, Priestley said, thought and sensation could not be separated from the body any more easily than breathing and moving could, or than the sound of a bell could have an existence apart from the material bell.

In the original Christian system (prior to the second century), good souls remained after death in a kind of limbo, in some place associated with God in heaven, awaiting resurrection. But in what condition? Priestley had trouble upholding "the dictates of reason" and still believing in "the sleep of the soul." How could the body decay in the grave, never to return to life, and the soul sleep, insensible, if it was to recover consciousness at some future point? He was left with the hope, supplied by the resurrection of Jesus, that the soul retained a consciousness of itself between death and eventual resurrection.[65]

Jefferson differed from Priestley in the details—notably, resurrection—but, like Priestley, he did not insist that any one alternative made complete sense. The question that kept coming up was whether the soul remained in the body after having been "deprived of the power of thought" in physical death, or whether the soul left the body—if it did, where did it go? "Can it be received in heaven while it's body is living on earth?" Jefferson posed to Dutch-born Unitarian François Adrian Van der Kemp the year before he died.[66] Epicurus taught that there was no afterlife, only nothingness, eternal sleep, and that the soul was as mortal as the body. As one recent scholar put it, "This is one of the few areas in which Jefferson's Christianity got the better of his Epicureanism."[67]

Medical studies mattered to Jefferson in his consideration of eternal truth, just as much as they mattered to his concern for physical well-being. In the 1825 letter to Van der Kemp—who had once told Jefferson that he wished to write a biography of the mortal Jesus, but never did so—Jefferson wrote that he was reading with pleasure, in French, "a most extraordinary book, that of M. Flourens on the functions of the nervous system in vertebrated animals." Flourens had removed part of the brain and discovered that the animal might suffer a loss of sight or smell as a result, but still survive. Jefferson acknowledged to Van der Kemp that the scientific study of sense perception was leading him to further ponder the nature of the soul. Spirit and flesh were relatable as part of medical discourse. The common denominator was sensation.

Even in his consideration of religion, then, Jefferson was able to draw upon a medical vocabulary. The philosophes from whom he took his cue for so much of his ideology had campaigned against the clerical order as if combating a disease. As Peter Gay has documented, their infected religion was a "sacred contagion," a "sick man's dream," a dangerous element in the air everyone breathed: "In the rhetoric of the Enlightenment, the conquest of nature and the conquest of revealed religion were one: a struggle for health. If the philosophes were missionaries, they were medical missionaries."[68]

Those who had earlier explored affective psychology, such as Spinoza and Descartes, had linked desires and appetites (sense) halfway to the soul, as "disturbances" which the soul suffered as a result of its union with the body.[69] For Jefferson, a clear line had to be drawn between the metaphysical and the physiological. As it was for the Swiss naturalist Charles Bonnet, it was for Jefferson. Bonnet wrote in his 1759 *Analytical Essay on the Faculties of the Soul*: "It is on and through the body that the soul acts. One must therefore always return to the physical side of Man as the first origin of everything that the soul experiences."[70]

The mind was that portion of the soul subject to analysis. It diverted from its understanding of nature when it began to embrace magical explanations. And for Jefferson, that would not do. He would look at such twenty-first-century technological breakthroughs as organ transplants, genetic coding, and forensic medicine as the triumph of the ideas he had early embraced. He would probably be just as shocked that a traditional belief in Biblical miracles, such as he dismissed, could continue to coexist with such science as ours.

From his days as a restless college student, when he admired the bold, freethinking critique of the established church posed by Lord Bolingbroke, to the end of his days, when he ruminated about the soul, Jefferson remained most comfortable with the deists' deity, the working Creator who balanced the universe, the intelligence behind mathematics and all its permutations—nature's God. Humankind made its own human history; only in death was there yet some uncertainty as to the nature of the living organism.

Whenever he challenged the established church, Jefferson's oppositional tone was full of fire and conviction; he was poised and prosecutorial. In this way, he remained a disciple of the age of Enlightenment, eager to comprehend pure morality and political justice in a completely natural world. He was loath to accept an institution that made believers cowardly or that caused people to be as afraid of intellectual progress as they were afraid of contesting the "truths" of a tradition filled with contradictions. To question the wisdom of the clergy, to say that organized religion was regressive, did not make him irreligious. To doubt that the mind of God was specially revealed to one or another leader of men, or embodied in a "Son," merely extended his search for a deeper knowledge.

He was fascinated by the life of the soul because he was concerned with human happiness. But in characterizing the soul, the Jefferson who challenged the Biblical word and scoffed at original sin did not build his argument on scientific rationalism alone. The nature of the soul was God's doing. Jefferson thereby distinguished between God's power and the human will without ever denying the former. He accepted that humans, as mortals, were powerless to arrest their collective fate; but he did not stop there. The capacity to understand the world and draw conclusions from it was best pursued with the aid of science, in conjunction with a sense of humility before God.

Awareness of God did not diminish freedom. The democrat-humanist saw himself and his neighbors as children of God, by which sentimental construction all sentient beings shared an essence: the potential for compassion and companionability. This led Jefferson to accept that if an ethical consciousness had been implanted in beings, then a postcorporeal consciousness of some kind could continue to bind souls together. Yet such a conviction was different from a concept of salvation. Salvation as imagined through mental deduction or, worse, an inspired faith, failed the test of reason. Otherwise, he would have believed that Hell existed, too. Jefferson knew he could not precisely establish what consciousness was; but in rationalizing a hereafter, he relished the puzzle posed by imagining its parameters.[71]

Still, he generally preferred tangible measures of knowledge. When, near the end, he used the metaphor of the mechanical timepiece to describe his exhausted state ("I am like an old watch, with a pinion worn here, and a wheel there, until it can go no longer"), Jefferson was not simply looking for a clever literary device. He had come to think of the human body as a kind of clock, albeit one constructed with sublime skill. As Denis Diderot, the least pious and most Epicurean of the French philosophes, had put it, a person who was not satisfied with observable order—who instead required invisible causes for visible effects—such a person was scarcely different from the peasant who attributed the motion of a clock to a spiritual being purportedly concealed within it.[72] Jefferson shared Diderot's perspective. But though he remained skeptical, he was too filled with sentiment to settle for atheism.

Jefferson admired the meticulous experimental philosophers of his time, and he felt equal contempt for all careless metaphysical constructions, which he dated to Plato. And so his religion was a "civilized" form of religion: Neither enthusiastic nor austere, it was tolerant (as the Quakers of his time and, ostensibly, the "primitive" Christians of Priestley's research were); it was wary of deceptions; it was dismissive of revelation. To Jefferson, revelation secured obedience, convention, and conformity, but did not lead to true knowledge of any kind. God was not revealed; the nature of God could be construed only slowly, and not by abstract speculation either, but by attention to the human sciences in the context of physical nature. Just as the mind's ideas corresponded to events within the body, and all partook of natural laws, science alone—given the progressive genius of human beings over time—might deduce natural causes, and thus provide a glimmering of the consciousness that animates the world.

The best proof that Jefferson believed in God comes in a letter to John Adams written the week of his eightieth birthday, in 1823. "I hold," Jefferson wrote, adding parenthetically, "(without appeal to revelation)," that "when we take a view of the Universe, in it's parts general or particular, it is impossible for the human mind not to perceive and feel a conviction of design, consummate skill, and indefinite power in every atom of it's composition." That the "heavenly bodies, so exactly held in their course" or the smallest observable creatures—"insects mere atoms of life"—were organized to function productively, constituted proof enough to him that a "superintending power" oversaw everything. The verbs Jefferson uses after the subject God are as convincing: "causes"; "designs"; and as predicate: "preserver and regulator" of life; "regenerator" of matter into "new and other forms." Mindful of all he saw as a student of science, Jefferson took God to be the mind of the universe.[73]

Jefferson did see the potential of the Judeo-Christian message to speak to enlightened moderns. Jesus of Nazareth, in that sense, represented renewal. But Old and New Testament alike contained far too many irrational claims. That is where, intellectually, his campaign against Christian self-deception began. Back in 1771, he had devised a model private library, his recommendations to a book collector of modest ambition: Under "History, Antient," he listed the Bible, along with classical and contemporary secular works; under "Religion," he listed the commonsense-bearing Xenophon and other ancients, "Locke's conduct of the mind in search of truth," and Lord Bolingbroke's "Philosophical Works," which exalted human reason and was highly distrustful of all theological speculation. Over the course of his life, Jefferson did not change his opinion as to what constituted "Religion," insofar as it unmistakably excluded the Bible.[74]

But in combating the dogmas of an established church, the radical Jefferson was not so radical that he rejected Jesus as a philosopher with insights into the afterlife. Though Jefferson was not very explicit about the way in which the oral ministry of Jesus had helped convince him that there was an afterlife, based on the more than one hundred references to heaven in the four gospels, he may have construed the hereafter as a permanent, vibrant sphere. In Matthew, which book Jefferson tends to favor in his "Life and Morals of Jesus," there is, for instance, the line: "For the kingdom of heaven is as a man traveling into a far country. . . ." In his routine correspondence, Jefferson often used the metaphor of life as a journey, and death as a welcome shore. A favorite verse of his, the closing sentiment in one of his later letters to John Adams, appears in the same chapter of Matthew, and on the very next page in his "Life and Morals," in which the wise and faithful prepare for the kingdom of heaven: "Well done, thou good and faithful servant." It indicates that there is a reward for a life of value. Jefferson the rationalist could just as easily have concluded that Jesus was a whimsical creation, but he did not; he found Jesus sublimely knowledgeable, and he believed in the future state Jesus spoke of as a reward.[75]

Though he would read a variety of ancient texts during his retirement, and go on to refine his thoughts about religion, Jefferson outlined his core beliefs to Joseph Priestley as early as 1803. He said he believed that Jesus, as a moral philosopher, had devoted his life to the reformation of Judaism to show his people "the incorrectness of their ideas of the deity . . . to bring them to the principles of a purer deism [i.e., monotheism], and juster notions of the attributes of god." Jesus had "purposely" omitted a clear explanation of his relationship to the divine essence—even the source of his inspiration—and had only one lesson to "inculcate" about the hereafter: that there was "a future state."[76]

Beyond that, Jefferson's intuitive understanding ceased, his philosophy drifted. He dreamt of passionate possibilities, but trusted only in the known world.

10

Engaging the Soul's Passions

I shall pass willingly to that eternal sleep which, whether with, or without dreams, awaits us hereafter.

JEFFERSON TO WILLIAM SHORT, MAY 5, 1816

Is it the Fourth?

JEFFERSON TO DR. DUNGLISON, JULY 3, 1826

At the beginning of 1825, Jefferson matter-of-factly informed Virginia physician Andrew Kean, who tended Monticello's residents when Thomas Watkins was gone from the neighborhood, "I have remaining but a short term of life that may be expected to be made up of infirmities."[1] As if his medical problems were not real enough, Jefferson almost suffocated to death in an avoidable freak accident in October of that year. An overconfident itinerant sculptor by the name of John Browere had come to Monticello to take a plaster cast of the patriarch's face for a life mask. He had purportedly done one of Lafayette, with marked success. The willing subject sat back while the sculptor covered his head and neck, and then left the plaster in place for an hour instead of the prescribed twenty minutes.

The family could not bear to witness Grandpapa with his face plaster-covered. Only Burwell Colbert, a grandson of Betty Hemings, and Browere himself were present, and it was Burwell who noted his master's suffering and jumped up. Browere's error required the emergency use of a chisel and mallet, which the sculptor handled with neither artistry nor subtlety. "I was taken in by Mr Browere," Jefferson wrote to his friend James Madison. He described the incompetent sculptor's confused rescue effort and his own exhaustion, adding (not without wit): "There became real danger that the ears would separate from the head sooner than from the plaster." Granddaughter Virginia, writing to her sister Ellen, damned Browere as "a vile plasterer." Jefferson concluded: "I now bid adieu for ever to busts and even portraits."[2]

Until Jefferson was close to death, he did not tell his family that he had been suffering from diarrhea, periodically, since early in his presidency, when he had first solicited Dr. Rush for advice. According to Jefferson Randolph, Grandpapa had not wished to worry the family. Perhaps, but diarrhea is not a pleasant subject, and Jefferson might have felt embarrassed talking about his condition to his nearest relatives, whom he saw day in and day out. He readily discussed his other ailments with these loved ones, but not the diarrhea. He was a man who resisted speaking about unpleasantness. He was not the garrulous John Adams, nor the effusive Charles Willson Peale, the latter of whom wrote Jefferson in 1813: "When your Son in Law Mr. [Thomas Mann] Randolph was in Philadelphia lately, I was indisposed with a Diarrhea." When fellow-sufferer Judge Roane of Richmond queried him about it, Jefferson denoted his problem "the visceral complaint."

Other than in writing to a physician, or to another victim, Jefferson might have thought such expression indelicate. Whatever the reason, he preferred not to talk about his diarrhea in his own house. As he aged, he grew increasingly compliant with worsening circumstances and was almost laconic when he wrote to Madison, his closest confidant on most issues, during the second half of 1825: "My rides to the University have brought on me great sufferings, reducing my intervals of ease from 45. to 20. minutes." His pen becomes lighter, less firm, at this point. "This is a good index of the changes which take place." When another bout with diarrhea instigated Jefferson's final illness, dysentery was at that moment rampant in Monticello's neighborhood.[3]

Irritability of the bladder, Jefferson's other serious medical condition in 1825—again, rarely broached but with physicians—necessitated self-application of a bougie to make urine flow pain-free. He described dysuria quite directly to his financial adviser and commercial agent in Richmond, Colonel Bernard Peyton, who made payments on his medical paraphernalia: "I am dragging on a tedious case of dysury coincident to senile frames attended with occasional pain, confining me to the house and obliging me to continue chiefly in a recumbent posture."

"Otherwise," Jefferson wrote next, in his draft copy of the letter, "my health is as good as ever." He crossed out "good" and replaced it with, "sound as ever." Did he consider "good" a misrepresentation? Did "sound," which one of Dr. Johnson's *Dictionary* definitions gives as "not failing," in effect mean "stable" to Jefferson, that is, an acceptable state given his "senile" condition? Yet Peyton interpreted "sound" at its full value, and replied to his client a few days later: "I was quite relieved & gratified to find your general health still sound, notwith-standing the pain & inconvenience you have been so long subject to. I sincerely hope it will not be of much longer continuance."[4] If his intense, chronic, ex-hausting diarrhea was not the sole cause of Jefferson's death, then it may have been a combination of diarrhea and an infection from the unsanitary bougies he inserted, on Dr. Dunglison's recommendation.

Of course, one cannot ignore the physical toll that Jefferson's worsening per-sonal finances must have taken on him. For years the planter had been frus-trated by the terms under which credit was negotiated and interest assessed. When he was newly wed, his father-in-law left him a sizeable estate, with a man-ageable debt. It became tied to Jefferson's own estate, and resulted in a liability that was only worsened by his effort to pay in depreciating paper currency dur-ing the Revolution. As others among his cohort also found, prices for tobacco and wheat fluctuated, and plantation profits never succeeded in solving the debt crisis.

Then he went abroad, and on his return five years later agreed to hold na-tional office. Owing to his long absences, crop management suffered. The problem of debt grew. In a letter to James Madison in 1789, he said that *"the earth belongs in usufruct to the living,"* that no generation should have the right to burden the next with inherited debt. Jefferson's dictum was a moral as much as a policy formulation, and he continued to live by its precepts—no matter how impractical it might be, as Madison assured him it was. As usual, Jefferson reacted emotionally to what he saw happening around him—the effects of debt on his society. Herbert E. Sloan puts it plainly in his study of Jefferson's views on this tender subject: "Crippled by debt, troubled in spirit, the Virginia gentry of the early nineteenth century presents a picture of moral and finan-cial exhaustion."[5]

Nonetheless, during his retirement Jefferson remained convinced that he possessed land and slaves worth well more than his accrued debts to European bankers. But he was wrong. The sale of lands in 1810, and his library in 1815, would have meant more had not the nation's economy taken a tumble in 1819–1820; but by then, Jefferson had secured additional loans from banks in Virginia and endorsed a fateful note on behalf of his luckless friend, Jeff Ran-dolph's father-in-law Wilson Cary Nicholas. Interest payments swelled.

As the year 1826 opened, only one possibility loomed that held out hope of rescue from his mounting debt and the preservation of Monticello as a home for Jefferson's surviving family: a lottery by which Jefferson would give up much of his other land. Lotteries had been made illegal in Virginia, and so the ex-president's friends had to fight in the legislature to make an exception. A humbled Jefferson wrote to his young ally Joseph Cabell and expressed his hope that the rules of the state could be bent slightly: "I can save the house of Monticello and farm adjoining to end my days and bury my bones." Jefferson's active enemies were silenced by the oratorical flourishes of those in the Assembly who hailed his "distinguished services" to the nation. The *Richmond Enquirer* reported: "His name was identified with every thing glorious in the history of our Republic." Thus Jefferson won enough votes of sympathy that a lottery was advertised that spring, to be managed by his grandson.[6]

By all accounts, Jefferson remained optimistic that the lottery was about to save him. Only after his death did its failure to raise sufficient funds make the sale of Monticello—and the majority of Monticello's slaves—inevitable. In the third week of June, just as he was urgently calling Dr. Dunglison to his side, he gave some indication of his residual uncertainty when he implored his grandson Jeff never to leave his mother—whether or not Martha retained possession of the mountain estate.[7]

A $500 contribution arrived from William Short, Virginian by birth and now of Philadelphia. In spite of distance, Jefferson's onetime law student and private secretary remained one of his most trusted friends.[8] A community of New Yorkers pledged an additional $7,500. As he held on, Jefferson's spirits were buoyed by the public show of support. Yet, in the words of Theognis, "No one can escape death by paying a ransom." Jefferson remained firm, if fatalistic. The tokens of love he received at the end of his days allowed his doctor to drug him less than he might otherwise have done.

Opium

A masculine culture that extolled displays of firmness and self-command did not obviate the need for pain-killing medicine. In the last days of June 1826, Dr. Dunglison prescribed the most common of painkillers, laudanum, an alcoholic solution of opium. The doctor administered it daily for the pain associated with his bedridden patient's debilitating diarrhea.

Tincture of opium, as laudanum is pharmacologically described, was first introduced into England in the sixteenth century and was recommended for diarrhea and sleeplessness as early as the seventeenth century. In the 1670s, the famed Dr. Sydenham swore by it: "Medicine would be a cripple without it." And Dr. Benjamin Rush, "the American Sydenham," attested: "OPIUM has a wonderful effect in lessening the fear of death. I have seen patients cheerful in their last moments, from the operation of this medicine upon the body and mind."[9] It was cheaper than alcohol and extremely easy to find in the Anglo-American world throughout Jefferson's adulthood, because of its great profitability. After Great Britain gained control of the state of Bengal in 1757, approximately 20 percent of the annual revenue of British India derived from the opium trade.

Opium is the starting material from which morphine and codeine are now extracted. Until the early twentieth century, however, laudanum was the primary medicinal formulation for opium, along with the less-potent paregoric, a camphorated tincture of opium produced in the decades after Jefferson's death. The essence of opium is contained in the seed capsule of the opium poppy *(Papaver somniferum),* and is composed of between 2 and 10 percent morphine. When the ripened capsule is pierced, a milky juice oozes from it. As the juice is dried in the air, it darkens, becoming sticky or crumbly: This is "raw opium," which can be further dried and powdered for medicinal use, or boiled and strained when it is to be smoked in an opium pipe.[10]

In his 1803 letter recommending a course of treatment to alleviate the president's bowel disorder, Benjamin Rush wrote: "To relieve the diarrhoea when troublesome, laudanum should be taken in small doses during the day, and in larger doses at bedtime so as to prevent your being obliged to rise in the night. . . . In cases of extreme pain, an injection composed of forty drops of laudanum mixed with a tablespoon of starch and half a pint of water will give ease." He was optimistic: "The laudanum when thus received into the system seldom affects the stomach with sickness or the head with pain afterwards."[11]

Many doctors recommended the very concentrated drug in small doses, though Jefferson's Harvard friend Dr. Benjamin Waterhouse advocated an even more restricted use. Preaching temperance, particularly among young adults, Waterhouse was concerned about the widespread use of narcotics, and he wrote of opium: "After destroying the energy of the stomach, it undermines the power of all the other organs in succession, even to the organ of *thought.*"[12] Certainly, he was not addressing Jefferson, a man who instinctively recoiled from a loss of self-control. He was concerned about younger people who took up the unhealthy habit of tobacco chewing and smoking and who might imitate the British poets of this period for whom impaired judgment was an acceptable risk as they sought to expand their creative possibilities.

Laudanum operated on both nervous and gastrointestinal systems. If taken too often or in large doses, it did more than block the sensation of pain, control diarrhea, and enable sleep; it decreased the depth and frequency of breathing, caused a loss of appetite, decreased the secretion of sex hormones, and impaired memory. Because in early-nineteenth-century America there was, in general, no moral stigma attached to the use of painkillers, the wide availability of laudanum led some despairing individuals to commit suicide by taking an overdose.

Addiction was known and feared, and opium was already considered more dangerous than alcohol. When "eaten" (a deceptive term, because it was actually consumed in liquid form), the morphine is poorly absorbable across the lining of the stomach, but in the intestines it is gradually absorbed into the bloodstream, and from there passes easily into the brain; thus, the ingested drug is slower to take effect than it is through pipe smoking, which delivers vaporized morphine almost instantly to the brain. "Eating," however, produces a prolonged sensation, and this explains its appeal to the creative writers who were enthusiasts.[13]

The Romantic poet Samuel Taylor Coleridge was an acknowledged opium addict, as was Thomas DeQuincey, whose *Confessions of an English Opium Eater* (1822) was an instant phenomenon. The poet John Keats, who had received medical training before he turned to publishing verse, was an occasional user. For such literary figures, opium played with past experience and produced new sensations; it stimulated visions, imaginative patterns, and dreams, which, in sentimental form, found their way into print at about this time. DeQuincey wrote that he timed each dose of laudanum so that he could walk the streets and mingle with the London crowds in the early evening when hyper-reality grew and the scale of his fantasies became exaggerated. He would then return home when the drug was about to have its narcotic effect. Indeed, cultivation of the opium poppy for this purpose goes back to antiquity: Greek physicians supplied it, and, in the second century A.D., the Roman emperor and moralist Marcus Aurelius was an opium addict.[14]

There is a generally known historical connection between opium and tea. In the second half of the eighteenth century, when the British East India Company began to offload Bengali opium at the southern Chinese port of Canton, in exchange for tea, London was able to reduce the amount of silver leaving the country (the former means of payment for China's tea). At the same time, the fast-growing Asian opium market discovered the pleasure of dipping American tobacco in an opium solution, and then smoking it. Chinese desire for the Virginia crop made possible increased imports of tea into Virginia, along with the sugar that went into every American cup. So the business that began in Bengal made the slave economy of the sugar-producing Caribbean all the more profitable.[15]

Why all this history? Opium, tobacco, sugar, and tea—exchangeable products indispensable to American consumerism and to the continuation of American slavery—became intertwined during the Revolutionary era. These vital products, which had long fed British economic power, were in Jefferson's fields, in his kitchen, and inside his body, for the greater part of his eighty-three years.

July 1: The Arrival of Henry Lee

The Lee family's history in America was already quite long at the outbreak of the American Revolution. As we have already discovered, though, the war hero "Light-Horse Harry" Lee went into financial decline in the 1790s, even as he served as a Federalist leader in Congress. The land-rich Lees were becoming land-poor when Harry's son and namesake, Henry Lee IV, became embroiled in a sensational sex scandal as notorious as Jefferson's suspected commerce with Sally Hemings.

This Henry Lee (1787–1837) grew up at Stratford, the estate usually associated with his younger half-brother, Robert E. Lee, of Civil War fame. Unlike his valiant Revolutionary father, Henry IV served without apparent distinction in the War of 1812, but retained his rank of major and used the title throughout his life. Burdened by his father's unsound financial choices, Major Henry Lee was nonetheless well schooled in the classics and had developed a talent for writing. At thirty, he married a wealthy cousin, and proceeded to alienate her by seducing her nineteen-year-old sister (who was at the same time his ward). Henry did not deny his behavior, and insisted that there was no reason for anyone to recoil from a tale of adultery in Virginia, where such things happened all the time among the wealthy. Henry Lee had a knack for making people uncomfortable. As he charged his accusers with hypocrisy, and schemed to marry off his sister-in-law to a friend he could manipulate, he lost his hold over the family's resources.[16]

By July 1824, when he opened a correspondence with the ailing Jefferson, Major Henry Lee had reconciled with his wife—who had acquired an embarrassing, nearly incapacitating opium habit—and had sold off the Lee mansion of Stratford. An outspoken supporter of Andrew Jackson's, he had undertaken to write campaign material on behalf of the candidate from Tennessee, and would eventually move to Nashville and compose Jackson's first inaugural address. But first, he hoped to make his mark as a writer by revisiting the *Memoirs* of his father. Gingerly, he courted Jefferson.

Lee advised Jefferson, in early May 1826, that he was editing his father's account of the Revolution, which in 1812 had called into question Jefferson's conduct as wartime governor of Virginia. Jefferson welcomed the opportunity to take another crack at rewriting history and to prove, with documentary evidence he kept at Monticello, that Lee's *Memoirs* had history wrong. When the son wrote that the account was neglectful of Jefferson's "foresight or energy," Jefferson jumped at the chance to widen an apparent opening. Lee proposed to visit Monticello.

"Were your father now living and proposing, as you are to publish a second edition of his Memoirs, I am satisfied he would give a very different aspect to the pages of that work which respect Arnold's invasion," Jefferson wrote on May 15. This was entirely consistent with his past approach to "candid" men whom he thought he might reclaim. In 1814, Jefferson had fantasized about getting one more chance to meet George Washington face-to-face, so that he could recover a lost trust: "These malignant insinuations should have been dissipated before his just judgment as mists before the sun," Jefferson imagined at that time. Using the same language in 1826, he assured that the late General Lee would eventually have come to see the validity of the Jeffersonian position by sifting from "the chaff of the rumors then afloat, rumors which vanished soon before the real truth, as vapors before the sun."

In a six-page letter to the younger Lee, Jefferson went into detail about his activities back in 1780–1781. All Lee had to do, he said, was to "turn to Girardin's history of Virginia" for an accurate published account copied from memoranda Jefferson had written at the time "on horseback, and on scraps of paper taken out of my pocket at the moment, fortunately preserved to this day, and now lying before me." It was a passionate appeal for justice from the son of his earlier traducer. "I would ask as much of your time at Monticello as would enable you to examine these papers at your ease. . . . All should be laid open to you without reserve, for there is not a truth existing which I fear, or would wish unknown to the whole world."[17]

Lee made his preparations, thanking Jefferson on May 25 for "the fairness of your explanations respecting my father." Acknowledging the value of getting all the details right, Lee vowed to do justice to the ex-president. On May 27, Jefferson wrote again, this time with minor adjustments to his narrative of 1780–1781. "I shall be happy to receive you at the time you mention or any other," Jefferson repeated graciously, eagerly, on May 30.[18]

One month later, on or just before July 1, Henry Lee rode up to Monticello, as Jefferson lay on his deathbed. Until powerful doses of laudanum became necessary, and the medication seriously clouded his thoughts, his mind remained clear. Notwithstanding his desperate condition, Jefferson felt the historic mission of converting a pen-wielding political adversary into a friend was important enough that he roused himself and invited Major Lee in to see him. Lee wrote to his patron Andrew Jackson from Monticello on that day, and reported that Jefferson was "confined to his bed with a severe Dysentary, which cannot but place so old a patient in great danger." Still, the unpredictable writer found Jefferson less sluggish than he had expected, and noted that Martha Jefferson Randolph "hover[ed] round his bed with grief at her heart." He turned to her at one point and ignorantly commented that it was wrong for her to entrust the care of so great an American to a foreigner such as Dunglison.

On the same day, that "foreigner" wrote with sober assurance to James Madison:

> Towards the termination of the last week [Mr. Jefferson] requested my advice in consequence of the increase of a diarrhoea to which he has been for years more or less subject, but which he has generally treated with too much indifference, and it was not until it had made serious inroads on his health that he had any communication with me on the subject. In the course of two or three days the complaint was considerably arrested, but the debility induced was so great as to give rise to symptoms, denoting, too unequivocally, the loss of that elasticity—that power of restoration the existence of which at an earlier period of life render similar affections but of trifling moment.

In short, Dunglison believed that Jefferson's complaint had mortal consequences because his body was too old to heal itself. "I much fear," the doctor concluded, "that without some speedy amelioration my worst apprehensions must soon be realized."[19]

Henry Lee's doubts notwithstanding, Robley Dunglison had a meritorious future in store for him—all of it connected in some way to his original sponsor in America, Thomas Jefferson. Increasingly heralded for his medical writings, and known around Charlottesville as "the walking dictionary," he would move to Philadelphia in the 1830s. There he would teach at the Jefferson Medical College, publish papers, and become one of the most productive members of the American Philosophical Society, which had been founded in 1743, the year of Jefferson's birth, by Benjamin Franklin. Jefferson himself, America's polymath after Franklin, was a member of the Society from 1780, and became its president concurrent with his vice presidency of the nation under John Adams. It is, perhaps, only fitting that the one grandson of Thomas Jefferson who chose medicine as his profession was the significantly named Benjamin Franklin Randolph.

From Franklin's day to Dunglison's, much of what the Philosophical Society did was to chart progress in the medical arts and in pure and applied science—very much in the spirit of Jefferson. Henry Lee, on the other hand, would end up attacking Jefferson in the fiercest terms, and go down in history as a ne'er do well with a poison pen. Whatever he saw among Jefferson's private papers had only a short-term effect. He completed the second edition of his father's *Memoirs* in 1827. But after Jeff Randolph published his grandfather's collected letters in four volumes in 1829, among which was a critical account of "Light-Horse Harry" Lee from the 1790s, intellect yielded to emotion; the son ceased feeling that Jefferson deserved soft treatment. Lee's next book was a ferocious diatribe that extended well beyond what his father wrote from debtor's prison: James Madison would call the 1831 *Observations on the Writings of Thomas Jefferson* "a vial of rage." A dying Jefferson had won Lee over, but only briefly.[20]

July 3: "Warn the Committee"

Jefferson "spoke freely of his approaching death," Dunglison recorded. As such, his celebrated role in the Revolution could not escape his fast fading thoughts—stimulated, no doubt, by Henry Lee's project. On July 3, after the doctor administered a dose of laudanum, his patient fell into a restless sleep. As the night wore on, Dr. Dunglison offered more laudanum, and Jefferson refused it.

Under the weakened effect of the drug, Jefferson began making hand gestures. It was as though he were composing documents of an urgent nature. Wartime was with him once again, and he was heard to say, "Warn the Committee to be on the alert!" During the Revolution, Committees of Safety had formed to reconnoiter and give notice of an imminent British or Tory attack.[21]

We know the kind of dreams laudanum produced. From the testimony of the Romantic poets who swallowed laudanum recreationally, we are told that an initial euphoria often led to displeasure upon awakening from stupor. Percy Bysshe Shelley consumed laudanum for his nervous headaches. Samuel Taylor Coleridge, who took it in widely varying doses, said that he suffered "horrors" and "degradation" from overuse of the drug. Edgar Allan Poe, in 1826 a student at the University of Virginia, reached out for laudanum in his later years to mitigate his private pain, and ended up a wasted talent.

Though an aid to the imagination, the opiate damaged judgment. Dreams are typically distortions, taking the substance of our lives and making it half-knowable. Reconstructed sense impressions take advantage of the mind's temporarily lax control. These reveries can draw forth hidden sorrows or force the individual to revisit old anxieties. In other words, dreams isolate the individual. That is what appears to have been happening to the dying Thomas Jefferson on July 3, as he revisited a momentous time in his public life: "Warn the Committee to be on the alert!"

Perhaps he brought to his chemically bent mind dramatic players, such as his best friend from college days, John Page, a leader of the Committee of Safety, and later a U.S. congressman. Page had written to Jefferson in Philadelphia in April 1776, pleading for the Continental Congress to declare the colonies independent. Jefferson, of course, did all he could to oblige him. A loyal Republican throughout his career, Page died in 1808, at the end of Jefferson's second term as president, after complaining about his financial woes. He punctuated his last letter with the words, "God bless you! then my dear Friend, for your Consolation. As to Death, I have long been prepared to meet it." Jefferson, at eighty-three, was as accepting of death as Page had been when they were sixty-five.[22]

The story of his unconscious murmurings about the Committee of Safety sounds so perfectly dramatic that it ought to be one of those meaningless myths that make up the founders' storied lives. But this anecdote, amid the fog of Jefferson's final days, was not one of those cooked up for later generations. "He remarked," Jefferson Randolph carefully recalled, "that the curtains of his bed had been purchased from the first cargo that arrived after the peace of 1782," that is, after American independence had been won and trade with England revived.

Jefferson's nostalgia for the Revolution was nostalgia for a fast diminishing sense of authenticity in American life. The unselfish Revolutionary spirit had always been real to him. From his perspective, the original thirteen states had made a genuine effort to draw closer together. In his retirement years, exhibiting the fatigue occasioned by their union, the fractious states were unsystematic at best in their attempt to remain together. Though the grandchild most like him lived comfortably in Boston in 1825–1826, Jefferson found himself exhibiting less patience with northerners' supposed vanities and more with southern clannishness.

The failing founder ruminated on the condition of his country, but he focused foremost on his immediate surroundings. Even as his mind returned to thoughts of the Revolution from whence his fame arose, his deepest concern lay with the future of his university. Nothing meant so much to him in his last days and years as that institution—fashioning the future meant even more than finding a Barlow or Johnson to write a "proper" history of political parties in America. In February 1826, Jefferson speculated that his friend of fifty years, former president James Madison, would step in and succeed him as its rector. In June he was counting on it. Only then would he rest easy.[23]

In harking back to the Revolution, Jefferson was in good company. Preparations were underway in every part of the Union to mark the first half-century of independence. As citizens paused to celebrate, the remembered Revolution enabled them to take a short respite from sectional politics. It had been years already since the second generation of leaders had taken over the demanding job of self-government from the Revolutionary generation; on July 4, 1826, they read the Declaration aloud in town after town, and fielded orators who reminisced about the "sacred cause," and pledged that Americans would act in such a way as to become a more "wise and liberal" people. They echoed Jefferson's words when they called 1776 a "consummation."[24]

Jefferson would see the Fourth, but he would not rise from his bed that day. On July 3, reclaiming images of an unforgettable past, he endured an arduous night of sleep, and prepared for the end. How telling that in his furious, opium-inspired acting out, he was moving his hand in the air, imagining himself writing—he was still doing all he could do to preserve the republic from harm. Though his troubled thoughts were illusory, they inform us, quite preciously, of what was running through his mind as he drifted away. He was still writing history—his own history—because it had not been done in his lifetime, at least not to his satisfaction.

July 4: Peculiar Recognitions

During those final days, his family was keeping well-intentioned neighbors out—for the sake of his comfort, they figured. Jeff Randolph and Dr. Dunglison took turns standing watch, and the scrupulous Burwell slept within earshot: A Hemings was present to respond immediately in the middle of the night if Jefferson called out or required medical intervention. Granddaughter Virginia and her new husband, West Point graduate Nicholas Philip Trist, were there, too, Nicholas having helped Jefferson organize his writings over the past year or two.

At one point on the eve of July 4, hearing a voice, Jefferson thought that the Reverend Frederick W. Hatch had asked to enter the room. Hatch was the rector of the Episcopal church in Charlottesville, with whom Jefferson had maintained friendly relations for several years. "I have no objection to see him, as a kind and good neighbor," Jefferson was said to have remarked, as if to indicate that he was not in need of religious solace, but amenable to human company. In fact, the man at the door was bursar Alexander Garrett, in whom Jefferson had obviously entrusted a good deal of his hopes for the university.[25]

As his consciousness faded, Jefferson was more than once roused to inquire whether it was yet midnight, and the Fourth of July. Dr. Dunglison heard him ask at 7:00 P.M. on July 3, and replied, "It soon will be"; to Nicholas Trist he repeated the question sometime later, and Trist answered falsely in the affirmative, out of sympathy, in the hope that he would rest easier. This was not, however, the last Jefferson spoke. He called out around 4:00 A.M. in "a strong and clear voice" to his servants (unnamed, but presumably including Burwell Colbert), words that were never recorded. Around 10:00 A.M. on the Fourth, Burwell interpreted a sign, and elevated his head against the pillow. Jefferson never spoke after that, his breathing faint until all stopped at fifty minutes past noon. His grandson closed his eyes.[26]

Jefferson's stout Revolutionary colleague John Adams was in his ninety-first year, alert, though immobile and nearly blind, when he rose on the fiftieth

Fourth of July. In the correspondence of their retirement years, the two former presidents habitually related their individual ills along with their philosophy. They tended to do so self-deprecatingly, and always good-naturedly.

"Too fat to last much longer," old Adams closed one letter to Jefferson in November 1823. Some months before, two days before his eightieth birthday, Jefferson previewed their common end when he finished one long letter with the words: "I join you cordially, and await [God's] time and will with more readiness than reluctance. May we meet there again, in Congress, with our antient Colleagues, and recieve with them the seal of approbation 'Well done, good and faithful servants.'"[27]

The Virginian's name was on Adams's lips in the early afternoon of July 4, 1826. Presumably it was a recognition of some kind that they were both seeing in the national anniversary. We will never know for sure what old Adams was thinking. That morning, he had uttered a clear and valid sentiment for the benefit of the people in his hometown of Quincy, Massachusetts: "Independence forever!" Though his garbled mention of Jefferson's name that afternoon has gone down in history as the polished and desirable "Jefferson survives," these are famous last words that Adams almost certainly *did not* speak. "Jefferson survives" has provided a snug ending for a good many books, but close investigation reveals that the one individual known to have been present in the room where Adams lay scrupulously maintained that his last words—something or other with respect to Jefferson—were "indistinctly uttered."[28]

Until then, John Adams's utterances were anything but indistinct. In 1813, in one of the letters he wrote to Jefferson discussing the doctrine of Theognis, the New Englander self-mockingly alluded to a recently published critique of a work he had written in younger years, when bright and ambitious. Feigning shock that anyone would still care about his political philosophy, or his past achievements at all, the oft-disparaged second president told the oft-heralded third president: "I am to become a great Man in my expiring moments."

Of course, he meant "expiring moments" to be understood as 1813, for he already felt washed up and could not conceive that he still had thirteen years of life ahead of him. "Theognis and Plato, and . . . Jefferson and I, must go down to Posterity together," he had added, "and I know not, upon the whole, where to wish for better company." Thanks to his wonderfully sardonic pen, the creative eulogists of 1826, and the numerous patriots and popular biographers who copied them, Adams and Jefferson have remained fairly inseparable in the historical imagination, where they both survive.[29]

So they died just four hours apart. Their "double apotheosis" was hailed as a miraculous event, a providential sign. When word of the two statesmen's deaths reached New York, a newspaper pronounced the coincidence "marvelous and enviable. . . It cannot be all chance." The orator Daniel Webster called out: "The great epic of their lives, how happily concluded!" In Fayetteville, North Carolina, another tribute-bearing speaker focused on the force of their intellects, proclaiming that, "to their last moments," these two national benefactors had retained minds that were, if "dethroned of the fancy and coruscations [flashes] of youth," still "active and sound." Their retirement years' letters were "like cities set on a hill, which could not be hid—and the American people were in the habit of looking up to them as the living epistles of practical liberty, to be read of all men." U.S. Attorney General William Wirt, who a few months earlier had turned Jefferson down when offered the position of president of the University of Virginia, extolled: "Is there a being, of heart so obdurate and skeptical, as not to feel the hand and hear the voice of Heaven in this wonderful dispensation?"[30]

As the Revolutionary generation passed on, its grown children watched, and wept. Writers such as Washington Irving, James Fenimore Cooper, Lydia Maria Child, and Catharine Maria Sedgwick penned historical novels that featured tragic friendships, deathbed scenes, and graveside meditations. Reassembling the building blocks of the American republic, these authors represented the population of the North American continent as a blend of cultures, immersed in a common, passionate quest for freedom. So in a very real sense, Romantic America was born as Thomas Jefferson was dying.

Among the second generation, and the one that followed it and led the nation into its Civil War, the double apotheosis was hard to ignore. On July 4, 1863, the momentous Battle of Gettysburg concluded. Taken by the news, President Lincoln addressed a crowd of expectant citizens who stood before the White House. Thinking back to his own youth, and to the events of July 4, 1826, he acknowledged the many "peculiar recognitions" that the Fourth of July evoked: "Precisely fifty years after they put their hands to the paper it pleased Almighty God to take both from the stage of action," he said of Adams and Jefferson. "This was indeed an extraordinary and remarkable event in our history."[31]

So how ought we to encounter the Adams-Jefferson double apotheosis today? We cannot make everything make perfect sense, as the Romantics tried to do. Ambiguity persists along with the finitude of the body and the limits on freedom. People manipulate history to ward off despair. Even science cannot help but mythologize nature to some degree. Though Adams's "Jefferson survives" is contrived in one respect, this does not make the double apotheosis a simple coincidence, or an event entirely beyond reason. There are millions who have seen and heard reports of near-death experiences in which patients who have died on the operating table perceive a "beyond" before being resuscitated.

Every generation produces stories that blur the boundary between temporality and eternity.

Doctors have recently taken note of the uncanny ability of dying patients to select a meaningful moment for death, especially anniversaries that bear personal significance. In this sense, the double apotheosis was not unique. A British study has tried to balance biological, psychological, and social factors in the dying process. Examining "disease trajectories," clinical researchers describe some outstanding examples in which death was postponed or hastened by the dying. One such episode even concerns a fiftieth anniversary.

Here are some of the study's findings:

1. An often agitated Catholic veteran of the Far East theater in World War II, who knew he was dying, played out a personal drama and confessed to a priest that he had participated in war atrocities. After receiving absolution, the veteran rested more easily, physically suffered less, and quietly awaited the fiftieth anniversary of VJ (Victory over Japan) Day. He died directly after seeing the anniversary commemorated on the television.
2. A young AIDS patient facing the onset of dementia fell into a coma and was expected to die in a few days. Comatose, he held on for three weeks; and although all cognitive capacity had abandoned him, he remained somehow aware of the approaching twentieth anniversary of his mother's death. They had been very close, the patient's surviving relatives explained knowingly, and so no one was surprised when he finally died on that day of personal significance.
3. A man, married sixty years, had just endured the death of his wife, only to collapse and die as her funeral was coming to an end. He had never been ill a day in his life, and presumably chose to die when life lost its greatest meaning.[32]

As for Adams and Jefferson, two exceptionally strong-willed individuals, it is not hard to imagine that the pathological cause of death was present for some time prior, and that the individual will somehow directed the final act. Thomas Jefferson's poignant (and verifiable) question on the night of July 3—"Is it the Fourth?" he pressed Dr. Dunglison, in what the doctor termed a "husky" voice— opens up the possibility that thoughts of anticipation triggered neurochemical changes. Or, perhaps, to put it in terms Jefferson understood, a "sympathy" acted on behalf of bodily and spiritual balance, connecting the simple fact of a date with his sense of the world. A decade before, he had complimented the forward-looking script of a Fourth of July orator: "I hope the example will be followed and make the 4th of July a revision of conduct and of recall to the principles which made it our birth-day."[33] In Jefferson's mind, the very idea of the Fourth of July remained a formative and transformative moment.

We should be allowed to return to the primacy of sensible nerves—of the "feeling" underlying the way of life and death in Jefferson's generation. As Théophile de Bordeu put it in his *Research on the History of Medicine* (1767), "Feeling is involved in all the functions [of the body]; it directs them all. It dominates over illnesses; it guides the action of remedies; it sometimes becomes so dependent upon the soul, that the soul's passions take the upper hand over all the changes of the body."[34] After all is said and done, eighteenth-century philosophical medicine explains what happened quite as satisfyingly as the latest studies. The "soul's passions" had animated Thomas Jefferson's activist mind for eighty-three years. Why should they not have directed his final moments as well?

"I Can Never Love Again"

Alexander Garrett, the university's bursar, was at Monticello on the afternoon of the Fourth. Except for the immediate family, with Henry Lee gone there were apparently no visitors on this fateful day. Garrett wrote to his wife at five o'-clock, with a sense of helplessness:

> Mr. Jefferson is no more, he breathed his last 10 minutes before 1 Oclock today allmost without a struggle. No one here but Col. [Sam] Carr & myself, both of us ignorant of shrouding, neither ever having done it, ourselves or seen it done, we have done the best we could, and I hope all is right. His remains will be buried tomorrow at 5 oclock PM, no visitations will be given, all comeing will be welcome *at the* grave. I understand Mrs. R[andolph] bears the loss as well as could be expected, perhaps better, she has not as yet shed a tear, could she do so it would go better with her, the rest of the family are much distressed I learn, all however is silence about the house.[35]

Martha Jefferson Randolph was reared by her father to be mentally strong. No doubt she watched as her son-in-law Nicholas Trist snipped off tufts of the deceased Thomas Jefferson's still reddish hair, as a souvenir for family members, before the body was prepared for burial.[36]

No one set forth details of the July 5 burial ceremony at the Monticello cemetery other than to take note of the weather, an intermittent rain. The Reverend Hatch conducted the service. The obelisk Jefferson had designed for his own tomb would be carved out of granite by workers at the university during the next days and weeks.

Sketch of original obelisk, marking Thomas Jefferson's grave. From great-granddaughter Sarah N. Randolph's family memoir, *The Domestic Life of Thomas Jefferson* (1871).

Martha sought to cope with this momentous death by collecting newspaper clippings and poems of lament published in her father's honor. One moved her so much that she wrote it down at the back of Jefferson's precious *Commonplace Book,* the loose pages of which she had saved and would pass down to Virginia and Nicholas Trist. The poem, by a favorite contemporary, Anna Letitia Barbauld, was nine stanzas in length and opened with the following:

Pure spirit! O where art thou now!
Oh whisper to my soul!
O let some soothing thought of thee,
This bitter grief control
'Tis not for thee these tears I shed
Thy sufferings now are o'er;
The sea is calm, the tempest past,
On that eternal shore.[37]

This was, whether consciously intended or not, an answer to the deathbed adieu her father had left her, the poem reproduced at the opening of this book. All pain and grief behind, Thomas Jefferson had reached the "eternal shore" that, as he put it, "crowns all my hopes, or which buries my cares." By every indication, he saw death as peace. He accepted it easily, because it took so many so swiftly, and took most at a far younger age. In his life, and especially in his retirement, he had only feared uselessness and incapacity.

Cornelia Randolph was visiting her sister Ellen in Boston in June, and so these two grown granddaughters were unable to attend the funeral. They had received word from home that their grandfather was sinking and that they might see him one last time if they hurried. But they had gone no farther than New York when word of his death on the Fourth reached them. Ellen described what it was like to see Monticello under these new circumstances:

He was gone. His place was empty. I visited his grave, but the whole house at Monticello, with its large apartments and lofty ceilings, appeared to me one vast monument. Yet I could not always feel that I should see him no more. I wandered the vacant rooms as if I were looking for him.

As she tarried in his bedroom, she reckoned that the best years of her life had been spent here, in his company. She stared at the chair she could ordinarily be expected to find him occupying. She gazed at his clothing—nothing had as yet been moved. Then she took small souvenirs from his writing table, including scraps of paper with his handwriting on them.

All seemed as if he had just quitted the rooms and there were moments when I felt as if I expected his return. For days I started at what seemed the sound of his step or his voice, and caught myself listening for both.

She remained some weeks with this "invisible presence," reflecting on how much she had always enjoyed walking alongside him. Finally, before leaving once again for Boston,

I quitted the home of my youth never to return. I can never again feel a local attachment. As far as this place is concerned I can never love again.[38]

Between Two Darknesses

Jefferson, dying, had his own sense of history's obligation to tell truths. But he had no special secrets to impart urgently at the end. With the exception of a sexual connection he did not talk about, the uncovered secrets in these pages are not so much awkward "truths" that he scrupulously, stealthily hid, but emendations of all that he willingly revealed at one point or another. His "secrets" were hidden in plain view in his mass of preserved papers, embodied in his choice of words, in a lost vocabulary we can piece back together once we notice it.

Of course, even if we of a later time do not quite know how to verbalize it, we have always known the secret of Jefferson's long-term success. The secular thinker defined individual and national progress alike as a search for knowledge and insight that could be applied to the cause of human betterment. He wanted tolerance and goodwill to symbolize liberty in America. Alongside his proactive message of civil charity, he advocated disengagement. He wanted that to symbolize liberty in America, too. Breathing the country air and feeling its salutary effect, knowing that government required but little from its citizens, was, to Jefferson, what sensing the presence of God was to others: It gave him faith, while pointing ahead.

The faith, the optimism, that he generated, substituted for conventional religious devotion. Pursuing order and consonance in an unstable world, he might be called a no-nonsense Romantic who venerated a mute god. Did not the well-ordered dreamworld of Monticello symbolize, after all, his eclecticism, if not his iconoclasm? Reorienting nature in order that he could become a greater part of it, he struggled with impermanence as he scrounged for tools and tinkered. In politics, he set forces in motion, doing what he knew would spark resentments, and then surveyed the results, sized up his options, and recalibrated. Indeed, all that he built, all that he wrote, created more longing in him; and the longing served only to further define unattainable perfection.

Thus he was principally responsible for any discontent he might have felt. Like anyone with a cause, he was all business. His life was one of compounded devotion. Dreaming his instinctively contentious dream, he could think of no occasion to express penitence or even, it appears, regret, except, perhaps, when he acknowledged himself a fated creature; in that sense, he was "a link reluctant in a fleshly chain," as Lord Byron classified the human condition. Precariousness of life was the key condition behind the evolution of all Jefferson's knowledge-worshipping ideals.

As a public planner, Jefferson strived, somewhat improbably, for a sentimental consensus among those who would extend education, encourage
achievement, and improve the overall quality of life in America. He articulated
this ideal beautifully at seventy-five, in 1818, in pithy remarks he prepared for
the Virginia legislature in support of the plan for his university: "Education
engrafts a new man on the native stock," he wrote, "and turns what in his nature was vicious and perverse into qualities of virtue and social worth."[39] With
broad support for his program, he trusted that honesty and industry would
spread. That, in the simplest terms, is Jefferson's definition of a working
democracy.

In seeking to create a "new man," he was in effect (ironically, then) employ-
ing a religious model—conversion—as he reached out with a broad plan of
mass self-improvement. His aim was to aid in reconstituting the physical and
moral health of those around him—an imperiled generation, as he saw it.
Keeping the "Revolution of 1800" alive, Jefferson's ostensibly learned successors
would avoid descent into a state of torpor (as manifest in impressionable "nervous persons" with "languid fibres"); clear-eyed, they would see beyond the
façade of proclaimed piety that masked intolerance; they would possess
strength enough to prevent reemergence of the cruel consensus that had stood
behind a grasping, encroaching, elite-driven political power. Jeffersonian
democracy derived from a prophetic, questioning mind, and a sensitive, self-
monitored body.

This book has asked readers to adjust their overall view and regard Thomas
Jefferson as one with an all-embracing medical curiosity, that is, to see him as
an inquiring physiologist.[40] As such, he does not dwell on abstractions, the way
some who doubted his capacity to rule once clamored. Nor is he necessarily
timid about sex. What makes the man so long symbolized in the metonym of
Head and Heart somewhat altered now is that Body communicates to us, too—
and not merely in the form of rhetoric Jefferson used, knowing that his constituency understood it. In their changing world of physical sensations, agony
and strife, Body displaced religiosity to a marked degree. More and more, from
the days of Dr. Tissot forward, the intellect was recognized as having a dependence on the material body for promoting human vitality (and, ultimately,
democracy). Or as Antonio Damasio has more recently put it, "Emotions play
out in the theater of the body."[41]

Why, then, has it taken so long to identify this "other" Jefferson? It is because he did not communicate that physicality, that sensationalism, without a
good bit of invention and disguise, just as we have shown that he hid a distinct
unease with regard to his political legacy by projecting his own anxiety onto

the people at large. What Jefferson hid, he hid in the hope that it would afford him peace.

Throughout his life, and in retirement especially, Jefferson came to understand that private repose and contentment could not be had but through discretion in speaking and writing. Beyond sponsorship of the new university, he did not wish to be immersed in public debate anymore. He did his best to restrain himself. He wrote, begging not to be quoted. He relied on his friends to fulfill his public objectives, but not in his name.

Now we must finally place this sentient, striving Jefferson beside the one so long familiar—the inspiring lover of liberty. For generations, he has been chiefly associated in the popular mind with lofty thoughts and memorable phrases. Of late, we find him presented as a canny political animal, which, of course, he was, too. Recently, the historian Joyce Appleby wrote trenchantly of his mixed legacy, as the slave owner who was a force for liberation: "That Jefferson carries the odium of slavery for his generation is a wry tribute to his status as the voice of America's better self."[42] *The voice of America's better self.* His disgust for artificial distinctions within society, his impatience with those who swallowed prescriptive texts without questioning—his dissidence was real. To rebuke him without acknowledging his willingness to stand public trial for his beliefs is to underestimate him. Appleby found in Jefferson an "introspective honesty" not matched by many others among the founders, in spite of his clear capacity to rationalize. I find this a daring, and marvelously provocative, statement.

At the end of his days, Jefferson retained his lifelong ability to use words to public advantage. The last message he consciously directed to his country recapped so many that had preceded: On June 24, 1826, he replied to the Washington, D.C., committee that had optimistically invited the eighty-three-year-old to attend their Fourth of July jubilee celebration. Blasting "monkish ignorance and superstition," as he had many times during his public life, Jefferson harkened back to the trials of the Revolution, warmly upholding "the blessings and security of self-government," and reiterating his "undiminished devotion" to human liberty.[43] Then he put his pen down, and without fear or regret got on with the process of dying.

The view provided here, of Jefferson as an old man looking back on life, is a rather more personal perspective than that which most historians have taken in appraising Jefferson's position among the founders. But I believe such a focus has been needed. Although Jefferson's words and values remain critical elements in Americans' overall sense of what makes this nation distinctive, the slow, building crescendo of Jefferson's already animated life story had not really been heard. His remarkable retirement years were of insufficient consequence to Jefferson studies, and I wanted to fill in some of what was missing.

But my goal has been larger than that. I set out to convey the imagination of an eighteenth-century man who read incessantly but safeguarded his inmost thoughts, who wrote letters every day but revealed something less than what the recipients of his letters (let alone we) would have liked. I have done my best to capitalize on clues. I have sought out every word he wrote that offers us some hint about his own sense of what he lived for. I will conclude my version of his life, then, with one final bit of Jeffersonian speculation on how the world would be after he was gone.

For help, I call upon the London-born novelist E. M. Forster, who lived for a time in Greece. When we think of a lifetime as a story, it is worth remembering one of Forster's observations. Reckoning birth as an experience that is forgotten, and death as an experience much anticipated but beyond comprehension, the novelist wrote simply: "Our final experience, like our first, is conjectural. We move between two darknesses."[44] That would seem, at first glance, a statement that the eighteenth-century man of science could live with.

But is it complete? Shortly before her own death, Abigail Adams received a pert letter from Thomas Jefferson in which he lightly meditated on the end of life and the beginning of the imagined next: "I heard once a very old friend," he narrated, "who had troubled himself with neither poets nor philosophers, say . . . in plain prose, that he was tired of pulling off his shoes and stockings at night, and putting them on again in the morning. The wish to stay here is thus gradually extinguished: but not so easily that of returning once in a while to see how things have gone on. Perhaps however one of the elements of future felicity is to be a constant and unimpassioned view of what is passing here."[45] So much for darknesses. I suggest it was not for mere literary effect that Jefferson wrote these words. He quested for light, and hoped to "see" what befell his country next.

That would be his "future felicity." Anyway, it was as close to divining as Thomas Jefferson got. He offers a generous quantity of bright sentiments for a man habitually accused of hiding himself. What makes him most unusual among historical figures is that so much of what he said and did over the long course of his life remains vivid. Jefferson dying did not spend his solitude speculating on darknesses. He appears to have foreseen that his would not be a voice in the dark, but one that would continue speaking to history, in encouraging tones, after his lifetime was spent.

Americans have a habit of focusing attention back while thinking of the present, looking to the founding era with the hope that it will shed light on the nation's democratic promise (or on its dim deficiencies). Few would dispute that this is a fruitful exercise, though it is always an uncertain one. To borrow Forster's imagery again, America's past is a darkness into which we can send back our brightest flares and even then hope to see only unequal pieces of a still life; whereas America's future is another darkness into which we can but imaginatively project a light that only flickers.

Thomas Jefferson possessed no better tools: We were the darkness to his flickering light. He looked backward and thought he could perceive the barbarity ("the throes and convulsions of the ancient world") that had preceded. In response, he sought to represent what was better: a civilizing, liberalizing spirit. He rejected traditional definitions of morality and modes of faith (submission), which he regarded as intellectual cowardice; and in its place he pursued self-knowledge (release), which he regarded as a republican trait. He wrote with intensity and application, and argued for responsible self-government—for eventual healing and balance.

Jefferson was more brazen than most Americans realize. Though it was often remarked upon that he was an indulgent host and an amiable acquaintance, he devoted little time to guesswork and pleasantries. He was purposeful in his dealings with others, as hardy and potent and nervy as one could be who abhorred all violence. He probably gave more attention to body than to soul. He dwelled relentlessly on knowable experiences, on carnal life, on doing.

He was a cool-seeming man with thoughts of fire, a force for the freedom of mind essential to a democracy. He was, just as deservedly, the father of black disillusionment; for he excluded African Americans from his republic of felicity. Yes, he respected the humanity of those whom he owned. Yes, he subscribed to what was then a common belief in a racial hierarchy. To single him out, we might just as well single out James Madison, no less distinguished a political figure (if less emotive in the minds of modern Americans). But we know Thomas Jefferson as a humanist, a man who detested apathy. And still he did not evaluate any more humane alternative to slavery than the one he presented just after the Revolution: mass deportation. He chose not to reconsider. He chose not to lead. He chose not to emancipate his mind.

I opened these pages with a passage from Edward Young, a favorite poet of Thomas Jefferson's. Let me close with lines from Young as well. Writing that human beings illogically sought and shunned death with equal resolve, the poet wished that they would spend less of life absorbed in vain pursuits and instead see Time for what it is.

The man who consecrates his hours
By vigorous effort, and an honest aim,

At once draws the sting of life and death;
He walks with nature; and her paths are peace.[46]

However Jefferson is to be judged by our time, I hope that more has been re-vealed in these pages of his living sensations than of his near dying sensations. With warm attachment, he built a majestic house that extended science and art, and a university that extended his mind. And that is where and how he tested, as an Epicurean, for the palpable feeling of tranquil permanent felicity

ACKNOWLEDGMENTS

Only one with a callous disregard for America's national treasures would fail to recognize the extraordinary competence that Daniel P. Jordan, Monticello's executive director for more than two decades, has brought to his job. I have Dan to thank not only for making the splendid new Jefferson Library accessible, but also for the warmth and intellectual enthusiasm he has conveyed over the years since I began to study in his neighborhood. During the summer of 2003, I received a generous research fellowship under the auspices of the International Center for Jefferson Studies.

The scope of scholarship that thrives at Monticello is impressive:

Cinder Stanton has produced studies of Jefferson and slavery, and Jefferson and literature. Her *Free Some Day: The African-American Families at Monticello* (2000) is outstanding, and her influence on my book has been pronounced. In *The Worlds of Monticello* (1993), Monticello's curator, Susan Stein, wrote about everything that Jefferson collected that holds any interest for me. She, too, has been consistently supportive. Bob Self, who has explored Monticello's recesses, opened up his country home, where he restores Jefferson's material world.

Jefferson Looney, editor of the new *Retirement Papers* series at the Jefferson Library, has a staggering knowledge of the republic of letters. As he moves ahead in publishing the many critical documents that pertain to Jefferson's retirement years, I hope my book will serve to attract more attention to the fine work already underway.

Conversations with Jill Anderson, also of the *Papers*, and research librarians Jack Robertson and Bryan Craig, made the investigative process friendlier and easier. Katherine Knisley, of the ICJS, coordinated everything so that my time as a fellow was productive. I am also grateful to Ann Lucas for sharing her inquiry into the travels of Ellen Wayles Randolph Coolidge; and to Andrew O'Shaughnessy, the new director of ICJS, for his encouragement.

Three other libraries were important in the research process: Alderman Library at the University of Virginia; the Huntington Library in San Marino, California; and the Library of Congress in Washington, D.C. For any historian who studies the republic of letters, nothing can replace access to personal texts and precious parchment.

A number of active scholars have contributed substantively to my work on Jefferson, and I wish to acknowledge their efforts as well: David Waldstreicher has a unique appreciation for the spirit of Jeffersonian Americans. I enjoy his scholarship, and I appreciate his good comments on key portions of the manuscript. Douglas Egerton aided in providing context on the subject of slavery and politics. Annette Gordon-Reed regularly challenges me to expand my understanding of Jefferson's long problematic race-consciousness. Joseph J. Ellis, attuned to Virginia-Massachusetts tensions, argues persuasively with regard to the Jefferson-Adams dialogue, and I bear in mind his incisive critique.

Classicist Tom Benediktson was of immense help as I sought to better appreciate what drew Jefferson's heart to ancient Greece. In his role as Dean of Arts & Sciences at the University of Tulsa, Tom has been encouraging on more than one front. Christine Ehrick and Andrew Grant Wood connected North and South American worldviews, as I aimed to encounter the varieties of knowledge and culture to which Jefferson was exposed. Jay H. Geller provided clarification of the career of Professor Ebeling of Hamburg, Germany; Laura Stevens gave a thoughtful review of the section on Jefferson's reading habits; and John Bowlin read and reacted to the chapter on Jefferson's religious views. My son Josh, now college-bound, freely gave his opinion on the readability of vital passages.

My partner, Nancy Isenberg, is a steady muse. This book was generated nearly as much by Nancy's lively historical perspective, and our relentless back-and-forth on daily walks, as by my own research and reflection. Watch for her forthcoming treatise on Aaron Burr!

I am especially grateful to two very understanding professionals who are devoted to the cause of history and who actively inspired the final product: Geri Thoma, my unfaltering literary agent, and the equally kind and resolute Liz Maguire, editor and publisher at Basic.

I leave for the ultimate acknowledgment my friend Peter Onuf, to whom I appreciatively dedicate this book. Peter has been a good-natured critic for more than a dozen years now. When I re-entered graduate school in quest of a Ph.D., after a "tentative" fifteen-year career in international business, the Thomas Jefferson Memorial Foundation Professor of History at the University of Virginia facilitated the transition and taught me how to think and write as a historian. I have been out of graduate school a good while now, but Peter never ceases to prompt, stimulate, and bring cheer. Excepting his extraordinary tolerance for differences in style and opinion, I do not know anyone quite so well formed for academe as he. This book is just part of what I owe, Big Guy.

ABBREVIATIONS

Adams-Jefferson Letters   *The Adams-Jefferson Letters: The Complete Correspondence between Thomas Jefferson and Abigail and John Adams*, ed. Lester J. Cappon (1959; rept. Chapel Hill, N.C., 1987).

Anas   *The Complete Anas of Thomas Jefferson*, ed. Franklin B. Sawvel (New York, 1903).

Bergh   *The Writings of Thomas Jefferson*, ed. Albert Ellery Bergh. 20 vols. (Washington, D.C., 1907).

Extracts   *Jefferson's Extracts from the Gospels*, ed. Dickinson W. Adams (Princeton, N.J., 1983).

Family Letters   *The Family Letters of Thomas Jefferson*, ed. Edwin Morris Betts and James Adam Bear, Jr. (Columbia, Mo., 1966).

Ford   *The Works of Thomas Jefferson*, ed. Paul Leicester Ford. 12 vols. (New York, 1905).

Inner Jefferson   Andrew Burstein, *The Inner Jefferson: Portrait of a Grieving Optimist* (Charlottesville, 1995).

Malone   Dumas Malone, *Jefferson and His Time*. 6 vols. (Boston, 1948–81).

Memorandum Books   *Jefferson's Memorandum Books: Accounts, with Legal Records and Miscellany, 1767–1826*, eds. James A. Bear, Jr. and Lucia C. Stanton (Princeton, N.J., 1997).

Notes on Virginia   Thomas Jefferson, *Notes on the State of Virginia*, ed. David Waldstreicher (New York, 2002).

Portable Jefferson   *The Portable Thomas Jefferson*, ed. Merrill D. Peterson (New York, 1975).

PTJ-Boyd   *Papers of Thomas Jefferson*, ed. Julian P. Boyd, et. al. 30 vols. to date. (Princeton, N.J., 1950 –).

Randall   Henry S. Randall, *The Life of Thomas Jefferson*. 3 vols. (New York, 1858).

Sowerby   *Catalogue of the Library of Thomas Jefferson*, compiled by E. Millicent Sowerby. 5 vols. (Washington, D.C., 1952–59).

TJP-Huntington Thomas Jefferson Papers, Huntington Library, San Marino, Calif.

TJP-LC Thomas Jefferson Papers, Library of Congress.

TJP-MHS Thomas Jefferson Papers, Massachusetts Historical Society.

TJP-WM Thomas Jefferson Papers, Tucker-Coleman Collection, College of William & Mary.

TJP-ViU Thomas Jefferson Papers, University of Virginia.

I have examined Jefferson's correspondence in his hand, generally on microfilm, in order to discern cross-outs and substitutions, and other indications of deliberation in the writing process. Whenever possible, I have cross-checked to see if a cited letter has been published, and have either cited both original and printed sources, or the printed source alone. Unpublished letters are indicated, of course, by the collection to which they belong. I have made an effort at consistency in displaying Jefferson's orthography and capitalization: He begins sentences with lower case letters, except for the pronoun "I". I have begun Jefferson's sentences with capitalization, for ease in reading.

NOTES

Postmortem

1. *Jefferson's Literary Commonplace Book,* ed. Douglas L. Wilson (Princeton, 1989), 102–103, 187.

2. Ibid., 102; TJ to Adams, June 1, 1822, Adams-Jefferson Letters, 577.

3. The most notable recent exception is Joseph J. Ellis, who treated these years in successive books on Adams and Jefferson. See Ellis, *Passionate Sage: The Character and Legacy of John Adams* (New York, 1993), chaps. 4 and 7, and *American Sphinx: The Character of Thomas Jefferson* (New York, 1997), chap. 5. Dumas Malone's classic six-volume biography of Jefferson, published between 1948 and 1981 and collectively titled *Jefferson and His Time,* is the starting point for any intelligent study. Malone's final volume, on the retirement years, is subtitled *The Sage of Monticello.*

4. Though less concerned with nuances in medical language than we are here, the scholars who have principally examined these matters are Daniel J. Boorstin, *The Lost World of Thomas Jefferson* (Chicago, 1948); Charles A. Miller, *Jefferson and Nature: An Interpretation* (Baltimore, 1988), chap. 2; and I. Bernard Cohen, *Science and the Founding Fathers* (New York, 1995), chap. 2. Roy Porter's posthumously published *Flesh in the Age of Reason* (London and New York, 2003 and 2004) came out only after I had finished writing; but the intellectual environment described in his work bears a remarkable connection to my evaluation of Jefferson's way of thinking.

5. Adams to TJ, March 2, 1816; TJ to Adams, April 2, 1816, *Adams-Jefferson Letters,* 464, 467.

6. Samuel Johnson, *A Dictionary of the English Language* (Philadelphia, 1813), n.p.

7. TJ to Charles Bellini, September 30, 1785, PTJ 8:569, here expressing his belief that Americans, simpler in their ways than the Europeans, succeeded in moral self-cultivation and could claim superiority on that basis. For further analysis of *happiness, delight,* and *felicity,* see *Inner Jefferson,* chap. 3.

8. Antonio Damasio, *The Feeling of What Happens: Body and Emotion in the Making of Consciousness* (New York, 1999), esp. chap. 9; Damasio, *Looking for Spinoza: Joy, Sorrow, and the Feeling Brain* (New York, 2003), 83ff. The author is head of the Department of Neurology at the University of Iowa Medical Center.

9. *Inner Jefferson*, esp. 255–257, 266–272. The sixty entries that concern mortality represent approximately 15 percent of the excerpts in the *Commonplace Book*.

10. TJ to Edward Rutledge, November 30, 1795, PTJ-Boyd 28:541.

11. TJ to Madison, April 27, 1795, PTJ-Boyd 28:339. Similarly, to his tobacco broker, Alexander Donald, a month later, stressing his return to the preferred occupation of farming: "I rarely take up a book, and never a pen if I can help it." TJ to Donald, May 30, 1795, PTJ-Boyd 28:366.

12. Jefferson's notes on a conversation with John Adams, February 15, 1798, PTJ-Boyd 30:113.

13. *Memorandum Books*, 2:1414–1417.

14. Short to TJ, August 14, 1819, TJP-MHS. To Dr. Benjamin Waterhouse even before that, Jefferson had grumbled that all "epistolary industry" was gone: "The aversion has been growing on me for a considerable time." TJ to Waterhouse, March 3, 1818, Ford 12:89.

15. TJ to Lafayette, October 28, 1822, Ford 12:255–256.

16. TJ to Katherine Duane Morgan, January 26, 1822, TJP-ViU.

17. Jefferson's original *Summary Journal of Letters* is in the Library of Congress.

18. TJ to Thomas Jefferson Randolph, February 8, 1826, *Family Letters*, 469; *Inner Jefferson*, 265–266; Sarah N. Randolph, *The Domestic Life of Thomas Jefferson* (Charlottesville, Va., 1978 [New York, 1871]), 429. Jefferson's deathbed adieu remained in the Jefferson family until 1932, and is today in a private collection. For its provenance, see letter from Laurence Gouverneur Hoes to John Fleming, May 27, 1954, at the James Monroe Museum.

19. Randall, 3:563; Randolph, *Domestic Life*, 431. For Jefferson as a violinist and lifelong lover of music, see Helen Cripe, *Thomas Jefferson and Music* (Charlottesville, Va., 1979).

20. John M. Bryan, ed., *Robert Mills, Architect* (Washington, D.C., 1989), 154–55; Mills to TJ, February 15; TJ to Mills, March 3, 1826, TJP-LC. Mills (1781–1855) designed the Washington Monument near the end of his life. Jefferson was an honorary member of the Bunker Hill Monument Association, at the invitation of the classical scholar and Massachusetts congressman Edward Everett of Massachusetts. See Everett to TJ, March 29, 1825, TJP-LC.

21. *Memorandum Books*, 1:415, 521. "Patty" was the nickname of Martha Wayles Jefferson; when Jefferson wrote of his wife to friends, he referred to her as "Patty."

22. *Inner Jefferson*, 60–62, 147.

23. Ibid., 63–66, 247.

24. Randall, 3:537, 543, 547.

25. TJ to Mills, March 3, 1826; to Macon, February 21, 1826; Macon to TJ, February 11, 1826, all in TJP-LC. Passing on a status report to a school chum of his early teenage years, Jefferson provided essential data: "I shall be 83. y. old on the 13th of the ensuing month of April. . . . disloc[atio]ns of both my wrists antient & recent with the advance of years have so far disabled my hands as to make writing all but impracticable to me." TJ to Thomas W. Maury, March 1, 1826, TJP-LC.

26. Randolph, *Domestic Life*, 416.

27. William Buchan, *Domestic Medicine* (London, 1781), 121–122. Jefferson owned the 1784 edition. Dr. Buchan's book eventually saw more than one hundred editions in print.

28. On the medical aspects of gender roles, see Ludmilla Jordanova, *Sexual Visions: Images of Gender in Science and Medicine between the Eighteenth and Twentieth Centuries* (Madison, Wisc., 1989); on the confluence of medicine and literature, see esp. Anne C. Vila, *Enlightenment and Pathology: Sensibility in the Literature and Medicine of Eighteenth-Century France* (Baltimore, 1998). For observations on gender and socialization in literature, the seminal work is Cathy N. Davidson, *Revolution and the Word: The Rise of the Novel in America* (New York, 1986). See chapter 4 below for a more detailed examination of these issues.

29. TJ to Cosway, December 27, 1820, in Helen Duprey Bullock, *My Head and My Heart: A Little History of Thomas Jefferson and Maria Cosway* (New York, 1945), 176–177. At an even more advanced age, Jefferson wrote similarly to François Adrian Van der Kemp: "The solitude in which we are left by the death of our friends is one of the greatest evils of protracted life. When I look back to the days of my youth it is like looking over a field of battle. All, all dead! and ourselves left alone midst a new generation whom we know not and who know not us." TJ to Van der Kemp, January 11, 1825, Ford 12:400. These lines add meaning to Jefferson's comment to Benjamin Waterhouse a few days earlier: Should a stumble, a fall, cut short life "and relieve me from the evils of dotage," death would not be a tragedy. "Come when it will, it will find me neither unready nor unwilling." TJ to Waterhouse, February 11, 1825, Ford 12:399.

30. Throughout his life, Jefferson indulged in metaphors of the sea when he wished to describe emotional challenge or emotional calm. Recently, Charles A. Miller published his study of this phenomenon; see his *Ship of State: The Nautical Metaphors of Thomas Jefferson* (Lanham, Md., 2003).

Chapter 1

1. Ford 12:399. Waterhouse (1754–1846) taught at Harvard Medical College from 1783 to 1812.

2. Three days after he wrote to Waterhouse, Jefferson responded to a letter from a Dutch friend, François Adrian Van der Kemp, expressing similar forlorn hopes: "The solitude in which we are left by the death of our friends is one of the great evils of protracted life." Ford 12:400.

3. Ernest Becker, *The Denial of Death* (New York, 1973), 26, 31.

4. Peale to TJ, May 2, 1815, TJP-LC; TJ to Adams, August 15, 1820, *Adams-Jefferson Letters*, 569. Similarly, "God bless you, and give you health, strength, good spirits, and as much of life as you think worth having." See TJ to Adams, June 1, 1822, in ibid., 579.

5. Randall 3:674. The word *tettered* denoted red, scaly, or crusted skin, as from eczema.

6. His language to Waterhouse repeated what he had written some months before to Charles Willson Peale: "I ride every day from 3. or 4. to 8. or 10. miles without fatigue, but I am little able to walk, and never further than my garden." TJ to Peale, July 18, 1824, TJP-LC. As to the fear that his mental faculties were also in rapid decline, see, for example, TJ to Edward Livingston, March 25, 1825, in which he declined comment on a code of laws, not from laziness but "an approvable caution for the age of fourscore and two. . . . The misfortune of a weakened mind is an insensibility of it's weakness." Overseer Edmund Bacon

bought Eagle on Jefferson's behalf in November 1820, when the horse was six years old. See James A. Bear, Jr., ed., *Jefferson at Monticello* (Charlottesville, Va., 1967), 62; *Memorandum Books*, 2:1371; also Joseph J. Ellis, *American Sphinx: The Character of Thomas Jefferson* (New York, 1997), 229–233.

7. Samuel X. Radbill, "The Autobiographical Ana of Robley Dunglison, M.D.," *Transactions of the American Philosophical Society* 53 (1963): 9–10.

8. Ibid., 26.

9. TJ to Wistar, June 21, 1807, Ford 9:78–85. Jefferson tended mostly to disparage medical theory, not medical practice. He remarked to a visiting Italian investigator on the subject of the "stranger's fever" common to southern seaports: "The absence of all medical theory and pretentions can alone claim any respect for the information from those unlearned, as myself, in the art." TJ to Dr. Eusebio Valli, May 9, 1816, TJP-LC; see also Daniel J. Boorstin, *The Lost World of Thomas Jefferson* (Chicago, 1948), 133–135. Yet Jefferson must still strike us as an eighteenth-century man, trusting in bleeding in cases of inflammation, and mercury in cases of syphilis.

10. *The Autobiography of Benjamin Rush: His 'Travels Through Life' Together with His Commonplace Book for 1789–1813,* ed. George W. Corner (Princeton, 1948), entry of July 27, 1796, 236; Rush to Hosack, June 20, 1812, *Letters of Benjamin Rush,* ed. L. H. Butterfield (Princeton, 1951), 2:1141–1142; on the Rush-Hosack dialogue, see Christine Chapman Robbins, *David Hosack: Citizen of New York* (Philadelphia, 1964), chap. 9; on competing ambitions among prominent American physicians, see Benjamin Waterhouse to TJ, March 26, 1813, TJP-LC; Carl Van Doren, *Benjamin Franklin* (New York, 1938), 110. The Franklin sayings are from 1733 and 1736 respectively. Jefferson occasionally used the word *surgeon* or *surgery* in a nonmedical context to convey a sense of butchery or reckless provocation, as in vilifying Britain for its unfeeling recourse to war: "Your government . . . ordered their surgeons to commence work upon us." See TJ to Alexander Donald, May 30, 1795, PTJ-Boyd 28:367.

11. "Dr. Dunglison's visits," TJP-LC; *The Jefferson-Dunglison Letters,* ed. John M. Dorsey, M.D. (Charlottesville, Va., 1960), 38; TJ to Dearborn, June 19, 1825, TJP-LC; TJ to Short, August 9, 1825, TJP-MHC; TJ to Bernard Peyton, August 29, 1825, TJP-MHC, requesting "6. full sized bougies[,] 12. of various sizes." Insertion of the bougie must have been uncomfortable. Jefferson would have moved the rigid, narrow tube through the urethral opening at the end of the penis until it reached the bladder. After visiting Monticello in 1824 and 1825, Lafayette sent a shipment of superior quality French elastic (more flexible) gum catheters; however, these did not arrive until after Jefferson's death. I am grateful to Dr. T. J. "Jock" Murray, Professor of Medical Humanities at Dalhousie Medical School, Halifax, Nova Scotia, for explaining how bougies and catheters were used in the early nineteenth century.

12. Radbill, "Autobiographical Ana," 26. For an overview of the state of medical knowledge and family care in this era, see Oscar Reiss, *Medicine in Colonial America* (Lanham, Md., 2000); also Lamar Riley Murphy, *Enter the Physician: The Transformation of Domestic Medicine, 1760–1860* (Tuscaloosa, Ala., 1991).

13. *Papers of Andrew Jackson,* ed. Sam B. Smith et al. (Knoxville, Tenn., 1980), 2:24, 102–103.

14. Mary Rawlings, *Ante-bellum Albemarle* (Charlottesville, Va., 1974), 71; John Hammond Moore, *Albemarle: Jefferson's County, 1727–1976* (Charlottesville, Va., 1976), 90; *American Farmer* (Baltimore), June 30, 1820. I wish to thank Cinder Stanton for bringing this newspaper to my attention.

15. TJ to Madison, January 28, 1821, *Republic of Letters*, 1829; *Memorandum Books*, 2:1369.

16. John Somerville to Jackson, February 4, 1822; Jackson to TJ, February 6, 1822, *Papers of Andrew Jackson*, 5:142–144.

17. *American Farmer*, June 30, 1820.

18. Watkins's commentary ("this whole course however will wear the face of trick and unfairness") makes plain that he believed the Jackson forces up to no good, and he presumed Jefferson in sympathy with his view. Watkins to TJ, October 16, 1823; TJ to Watkins, November 9, 1823, TJP-LC. Jefferson had already given Watkins a letter of introduction to Senator Nathaniel Macon stating that "his political principles are yours & mine." See TJ to Macon, October 10, 1823, TJP-LC. Expecting a long absence or perhaps that Watkins would never return, Jefferson settled his accounts with the doctor, paying him fifty dollars on October 5. See *Memorandum Books*, 2:1399.

19. Watkins to TJ, September 27, 1824, TJP-LC.

20. Malone, 6:431–432.

21. Watkins to TJ, September 27, 1824, TJP-LC.

22. TJ to Watkins, October 16, 1824, TJP-LC.

23. Crawford's debility could have been kept hidden from the public. He recovered, but only very slowly. In the summer of 1824, Crawford supporter and longtime Jefferson admirer Margaret Bayard Smith wrote of the Georgian, now her Washington neighbor: "It is surprising to me that his temper is not soured or irritated by these repeated attacks of Malevolence and disease; instead of which he is now more mild and indulgent to his opponents, more patient, gentle and affectionate to his family than ever." While others were pitying his condition, she affirmed: "He . . . will, I trust, be soon quite well." Margaret Bayard Smith, *The First Forty Years of Washington Society*, ed. Gaillard Hunt (New York, 1906), 165–166.

24. Politics and scientific inquiry were hard to separate for other reasons. The best minds of the Revolutionary generation tended to legitimize political arguments with extended metaphors from science. Perhaps most prevalent among such rhetorical constructions were metaphors from astronomy. As the Revolution approached, a variety of political commentators analogized the shifting center of gravity in the solar system to America's separation from England; in philosophic minds the new nation was "a new primary planet in the system of the world." In support of the federal Constitution, James Madison and others strengthened their arguments with respect to federal-state relations by associating the system of government with the "attractive principle," "centrifugal force," and planetary orbits. There is good reason to associate Jefferson's evocation of "laws of nature," in the Declaration and elsewhere, with Newtonian laws of motion: Physical phenomena and human morality were equally facts of nature to him. Political equilibrium as a concept clearly has a scientific referent. See I. Bernard Cohen, *Science and the Founding Fathers* (New York, 1995), 36–40,

150–153, 257–260; George E. Rosen, "Political Order and Human Health in Jeffersonian Thought," Bulletin of History of Medicine 26 (1952): 32–44; Charles A. Miller, *Jefferson and Nature: An Interpretation* (Baltimore, 1988), 91.

25. Courtney R. Hall, "Jefferson on the Medical Theory and Practice of His Day," *Bulletin of the History of Medicine* 31 (1957): 242–244; Silvio A. Bedini, *Jefferson and Science* (Charlottesville, Va., 2002), 57–59; Wyndham B. Blanton, *Medicine in Virginia in the Nineteenth Century* (Richmond, Va., 1933), 133, 260.

26. Watkins to TJ, May 14, 1825, TJP-LC.

27. Ibid., May 11, 1825, TJP-LC.

28. Samuel Johnson, *A Dictionary of the English Language* (Philadelphia, 1813), n.p.

29. *Memorandum Books* 1:207–209, entries of August 4, September 5, October 14, and October 28, 1770. Patty Jefferson was previously married to Bathurst Skelton, whom Jefferson had known in college; the couple had one child, a boy who died shortly before Jefferson married the widow Skelton in 1772—there is no reason, however, to suspect that Patty carried a sexually transmitted disease; TJ to John Banister, Jr., October 15, 1785, *Portable Jefferson*, 393.

30. I wish to thank Dr. Joan Witkin of Columbia University School of Physicians and Surgeons, Dr. Herb Chase and Dr. Susan Lederer of Yale University School of Medicine, and especially Dr. T. J. "Jock" Murray of Dalhousie Medical School, Halifax, Nova Scotia, for their help in evaluating Jefferson's medical condition.

31. *The Jefferson-Dunglison Letters,* 96.

32. Bear, *Jefferson at Monticello,* 73.

33. James Maury to TJ, April 29, 1815; TJ to Maury, June 15, 1815, TJP-LC.

34. Jock Murray, "Thomas Jefferson and Medicine," *Journal of Medical Biography* 5 (August 1997): 154; TJ to Peale, July 18, 1824, TJP-LC.

35. TJ to Ellen Wayles Randolph, October 25, 1808, and to Martha Randolph, November 1, 1808, *Family Letters,* 354–56; TJ to Benjamin Rush, August 17, 1811, Ford 11:212–213; TJ to Dr. Brown, November 13, 1813, TJP-LC.

36. TJ to Martha Randolph, August 21, 1818, and August 24, 1819; TJ to Francis W. Eppes, September 11, 1818, *Family Letters,* 426, 427, 431; TJ to Henry Dearborn, October 27, 1818, TJP-LC; Hannah (Poplar Forest slave) to TJ, November 15, 1818, TJP-MHS; *Memorandum Books,* 2:1346, 1357. For an in-depth study of the springs, see Charlene M. Boyer Lewis, *Ladies and Gentlemen on Display: Planter Society at the Virginia Springs, 1790–1860* (Charlottesville, Va., 2001).

37. TJ to Rush, February 28, 1803, Ford 9:453–454; Rush to TJ, March 12 and May 5, 1803, *Letters of Benjamin Rush,* ed. L. H. Butterfield (Princeton, 1951), 2:856–859, 863–864. An "oak gall" is a swollen mass formed on the oak tree after parasites puncture the bark and lay eggs inside. Although Rush's remedies, from a modern perspective, tended to be in large measure ineffective and, at times, even harmful, Jefferson trusted him implicitly, ordering the doctor's complete works for the new University of Virginia library. See TJ to William Hilliard, June 3, 1825, TJP-LC.

38. Roy Porter, "Consumption: Disease of the Consumer Society?" in John Brewer and Roy Porter, eds., *Consumption and the World of Goods* (London, 1993), 58–80.

39. John M. Holmes, *Thomas Jefferson Treats Himself* (Fort Valley, Va., 1997), 43. Peter Hatch of Monticello cautions that there is no definite indication that Jefferson grew rhubarb specifically to take for diarrhea.

40. James Ewell, *The Medical Companion* (Philadelphia, 1819), 416.

41. TJ to Roane, July 18, 1822, TJP-LC; Jefferson owned a London, 1705, edition of *The Whole Works of That Excellent Practical Physician, Dr. Thomas Sydenham.* See Sowerby, 1:410–411.

42. Sir John Sinclair, *The Code of Health and Longevity* (London, 1818 [4th ed.; 1st edition 1802]), 220–231. Jefferson maintained a correspondence with Sinclair during his retirement.

43. William Buchan, *Domestic Medicine* (London, 1781), 338–342.

44. Sowerby, 1:405–406; Ludmilla Jordanova, "The Popularisation of Medicine: Tissot on Onanism," in Jordanova, *Nature Displayed: Gender, Science and Medicine, 1760–1820* (London, 1999), 105. The full title of *Tissot's Advice* was *Tissot's Advice to the People in General, with Regard to Their Health.*

45. "Une habitude rigoureuse est une véritable servitude." "J'ai connu des Gens de Lettres tellement asservis à leur régime que leur esprit étoit dans la plus complete dépendance du corps." S. A. D. Tissot, *De la Santé des Gens de Lettres* (Lausanne, Switzerland, 1775), 236.

46. Ibid., 67–74, 125, 236.

47. Anne C. Vila, *Enlightenment and Pathology: Sensibility in the Literature and Medicine of Eighteenth-Century France* (Baltimore, 1998), chap. 3; Tissot, *De la Santé des Gens de Lettres,* 83–84; TJ to Rush, August 17, 1811, Ford 11:212–213. From Liverpool, England, Virginian James Maury, who had been Jefferson's school chum back in the 1750s, confided in his old friend in 1822 that his son and namesake "has, for many years, labored under nervous affections to such a degree as greatly to have impeded his progress in acquirements equal to my original expectations." What Maury's problem was, the father does not say, though it shows that a range of unsuccessfully treated "nervous affections" existed, and whether from a passion for learning or other, less noble cause, was thought to have the same deleterious effect on the body (Maury to TJ, June 24, 1822, TJP-LC).

48. Benjamin Waterhouse, M.D., *Cautions to Young Persons Concerning Health in a Public Lecture Delivered . . . Nov. 20, 1804* (Cambridge, Mass., 1805), 7–10, 16.

49. Ewell, *The Medical Companion,* 366.

50. TJ to Charles Yancey, January 6, 1816, Ford 11:494. A recent arrival from England named Joseph Coppinger used a combination of moral reasoning and patriotic notions to interest Jefferson in investing in a large-scale brewing operation, saying that this industry "should be ranked among the first objects of [America's] domestic and political economy." Jefferson replied that though he concurred with the "desirableness to introduce a taste for malt liquors instead of that for ardent spirits," he did not "think it a case where a company need form itself on patriotic principles merely, because there is a sufficiency of private capital which would embark itself in the business." He was content to brew on a small scale: "I am lately become a brewer for family use." To learn this skill, he relied on a Norfolk brewer he was quite partial to, Captain Joseph Miller. See Coppinger to TJ, April 6, 1815; TJ to Coppinger, April 25, 1815; TJ to Miller, June 26, 1815, all in TJP-LC. Jefferson distilled whiskey "out of our worst toll wheat," largely for the consumption of laborers. See Bear, *Jefferson at Monticello,* 56.

51. Elizabeth Trist to Catharine Wistar Bache, August 22, 1814, Papers of the American Philosophical Society, Philadelphia (microfilm); TJ to Craven Peyton, August 12, 1821, TJP-ViU.

52. Waterhouse, *Cautions to Young Persons Concerning Health,* esp. 23–30; TJ to Waterhouse, June 26, 1822, Ford 12:241, concerning a later but similarly inspired pamphlet.

53. See especially G. J. Barker-Benfield, *The Horrors of the Half-Known Life: Male Attitudes Toward Women and Sexuality in Nineteenth-Century America* (New York, 2000 [1974]), chap. 6.

54. Helen Lefkowitz Horowitz, *Rereading Sex: Battles over Sexual Knowledge and Suppression in Nineteenth-Century America* (New York, 2002).

55. Adam Smith, *The Theory of Moral Sentiments* (Amherst, N.Y., 2000 [1759]), 209.

56. TJ to William Short, October 31, 1819, *Extracts,* 390.

57. TJ to W. H. Torrance, June 11, 1815, TJP-LC.

58. George Cheyne, *The English Malady* (facsimile reprint of 1733 edition), ed. Roy Porter (London, 1991), pt. 3, chap. 1; Sinclair, *The Code of Health and Longevity,* 19.

59. Waterhouse, *Cautions to Young Persons Concerning Health,* 7–8, 13. On the linkage between eighteenth-century intellectual life, digestive disorders, and the opening of restaurants in the pursuit of health, see Rebecca L. Spang, *The Invention of the Restaurant: Paris and Modern Gastronomic Culture* (Cambridge, Mass., 2000), chap. 1.

60. Ellen Coolidge Letterbook, Special Collections, ViU; Waterhouse, *Cautions to Young Persons,* 18.

61. Rush to Vine Utley, June 25, 1812, *Letters of Benjamin Rush,* 2:1142–1143.

62. TJ to Utley, March 21, 1819, Ford 12:117; Utley to TJ, March 18, 1822, TJP-MHS. Dr. Utley advised Jefferson at this time that he had adopted Jefferson's habit of daily bathing his feet in cold water to prevent colds. For Jefferson's ideas related to coffee drinking, see also TJ to Edmund Rogers, February 14, 1824, TJP-WM.

63. Waterhouse, *Cautions to Young Persons Concerning Health,* 10.

64. TJ to Charles Bellini, September 30, 1785, PTJ-Boyd 8:569. Jefferson's Enlightenment ideology dictated that awakening reason, the illimitable pursuit of a knowledge of nature, was another way to describe the process by which human beings developed in self-knowledge. Jefferson held that progress—the acquisition of knowledge—was by definition conducted under a condition of vitality, or advancing health.

Chapter 2

1. Randall, 3:546–548; Gordon Jones and James A. Bear, Jr., "Thomas Jefferson's Medical History," 1979, an unpublished manuscript at the Jefferson Library, Monticello.

2. Merrill D. Peterson, ed., *Visitors to Monticello* (Charlottesville, Va., 1989), 79, citing the 1817 visit of Lieutenant Francis Hall.

3. TJ to James Monroe, March 18, 1785, PTJ-Boyd 8:43; TJ to James Maury, June 15, 1815 (scored through section of draft letter), TJP-LC; Peter Gay, *The Enlightenment: An Interpretation,* vol. 2, *The Science of Freedom* (New York, 1969), 8, 12.

4. Gay, *The Enlightenment,* 2:14–15, 23; Carl Binger, *Revolutionary Doctor: Benjamin Rush, 1746–1813* (New York, 1966). The Rush family owned a Pennsylvania estate called "Sydenham."

5. Among his French holdings were works by Pierre Jean Georges Cabanis (1757–1808), whom he knew in France and whose books he eagerly sought; he acquired French studies of venereal disease, varieties in the human constitution, new treatments for diseases, and pharmacology. But he, like many of his peers, took a comparable interest in medical knowledge derived from classical antiquity; he owned, for instance, the works of Hippocrates in Greek and Latin, and other medical texts published in the sixteenth and seventeenth centuries in those languages. See Sowerby, 1:395–396, 400–401, 412, 434–435. On the influence of the ancients, see also Jones and Bear, "Thomas Jefferson's Medical History," chap. 4. Jones and Bear write of Cabanis, "Perhaps if Cabanis had not died so young in 1808 he would have fired Jefferson's interest in the years of his retirement."

6. *Philosophical Writings of Étienne Bonnot, Abbé de Condillac,* trans. Franklin Philip (Hillsdale, N.J., 1982), 157–167; Ernst Cassirer, *The Philosophy of the Enlightenment* (Princeton, 1951 [1932]), 102–105. Relating each of the five senses to the mind by presenting them separately as they would respond in a body deprived of all the other senses, Condillac demonstrates his powers of analysis. "A sensation is not yet an idea," he writes, "insofar as it is considered only as a feeling limited to modifying the mind. . . . [If] feelings exist only in the memory that recalls them, they become ideas." *Philosophical Writings,* 167.

7. TJ to Abigail Adams, January 11, 1817, *Adams-Jefferson Letters,* 504. For a useful discussion of the philosophical range of meaning within which "imagination" was understood in Jefferson's lifetime, see Mark Johnson, *The Body in the Mind: The Bodily Basis of Meaning, Imagination, and Reason* (Chicago, 1987), chap. 6.

8. For a balanced discussion of this phenomenon, see Patrick H. Hutton, *History as an Art of Memory* (Hanover, N.H., 1993).

9. TJ to Rush, Aug. 17, 1811, Ford 9:329; *Notes on Virginia,* Query XIV, 175–176.

10. Rush to TJ, March 12, 1801, *Letters of Benjamin Rush,* 2:831–833; TJ to Rush, March 24, 1801, Ford 9:230; TJ to Madison, February 8, 1798, *Republic of Letters,* 1020; TJ to Adams, June 15, 1813, and August 15, 1820, *Adams-Jefferson Letters,* 331, 567–568. It is possible that Jefferson borrowed his "I feel, therefore I exist" from the French philosopher whose work he translated and arranged for U.S. publication. The first part of Destutt de Tracy's *Elements d'Idéologie* contains this statement: "To pass a judgment, true or false, is an act of thought; this act consists in feeling. . . . To think, as you see, is always to feel, and is nothing other than to feel."

11. *Medical Extracts of the Nature of Health, with Practical Observations: and the Laws of the Nervous and Fibrous Systems,* vol. 2 (London, 1796), xxviii–xxx, 139–141, 307–311; George Cheyne, *The English Malady* (facsimile reprint of 1733 edition), ed. Roy Porter (London, 1991), part I, preface, and chap. 7.

12. Anne C. Vila, *Enlightenment and Pathology: Sensibility in the Literature and Medicine of Eighteenth-Century France* (Baltimore, 1998), 31–35. As Bonnet phrased it, one must always "return to the physical side of Man as the first origin of everything" that the mind or

soul experienced. I use the dual terms "mind or soul" here, because in their original texts both Condillac and Bonnet use the term *l'âme,* which is rendered both ways in modern translations.

13. TJ to James Monroe, May 20, 1782, TJP-LC, facsimile reproduced in *Inner Jefferson,* 119; TJ to Elbridge Gerry, January 26, 1799, *Portable Jefferson,* 479. Similarly, in a letter to Joel Barlow upon his retirement, Jefferson quoted from a conversation he had had with George Washington, in which the first president demonstrated his distaste for aristocracy by saying "No! not a fibre of it must be retained." TJ to Barlow, October 8, 1809, Ford 11:122n; Angelica Goodden, *The Complete Lover: Eros, Nature, and Artifice in the Eighteenth-Century French Novel* (Oxford, 1989), 89. Also see G. S. Rousseau, "Nerves, Spirits, and Fibres: Towards Defining the Origins of Sensibility," in R. F. Brissenden and J. C. Eade, eds., *Studies in the Eighteenth Century III* (Canberra, 1976).

14. Wilkes's quote is by way of Jay Fliegelman, *Declaring Independence: Jefferson, Natural Language, and the Culture of Performance* (Stanford, Calif., 1993), 187–188; TJ to Samuel Wells, May 12, 1819, Bergh 1:180. In his joint eulogy of Jefferson and Adams in 1826, Attorney General William Wirt termed John Adams's letter-writing style "plain, nervous, and emphatic." In his *Traité de la Fureur Uterine* (1771), Bienville used "nervous" to mean "endowed with extraordinary mental or cognitive capabilities." See G. S. Rousseau, "Nymphomania, Bienville, and the Rise of Erotic Sensibility," in Paul-Gabriel Boucé, ed., *Sexuality in Eighteenth-Century Britain* (Manchester, England, and Totowa, N.J., 1982), 104. For a straightforward history of developments in the study of the nerves, see John D. Spillane, *The Doctrine of the Nerves* (Oxford, 1981).

15. "First Inaugural Address," *Portable Jefferson,* 291; TJ to Thomas Cooper, November 29, 1802, Bergh 10:341.

16. Declaration of Independence, in *Portable Jefferson,* 235; TJ to George Thompson, June 22, 1825, TJP-Huntington. In his draft of the letter to Thompson, Jefferson at first wrote "agonises" in place of "convulses," but crossed out the former in preference for the latter.

17. On the metaphorical use of "harmony" in conjunction with bodily and medical analogies, see Helen Haste, *The Sexual Metaphor* (Cambridge, Mass., 1994), 39–48.

18. *Notes on Virginia,* Query V, 96; Richard Harrison Shryock, *Medicine and Society in America, 1660–1860* (New York, 1960), 69–70. There are at least seven instances of Jefferson's use of "convulsion" in his *Notes on Virginia.*

19. TJ to François Adrian Van der Kemp, February 9, 1818, TJP-LC. As president, Jefferson notably used the word *agitation* in references to political threats he perceived: in the first inaugural address; in the Burr conspiracy; and in negotiations over the Louisiana Purchase, wherein his October 1803 Third Annual Message to Congress alluded to "extraordinary agitation produced in the public mind."

20. TJ to Cosway, October 12, 1786, *Portable Jefferson,* 408.

21. Eli F. Brown, M.D., *The Eclectic Physiology* (Cincinnati and New York, 1884), chaps. 11 and 12.

22. Our language and culture is awash in medical prescriptions that have shed their original, scientific character and acquired a literary or culturally twisted definition. Think of "workaholic," "shock therapy," "miracle drug," "poison," "anemic," "contagious," "immunize,"

"amputate"—words used metaphorically in a variety of nonmedical contexts. Popular remedies—such as "chicken soup" and "Band-Aid"—are attached to conversations that bear no
relationship to medical conditions; still, their application may on occasion reveal some
greater cultural significance because of their original reference. By studying the context of
repeated words, common phrases, and other subjective elements of culture, we can better
understand what produced anxiety, what inspired hope, under medically unpromising conditions. For Jefferson, biomedical formulations happen to be literally descriptive of a mindset, which he expressed boldly in certain public addresses and more obliquely in personal
documents. I am grateful to Professor Allan Harkness of the Department of Psychology,
University of Tulsa, for prompting my thoughts on this subject.

23. [Margaret Bayard Smith], *The First Forty Years of Washington Society,* ed. Gaillard
Hunt (New York, 1906), 6–7. Similarly, the painter and playwright William Dunlap recorded
in his diary in 1806: "Thomas Jefferson, is a tall man, say 6 feet & thin. His hair which has
been red is now grey & is worn in negligent disorder, tho not ungracefully. His complexion
is ruddy & his eye (a hazle) very animated. He converses with ease & vivacity, possessing true
politeness, which places his guests perfectly at their ease." See *Diary of William Dunlap
(1766–1839)* (New York, 1930), 2:388. On the antecedents of that male softness Jefferson exemplified, see G. J. Barker-Benfield, *The Culture of Sensibility: Sex and Society in Eighteenth-
Century Britain* (Chicago, 1992), chap. 3.

24. *Inner Jefferson,* 211–212.

25. Randall, 3:230–234, 345.

26. TJ to James Sullivan, June 19, 1807, Ford 10:422.

27. TJ to Edward Carrington, January 16, 1787, PTJ-Boyd 11:49; TJ to Abigail Adams,
February 22, 1787, *Adams-Jefferson Letters,* 173; TJ to George Washington (Opinion on the
French Treaties), April 28, 1793, *Portable Jefferson,* 270; TJ to John Adams, August 1, 1816,
Adams-Jefferson Letters, 484.

28. TJ to Samuel Kercheval, July 12, 1816, *Portable Jefferson,* 558–561.

29. It is not too much of a stretch to conclude that sympathy and generosity, the central
conceit of American foreign policy, originated in Thomas Jefferson's language of bodily sensations that he and other patriots connected with moral reformation on a global scale. I have
written at length on this subject; see Andrew Burstein, "The Political Character of Sympathy," *Journal of the Early Republic* 21 (Winter 2001): 601–632; and Burstein, *Sentimental
Democracy: The Evolution of America's Romantic Self-Image* (New York, 1999).

30. Eric T. Carlson et al., eds., *Benjamin Rush's Lectures on the Mind* (Philadelphia, 1981),
238–244.

31. TJ to Clinton, May 1, 1815, TJP-LC; Arthur May, *An Inaugural Dissertation on Sympathy* (Philadelphia, 1799). Much as philosophic medicine sought to explain nervous sympathies, there remained something mysterious about them. Jefferson began one letter to
John Adams, at a time when they were communicating irregularly, by remarking on the coincidence of his being in the process of writing to Adams just when Adams's most recent letter came to hand: "The simultaneous movements in our correspondence have been really remarkable on several occasions. It would seem as if the state of the air, or state of the times,
or some other unknown cause produced a sympathetic effect on our mutual recollections."

TJ to Adams, August 10, 1815, *Adams-Jefferson Letters,* 452.What actuated these sympathies could only be guessed at, and here Jefferson's use of the term was comparable to modern-day assumptions about extrasensory perception. In fact, though, Jefferson's generation had inherited from the prior century the notion of internal sympathies as sensations "natural to the faculties," sensations that acted on behalf of bodily and spiritual balance in order to sustain one's health and vigor. It was by way of sympathies that "the rational Soul and the sensitive [i.e., sensory] Soul communicate their passions to each other." The passage goes on to say, in terms that would evolve into those that Jefferson's generation recognized, "that the Sensitive Appetite should be enlightened by the Imagination, and that the Imagination should onely [sic] take cognizance of things sensible." Sieur de la Chambre, *The Art How to Know Men,* trans. John Davis (London, 1665), 99–100 and passim.

32. For insights into Jefferson's relationship with the Scottish Enlightenment, see Barker-Benfield, *The Culture of Sensibility;* Garry Wills, *Inventing America: Jefferson's Declaration of Independence* (Garden City, N.Y., 1978); Jean Yarbrough, *American Virtues: Thomas Jefferson on the Character of a Free People* (Lawrence, Kans., 1998); and, generally, Jane Rendall, *The Origins of the Scottish Enlightenment* (New York, 1978).

33. George E. Rosen, "Political Order and Human Health in Jeffersonian Thought," *Bulletin of the History of Medicine* 26 (1952): 32–44. On the "pathology of passion," see Goodden, *The Complete Lover,* chap. 3.

34. TJ to Cosway, October 12, 1786, *Portable Jefferson,* 410; Samuel Johnson, *Dictionary of the English Language* (Philadelphia, 1813), n.p. Similarly, to Lafayette, Jefferson wrote on February 14, 1815: "The cement of the Union is in the heart-blood of every American." Ford 11:461. Again, we are trying to establish what it was that made Jefferson's imagination, his emotional world, different from ours, and to show how his attention to human physiology is a significant part of that determination. Just as Jefferson's world was responsive to the anatomized culture of sensibility as a guide to right social conduct, ours might be described as the "age of self-esteem." One could easily conclude that every contingency of modern daily life obliges us to measure our self-esteem and "get in touch with our feelings" in order to develop pride in our purposes. That is how we have to look at Jefferson's generation, too, as it responded to a medicalized social environment. What they were doing to adapt amid life's unavoidable anxieties was the equivalent of our "getting in touch with feelings." The same cultural concept has been expressed historically as "self-improvement," and taught as often in a religious as in a secular context. In more recent times, "self-esteem" has involved tailoring the self to prepare better for a fulfilling relationship with a mate. Though not precisely comparable, "sensibility" took on this kind of role: A sensible person, unselfish, compassionate, and a tender and zealous friend, was poised to benefit himself or herself and all those with whom he or she came in contact.

35. TJ to James Maury, June 15, 1815, TJP-LC.

36. A related, psychologically wrought, and politically charged term, *intrigue,* or *intriguer,* combined self-interest with the exercise of unrestrained passion.

37. *Notes on Virginia,* Query XIX, 171. To Dr. Benjamin Rush, who had courageously if unsuccessfully battled yellow fever, Jefferson wrote: "Most evils are the means of producing some good. The yellow fever will discourage the growth of great cities in our nation; and I

view great cities as pestilential to the morals, the health, and the liberties of man." TJ to Rush, September 23, 1800, *Extracts*, 319; similarly, to Dr. Wistar he wrote of his reluctance to send his grandson to school in Philadelphia: "I am not a friend to placing young men in populous cities, because they acquire there habits and partialities which do not contribute to happiness of their after life." TJ to Wistar, June 21, 1807, Ford 10:423.

38. See Carole Shammas, "The Space Problem in Early United States Cities," *William and Mary Quarterly* 57 (July 2000): 505–542, quote at 506, chart at 509. Shammas points out that American cities were densely packed (comprising only 1.2 to 1.5 square miles of land), because although there was plenty of room to expand and still allow the working population to commute on foot, local government was unwilling to pave roads into new areas or to pay for other improvements. The result was the constant subdivision of town lots, adding new residential units in alleys, tearing up yards; the average number of persons per dwelling in New York and Philadelphia was seven in the period 1789–1800, and nine in Boston. The worst of the lower-class wards were noted for their "nauseous stenches."

39. TJ to Alexander Donald, May 30, 1795, TJP-Boyd 28:368; TJ to Lafayette, November 4, 1823, Ford 12:323.

40. Drew R. McCoy, *The Elusive Republic: Political Economy in Jeffersonian Virginia* (Chapel Hill, N.C., 1980), 21–22.

41. Jefferson did not object to the economic principles that brought on market fluctuations, unless they subverted the will of the people; but he identified public happiness most distinctly in terms of the fruits of human labor and concepts of social justice that easily translate into the tenets of modern liberalism.

42. See Alexis de Tocqueville, *Democracy in America* (New York, 1945), 1:276–280, ending with a quotation from Jefferson, which Tocqueville interpreted in his own way.

43. *Notes on Virginia*, Query XIV, 171–172.

44. I have relied here on the impressive research of Louis S. Greenbaum, "Thomas Jefferson, the Paris Hospitals, and the University of Virginia," *Eighteenth-Century Studies* 26 (Summer 1993): 607–626. In a vivid letter to Dr. Thomas Cooper, Jefferson described his plan for construction of the professors' pavilions, lecture rooms, and student dormitories, "the whole connected by a covered colonnade." TJ to Cooper, September 1, 1817, TJP-ViU.

45. TJ to Joseph Priestley, January 18, 1800, Ford 9:96–98. These arguments are repeated in the September 1, 1817, letter to Thomas Cooper: "The situation of Charlottesville is in a mountainous, healthy, fertile country, delicious climate, good water, cheap subsistence, an independent yeomanry, many wealthy persons, good society, and free as air in religion and politics." On the geography of disease as studied in Jefferson's time, see esp. Alan Bewell, *Romanticism and Colonial Disease* (Baltimore, 1999), 29–51. Bewell examines how "medical cartography" accompanied colonialism in general, and how entire cultures were judged on the basis of disease transmission—what he calls "a radical medicalization of the globe." Jefferson's pathogenic evaluation of coastal versus piedmont Virginia accords perfectly with this mindset: The air was regarded as the medium of fevers, and "ventilation" acquired a special status; therapy included a "change of air." Ibid., 30–31.

46. TJ to Tazewell, cited in Frank Edgar Grizzard, Jr., "Documentary History of the Construction of the Buildings at the University of Virginia, 1817–1828" (Ph.D. diss., University of Virginia, 1996), chap. 1; TJ to William H. Crawford, June 20, 1816, Ford 11:538.

47. TJ to White et al., Trustees for the Lottery of East Tennessee College, May 6, 1810, Bergh 12:387.

48. TJ to Joseph Priestley, January 18, 1800, Ford 9:96–98. He led his list with the following academic specialties: Botany, Chemistry, Zoology, Anatomy, Surgery, Medicine, Natural Philosophy. See also the detailed plan recommended to the Virginia legislature, dated September 7, 1814, in Jefferson's hand, meant to be transmitted through his nephew Peter Carr. In this lengthy document, Jefferson categorizes curriculum at all levels of education, and categorizes professorships; under the sciences, half of the professorships relate to scientific investigation: "Mathematics pure," "Physico-Mathematics," "Physics," "Anatomy," "Medicine, theory," "Chemistry," "Zoology," "Botany," "Mineralogy." TJP-LC.

49. Randall, 3:512; Samuel X. Radbill, "The Autobiographical Ana of Robley Dunglison, M.D.," *Transactions of the American Philosophical Society* 53 (1963): 21.

50. TJ to Joseph Cabell, January 11, 1825, TJP-ViU.

51. TJ to Charles Yancey, January 6, 1816, Ford 11:494.

52. See the testimony of Professor George Tucker, in Randall, 3:463–464.

53. TJ to Dr. Dunglison, June 29, 1825, TJP-LC. "Thread"—as in "thread of their studies"—can be regarded as an alternative form of the medical metaphor of nerve "fibre." Jefferson used this word in many other instances, as when his daughter Maria died in 1804 and he wrote his consoling friend John Page that Martha's life was the "slender thread" on which his future prospects hung; and when he told Dr. Waterhouse in January 1825 that, in his fragile physical state, a slight misstep would "cut short the toughest thread of life." He added, in the letter to Dunglison, that the academic schedule was established for the students' own good, "with the sole view of rendering them worthy in themselves, valuable members of society, and fit successors of their fathers in the govmt of their country." Sons would become fathers, responsible for preserving the health and well-being of the republic; the "thread," in that sense, would strengthen.

Chapter 3

1. Samuel X. Radbill, "The Autobiographical Ana of Robley Dunglison, M.D.," *Transactions of the American Philosophical Society* 53 (1963): 26; Sarah N. Randolph, *Domestic Life of Thomas Jefferson* (Charlottesville, Va., 1978 [New York, 1871]), 400–401; Lucia Stanton, *Free Some Day: The African-American Families of Monticello* (Charlottesville, Va., 2000), 120–122. Jefferson frequently invited other professors and their families to dinner at this time, in addition to Dr. Dunglison. See George Tucker, *The Life of Thomas Jefferson* (Philadelphia, 1837), 2:487.

2. Malone 6:164–165; TJ to James Monroe, June 23, 1823, TJP-LC.

3. James A. Bear, Jr., ed., *Jefferson at Monticello* (Charlottesville, Va., 1967), 3–4, 46, 50–51.

4. Merrill Peterson, ed., *Visitors to Monticello* (Charlottesville, Va., 1989), 111–113.

5. Martha Randolph to Ellen Randolph Coolidge, August 2, 1825, Ellen Coolidge Correspondence, Special Collections, ViU.

6. Peterson, *Visitors to Monticello,* 97–101; William Maclay, *The Journal of William Maclay* (1890; reprint, New York, 1965), August 29, 1789, 140; Randolph, *Domestic Life,* 392.

7. TJ to Cary & Lea, June 27, 1822, TJP-LC.

8. TJ to Say, March 2, 1815, TJP-LC. Compare earlier remarks on central Virginia to a close friend from his time in France: "A genial climate, a grateful soil, gardens planted by nature, liberty, safety, tranquility and a very secure and profitable revenue from whatever property we possess." TJ to Madame de Tessé, September 6, 1795, PTJ-Boyd 28:452.

9. TJ to Barton, February 26, 1815; to Rodney, March 16, 1815, TJP-LC.

10. Ellen Wayles Coolidge Diary of a Trip to London, MHS, entry of January 11, 1839.

11. "The Autobiography of Peachy R. Gilmer," in Malone 6:157.

12. TJ to the Chevalier Pio, June 13, 1817, TJP-WM.

13. Stanton, *Free Some Day,* 125.

14. Randall 3:327n; Malone 6:453.

15. Thomas Jefferson Randolph memoir, Special Collections, ViU.

16. TJ to Wistar, June 21, 1807, Ford 10:423.

17. TJ to Jefferson Randolph, November 24, 1808, *Family Letters,* 363–365.

18. Peale to TJ, May 2, 1815, TJP-LC.

19. TJ to Eliza House Trist, February 1, 1814, TJP-ViU.

20. Malone, 6:161; TJ to Wistar, October 22, 1815, TJP-LC.

21. Thomas Jefferson Randolph memoir, Special Collections, ViU. Accounts of the stabbing incident uniformly identify Bankhead as the instigator. See Joseph Carroll Vance, "Thomas Jefferson Randolph" (Ph.D. diss., University of Virginia, 1957), 61–70.

22. Vance, "Thomas Jefferson Randolph," 92.

23. Thomas Jefferson Randolph memoir, Special Collections, ViU.

24. Virginia Randolph Trist to Ellen, June 27, 1825, Ellen Coolidge Correspondence, Special Collections, ViU; Susan R. Stein, *The Worlds of Monticello* (New York, 1993), 280.

25. Malone 6:456.

26. TJ to Thomas Cooper, March 9, 1822, TJP-LC. Cooper was a professor at South Carolina College whom Jefferson had earlier sought to attract to the University of Virginia. See Malone 6:365–380 for controversy surrounding Cooper.

27. On this last category especially, see Jan Lewis, *The Pursuit of Happiness: Family and Values in Jefferson's Virginia* (Cambridge, 1983), chap. 4.

28. TJ to Everett, July 21, 1825, TJP-LC.

29. Virginia Randolph Trist to Ellen, June 27, 1825, Ellen Coolidge Correspondence, Special Collections, ViU.

30. Cornelia J. Randolph to Lizzie Rivinus, June 7, 1864, TJP-LC.

31. Ellen to Nicholas Trist, November 17, 1822, Trist Papers, LC; TJ to Cosway, October 12, 1786, *Portable Jefferson,* 403.

32. TJ to Short, May 5, 1816, TJP-LC.

33. Abigail Adams to TJ, December 15, 1816; TJ to Abigail Adams, January 11, 1817, *Adams-Jefferson Letters,* 500.

34. Ellen to TJ, December 12, 1821, photocopy at the Jefferson Library, Charlottesville (original in a private collection).

35. Dr. Watkins to TJ, September 27, 1824, TJP-LC.

36. Ellen to TJ, November [before the 9th], 1801, January 15 and 29, 1808; TJ to Ellen, October 19, 1807, December 20, 1808, *Family Letters,* 211–212, 312, 321, 324, 373; undated samples of poetry in TJP-LC.

37. TJ to Eliza House Trist, February 1, 1814, TJP-ViU. Visiting Virginia, Mrs. Trist six months later echoed and enlarged on Jefferson's remark: "Ellen is perhaps one of the best Educated Girls in America a perfect Mistress of the french Italian and Spanish languages." Mrs. Trist to Catharine Wistar Bache, August 22, 1814, Papers of the American Philosophical Society, Philadelphia (microfilm).

38. TJ to Ellen, March 14, 1816, *Family Letters,* 412.

39. Ellen to TJ, March 19, 1816, *Family Letters,* 414. There is little doubt that Ellen could have expressed her view of politics with conviction and insight but simply refrained from comment. Her grandfather undoubtedly understood her real reason for adopting this pose.

40. Ellen to Francis Eppes, April 5, 1821, Eppes Family Papers, Special Collections, ViU.

41. TJ to Ellen, November 14, 1825, *Family Letters,* 461–462.

42. Ellen to TJ, December 26, 1825, *Family Letters,* 464–465.

43. Adams to TJ, December 1, 1825, *Adams-Jefferson Letters,* 611.

44. Jack McLaughlin, *Jefferson and Monticello: Biography of a Builder* (New York, 1990), chap. 10; Miller, *Jefferson and Nature,* 116.

45. Wills added: "There can never be another Monticello—a building that is ancient and modern, regular and irregular, classical and romantic, formal and informal, efficient and impractical." See Garry Wills, *Mr. Jefferson's University* (Washington, D.C., 2002), 71, 77.

46. Peterson, *Visitors to Monticello,* 74–75; *Notes on Virginia,* Query VII, 135–136; Malcolm Kelsall, *Jefferson and the Iconography of Romanticism: Folk, Land, Culture and the Romantic Nation* (New York, 1999), 173–174.

47. "Ideas on the subject of a Meridian for the University," September 30, 1825, TJP-LC. I wish to thank physics professor Louis Bloomfield of the University of Virginia for helping to interpret Jefferson's design. In Impressionism, as in Jefferson's language and thought, sensation is fundamental. It derives from the understanding that art arose from the impressions conveyed by a communicative nature.

48. TJ to Judge Augustus B. Woodward, April 3, 1825, Ford 12:408.

49. TJ to Edward Livingston, March 25, 1825, TJP-LC.

50. Those who have traced the long course of Jefferson's effort to bring an institution of higher education to his state, to secure its site in his own neighborhood, and shape it in accordance with his most deeply held principles, include Frank Edgar Grizzard, Jr., "Documentary History of the Construction of the Buildings at the University of Virginia, 1817–1828" (Ph.D. diss., University of Virginia, 1996); Richard Guy Wilson, ed., *Thomas Jefferson's Academical Village: The Creation of an Architectural Masterpiece* (Charlottesville, Va., 1993); Virginius Dabney, *Mr. Jefferson's University: A History* (Charlottesville, Va., 1981); Philip Alexander Bruce, *History of the University of Virginia, 1819–1919* (New York, 1920).

51. TJ to Correa da Serra, November 25, 1817, TJP-LC; Bergh 15:155–157. Even as a politician, Jefferson was thought of as an eccentric by those who found his projects "vision-

ary"—a word that was then defined as "imaginary; not real; seen in a dream." Samuel Johnson, *Dictionary* (Philadelphia, 1813), n.p.

52. TJ to Lafayette, February 14, 1815; TJ to Monroe, March 29, 1823, TJP-LC.

53. TJ to Caspar Wistar, June 21, 1807, Ford 10:423.

54. TJ to Clinton, March 19, 1822, TJP-LC. On financial affairs and the establishment of the university, see especially Grizzard, "Documentary History of the Construction of the Buildings at the University of Virginia, 1817–1828."

55. TJ to Martha Randolph, January 5, 1808, *Family Letters*, 319.

56. Malone, 6:169–184; TJ to John Barnes and TJ to Secretary of the Treasury Alexander Dallas, both on April 18, 1815, TJP-LC; TJ to Kosciusko, June 28, 1814, TJP-ViU. The debts to Short and Kosciusko totaled $15,730. An 1851 fire consumed the majority of Jefferson's donated books, though a good number have been preserved to this day.

57. TJ to Charles Yancey, January 6, 1816, TJP-LC.

58. Malone, 6:301–315; Herbert E. Sloan, *Principle and Interest: Thomas Jefferson and the Problem of Debt* (Oxford, 1995), 26–28 and chap. 6; William R. Taylor, *Cavalier and Yankee: The Old South and American National Character* (New York, 1961), 126–127, 131–132; Merrill D. Peterson, *The Jefferson Image in the American Mind* (Charlottesville, Va., 1998 [1960]), 122–127.

59. TJ to Thomas Jefferson Randolph, February 8, 1826, *Family Letters*, 469.

Chapter 4

1. [Eliza Foster], *Yorktown: An Historical Romance* (Boston, 1826). Though its author was the daughter of the prominent novelist Hannah Webster Foster, and the book was released in two volumes, *Yorktown* received scant notice and went through a single modest printing; only a few copies survive.

2. The mixture of social events and politics in Washington, from the time of Jefferson through the time of Jackson, is the subject of Catherine Allgor, *Parlor Politics: In Which the Ladies of Washington Help Build a City and a Government* (Charlottesville, Va., 2000). Allgor uses Dolley Madison as a model of competence in this regard, while supplying evidence of Jefferson's general discomfort with strong women and his preference that their influence remain behind "the domestic line."

3. TJ to Gallatin, January 13, 1807, Ford 10:339.

4. Ellen Wayles Coolidge Letterbook, Manuscripts Division, ViU.

5. Ellen Wayles Coolidge Diary of a Trip to London, MHS, entry of July 11, 1838.

6. Rush to Rebecca Smith, May 1792, *Letters of Benjamin Rush*, ed. Butterfield, 1:617; *Thoughts upon Female Education* (Philadelphia, 1787).

7. Eric T. Carlson et al., eds., *Benjamin Rush's Lectures on the Mind* (Philadelphia, 1981), 686–689, 695.

8. On this subject, see William Howard Adams, *The Paris Years of Thomas Jefferson* (New Haven, Conn., 1997), 75–77 and chap. 7; Gilbert Chinard, *Trois amitiés françaises de Jefferson* (Paris, 1927); Dena Goodman, *The Republic of Letters: A Cultural History of the French Enlightenment* (Ithaca, N.Y., 1994).

9. G. J. Barker-Benfield, *The Culture of Sensibility: Sex and Society in Eighteenth-Century Britain* (Chicago, 1992), chap. 7.

10. Jefferson was very much at home among women, never at a loss for charming conversation, but he was perfectly comfortable justifying traditional roles. In Jefferson's construct, men needed that social authority, and he was more than willing to deny women legal rights in the course of protecting the position of men; for public men had to neutralize what was already, in this time, referred to as "anxiety." Inside and outside the home alike, they had to show a "magnanimous" side, earning trust while achieving self-respect. For the critical usage of *magnanimity* in defining masculine courtesy, morality, and stature in early American political culture, see Andrew Burstein, *Sentimental Democracy: The Evolution of America's Romantic Self-Image* (New York, 1999).

11. Ellen Wayles Coolidge Letterbook, Special Collections, ViU.

12. Once again, Dr. Rush wrote an (earlier) instructive letter to Rebecca Smith stressing appropriate female comportment: "The qualities necessary to pleasing in company are *good nature, good sense,* and *wit*. I have set them down in the exact order in which they prove most acceptable in company. It is only when this order is inverted that we fail of pleasing." Wit, he explained, entertains well enough, but "only by *exhilarating* the spirits and never by conveying any solid or durable pleasure into the mind. Its effects upon company are like the operation of brandy upon the human body. It is a cordial, proper only in dull weather or in sickness, but always hurtful when used every day." Rush to Smith, July 1, 1791, *Letters of Benjamin Rush,* 1:585.

13. Isaac Briggs to TJ, March 30, 1816; TJ to Briggs, April 17, 1816, TJP-LC. On the other hand, Jefferson did not always succumb to this kind of language. He responded with standard expressions of sympathy, but nothing more, when the daughter of his former Washington, D.C., dentist wrote to inform him of her father's death and the dire circumstances in which the widow and children were left. Her pathos, on hearing the tragic news, equally echoed the tone of a sentimental novel: "Alas! the heart-rending intelligence arrived that he was no more—Oh sir, picture to yourself our agony—our distraction—deprived of our staff—my Mamma left in a state of ill health, with 5 children to support and educate, without the means. Pardon me, honoured Sir . . . you will excuse a young female who has been raised with the tenderest care, and from infancy taught to believe that she should one day be independent of the unfeeling world." Susan Maria Bruff to TJ, March 31, 1816; TJ to Bruff, April 17, 1816, TJP-LC; *Memorandum Books,* 2:1093, 1144, 1235. Of the many studies in literary sensibility, one in particular offers a pointed examination of nervous physiology and female character; see Ann Jessie Van Sant, *Eighteenth-Century Sensibility and the Novel: The Senses in Social Context* (Cambridge, 1993); also helpful is John Mullan, *Sentiment and Sociability: The Language of Feeling in the Eighteenth Century* (Oxford, 1988).

14. TJ to Burwell, March 14, 1818, TJP-LC. This letter is reproduced in Ford, 12:90–93, but lacks the crucial list of novels appended to it. Note, too, that Jefferson refused a later request from Baltimore for his opinions on female education because he did not know the writer personally and assumed that whatever he wrote would be leaked to the newspapers and receive wide distribution. (TJ to A. and J. W. Picket, September 25, 1821, TJP-WM.)

15. *American Minerva,* March 24, 1795. Webster was the editor of this newspaper. Of course, Jefferson, Webster, and, indeed, the vast majority of men, did not appreciate Mary Wollstonecraft's sardonic observation in her 1792 *A Vindication of the Rights of Women:* "Dependence is called natural." She understood, for example, that playing with dolls occurred by imitation rather than was automatic. When she put gender inequality in the terms the physiologists employed—"the sedentary life which [girls] are condemned to live, whilst boys frolic in the open air, weakens the muscles and relaxes the nerves"—she was arguing that there did not have to be "exquisite sensibility"; it was taught and enforced behavior. *A Vindication of the Rights of Women* (New York, 1992), 129, 131.

16. Jefferson is quite obviously responsive to widely prevailing, gender-specific rules of behavior that were meant to keep society safe from moral decay. The emphasis on female modesty in didactic literature around this time is addressed in numerous studies. A carefully drawn overview can be found in C. Dallett Hemphill, *Bowing to Necessities: A History of Manners in America, 1620–1860* (New York, 1999), chap. 6. For two potent recent critiques of the early republican ideology with respect to womanhood, see Pauline Schloesser, *The Fair Sex: White Women and Racial Patriarchy in the Early American Republic* (New York, 2002), and Nancy Isenberg, *Sex and Citizenship in Antebellum America* (Chapel Hill, N.C., 1998). Quote from Tissot's 1772 *Essay on Onanism* in Ludmilla Jordanova, *Nature Displayed: Gender, Science and Medicine, 1760–1820* (London, 1999), 111.

17. This level of anxiety is profoundly drawn in the novels of Charles Brockden Brown, who repeatedly links the self-destructive imagination to deadly disease. Fever, contagion, fear of the dark, mental confusion, and the breakdown of social norms are crucial elements in *Wieland* (1798), *Ormond* (1799), and *Arthur Mervyn* (1799–1800). See esp. Bryan Waterman, "*Arthur Mervyn's* Medical Repository and the Early Republic's Knowledge Industries," *American Literary History* 15 (Summer 2003); also Julia Stern, "The Politics of Tears: Death in the Early American Novel," in Nancy Isenberg and Andrew Burstein, eds., *Mortal Remains: Death in Early America* (Philadelphia, 2003), 108–119. Note, too, the discourse concerning the "masculine" features of scientific study and "feminine" features of the literary life, which came to light within Brown's social circle and grew to be more fixed as the nineteenth century progressed. See John Limon, *The Place of Fiction in the Time of Science: A Disciplinary History of American Writing* (Cambridge, 1990), chap. 2.

18. [Anna Letitia Barbauld], *Eighteen Hundred and Eleven, a Poem* (Boston, 1812). In a Jeffersonian cadence, she praises America as the successor to British greatness—America where the British seed sprouts: "Nations beyond the Apalachian hills / Thy hand has planted and thy spirit fills." To Priestley, she composed a supportive poem amid his trials: "Thy country owes thee. Calm thou can'st consign it / To the slow payment of that distant day, / If distant, when thy name, to freedom's join'd, / Shall meet the thanks of a regenerate land." See *The Works of Anna Lætitia Barbauld* (London, 1825), 1:183–184. She was also an early abolitionist.

19. *Evenings at Home; or, the Juvenile Budget Opened* (Philadelphia, 1802), quotes at 1:60–61. *Evenings at Home* was written in collaboration with her brother, John Aikin.

20. Maria Edgeworth, *Castle Rackrent,* ed. George Watson (London, 1964), 10–11, 95–96. There is a considerable body of literary criticism relating to *Castle Rackrent,* including Cóilín

Owens, *Family Chronicles: Maria Edgeworth's* Castle Rackrent (Dublin, 1987) and Brian Hollingworth, *Maria Edgeworth's Irish Writing: Language, History, Politics* (New York, 1997), chap. 4.

21. See, in particular, James S. Rodgers, "'Life' in the Novel: *Tristram Shandy* and Some Aspects of Eighteenth-Century Physiology," *Eighteenth-Century Life* 6 (October 1980): 1–20. Recognizing the importance of his understanding of physiology, Sterne's outstanding twentieth-century biographer, Wilbur L. Cross, wrote that as Sterne approached his writing, Rabelais "rested at his elbow for hints, and [Dr. John] Burton's *Anatomy,* I fear, lay wide open in front of him." See Cross, *The Life and Times of Laurence Sterne* (New York, 1967 [New Haven, Conn., 1925]), 278. Burton was caricatured in the novel as "Dr. Slop." I devote an entire chapter to Jefferson and Sterne in *The Inner Jefferson.*

22. See, for example, TJ to Thomas Jefferson Randolph, November 24, 1808, *Family Letters,* 363; TJ to Benjamin Rush, January 3, 1808, Bergh 11:413. By humor, Jefferson chiefly meant smooth temperament or good-natured disposition; but he also meant to privilege cheerfulness over a strict, unsympathetic, humorless moralizing.

23. Randall, 3:343.

24. Audrey Bilger, *Laughing Feminism: Subversive Comedy in Frances Burney, Maria Edgeworth, and Jane Austen* (Detroit, 1998), chap. 1, quote at 23.

25. We should recall, in this context, Jefferson's recurrence to clever wordplay. His metaphorical inventions make him closer in spirit to subsequent writers of the nineteenth century than to past moralists. As explained in Chapter 2 above, he clearly understands language as a sensual vehicle. See Michael West, *Transcendental Wordplay: America's Romantic Punsters and the Search for the Language of Nature* (Athens, Ohio, 2000), esp. 50–56; and *Inner Jefferson,* 126–130.

26. Maria Edgeworth, *Belinda* (New York, 1967), 9.

27. Ibid., 4, 117–128.

28. Ellen to Nicholas Trist, January 20, 1823, Trist Papers, LC. For a good understanding of Ellen's concept of success in gendered (and regional) terms, see Jan Lewis, *The Pursuit of Happiness: Family and Values in Jefferson's Virginia* (Cambridge, 1983), chap. 4 and "Conclusion."

29. Edgeworth, *The Absentee* (New York, 1999), 121.

30. Ibid., 37, 39; Elizabeth Kowaleski-Wallace, *Their Fathers' Daughters: Hannah More, Maria Edgeworth, and Patriarchal Complicity* (New York, 1991), chap. 4, quote at 117. Maternal energy, Kowaleski-Wallace further notes, is not free-wheeling, but "harnessed," in this Edgeworthian-Jeffersonian sphere. And the father's (or, in our case, the grandfather's) pedagogical influence lies in eliciting a cooperative spirit, or, quoting Edgeworth on her own father, "without force or fictitious excitements, the taste for knowledge, and the habits of application, were induced by example, and conformed by sympathy." Ibid., 118, 121. With a slightly different perspective, Mitzi Meyers openly questions what she calls the "reductive mythology of Maria Edgeworth as daddy's little good girl, docilely ventriloquizing paternal ideas." She sees, rather, "the 'good' daughter's wicked pen" in action, and in *Belinda* especially, "the vulnerability of patriarchal authority." See Meyers, "My Art Belongs to Daddy? Thomas Day, Maria Edgeworth, and the Pre-Texts of *Belinda:* Women

Writers and Patriarchal Authority," in Paula R. Backscheider, *Revising Women: Eighteenth-Century "Women's Fiction" and Social Engagement* (Baltimore, 2000), 104–146. For another nuanced perspective on the father-daughter relationship, see Caroline Gonda, *Reading Daughters' Fictions, 1709–1834: Novels and Society from Manley to Edgeworth* (Cambridge, 1996), chap. 6.

31. Autobiographical writings, July 13, 1828, Ellen Coolidge correspondence, Special Collections, ViU.

32. O. Elizabeth McWhorter Harden, *Maria Edgeworth's Art of Prose Fiction* (The Hague, Netherlands, 1971), 104–105, and Harden, *Maria Edgeworth*, 18–21.

33. Martha Jefferson Randolph to TJ, November 24, 1808, *Family Letters*, 361. Curiously, Jefferson did not like the adventure-filled novels of Sir Walter Scott, though his granddaughters read and admired these as well. See Randall, 3:448. A reference work published at the peak of Edgeworth's popularity begins its entry for the author by not listing her accomplishments but by noting her as "the daughter of Richard Lovell Edgeworth, esq., of Edgeworthtown, Ireland, a gentleman distinguished in the literary world." Hailing the daughter as an "eminent" novelist, the entry adds that "one of her objectives has been to perfect the system of female education, in which she has in part succeeded." *Universal Biographical Dictionary* (New York, 1825), 427.

34. *Castle Rackrent*, 2.

35. Jack McLaughlin, *Jefferson and Monticello: The Biography of a Builder* (New York, 1988), 326–327. I am grateful to Robert Self, restoration specialist at Monticello, for demonstrating how Jefferson's louvered shutters were deployed. Malcolm Kelsall similarly remarks on Jefferson's self-protective attachment to Monticello as "not just a place in which to live the good life; it is an anchor in a storm." See Kellsall, *Jefferson and the Iconography of Romanticism: Folk, Land, Culture and the Romantic Nation* (London, 1999), 115. The time of Jefferson's regular dinner is established in TJ to Mason L. Weems, August 2, 1815, TJP-Huntington.

36. Randall, 3:478.

37. TJ to William Cardell, January 27, 1821, TJP-ViU. Cardell had written to announce that Jefferson had been named an honorary member of the American Academy of Language and Belles Lettres.

38. From an unpublished 1856 letter to biographer Henry S. Randall, in Ellen Wayles Coolidge Letterbook, Special Collections, ViU.

39. Lafayette to TJ, December 20, 1823, *The Letters of Lafayette and Jefferson,* ed. Gilbert Chinard (Baltimore, 1929), 419.

40. On these subjects, see esp. TJ to Adams, January 24 and July 5, 1814; January 11 and August 1, 1816, *Adams-Jefferson Letters*, 421–425, 431, 458–459, 483–485. Jefferson's best literary assault on Napoleon attributes the popularity of his "iron despotism" to "the indulgence of passion against principle" among the French. See TJ to Benjamin Austin, February 9, 1816, TJP-LC.

41. TJ to Rush, August 17, 1811, Ford 11:211–212.

42. TJ to Abigail Adams, August 22, 1813, *Adams-Jefferson Letters*, 367; James Bear, Jr., ed., *Jefferson at Monticello* (Charlottesville, Va., 1967), 12.

43. Randall, 3:342–345; TJ to François Adrian Van der Kemp, February 9, 1818, TJP-LC; TJ to Frederic Mayo, March 15, March 25, and April 9, 1819, TJP-MHS; Malone, 6:292–294.

44. *Inner Jefferson,* 32.

45. Merrill D. Peterson, ed., *Visitors to Monticello* (Charlottesville, Va., 1989), 21–32.

46. Before the Revolution, Jefferson wrote to a young friend in defense of the moral potential of fiction: "If the painting be lively, and a tolerable picture of nature, we are thrown into a reverie, from which if we awaken it is the fault of the writer." He goes on in this letter to point to Shakespeare and Sterne as examples of writers who deliver sentiment in such a way that it encourages "the sympathetic emotion of virtue." TJ to Robert Skipwith, August 3, 1771, *Portable Jefferson,* 349–351.

47. For reasons not explained, Randall does not acknowledge that Godwin's *Caleb Williams* appears on Jefferson's approved list of novels.

48. TJ to Burwell, March 14, 1818, TJP-LC; *Evenings at Home,* 1:65. Jefferson wrote in 1815 to the teacher of his grandson Francis Eppes: "French is now become an indispensable part in modern education. It is the only language in which a man of any country can be understood out of his own." The grandfather wanted Francis to spend time at Monticello so that he could converse with Jefferson's daughter Martha Randolph, who spoke French, he assured, "as a native." See TJ to ___ Holcombe, May 31, 1815, TJP-LC. Note, too, that Maria Edgeworth's novels contain a liberal sprinkling of French in the dialogue of her genteel female characters.

49. William Godwin, *Things as They Are: Or, the Adventures of Caleb Williams* (New York, 1988), 27, 37, 83. A substantial amount of scholarship exists that examines the sentimental novel and culture of sensibility from a literary perspective. One of those who "deified" female sensibility was Anna Letitia Barbauld. Hannah More's paradigmatic poem "Sensibility" focused on the female nervous constitution: "Where glow exalted sense, and taste refin'd, / There keener anguish rankles in the mind: / There feeling is diffus'd thro' ev'ry part, / Thrills in each nerve, and lives all the heart." See Barker-Benfield, *Culture of Sensibility,* quotes at 264–265.

50. Godwin, *Caleb Williams,* 1:52.

51. Ibid., 1:109 (chap. 12, quote).

52. Ibid., 1:111–113.

53. The same language reappears often. Later in the novel, Caleb reads with poignant apprehension news of the imprisonment of a faithful friend, an old woman persecuted in his place, because she will not inform on him: "With what sensations did I ruminate upon this paper?" he says. "Every word of it carried despair to my heart." And as he ruminates over his years of turmoil: "My sensations at certain periods amounted to insanity." There are more instances in which the sentimental assumptions of the day are voiced in the political context that Godwin and Jefferson share, and in which sensations can evoke good as well as dangerous results. One further example will suffice. When, early in their relationship, Caleb says to Falkland at a moment of heartfelt communion, "The world was made for men of sense [i.e., sensation] to do what they will with," he is saying that the superior man is the one who responds to his deepest humanity. Falkland instinctively replies: "You instruct me well. You have a right notion of things, and I have great hopes of you. I will be more of a man." He

means a man of generous sentiments. But all of a sudden, as Caleb utters the word *justice*, Falkland retracts and exchanges sympathy for vengeance: "'How came this conversation?' cried he. 'Who gave you a right to be my confidant? Base, artful wretch that you are! learn to be more respectful! Are my passions to be wound and unwound by an insolent domestic?" Social justice cannot be realized without an inner reformation, that is, a transformation of nearly sublime proportions. See Ibid., 1:112–113, 279, 316.

54. Ibid., 1:141–142.

55. Ibid., 2:279.

56. Ibid., 3:334–335.

57. Ibid., 1:197; Ellen Coolidge to Henry S. Randall, March 13, 1856, Ellen Wayles Coolidge Letterbook, Special Collections, ViU; B.J. Tysdahl, *William Godwin as Novelist* (London, 1981), chap. 5; Burstein, *Sentimental Democracy,* 310.

58. Godwin, *Caleb Williams,* 2:264.

59. TJ to Roger C. Weightman, June 14, 1826, in *Portable Jefferson,* 585. The "booted and spurred" image is not original, but the political sentiment is vintage Jefferson as much as it is vintage Godwin.

60. The comparison is provocatively drawn in Gay Clifford, "*Caleb Williams* and *Frankenstein:* First-Person Narratives and 'Things as They Are,'" *Genre* 10 (Winter 1977): 601–617. See also Pamela Clemit, *The Godwinian Novel: The Rational Fictions of Godwin, Brockden Brown, Mary Shelley* (Oxford, 1993), chap. 5. In the year of Jefferson's death, Mary Shelley published a novel, *The Last Man,* which took medical concerns to a new dimension in predicting the end of the human race in an epidemic. Other themes common to the father and daughter authors pertain directly to our discussion: Godwin and Shelley express a heightened concern with physiological sensations, and the threats their characters perceive are described as "convulsive."

61. Kenneth W. Graham, *William Godwin Reviewed: A Reception History, 1783–1834* (New York, 2001), 85–90. Hazlitt's review was published in *The Examiner.*

Chapter 5

1. Barrow was a Baptist minister, Virginia-bred, and politically friendly to Jefferson, who migrated to Kentucky prior to Jefferson's presidency and preached against slavery.

2. From "Life among the Lowly, No. 3," *Pike County (Ohio) Republican,* December 25, 1873, reproduced in Annette Gordon-Reed, *Thomas Jefferson and Sally Hemings: An American Controversy* (Charlottesville, Va., 1997), 249–252; on the Gillette family, see Lucia Stanton, *Free Some Day: The African-American Families of Monticello* (Charlottesville, Va., 2000), 87–96.

3. As published in *Nature* 396 (November 5, 1998).

4. The Woodson family has long and firmly claimed that Thomas Woodson was the first child of Jefferson and Hemings, born shortly after his parents returned from France in 1789. Jefferson was alleged to have spirited his mixed-race son from Monticello, depositing him on the Woodson plantation. There is no record of the birth (Sally Hemings's subsequent births were all recorded by Jefferson in his *Farm Book*), and DNA did not establish a genetic link

between Jefferson and Woodson. Four genetic types were considered: Jefferson, Hemings, Woodson, and Carr. The Woodson Y-haplotype was in fact similar to, though not identical with, the Carr Y-haplotype—the Carr DNA represented two of Jefferson's nephews who, until Jefferson's genetic link was convincingly established, were traditionally thought to be probable partners of Sally Hemings. Because of its similarity, the DNA of Thomas Woodson and the Carrs can be presumed to derive from a community in common in England. See Fraser D. Neiman, "Coincidence or Causal Connection? The Relationship between Thomas Jefferson's Visits to Monticello and Sally Hemings's Conceptions," *William and Mary Quarterly* 57 (January 2000): 201n. Neiman's article offers a statistical model in an effort to prove that Jefferson fathered all six of Hemings's children.

5. Eyler Robert Coates, ed., *The Jefferson-Hemings Myth: An American Travesty* (Charlottesville, Va., 2001).

6. "Life Among the Lowly, No. 1," *Pike County (Ohio) Republican,* March 13, 1873, at the Ohio Historical Society, Columbus. Note that Israel Jefferson and Madison Hemings were boyhood playmates.

7. Gordon-Reed, *Thomas Jefferson and Sally Hemings,* chap. 1.

8. Thomas Jefferson Memorial Foundation Research Committee, *Report on Thomas Jefferson and Sally Hemings* (Charlottesville, Va., January 2000); Joshua D. Rothman, *Notorious in the Neighborhood: Sex and Families Across the Color Line in Virginia, 1787–1861* (Charlottesville, Va., 2003), 48; James A. Bear, Jr., ed., *Jefferson at Monticello* (Charlottesville, Va., 1967), 102.

9. Malone 1:153–155, 448–449; Gordon-Reed, *Thomas Jefferson and Sally Hemings,* 60–62, 141–147.

10. Robert Richardson to TJ, March 31, 1824; TJ to Richardson, April 20, 1824, both in TJP-WM. It was in July 1803, after his short-lived notoriety, that an intoxicated Callender fell into the James River, in Richmond, and drowned.

11. See Joshua D. Rothman's assessment of Jefferson's silence, in *Notorious in the Neighborhood,* 50–51; also Joseph J. Ellis, "Jefferson: Post-DNA," *William and Mary Quarterly* 57 (January 2000): 125–138.

12. An earlier apologia for the lack of an exhaustive study of the Jefferson-Hemings question was published under the title "The Seductions of Thomas Jefferson," in *Journal of the Early Republic* 19 (Fall 1999): 499–509. I presented a further elaboration of the problem in "Jefferson's Rationalizations," as part of a forum in the *William and Mary Quarterly* 57 (January 2000): 183–197; and I participated in a public conversation before the DNA results were published, as transcribed in "Three Perspectives on America's Jefferson Fixation," *The Nation,* November 30, 1998, 23ff.

13. Peter A. Dorsey, "To 'Corroborate Our Own Claims': Public Positioning and the Slavery Metaphor in Revolutionary America," *American Quarterly* 55 (September 2003): 353–379. In an earlier work, I take the slavery metaphor back to the Stamp Act movement of the mid-1760s, noting a Boston minister's sermon celebrating the repeal of the act and escape from figurative enslavement. "Even our slaves rejoice," he proclaimed, mixing the non-racial with a racial metaphor, "as tho' they had received their manumission." See Andrew

Burstein, *Sentimental Democracy: The Evolution of America's Romantic Self-Image* (New York, 1999), 54–56, 59–60.

14. The foregoing discussion is drawn in large measure from Woody Holton, *Forced Founders: Indians, Debtors, Slaves, and the Making of the American Revolution in Virginia* (Chapel Hill, N.C., 1999), chap. 5; and Sylvia R. Frey, *Water from the Rock: Black Resistance in a Revolutionary Age* (Princeton, 1991), chaps. 2 and 5. Frey concludes with a revealing parable, relating how, under siege at Yorktown, Cornwallis expelled the black followers of his army in order to preserve the food supply. They had been taken in, reported a Hessian officer, only "to despoil the countryside." Ibid., 170.

15. For clarification, see Pamela Regis, *Describing Early America: Bartram, Jefferson, Crèvecoeur and the Influence of Natural History* (Dekalb, Ill., 1992). Regis explores taxonomic classification as Jefferson and his generation employed it. She draws the boundaries of knowledge, explaining racist generalizations in terms of the categories of natural history that encompassed human beings. A genre of "manners and customs" descriptions was popular and persuasive at this time, a shorthand for determining how best to live on and exploit the land; it was too abstract to provide means for living in harmony with other races. There was a pronounced tension in such texts between cultural narrative and static taxonomic description that we can apply to our examination of Jefferson's failure to rationalize African American rights.

16. On Wythe's attitude, see Philip D. Morgan, "Interracial Sex in the Chesapeake and the British Atlantic World, c. 1700–1820," in Jan Ellen Lewis and Peter S. Onuf, eds., *Sally Hemings and Thomas Jefferson: History, Memory, and Civic Culture* (Charlottesville, Va., 1999), 58–59; Jefferson's characterization of his mentor is in a letter to biographer John Saunderson, August 31, 1820, Bergh 1:165 (Appendix).

17. *Notes on Virginia*, Query VIII, 139; Query XIV, 176–177, 180; Elise Lemire, *"Miscegenation": Making Race in America* (Philadelphia, 2002), 28; on the eighteenth century's understanding of the orangutan's behavior, see John Chester Miller, *The Wolf by the Ears: Thomas Jefferson and Slavery* (Charlottesville, Va., 1991 [New York, 1977]), 54–55.

18. J. C. Lavater, *Essays on Physiognomy; for the Promotion of the Knowledge and the Love of Mankind* (Boston, 1794), quotes at 48, 86–87, 114–115. This is the first American edition; *The Pocket Lavater, or, The Science of Physiognomy* (New York, 1817), quotes at 28, 29, 33. With similar self-assurance, Lavater pronounced on gender differences: "Man is the most firm, woman the most flexible. . . . Man stands stedfast, woman gently retreats. Man surveys and observes, woman glances and feels. Man is serious, woman is gay." *Essays on Physiognomy*, 178; [Charles Caldwell], *An Essay on the Truth of Physiognomy, and Its Application to Medicine* (Philadelphia, 1807), 35; *Autobiography of Charles Caldwell, M.D.* (New York, 1968 [Philadelphia, 1855]), quotes at 44–45; Ray L. Birdwhistell, "Background Considerations to the Study of the Body as a Medium of 'Expression,'" in Jonathan Benthall and Ted Polhemus, eds., *The Body as a Medium of Expression* (London, 1975), 36–54. On the antecedents of Anglo-American prejudice against dark-skinned people, see Alden Vaughan, "The Origins Debate: Slavery and Racism in Seventeenth-Century Virginia," in Vaughan, *Roots of American Racism: Essays on the Colonial Experience* (New York, 1995), chap. 7; and Winthrop D.

Jordan, *White over Black: American Attitudes Toward the Negro, 1550–1812* (Chapel Hill, N.C., 1968).

19. *Notes on Virginia,* Query XVIII, 195; Morgan, "Interracial Sex in the Chesapeake and the British Atlantic World"; Anne C. Vila, *Enlightenment and Pathology: Sensibility in the Literature and Medicine of Eighteenth-Century France* (Baltimore, 1998), 47, 66–67.

20. Quoted in Ira Berlin, *Slaves Without Masters: The Free Negro in the Antebellum South* (New York, 1974), 101.

21. On the foregoing issues, I have drawn on a number of studies, prominent among them Larry E. Tise, *Proslavery: A History of the Defense of Slavery in America, 1701–1840* (Athens, Ga., 1987); James Oakes, *The Ruling Race: A History of American Slaveholders* (New York, 1982), and Oakes, "Why Slaves Can't Read: The Political Significance of Jefferson's Racism," in James Gilreath, ed., *Thomas Jefferson and the Education of a Citizen* (Hanover, N.H., 1999), 177–192; Jan Lewis, "The Problem of Slavery in Southern Political Discourse," in David Thomas Konig, ed., *Devising Liberty: Preserving and Creating Freedom in the Early American Republic* (Stanford, Calif., 1995), 265–297; Bruce Dain, *A Hideous Monster of the Mind: American Race Theory in the Early Republic* (Cambridge, Mass., 2002); Lemire, "*Miscegenation*"; Berlin, *Slaves Without Masters;* David Brion Davis, *The Problem of Slavery in the Age of Revolution, 1770–1823* (Ithaca, N.Y., 1975); Jordan, *White Over Black.* On northern conditions in particular, see Gary B. Nash, *Forging Freedom: The Formation of Philadelphia's Black Community, 1720–1840* (New York, 1991); James O. Horton and Lois Horton, *In Hope of Liberty: Culture, Community, and Protest among Northern Free Blacks, 1700–1860* (New York, 1997); cogent summaries of relevant questions can be found in Matthew Mason, "The Battle of the Slaveholding Liberators: Great Britain, the United States, and Slavery in the Early Nineteenth Century," *William and Mary Quarterly* 59 (July 2002): 665–696; Joanne Pope Melish, "The 'Condition' Debate and Racial Discourse in the Antebellum North"; and James Brewer Stewart, "Modernizing 'Difference': The Political Meanings of Color in the Free States, 1776–1840," in *Journal of the Early Republic* 19 (Winter 1999): 651–672, 691–712.

22. *Notes on Virginia,* Query XVIII, 195–196.

23. See esp. Malone 2:94–98; Adams to TJ, May 22, 1785, *Adams-Jefferson Letters,* 21.

24. TJ to David Barrow, May 1, 1815, TJP-LC.

25. Douglas R. Egerton, "The Empire of Liberty Reconsidered," in James Horn et al., eds., *The Revolution of 1800: Democracy, Race, and the New Republic* (Charlottesville, Va., 2002), 309–330; Garry Wills, "*Negro President*": *Jefferson and the Slave Power* (Boston, 2003), chap. 2; Paul Finkelman, *Slavery and the Founders: Race and Liberty in the Age of Jefferson* (Armonk, N.Y., 1996), 126–127.

26. On the conditions faced by Virginians, and their perception of life under the Virginia Dynasty of presidents in general, see Daniel P. Jordan, *Political Leadership in Jefferson's Virginia* (Charlottesville, Va., 1983).

27. Malone 6, chap. 23, quote at 334; Miller, *The Wolf by the Ears,* chap. 26; Peter S. Onuf, *Jefferson's Empire: The Language of American Nationhood* (Charlottesville, Va., 2000), chap. 4 and 185–188.

28. TJ to Clement Caine, September 16, 1811, Ford 11:214–216.

29. Mason, "Battle of the Slaveholding Liberators."

30. Douglas R. Egerton, *He Shall Go Out Free: The Lives of Denmark Vesey* (Madison, Wisc., 1999).

31. TJ to Chastellux, September 2, 1785, *Portable Jefferson*, 387. For a nice comparison, consult French traveler Michel Chevalier's remarks, written eight years after Jefferson's death: "The Virginian of pure race is frank, hearty, open, cordial in his manners, noble in his sentiments, elevated in his ideas; he is a worthy descendant of the English gentleman. Surrounded from infancy by his slaves who relieve him from all personal exertion, he is rather indisposed to activity, even indolent." And: "The Yankee, on the contrary, is reserved, cautious, distrustful; he is thoughtful and pensive, but equable; his manners are without grace, modest but dignified, cold and often unprepossessing; he is narrow in his ideas but practical." Chevalier, *Society, Manners, and Politics in the United States,* ed. John William Ward (Garden City, N.Y., 1961), 103–104.

32. Onuf, *Jefferson's Empire,* chap. 5, quote at 169.

33. [Lemuel Hopkins], *Guillotina, For the Year 1798,* broadside in the *Connecticut Courant* (1798), at the Huntington Library, San Marino, Calif.

34. TJ to Banneker, August 30, 1791, *Portable Jefferson,* 454; Onuf, *Jefferson's Empire,* 169.

35. See Henry Louis Gates, Jr., *The Trials of Phillis Wheatley* (New York, 2003).

36. *Letters of the Late Ignatius Sancho, an African* (New York, 1998), Letter XXVI, 63–64. Sancho also wrote of his relationship with his wife: "I am her barometer—if a sigh escapes me, it is answered by a tear in her eye;—I oft assume a gaiety to illumine her dear sensibility with a smile." Ibid., Letter LIII, 103. The collection was first published in London, in 1782.

37. TJ to Joel Barlow, October 8, 1809, Ford 11:220–221; *Notes on Virginia,* Query XIV, 180.

38. James Baldwin, *Another Country* (New York, 1963), 418–419.

39. See esp. P. J. Staudenraus, *The African Colonization Movement, 1816–1865* (New York, 1961).

40. TJ to Samuel Kercheval, July 12, 1816, *Portable Jefferson,* 559.

41. Later transcription of an 1826 essay, in Ellen Wayles Coolidge Letterbook, Special Collections, ViU; TJ to Thomas Jefferson Randolph, February 4, 1826, TJP-WM.

42. Hemings to TJ, November 18, 1819; TJ to John Hemings, November 14 and 27, 1819; TJ to Yancey, November 10, 1818; Hannah to TJ, November 15, 1818, all in TJP-MHS; Kyle Bentley Norwood, "'After Glory Run': Slave Life at Thomas Jefferson's Bedford County Plantation, 1800–1830" (master's thesis, University of New Mexico, 1994). Correspondence between Jefferson and Yancey, and Hannah's letter, are also to be found in *Thomas Jefferson's Farm Book,* ed. Edwin Morris Betts (Charlottesville, Va., 1999).

43. TJ to John Hemings, August 17, 1825, TJP-MHS.

44. Stanton, *Free Some Day,* 60–63.

45. TJ to William O. Callis, May 8, 1795, PTJ-Boyd 28:346–347n. As it turned out, Nance's daughter Critta was purchased by Thomas Mann Randolph, and lived nearby, until she came to Monticello upon Jefferson's final retirement. Nance's son, Billy, remained on the Louisa County plantation. Critta married her cousin Burwell Colbert, Jefferson's close companion at the end of his life. See Stanton, *Free Some Day,* 124.

46. Martha Randolph to Ellen Coolidge, August 2, 1825, Ellen Coolidge Correspondence, Special Collections, ViU.

47. Ellen to TJ, August 1, 1825, *Family Letters,* 454.

48. TJ to David Barrow, May 1, 1815, TJP-LC. Jefferson felt compelled to add that the conscience of the master required immediate development, and both the training of master and training of slave for their ultimate separation required a good amount of time and care. "Some progress is sensibly made in it; yet not so much as I had hoped and expected," when first advancing his thoughts in *Notes on Virginia.*

49. Merrill D. Peterson, *The Jefferson Image in the American Mind* (Charlottesville, Va., 1998 [1960]), 171–174.

50. TJ to Humphrey, June 15, 1816, TJP-LC.

51. TJ to Coles, August 25, 1814, in *Portable Jefferson,* 544–547; Malone 6:320–324. I wish to thank Tom Benediktson for his expanded translation of the Vergil quote. (Note that I have changed the *ferruncingi* of the Peterson edition to the correct *ferrum cingi.*) On the troubling perception of Jefferson's apparent hypocrisy, see also Paul Finkelman, "Jefferson and Slavery: 'Treason against the Hopes of the World,'" in Peter S. Onuf, ed., *Jeffersonian Legacies* (Charlottesville, Va., 1993), 181–221.

52. Except, ironically, Washington, D.C. At the very moment that Jefferson penned the letter, the national capital was in the hands of British soldiers. Jefferson obviously could not yet have known.

53. TJ to Louis Girardin, March 27, 1815, TJP-LC; to Cabell, January 31, 1814, TJP-ViU.

54. TJ to Cabell, January 6, 1818, TJP-WM; to David Barrow, May 1, 1815, TJP-LC.

55. *Autobiography,* draft in Jefferson's hand, at the Library of Congress Web site.

56. See Frank Shuffelton, "Thomas Jefferson: Race, Culture, and the Failure of Anthropological Method," in Shuffelton, ed., *A Mixed Race: Ethnicity in Early America* (New York, 1993), 257–277; Alexander O. Boulton, "The American Paradox: Jeffersonian Equality and Racial Science," *American Quarterly* 47 (September 1995): 467–492; also Regis, *Describing Early America,* chap. 1. Linnaeus's system was based upon differences in the sexual organs of plants; Jefferson's system of racial distinction was also sexual, though he might not have recognized it as such.

57. Jefferson's dissatisfaction with the small-scale operation of the American Colonization Society, founded in 1816, related to his preference for a massive, not a piecemeal, relocation program. See Peter S. Onuf, "'Every Generation Is an Independant Nation': Colonization, Miscegenation, and the Fate of Jefferson's Children," *William and Mary Quarterly* 57 (January 2000): 153–170, esp. 161–165.

58. See Andrew Burstein, *America's Jubilee* (New York, 2001), chap. 1.

59. Lafayette to TJ, October 1, 1824, *Letters of Lafayette and Jefferson,* ed. Gilbert Chinard (Baltimore, 1929), 424; [Frances Wright], *Views of Society and Manners of America* (London, 1821), 62–76, quotes at 70–71, 75. This volume, at Special Collections, ViU, is the very copy Jefferson owned.

60. Celia Morris Eckhardt, *Fanny Wright: Rebel in America* (Cambridge, Mass., 1984), 2–3, 84ff; Lucia Stanton, "Looking for Liberty: Thomas Jefferson and the British Lions," *Eighteenth-Century Studies* 26 (Summer 1993): 649–668, quote at 664.

61. Eckhardt, *Fanny Wright*, 65, 69.

62. TJ to Lafayette, December 26, 1820, and Lafayette to TJ, July 1, 1821, *Letters of Lafayette and Jefferson*, 402, 407.

63. Lafayette to TJ, June 1, 1822; TJ to Lafayette, November 4, 1823, *Letters of Lafayette and Jefferson*, 409, 415–416.

64. Jefferson's draft of welcoming speech, November 4, 1824, TJP-LC.

65. Wright to Martha Randolph, December 4, 1824, TJP-LC (Randolph Family Manuscripts); Wright to TJ, July 26, 1825, TJP-WM.

66. TJ to Wright, August 7, 1825, TJP-LC.

67. Everett to TJ, April 16, 1826, TJP-LC.

68. Heaton to TJ, April 20, 1826; TJ to Heaton, May 20, 1826, TJP-LC.

69. Frances Trollope, *Domestic Manners of the Americans* (New York, 1927 [1832]), 23–25, 57.

70. Lafayette to TJ, February 25, 1826, *Letters of Lafayette and Jefferson*, 437–438.

71. *Summary Journal of Letters*, TJP-LC.

72. Gail Weiss, "The Body as a Narrative Horizon," and William A. Cohen, "Deep Skin," in Jeffrey Jerome Cohen and Gail Weiss, eds., *Thinking the Limits of the Body* (Albany, N.Y., 2003), 25–35, 63–82.

73. *Notes on Virginia*, Query XIV, 174–176; Oakes, "Why Slaves Can't Read," 183, 348 n. 15.

74. The phrase "eternal monotony" comes from *Notes on Virginia*, Query XIV, 176; on the calculations relative to white and mulatto status under the law, see TJ to Francis Gray, March 4, 1815, TJP-LC, also reproduced in Lewis and Onuf, eds., *Sally Hemings & Thomas Jefferson*, 262–263; and Gray to TJ, March 24, 1815, TJP-LC; Jefferson uses the word *deportation* in his 1821 *Autobiography*, draft online at the Library of Congress Web site.

75. Michel Foucault, *The History of Sexuality*, vol. 1, *An Introduction* (New York, 1978), 146–148.

76. Peter W. Bardaglio, *Reconstructing the Household: Families, Sex & the Law in the Nineteenth-Century South* (Chapel Hill, 1995), 48–63; Rothman, *Notorious in the Neighborhood*; Deborah Gray White, *Ar'n't I a Woman: Female Slaves in the Plantation South* (New York, 1985); *Notes on Virginia*, Query XIV, 176.

77. Rothman, *Notorious in the Neighborhood*, chap. 5.

78. James A. Bear, Jr., ed., *Jefferson at Monticello* (Charlottesville, Va., 1967), 4. Half of Betty Hemings's children were fathered by white men, half by black men.

79. See esp. Lemire, "*Miscegenation*," chap. 1. The word *miscegenation* was not coined until 1864; prior to that the same notion was referred to as "amalgamation." Ibid., 4.

80. We must always consider that Jefferson did not hold himself to precisely the same standard of treatment toward blacks and mulattos as he was prescribing for society at large—a question to be taken up in the next chapter. I thank David Waldstreicher for tempting me with a different viewpoint, and for reminding me that it makes sense to regard Jefferson as a writer with a political strategy, whose stated beliefs may reflect political objectives as much if not more than personal preferences.

Chapter 6

1. For a good overview of the sexual literature of the Enlightenment and the widespread effects of sexual knowledge, see Peter Wagner, *Eros Revived: Erotica of the Enlightenment in England and America* (London, 1988).

2. On Jefferson and his wife, see *Inner Jefferson,* chap. 2; on Maria Cosway and the other women with whom he interacted in France, see ibid., chap. 3. Jefferson expressed conventional misogyny in certain entries in the *Commonplace Book* of his younger years, and he expressed an equally conventional embrace of marital fidelity in adulthood. For a useful discussion, see Ruth H. Bloch, "Changing Conceptions of Sexuality and Romance in Eighteenth-Century America," *William and Mary Quarterly* 60 (January 2003): 13–42.

3. See Nancy Isenberg, "Death and Satire: Dismembering the Body Politic," in Nancy Isenberg and Andrew Burstein, eds., *Mortal Remains: Death in Early America* (Philadelphia, 2003), 71–90.

4. Devotion to kin belonged to a system of sympathetic benevolence and creative self-fashioning that Jefferson exemplified. On the emergence of this way of life, see esp. G. J. Barker-Benfield, *The Culture of Sensibility: Sex and Society in Eighteenth-Century Britain* (Chicago, 1992).

5. TJ to Martha, May 12, 1793; to Thomas Jefferson Randolph, October 24, 1808; to Ellen, December 20, 1808; to Cornelia, December 26, 1808, *Family Letters,* 117, 353, 373, 374.

6. Martha to TJ, February 17, 1809; TJ to Martha, February 27, 1809, *Family Letters,* 382, 385–386.

7. Henry Wiencek, *An Imperfect God: George Washington, His Slaves, and the Creation of America* (New York, 2003), 84–86.

8. Madison Hemings reported that his mother became pregnant in 1789 while still in Paris and bore her first child in Virginia, though it "lived but a short time." Whether or not there was a child, and it was Jefferson's child, as Madison believes (the efficient personnel manager Jefferson failed to record such a birth in his farm log), Jefferson does record each of Sally's other births, beginning in the autumn of 1795. This was ten months after Jefferson had retired from Washington's cabinet and had no further plans to return to national office; that is, it was a time when he believed his actions would not be subject to public scrutiny. See also Annette Gordon-Reed's argument with regard to James and Sally Hemings's prospects for freedom in France, *Thomas Jefferson and Sally Hemings: An American Controversy* (Charlottesville, Va., 1997), 173–174; for more detail on the life of James Hemings, see Lucia Stanton, *Free Some Day: The African-American Families of Monticello* (Charlottesville, Va., 2000), 126–128.

9. Even after her marriage, whenever Jefferson returned from the national capital to live at Monticello, Martha and family would move back in to be with him. She was, therefore, nearby during Sally Hemings's pregnancies.

10. The only other conceivable explanation is that, at some point, she approached Sally and asked who her lover was, and Sally refused to say; and at some other point she approached her father and asked *him* who he thought Sally's lover was, and he directed her

away from himself. But it is far more reasonable to believe that, as on other southern planta-tions, family did not easily talk about the master's sexual habits; Martha's chatty letters to her daughters in the late 1810s and 1820s suggest more than a little curiosity in matters of social connections, belles and beaux.

11. Mary Wollstonecraft protested that in the language of patriarchy, "She was created to be the toy of man, his rattle, and it must jingle in his ears whenever, dismissing reason, he chooses to be amused." And a bit later, "They [again, women] were made to be loved, and must not aim at respect, lest they should be hunted out of society as masculine." *A Vindica-tion of the Rights of Woman* (New York, 1992), 118–119.

12. M. D. T. de Bienville, *Nymphomania, Or, a Dissertation Concerning the Furor Uterinus* (London, 1775), 163–164.

13. Eric Carlson et al., eds., *Benjamin Rush's Lectures on the Mind* (Philadelphia, 1981), 696.

14. Roy Porter, "Mixed Feelings: The Enlightenment and Sexuality in Eighteenth-Century Britain," in Paul-Gabriel Boucé, ed., *Sexuality in Eighteenth-Century Britain* (Manchester, England, and Totowa, N.J., 1982), 16; on the bawdy humor associated with female sexual knowledge and behavior, and its tempering in the post-Revolutionary period, see Richard Godbeer, *Sexual Revolution in Early America* (Baltimore, 2002), chap. 8.

15. G. S. Rousseau, "Nymphomania, Bienville, and the Rise of Erotic Sensibility," in Paul-Gabriel Boucé, ed., *Sexuality in Eighteenth-Century Britain,* 109; Roy Porter, "The Literature of Sexual Advice before 1800," in Porter and Mikulas Teich, eds., *Sexual Knowledge, Sexual Science: The History of Attitudes to Sexuality* (Cambridge, 1994), 134–156, quote at 145. Sex was also prescribed as a cure for melancholy.

16. S. A. D. Tissot, *Onanism: Or, a Treatise upon the Disorders Produced by Masturbation* (London, 1766), pt. 2, sec. 6. In the Book of Genesis, Onan was the man who "spilled his seed" and incurred God's wrath for doing so, in failing to have sexual relations with his brother's widow.

17. Oscar Reiss, *Medicine in Colonial America* (Lanham, Md., 2000), 87, 254, citing Dr. A. F. M. Willich's 1800 *Lectures on Diet and Regimen* and A. Richerand's 1808 *Elements of Phys-iology.* On warnings of the dangers of masturbation as expressed in books containing med-ical advice, see esp. Paula Bennett and Vernon A. Rosario II, eds., *Solitary Pleasures: The His-torical, Literary, and Artistic Discourses of Autoeroticism* (New York, 1995). Jefferson owned the oft-reprinted, anonymously authored *Onania; or, The Heninous Sin of Self-Pollution and All Its Frightful Consequences.* See Sowerby, 1:422.

18. Tissot, *Onanism,* 58, 83. The characterization Tissot repeats here borrows in part from the work of the Swiss physiologist Dr. Albrecht von Haller (1708–1777).

19. Though the DNA results of 1998 produced new excitement concerning love across racial lines at Monticello, the impetus provided by biographer Fawn Brodie a generation ear-lier had never really faded. See Brodie, *Thomas Jefferson: A Biography* (New York, 1974). Her book, though compelling on many levels, is marred by its distortion of eighteenth-century meanings. Her crusade to link Jefferson and Hemings romantically led her to speculate too often without evidence.

20. Laurence Sterne, *A Sentimental Journey Through France and Italy* (London, 1770), 208.

21. A related facet of eighteenth-century culture may be a bit harder for the modern mind to digest. Because childbirth could be quite deadly, wives who did not wish to endure additional pregnancies were at times relieved when lustful husbands took mistresses, providing their extramarital sex lacked emotional depth. The trope of the servant holding on to her virtue until her master finally sees her as an emotional equal and agrees to make her his bride is mainly fiction; though it did occur, it clearly did not occur at Monticello. See Porter, "Mixed Feelings," 1–27; Ludmilla Jordanova, "Naturalizing the Family: Literature and the Bio-medical Sciences of the Late Eighteenth Century," in Jordanova, *Nature Displayed: Gender, Science and Medicine, 1760–1820* (London, 1999), 172–173; Karen Harvey, "The Century of Sex? Gender, Bodies, and Sexuality in the Long Eighteenth Century," *The Historical Journal* 45 (2002): 899–916.

22. Ann Twinam, *Public Lives, Private Secrets: Gender, Honor, Sexuality, and Illegitimacy in Colonial Spanish America* (Stanford, Calif., 1999). An interesting element in developmental differences between Anglo-American and Spanish-American race relations is that, despite a common concern with "purity of blood," *limpieza de sangre,* the Spanish found ways to maintain the social status quo with less attention paid to physiognomy and more to the porousness of social boundaries. Acceptance followed exhibitions of family solidarity; honor negotiations superseded other categories. Twinam writes: "Honor was the reason that eighteenth-century Latin Americans wanted to pass, for it was the matrix through which Hispanic canons of birth and *limpieza de sangre,* which defined hierarchy, were made evident. To lack honor was simply to be disqualified from most positions of political, economic, and social prestige. Honor was a public phenomenon and constantly subject to challenge, for it could be threatened, lost, gained, and regained." Ibid., 337–338.

23. The seminal work is Bertram Wyatt-Brown, *Southern Honor: Ethics and Behavior in the Old South* (New York, 1982). My *Passions of Andrew Jackson* (New York, 2003) notes the extensive interactions between post-Revolutionary southern culture and Spanish government, while focusing attention on the Carolina-born Jackson's inherited sense of honor.

24. Thomas Jefferson Memorial Foundation Research Committee, *Report on Thomas Jefferson and Sally Hemings.*

25. To be clear, sex has always been in some way associated with social taboos. Christian doctrine stigmatized fornication, adultery, and sodomy as sins; colonial Americans (especially in New England) developed a legal system that punished deviance. Of course, no one familiar with Jefferson's political or cultural inclinations would suggest that he inherited any share of his sexual outlook from Puritan New England. Before the Victorians, sex before marriage was quite common, and was condoned if the couple intended to enter into holy matrimony. The medical Enlightenment further eroded the strength of biblical prohibitions against nonmarital sex by privileging a morality rooted in scientists' understanding of health. At this time, only the "libertine" was targeted as a male who was out of control and became something of a social pariah.

26. Xenophon, *Conversations of Socrates,* ed. Robin Waterfield (London, 1990), quote at 163.

27. Karl Lehmann, *Thomas Jefferson, American Humanist* (Charlottesville, Va., 1985 [New York, 1947]), quote at 46; Moses Hadas, *A History of Greek Literature* (New York, 1950),

chap. 9; Leo Strauss, *Xenophon's Socrates* (South Bend, Ind., 1998); Carl J. Richard, *The Founders and the Classics: Greece, Rome, and the American Enlightenment* (Cambridge, Mass., 1994); Erin Shalev, "Ancient Masks, American Fathers: Classical Pseudonyms during the American Revolution and Early Republic," *Journal of the Early Republic* 23 (Summer 2003): 151–172. For Greek holdings in Jefferson's library, see Sowerby 2:31–32, 3:23–24, 4:450–451.

28. TJ to John Brazier, August 24, 1819, TJP-LC, also in Bergh 15:207–211.

29. *Inner Jefferson*, 66, 88–89, 106; Lehmann, *Thomas Jefferson, American Humanist*, 148–155.

30. Randall, 1:383.

31. In the rather abundant literature that exists on this subject, common streetwalkers were carefully distinguished from respectable prostitutes, who were often skilled in music and conversation. In Xenophon, where it comes to the world of the privileged prostitute, eros and highbrow philosophy mingle. The *hetaera* (escort) was contracted for a period of time; the disreputable *pornoi* rented simply for the sexual act. Certain courtesans grew famous as the constant companions of politicians and philosophers. These relationships became embarrassing only when wives felt abandoned; and then the public automatically sympathized with the upper-class woman whose status had been threatened by a lower-class woman's greater charms. Physical separation of the two worlds was an essential principle for the Greeks: To avoid being insulted, the wife and the *hetaera* were never to be brought in contact with one another. Interestingly, too, young upper-class men, before marriage, had little contact with women of their same class and age. Those who could afford it received an education in the ways of the flesh from prostitutes. See Michel Foucault, *The History of Sexuality*, vol. 2, *The Use of Pleasure* (New York, 1985), 143–165; John Scarborough, *Facets of Hellenic Life* (Boston, 1976); James N. Davidson, *Courtesans and Fishcakes: The Consuming Passions of Classical Athens* (New York, 1997), chap. 3; Daniel Ogden, *Greek Bastardy in the Classical and Hellenistic Periods* (Oxford, 1996), 103.

32. Note that among the leading voices in the modern effort to publicize the positive features of the Jefferson-Hemings relationship, the Woodson family voice has been perhaps the strongest. The late Robert Cooley, an accomplished Virginia attorney and Woodson descendant, spoke of Sally Hemings as a woman whom Jefferson deeply loved, his "substitute wife." Yet the Woodson family claim of a genetic link was disproved in the 1998 study, rendering the oral history conveyed by Cooley suspect.

33. Davidson, *Courtesans and Fishcakes*, 88–90. As to Jefferson's knowledge of Greek pornography, we have no evidence but guilt by association. While courting the married Maria Cosway in Paris in 1786, he was nearly as often in the company of Mrs. Cosway's much older friend, the Greek scholar and pornographer d'Hanquerville, who published widely on the erotic in classical antiquity and corresponded familiarly with Jefferson. See *Inner Jefferson*, 79.

34. Ogden, *Greek Bastardy*, 64–65; Scarborough, *Facets of Hellenic Life*, 189.

35. Davidson, *Courtesans and Fishcakes*, 98, 102; Ogden, *Greek Bastardy*, 72–74; for a brief period of time, the historian Diogenes Laertius recorded, citizenship law was changed to permit a man to have legitimate children with two women, legitimizing those born of a con-

cubine; Aristotle's will, in Mary R. Lefkowitz and Maureen B. Fant, *Women's Life in Greece and Rome* (Baltimore, 1982), 36–37. Jefferson himself appears not to have openly used the term *concubine;* the only obvious written reference is a technical one in a letter to Thomas Cooper, in which he cited his *Legal Commonplace Book* and confined himself to concubinage under Biblical law. See TJ to Cooper, February 10, 1814, Bergh 14:94, 96.

36. In some scholarship, *notheia* is also associated with the word *skotios,* or "born in the dark," which in Euripides has the meaning "concubinal," "illegitimate."

37. Euripides and others were known to protest that *nothoi* "in no way fall short of legitimates, but just ail under the law." Indeed, the rich who became involved sexually with poor girls and produced bastards were somehow able to land on their feet; the poor might at times be thought to have borne bastards even when they did not, because any woman given in marriage without a dowry was thought to have been given in concubinage rather than in matrimony. There are further parallels worth mentioning: In Greek drama, *nothos* (bastard) is almost identical to *nosos* (disease), and invited witty word associations between the two in classical literature. The association of Africanness with a "taint," or disease, in Jefferson's writing, constitutes another interesting—and disturbing—connection here. See Ogden, *Greek Bastardy,* 15–17, 25–26, 39, 42, 91–93, 204–207.

38. Davidson, *Courtesans and Fishcakes,* 30–31.

39. TJ to Short, October 31, 1819, *Extracts,* 388, and in Bergh 15:219–220.

40. Tissot, *Onanism,* 50; George A. Panichas, *Epicurus* (Boston, 1967); Léon Robin, *Greek Thought and the Origins of the Scientific Spirit* (New York, 1967 [Paris, 1928]), 323–340; Scarborough, *Facets of Hellenic Life,* 207. Certain Roman republicans adopted Epicurus as their own. Jefferson's adoration of the poet Horace, who, like Jefferson, philosophized from his country villa, was, in Karl Lehmann's words, "above all caused by his profession of Epicurean ethics." Lehmann, *Thomas Jefferson, American Humanist,* 60, 139.

41. Martha C. Nussbaum, *The Therapy of Desire: Theory and Practice in Hellenistic Ethics* (Princeton, 1994), chap. 4; E. Zeller, *The Stoics, Epicureans and Sceptics,* trans. Oswald J. Reichel (New York, 1962), 425–429; Robert M. Strozier, *Epicurus and Hellenistic Philosophy* (Lanham, Md., 1985), 51–97. Epicurus accepted the validity of every sensation, saying: "If you reject any . . . sensation, feeling, and intuitive presentation, you overthrow the remaining sensations by this unfounded opinion." Strozier, 63.

42. Nussbaum, *The Therapy of Desire,* 149–154; Zeller, *The Stoics, Epicureans and Sceptics,* 485–498; Panichas, *Epicurus,* 105–107. "Intercourse never helped anyone, and it's lucky if it does no harm," Epicurus is meant to have said. He was concerned about the development of excessive desire, beyond what was natural, and that proved unsatisfiable. The Greeks were known to admire the self-restraint of their great athletes, who practiced sexual abstinence and ate cheese and figs when preparing for a contest. See Elizabeth Abbott, *A History of Celibacy* (New York, 1999), 209–211. No one in Jefferson's time would have regarded Epicureanism as restrictive. It is therefore quite doubtful that Jefferson, as a self-styled Epicurean, would have found himself hindered by a few superficial remarks, attributed to Epicurus, that protested overindulgence in sexual activity—for he would not have thought his own sexual activity part of a pathology. Indeed, as we know, it was for the sake of health that sex was recommended to men of intellectual attainments.

43. TJ to Adams, June 27, 1813; Adams to TJ, July 9 and August 14, 1813, *Adams-Jefferson Letters,* 335, 350–352, 365. On Theognis as an interpreter of the aristocratic temperament, see Veda Cobb-Stevens, "Opposites, Reversals, and Ambiguities: The Unsettled World of Theognis," in Thomas J. Figueira and Gregory Nagy, eds., *Theognis of Megara: Poetry and the Polis* (Baltimore, 1985), 159–175. For a modern translation of the lines Adams and Jefferson are discussing, see A. W. H. Adkins, *Poetic Craft in the Early Greek Elegists* (Chicago, 1985), 135. And for a good summary of the thinking of Theognis, gleaned from his poetry, and in particular his elevation of judgment over the tug of the heart, see C. M. Bowra, *Early Greek Elegists* (London, 1938), 139–170.

44. Adams to TJ, September 2, 1813, *Adams-Jefferson Letters,* 371. Again on September 15, Adams ruminated on the same subject, before Jefferson was able to reply.

45. TJ to Adams, June 27 and October 28, 1813, *Adams-Jefferson Letters,* 335, 387.

46. See especially John M. Lewis, "Eros and the Polis in Theognis Book II," in Figueira and Nagy, eds., *Theognis of Megara,* 197–222. In analyzing the state of confusion that Theognis perceives, Lewis notes significantly that "Eros is also a breeder of hubris."

47. Ocellus is the presumed author of the 5th century B.C. text *On the Nature of the Universe,* which asserts the eternal nature of an uncreated universe and the indestructibility of the human race. Two years after their exchange, Adams read and took notes on the work of Ocellus, and showed an interest in that which related to the question of race mixing: "With fear and trembling," he would write in 1815, "I must add the Planters in my beloved Country to forbid familiarities between their Boys and their Negro Girls." See Constance B. Schultz, "John Adams on 'The Best of All Possible Worlds,'" *Journal of the History of Ideas* 44 (October–December 1983): 561–577, quote at 571.

48. Jefferson also uses the word *oestrum* in *Notes on Virginia* (Query XIV, p. 178) in the course of denying to blacks a poetic soul. He wrote: "Among the blacks is misery enough, God knows, but no poetry. Love is the peculiar oestrum of the poet."

49. Tissot, *Onanism,* 51.

50. TJ to Adams, Oct. 28, 1813, *Adams-Jefferson Letters,* 387–389.

51. TJ to Cathalan, July 21, 1787, PTJ-Boyd 11:605–606.

52. Cathalan to TJ, July 8, 1817; Monroe to TJ, February 13, 1818; TJ to Cathalan, January 18, 1818; TJ to Monroe, October 14, 1817, and February 21, 1818 (the extensively quoted letter), all in TJP-LC.

53. Madison to TJ, October 20, 1797, *Republic of Letters,* 993.

54. TJ to John Banister, Jr., October 15, 1785, PTJ-Boyd, 8:636–637; see also TJ to Walker Maury, August 19, 1785, ibid., 409–410. Compare the tone of the medical doctor and famed satirist Bernard Mandeville (1670?–1733), in his *A Modest Defence of Publick Stews: Or an Essay upon Whoring.*

55. Jefferson was reflecting a common understanding of the time with regard to private vs. public sexuality. Privacy conjured a protected domesticity, an acceptance of behavior not meant to be seen; on the other hand, separation of male and female was required outside the home, which is why the term "public women" or *"filles publiques"* was a code word for prostitution. See Jordanova, "Naturalising the Family," in Jordanova, *Nature Displayed,* 180.

56. Ellen to Virginia Randolph, August 4, 1819, Ellen Coolidge Correspondence, Special Collections, ViU. In later years, touring Europe, she identified, as her grandfather had in the mid-1780s, with *A Sentimental Journey:* "I am worse off than Sterne with his six shirts and one pair of black satin unmentionables." Ellen Wayles Coolidge Diary of a Trip to London, MHS, entry of July 9, 1838.

57. Ellen to Martha Randolph, June 26, 1825, Ellen Coolidge Correspondence, Special Collections, ViU. Ellen and Joseph Coolidge remained close to the Bulfinch family of Boston; Thomas Bulfinch (1796–1867) achieved fame in the 1850s as author of the extremely popular, long in print *Bulfinch's Mythology,* and served as literary agent on behalf of Ellen's sister Cornelia, who wrote a book on house plants.

58. Mary Randolph to Ellen Coolidge, July 29, 1827, Ellen Coolidge Correspondence, Special Collections, ViU.

59. Unusual arrangements were not new, as we can see in relating the manner by which Sally Hemings's older brother Robert Hemings obtained his freedom in 1794. He was Jefferson's body servant back in 1775–76 in Philadelphia, but remained behind when Jefferson traveled to Europe in 1784, and hired himself out. Bob met his wife (an enslaved woman in Fredericksburg) in this way, and in effect bought his own freedom when his wife's owner advanced Bob the money he needed to pay Jefferson, which Bob paid back a few years later. See Stanton, *Free Some Day,* 118; *Memorandum Books,* 1:342n, 2:923.

60. This is essentially the conclusion of Stanton, *Free Some Day,* 143.

61. Thomas Jefferson Memorial Foundation Research Committee, *Report on Thomas Jefferson and Sally Hemings*; compendium of correspondence relating to Ellen's Sally (whose surname Cottrell dates to her marriage contract of 1846), and including excerpts from the Nicholas Trist Papers, Library of Congress, regarding Thomas H. Key, also Ellen Coolidge to Jane N. Randolph, April 1835, ViU, all generously provided by Cinder Stanton, Monticello; while acknowledging that it is unclear whether Cottrell is Sally's maternal, paternal, or a marital surname prior to 1846, Stanton believes that Ellen's Sally is more likely to have been of a family other than the Hemingses; Shannon Lanier and Jane Feldman, *Jefferson's Children: The Story of One American Family* (New York, 2000), 128-29, with photo of an elderly Ellen Hemings (Roberts).

62. Upon the death of Burwell Colbert's wife and first cousin, Critta, in 1819, Ellen asked her mother to see that one of the now motherless children could be placed in her care: "I am more than ever anxious," she wrote, "to have it in my power to befriend, and educate as well as I can, one of these children." See Stanton, *Free Some Day,* 124.

63. William Faulkner, *Absalom, Absalom!* (New York, 1986), quote at 126.

64. Jan Ellen Lewis, "The White Jeffersons," in Jan Ellen Lewis and Peter S. Onuf, eds., *Sally Hemings and Thomas Jefferson: History, Memory, and Civic Culture* (Charlottesville, Va., 1999), chap. 6, quotes at 154–155.

65. As published in James Parton, *Life of Thomas Jefferson* (Boston, 1874), 568–570.

66. Frank Edgar Grizzard, "'A Perilous and Grievous Burden': The Dilemma of the Antislavery Slaveholder in Virginia during the Early National Period: A Case Study of General John Hartwell Cocke of Bremo" (master's thesis, University of Virginia, 1989). In the 1840s, Cocke bought an Alabama cotton plantation, where he experimented with black self-government. His 1853 diary entry is dated from Alabama.

67. Diary entries of January 26, 1853, and April 23, 1859, Cocke Papers, Special Collections, ViU.

68. Frank Carr to Cocke, July 8, 1826, Cocke Papers, Special Collections, ViU.

69. *Daily Scioto (Ohio) Gazette,* August 1, 1902, cited in Thomas Jefferson Memorial Foundation Research Committee, *Report on Thomas Jefferson and Sally Hemings.* In the same newspaper, Eston's skin was described as "light bronze." Another Ohio newspaper, the *Chilicothe Leader* (January 26, 1887), noted that he was "very slightly colored." His wife, Julia Isaacs, was the daughter of a Jewish merchant of Charlottesville, and a free woman of color.

70. Randall 3:537. The author's statement suggests that it was not until 1826, when Jefferson was in a weakened condition and required assistance to walk, that the family became aware of his chronic diarrhea.

71. Peter W. Bardaglio, *Reconstructing the Household: Families, Sex & the Law in the Nineteenth-Century South* (Chapel Hill, N.C., 1995), 66–78. The effort to appear fair-minded toward black defendants is not meant to discount the outrageous inequity of a legal system in which blacks could not impeach the testimony of whites, but could only testify against statements made by other blacks. On the courts' reluctance to prosecute white men for sex across the color line, see Joshua D. Rothman, *Notorious in the Neighborhood: Sex and Families Across the Color Line in Virginia, 1787–1861* (Charlottesville, Va., 2003). The author consistently demonstrates that class was a major factor in acceptance (versus suspicion) of the motives of the couples involved.

72. This is the reasoning, as well, of Rothman, *Notorious in the Neighborhood,* 19–20; Sharon Block emphasizes the absence of legal constraints on the master, noting in general that an enslaved woman would have to draw upon the authority of another patriarchal figure for her case to receive publicity; see Block, "Lines of Color, Sex, and Service: Comparative Sexual Coercion in Early America," in Martha Hodes, ed., *Sex, Love, Race: Crossing Boundaries in North American History* (New York, 1999), 141–163. It is also worth mentioning a curious statistic in a study on rape charges in Pennsylvania during this period: Before 1794, juries convicted in 34.8 percent of cases heard, but between 1794 and 1800—the years when Sally Hemings conceived most of her children, in Virginia—the conviction rate went down to 18.2 percent. The authors of the study write: "The close of the century appears to have been a time of greater tolerance of sexual aggression." See Jack Marietta and G. S. Rowe, "Rape, Law, Courts, and Custom in Pennsylvania, 1682–1800," in Merril D. Smith, ed., *Sex Without Consent: Rape and Sexual Coercion in America* (New York, 2001), 81–102, quote at 88; also Wiencek, *An Imperfect God,* 305–307. Clarence Walker writes: "We have no record of the Sally Hemings-Thomas Jefferson affair. But what we do know about slavery and the sexual exploitation of black women under that system makes it easy to believe that the Hemings-Jefferson relationship was exploitative, with a powerful white man taking advantage of a powerless black female." Walker, "'Denial Is Not a River in Egypt,'" in Lewis and Onuf, eds., *Sally Hemings and Thomas Jefferson,* 190; on sexual strategies used by owners and slaves, see Deborah Gray White, *Ar'n't I a Woman? Female Slaves in the Plantation South* (New York, 1985).

73. Sarah C. Maza, *Servants and Masters in Eighteenth-Century France* (Princeton, 1983), chaps. 3–6, quote at 157. Maza defines female servants as unmarried but unavail-

able except to their masters (or else given away only at their master's whim). Though there was a decline in the percentage of illegitimate pregnancies that were assignable to master-servant relations during the second half of the eighteenth century (rough estimates put the figure at 10–30 percent prior to 1750), more French men went outside the household and set up apartments in town for their working-class mistresses. This was not an option available to Jefferson.

74. A host of popularizers (novelists, playwrights, journalists) made such claims in the immediate aftermath of the DNA revelation in 1998–1999. For documentation, see Andrew Burstein, "Jefferson's Rationalizations," *William and Mary Quarterly* 57 (January 2000), 192–194.

75. Annette Gordon-Reed has supposed that the reputedly "dashing" Hemings may have felt she deserved Jefferson's love, that as a teenage maid in Paris she learned to think of herself as "special," and that "seeing herself differently may have changed the way others, including Thomas Jefferson, saw her." Though I am not insisting that this could not have been true, I have found no firm evidence to bolster the speculation that Hemings exercised influence over Jefferson's heart and mind. Professor Gordon-Reed identifies Jefferson's understanding of *concubine* as "whore" in a communication with James Madison concerning the sexual demands of a visiting diplomat; she also records the neutral use of *concubine* by Madison Hemings to describe his mother's relationship to Jefferson. This does not translate as "love." Gordon-Reed, *Thomas Jefferson and Sally Hemings*, 163–164, 231–232. If we are to infer that his servant was not primarily a sexual object in Jefferson's life, additional evidence needs to be collected.

76. TJ to Bellini, September 30, 1785, PTJ-Boyd 8:569.

77. Gerald W. Gawalt, "'Strict Truth': The Narrative of William Armistead Burwell," *The Virginia Magazine of History and Biography* 101 (January 1993): 118–120.

78. Freud would have a field day with this material. The lack of available evidence, however, places it beyond the bounds of our discussion; and regardless, if an eighteenth-century man did not make Freudian connections, there must be limits to the efficacy of Freudian analysis here.

79. John D'Emilio and Estelle B. Freedman, *Intimate Matters: A History of Sexuality in America* (New York, 1988), 103. See also Block, "Lines of Color, Sex, and Service."

Chapter 7

1. Yancey (1770–1857), a Buckingham County, Virginia, plantation owner and lieutenant colonel in the state militia during the War of 1812, was an important member of the Virginia legislature, on and off, from the 1790s through the 1830s.

2. On the political activity of Jeffersonian partisans, with attention to their efforts to appear nationalistic, see esp. David Waldstreicher, *In the Midst of Perpetual Fetes: The Making of American Nationalism, 1776–1820* (Chapel Hill, N.C., 1997), chap. 4; Saul Cornell, *The Other Founders: Anti-Federalism and the Dissenting Tradition in America, 1788–1828* (Chapel Hill, N.C., 1999); Noble E. Cunningham, Jr., *The Jeffersonian Republicans: The Formation of Party Organization, 1789–1801* (Chapel Hill, N.C., 1957); more generally, see James Roger

Sharp, *American Politics in the Early Republic* (New Haven, Conn., 1993); and Stanley Elkins and Eric McKitrick, *The Age of Federalism: The Early Republic, 1788–1800* (New York, 1993).

3. TJ to P. N. Nicholas, April 7, 1800, Bergh 10:163.

4. TJ to Madison, August 30, 1823, *Republic of Letters*, 1875–1877. Jefferson gave Madison a thorough rundown of events leading to his authorship of the Declaration, and acerbically countered Pickering's suggestion that Jefferson's ideas were irrelevant, and the document nothing without Congressional editing: "Timothy thinks the instrument [the Declaration] the better for having a fourth of it expunged. He would have thought it still better had the other three-fourths gone out also, all but the single sentiment (the only one he approves), which recommends friendship to his dear England, whenever she is willing to be at peace with us." Madison answered on September 6: "Nothing can be more absurd than the cavil that the Declaration contains known and not new truths. The object was to assert not to discover truths, and to make them the basis of the Revolutionary Act." Compare this to Jefferson's posture in an 1809 letter resisting publication of his collected writings. (TJ to John W. Campbell, September 3, 1809, Ford 11:115–117.) Garry Wills has recently resurrected Pickering, revealing the sources of his and Jefferson's mutual hostility. See Wills, *"Negro President": Jefferson and the Slave Power* (Boston, 2003). As to Adams's perspective on his and Jefferson's relative contributions to the Declaration, see Joseph J. Ellis, *Passionate Sage: The Character and Legacy of John Adams* (New York, 1993), 63–65; and Ellis, *American Sphinx: The Character of Thomas Jefferson* (New York, 1997), 243–246.

5. In spite of Jefferson's habit of using written notes to certify his memory, one scholar has supplied evidence of Jefferson's misremembering. See Charles R. Ritcheson, "The Fragile Memory: Thomas Jefferson at the Court of George III," *Eighteenth-Century Life* 6 (January and May, 1981): 1–16.

6. For a good presentation of the electoral crisis, see Sharp, *American Politics in the Early Republic*, chap. 12; and Joanne B. Freeman, "Corruption and Compromise in the Election of 1800," in James Horn, Jan Ellen Lewis, and Peter S. Onuf, eds., *The Revolution of 1800: Democracy, Race, and the New Republic* (Charlottesville, Va., 2002), 87–120. The word *civil*, in Jefferson's time, meant "civilized" as well as "political"; significantly, it also meant "other than ecclesiastical." The Twelfth Amendment, passed in 1804, insured that future presidential and vice presidential candidates were voted on separately, and did not compete for votes.

7. "First Inaugural Address," *Portable Jefferson*, 293.

8. TJ to Roane, September 6, 1819, Bergh 15:212 and TJP-LC.

9. Barry to TJ, June 15, 1822, TJP-LC; TJ to Barry, July 2, 1822, Bergh 15:388–390 and TJP-LC.

10. For a nuanced view of Jefferson's thoughts on the politicization of his contribution to the Declaration and its relative importance, see Pauline Maier, *American Scripture: Making the Declaration of Independence* (New York, 1997); also see Carl L. Becker, *The Declaration of Independence: A Study in the History of Political Ideas* (New York, 1922); Robert M. S. McDonald, "Thomas Jefferson's Changing Reputation as Author of the Declaration of Independence," *Journal of the Early Republic* 19 (Summer 1999): 169–196; Robert E. McGlone, "Deciphering Memory: John Adams and the Authorship of the Declaration of Independence," *The Journal of American History* 85 (September 1998): 411–438.

11. Trumbull to TJ, October 17, 1823, TJP-LC.

12. TJ to Adams, July 9, 1819; Adams to TJ, June 22, July 21, and July 28, 1819, *Adams-Jefferson Letters*, 542–546; Maier, *American Scripture*, 172–177.

13. TJ to Barry, July 2, 1822, Bergh 15:388–390.

14. *The Pennsylvania Magazine*, April 1776.

15. Ebeling to TJ, July 30, 1795, TJP-LC; also in PTJ-Boyd 28:423–427.

16. TJ to William Branch Giles, sometime after October 15, 1795, the day Jefferson received Ebeling's letter, TJP-LC; also in PTJ-Boyd, vol. 28.

17. Jefferson did not initially include the heady phrase "timid whigs who prefer tranquility to freedom" in his draft, but inserted it above the line, with a caret. He apparently wished to emphasize his view that monarchy was a real possibility, and to make the statement more powerful. Note, too, that this unusual use of "tranquility" was repeated when Jefferson rationalized the loss of George Washington's friendship and trust by saying that, in retirement, Washington no longer possessed "the firm tone of mind for which he was remarkable. . . . It's energy was abated. . . . A desire for tranquility had crept on him," so that he let others think for him. See *Anas*, 39–40.

18. Yet Jefferson long retained his suspicion about newspaper culture, writing with telling sarcasm to an aspiring editor: "To your request of my opinion of the manner in which a newspaper should be conducted, so as to be most useful, I should answer, 'by restraining it to true facts & sound principles only.' Yet I fear such a paper would find few subscribers." TJ to John Norvell, June 14, 1807, Ford 10:417. At the end of his life, too, he continued to express these thoughts, thanking an associate for his discretion: "You have done very right in not publishing my letter of Apr. 21. I should have had immediately a whole kennel of scribblers attacking me in the newspapers. . . . Let us avoid by all means the cheapening ourselves in the newspapers." (TJ to A. S. Brockenbrough, June 25, 1825, TJP-LC.) On the expansion of newspapers and the rise of newspaper culture (and on Norvell's career), see Jeffrey L. Pasley, *"The Tyranny of Printers": Newspaper Politics in the Early Republic* (Charlottesville, Va., 2001).

19. Jefferson's anonymous authorship of the controversial Kentucky Resolution, a states' rights document, in 1798, follows this pattern. He did not sign his name to the Ebeling notes, and he made no record either in the Summary Journal of Letters that he kept at Monticello. The research of the editors of the *Papers of Thomas Jefferson* with regard to the Jefferson-Ebeling correspondence (or lack thereof) is in PTJ-Boyd 28:427–428, 510. Letters Ebeling received are no longer extant.

20. Bentley to TJ, October 30, 1815; TJ to Bentley, December 28, 1815, TJP-LC. On Bentley's life and curious career, see Richard D. Brown, *Knowledge Is Power: The Diffusion of Information in America, 1700–1865* (New York, 1989), chap. 8.

21. TJ to Washington, May 23, 1792, PTJ-Boyd 23:538; TJ to Lafayette, March 1, 1801, Bergh 10:213; TJ to John B. Colvin, September 20, 1810, Ford 11:148–149. Similarly, Jefferson's protégé James Monroe would write to him in 1819, after Andrew Jackson loosely interpreted his orders and took an army across an international boundary, invading Spanish Florida: "Had General Jackson been brought to trial for transcending his orders, I have no doubt that the interior of the country would have been much agitated, if not convulsed by appeals to sectional interests." Monroe to TJ, February 8, 1819, TJP-LC.

22. TJ to Robert Williams, November 1, 1807, Ford 10:527.

23. *Inner Jefferson*, chap. 6.

24. TJ to Cooper, November 29, 1802, Ford 9:403.

25. TJ to Lafayette, February 14, 1815, Ford 11:460. Similarly, Jefferson described the Franco-American diplomatic impasse of the late 1790s, the XYZ affair, as a "delusion." See TJ to William B. Giles, March 23, 1801, Ford 9:223. It is also interesting that Jefferson criticized physicians' reliance on untested theories as "bewitching delusions." TJ to Caspar Wistar, June 21, 1807, Ford 10:428. Conceptually, "delusion" contrasted with an attachment to "justice," and Jefferson was always comfortable in saying that, as an executive, he had never carried out an act of injustice.

26. TJ to Smith, August 2, 1823, and December 19, 1823, Ford 12:300–302.

27. *Anas*, 23–24, 38; TJ to Cabell, February 26, 1818, in Malone 6:275.

28. This tells us something else as well: Jefferson's consistently rationalized (less passionately felt) responses to slavery-related correspondence contrasts with the mood and spirit he brought to letters that concerned his historical reputation, indicating that slavery was far less personal and troubling to him.

29. TJ to Logan, June 20, 1816, TJP-LC.

30. Short to TJ, April 23, 1816, TJP-LC.

31. TJ to Short, May 5, 1816, TJP-LC.

32. TJ to Martha Randolph, January 23, 1799; to Maria Jefferson Eppes, February 7, 1799, *Family Letters*, 172–173; TJ to Wistar, June 21, 1807, Ford 10:429.

33. TJ to Short, May 5, 1816, TJP-LC.

34. Terrell to TJ, May 31, 1825; TJ to Terrell, June 23, 1825, TJP-LC. Many around the country were aware that Jefferson kept his papers in good order, and in his late years he received not infrequent requests to make use of them. Another correspondent held exaggerated expectations from Jefferson's research into North American Indian cultures. Jefferson redirected him, while indicating that certain old volumes he had purchased from Virginia estates were to be deposited in the University of Virginia library, "where they [would] be most likely to be preserved with care." As to the larger principle: "I agree with you that it is the duty of every good citizen to use all the opportunities which occur to him for preserving documents relating to the history of our country, . . . but there is a time, and that time has come with me, when these duties are no more, when age and the wane of mind & memory and the feebleness of the powers of life pass them over, as a legacy, to younger hands." TJ to Hugh P. Taylor, October 4, 1823, TJP-LC.

35. TJ to Van der Kemp, January 11, 1825, Ford 12:400. Van der Kemp had protested that Jefferson allowed so little among his "valuable writings" to slip into the public journals. See Van der Kemp to TJ, December 28, 1824, TJP-LC.

Chapter 8

1. Tucker, *The Life of Thomas Jefferson, Third President of the United States*, 2 vols. (Philadelphia, 1837), 2:502. The title page of Tucker's biography identifies him in his position as "Professor of Moral Philosophy in the University of Virginia."

2. Leonard Baker, *John Marshall: A Life in Law* (New York, 1974); also James F. Simon, *What Kind of Nation: Thomas Jefferson, John Marshall, and the Epic Struggle to Create a United States* (New York, 2002); TJ to Madison, June 21, 1798, *Republic of Letters*, 1060.

3. The preceding is drawn, in large measure, from James Woodress, *A Yankee's Odyssey: The Life of Joel Barlow* (Philadelphia, 1958).

4. TJ to Barlow, May 3, 1802, TJP-LC and Ford 9:370–372.

5. *Anas*, 24.

6. TJ to Barlow, October 8, 1809, Ford 11:120–124.

7. John Marshall, *The Life of George Washington*, vol. 5 (Philadelphia, 1807), 672.

8. Joseph Dougherty to TJ, April 7, 1815; TJ to Milligan, May 6, 1815, TJP-LC. At $17.50 for the set, it was the most expensive book purchase he made in the order to Milligan.

9. Carr to TJ, December 1, 1815, TJP-LC; William Wirt, *Life of Patrick Henry* (Hartford, Conn., 1832 [1817]), 105–109. Friendly correspondents Dr. Benjamin Waterhouse and John Adams reported to Jefferson on their state's reaction to the controversy generated by Wirt's book. To sympathetic Richmond newspaper editor Thomas Ritchie, Jefferson wrote in this regard: "I think a state, like an individual, should be the last to praise itself. . . . It has been said, and I am afraid not entirely without foundation, that ours is the most boasting and braggadocio nation on earth." TJ to Ritchie, March 20, 1818, TJP-LC. See also Ellis, *Passionate Sage*, 101–105.

10. TJ to William Johnson, June 12, 1823, TJP-LC.

11. *Anas*, 25, 36–40.

12. Marshall, *Life of George Washington*, 5:777–778.

13. Ibid., 5:352–360.

14. *Anas*, 23–24, 44–45.

15. Ibid., 25.

16. Ibid., 43.

17. Ibid., 113. The substance is repeated in another conversation with Lear a short time later. See ibid., 117–118.

18. *Inner Jefferson*, 235–236.

19. William D. Brewer, *The Mental Anatomies of William Godwin and Mary Shelley* (Madison, N.J., 2001), 41–43; William Godwin, *Things as They Are: Or, the Adventures of Caleb Williams* (New York, 1988), 325.

20. Malone, 1:314–369.

21. *The Revolutionary War Memoirs of General Henry Lee*, ed. Robert E. Lee (New York, 1998 [1869]), 118, 286, 290, 296. Robert E. Lee, a son of the Revolutionary War general, contributed a biography of his father to his 1869 edition of the 1812 memoir.

22. Ibid., 303, 308, 397; on Lee's inflated sense of his own importance, see John Buchanan's narrative of the southern campaign, *The Road to Guilford Courthouse: The American Revolution in the Carolinas* (New York, 1997).

23. *The Revolutionary War Memoirs of General Henry Lee*, 300, 505.

24. Ibid., 90–91, 501.

25. Louis Hue Girardin, *The History of Virginia* (Petersburg, Va., 1816), 498–505 and Appendix, xi–xii; Malone, 6:218–222. As part of his discussion, Malone gives details of other wartime episodes the previously published history of which Jefferson sought to correct.

26. On the circumstances surrounding Delaplaine's project, and criticisms of his "national biography," see Scott E. Casper, *Constructing American Lives: Biography and Culture in Nineteenth-Century America* (Chapel Hill, N.C., 1999), 41–46.

27. TJ to Delaplaine, July 26, 1816, and October 30, 1817, TJP-LC. Insisting that his submission of a "written opinion" was a "singular case" of consenting to make a direct public statement about historical controversy, Jefferson reminded Delaplaine in 1821 that "it was for a very special reason." Otherwise, he held to his standard practice of avoiding exposure: "A desire for tranquility & aversion to place myself before the public in any form dictate this law to me." TJ to Delaplaine, January 29, 1821, TJP-LC.

28. Ellen to Henry S. Randall, March 13, 1856, Ellen Coolidge Letterbook, Special Collections, ViU.

29. TJ to Stephen Cathalan, July 3, 1815, TJP-LC.

30. Ibid.

31. Hamilton to Edward Carrington, May 26, 1792, *Papers of Alexander Hamilton*, ed. Harold C. Syrett (New York, 1961–1987), 11:440.

32. TJ to Madison, September 8, 1793, *Republic of Letters*, 818.

33. The argument presented by William Ian Miller in *The Mystery of Courage* (Cambridge, Mass., 2000) prompted the foregoing discussion. Sun Tzu quote is at p. 165.

34. William Johnson, *Sketches of the Life and Correspondence of Nathanael Greene, Major General of the Armies of the United States in the War of the Revolution* (Charleston, S.C., 1822), 1:v, x.

35. TJ to Johnson, October 27, 1822, TJP-LC.

36. Johnson, *Sketches of the Life and Correspondence of Nathanael Greene*, 2:447, 457, 461–462.

37. Ibid., 2:464.

38. TJ to Johnson, October 27, 1822, TJP-LC.

39. TJ to Johnson, March 4, 1823, TJP-LC and Ford 10:247.

40. Ibid.

41. Simpson to TJ, October 20, 1824; TJ to Simpson, October 27, 1824, TJP-Huntington. As editor of the *Columbian Observer*, and trained by Jeffersonian enthusiast William Duane, longtime editor of the *Aurora*, Simpson's political credentials were certainly good; it is possible, though, that Jefferson considered him too radical, and thus incapable of arguing to the readership Jefferson wished to sway. In addition, Simpson's paper was decidedly pro-Jackson, and Jefferson was lukewarm at best about the Tennessean's presidential ambitions. On Duane and Simpson, see Pasley, "*The Tyranny of Printers*." By this point in his life, Jefferson appears to have classified newspaper editors as a breed of inferior writers. Typically members of a younger generation, they were remote from the Revolutionary moment. Jefferson was tired of newspapers. He would settle for no one of a lesser stature or proven literary-historical talent than a Joel Barlow or a William Johnson. These men knew precisely what he wanted and would have been of one mind with him.

42. The Batture was a part of the Mississippi riverbed, submerged part of the year, reclaimable, and very valuable. The controversy concerned the question of whether this marginal land was private or public property. See Malone 6:55–73, quote from a letter to William B. Giles, at p. 63.

43. TJ to Monroe, March 27, 1824, TJP-LC.

44. TJ to Adams, January 21, 1812, *Adams-Jefferson Letters*, 291.

45. TJ to Livingston, April 4, 1824, TJP-LC.

46. Ibid., March 25, 1825, TJP-LC.

Chapter 9

1. Randall, 3:559–561; Jan Lewis, *The Pursuit of Happiness: Family and Values in Jefferson's Virginia* (Cambridge, 1983), 40–43.

2. "First Inaugural Address," *Portable Jefferson*, 295; in his second inaugural address, Jefferson referred to "that Being in whose hands we are, who led our forefathers, as Israel of old, from their native land." He frequently alluded to God's "kind providence." Also see Charles B. Sanford, *The Religious Life of Thomas Jefferson* (Charlottesville, Va., 1984), 1–6; Randall 3:553–555.

3. Jefferson wrote quintessentially in this regard to Charles Clay, an old acquaintance who had earlier served as rector of nearby St. Anne's parish: "I not only write nothing on religion, but rarely permit myself to speak on it, and never but in reasonable society." TJ to Clay, January 29, 1815, *Extracts*, 363.

4. TJ to Wendover, March 13, 1815, TJP-LC. Instead, he sent a half-page letter, neutral in tone, complimenting the "able proofs adduced by the eloquent author from Scriptural sources, in justification of a war so palpably supported by reason."

5. Benjamin Rush reminds John Adams of the story, originally told to him by Adams. See Rush to Adams, June 4 and 27, 1812, *Letters of Benjamin Rush*, 2:1128, 1144.

6. *Notes on Virginia*, Query XVII, 192.

7. TJ to Rush, September 23, 1800, *Extracts*, 320.

8. See esp. Thomas E. Buckley, "The Political Theology of Thomas Jefferson," in Merrill D. Peterson and Robert C. Vaughan, eds., *The Virginia Statute for Religious Freedom: Its Evolution and Consequences in American History* (Cambridge, U.K., 1988), 75–107.

9. TJ to Ely, June 25, 1819, *Extracts*, 387. Ely, a graduate of Yale, was the namesake of that college's former president, Congregationalist Ezra Stiles, whom Jefferson had met in the early 1780s and with whom he had sociably corresponded.

10. Paul K. Conkin, "The Religious Pilgrimage of Thomas Jefferson," in Peter S. Onuf, ed., *Jeffersonian Legacies* (Charlottesville, Va., 1993), 19–47, quote at 47. This is a concise yet quite comprehensive discussion of Jefferson's views.

11. Mark A. Beliles, "The Christian Communities, Religious Revivals, and Political Culture of the Central Virginia Piedmont, 1737–1813," in Garrett Ward Sheldon and Daniel L. Dreisbach, eds., *Religion and Political Culture in Jefferson's Virginia* (Lanham, Md., 2000), 3–40; Nathan O. Hatch, *The Democratization of American Christianity* (New Haven, Conn., 1989); Edwin S. Gaustad, *Sworn on the Altar of God: A Religious Biography of Thomas Jefferson* (Grand Rapids, Mich., 1996).

12. On deism in Jefferson's culture, see Richard Beale Davis, *Intellectual Life in Jefferson's Virginia, 1790–1830* (Chapel Hill, N.C., 1964), 123–128; A. Owen Aldridge, "Natural Religion and Deism in America before Ethan Allen and Thomas Paine," *William and Mary*

Quarterly 54 (October 1997): 835–848; Thomas C. Thompson, "Perceptions of a 'Deist Church' in Early National Virginia," in Sheldon and Dreisbach, eds., *Religion and Political Culture in Jefferson's Virginia*, 41–58; Sanford, *The Religious Life of Thomas Jefferson*, 128.

13. See Robert M. S. McDonald, "Was There a Religious Revolution of 1800?" in James Horn, Jan Ellen Lewis, and Peter S. Onuf, eds., *The Revolution of 1800: Democracy, Race, and the New Republic* (Charlottesville, Va., 2002), 173–198.

14. Jenny Graham, *Revolutionary in Exile: The Emigration of Joseph Priestley to America, 1794–1804* (Philadelphia, 1995), quote at p. 44.

15. Joseph Priestley, *An History of the Corruptions of Christianity* (New York, 1974 [Birmingham, Eng., 1782]), 1:vii, 2–4. Facsimile of the first edition.

16. Ibid., 25–27, 34–35.

17. Looking for the earliest origins of the Trinity, Priestley wrote: "Justin Martyr, who is the first that we can find to have advanced the doctrine of the divinity of Christ, says, 'He who appeared to Abraham, and to Isaac, and to Jacob, was subordinate to the Father, and minister to his will.'" Ibid., 47–48.

18. Ibid., 46–68.

19. In Greek myth, Cerberus was a three-headed dog guarding the entrance to Hades.

20. TJ to Rev. James Smith, December 8, 1822, TJP-LC.

21. Priestley, *An History of the Corruptions of Christianity*, 172–173.

22. Priestley put it this way: "Since, then, the great object of our Lord's mission was to teach the doctrine of a resurrection to a future immortal life, we see the necessity of his own death and resurrection as *a proof of his doctrine*. For whatever he might have *said*, or *done* while he lived, he could not have given the most satisfactory proof even of his own belief of a resurrection, unless he had actually died in the full expectation of it." Ibid., 173.

23. TJ to Priestley, April 9, 1803, *Extracts*, 328–329n.

24. TJ to Priestly, March 21, 1801, *Portable Jefferson*, 483–485.

25. Graham, *Revolutionary in Exile*, 164–165.

26. *Literary Commonplace Book*, 46; Douglas L. Wilson, "Jefferson and Bolingbroke: Notes on the Question of Influence," in Sheldon and Dreisbach, eds., *Religion and Political Culture in Jefferson's Virginia*, 107–118.

27. *The Autobiography of Benjamin Rush: His 'Travels Through Life' Together with His Commonplace Book for 1789–1813*, ed. George W. Corner (Princeton, 1948), 294.

28. TJ to Thomson, January 9, 1816, *Extracts*, 364–365.

29. Lehmann, *Thomas Jefferson, American Humanist*, 84–86. The Epicurean way of life that Jefferson sought to enjoy was that which commenced with an understanding of the importance of sensations, and which opened his mind to the pleasures of the imagination. It is in this vein, too, that we need to consider his disgust with Plato, who held that the highest good came not through an understanding of the natural world but through access to a transcendental world: The mystifying character of that world and the selectivity of its beneficiaries were what Jefferson rejected. Epicurus was his antidote to all such irrational constructs.

30. TJ to Thomson, January 29, 1817, *Extracts*, 384.

31. TJ to Rush, September 23, 1800, *Extracts*, 320. Years later, as the War of 1812 approached, Rush was reminded of the problem with conservative clergy and its role, along

with Federalist politicians, in defying popular resistance to tyranny: "Our country has twice declared itself independent of Great Britain," he wrote Jefferson. "Once in 1776 and again in 1800. In the former the legislatures, the bench, the bar, and the clergy were nearly all *united* in producing that event. In the latter year the legislatures, the bench, the bar, and the clergy were nearly all *opposed* to it." Rush to TJ, August 26, 1811, *Letters of Benjamin Rush,* 2:1099–1100. The phrase *genus irritabile vatum* derives from the epistles of Horace.

32. Gaustad, *Sworn on the Altar of God,* 90–93.

33. *Portable Jefferson,* 235, 251–253, 295.

34. Ibid., 252; Isaac Kramnick, "Eighteenth-Century Science and Radical Social Theory: The Case of Joseph Priestley's Scientific Liberalism," *Journal of British Studies* 25 (January 1986): 1–30, quote at p. 19.

35. Kramnick, "Eighteenth-Century Science and Radical Social Theory," 20.

36. TJ to Thomas Leiper, January 21, 1809, Ford 11:89.

37. TJ to Cooper, September 1, 1817, TJP-ViU. In Jefferson's time, *to brawl* meant to argue noisily and disruptively.

38. TJ to Smith, August 6, 1816, *Extracts,* 376; TJ to Adams, May 5, 1817, *Adams-Jefferson Letters,* 512.

39. Waterhouse to TJ, June 8, 1822, TJP-LC.

40. TJ to Waterhouse, June 26 and July 19, 1822, TJP-LC and Ford 12:241–244. Jefferson may as well have been encouraged by the opinion of his granddaughter Ellen, who observed from Washington half a year before that a Unitarian had been elected as chaplain of the House of Representatives: "The progress of Unitarianism is too evident to be disavowed." Ellen to TJ, December 12, 1821, photocopy at the Jefferson Library, Charlottesville (original in a private collection). On his blatant rebuke of the "priesthood," note his plainspoken manner with the Rev. Charles Clay, back in 1815: "I abuse the priests indeed, who have so much abused the pure and holy doctrines of their master, and who have laid me under no obligations of reticence as to the tricks of their trade." TJ to Clay, January 15, 1816, *Extracts,* 363.

41. TJ to Hatch, May 12, 1822, TJP-MHS; S. Alen Chambers, Jr., *Poplar Forest and Thomas Jefferson* (Charlottesville, Va., 1993), 145.

42. TJ to Fellows, March 9, 1826, TJP-LC.

43. See Jean M. Yarbrough, *American Virtues: Thomas Jefferson on the Character of a Free People* (Lawrence, Kan., 1998), esp. 29–48, 177–184; Andrew Burstein, "The Political Character of Sympathy," *Journal of the Early Republic* 21 (Winter 2001): 610–613; Roy Porter, *Flesh in the Age of Reason* (London and New York, 2003 and 2004), chap. 23.

44. The precise date of its completion is unknown, but 1820 appears to be the most probable date. See *Extracts,* 38.

45. The greater portion of Matthew is cited in the first half, and the greater portion of Luke in the latter half, of Jefferson's text. There are fewer extracts from Mark, and the fewest from John.

46. John 11:25.

47. From abstract of Isaac Newton's *Philosophiae Naturalis Principia Mathematica,* trans. Andrew Motte.

48. TJ to John Adams, May 5, 1817, *Adams-Jefferson Letters,* 512.

49. TJ to William Short, August 4, 1820, *Extracts,* 396.

50. Claiming the perceptiveness to see the real teachings of Jesus through "the fictions of his pseudo-followers," Jefferson listed his rational objections to all that passed for Christianity, which he considered adulterations: "The immaculate conception of Jesus, his deification, the creation of the world by him, his miraculous powers, his resurrection and visible ascension, his corporeal presence in the Eucharist, the Trinity, original sin, atonement, regeneration, election, orders of Hierarchy, &c." Although a part of one of his unguarded letters to William Short, this list was not sent, but was an asterisked addendum, kept in Jefferson's personal correspondence records, presumably intended for eventual, posthumous publication. See TJ to Short, October 31, 1819, TJP-LC and *Extracts,* 391.

51. *Extracts,* 167–187.

52. Reinhold Niebuhr, *The Nature and Destiny of Man: A Christian Interpretation* (New York, 1941), 2:28, 44–48, 56.

53. Daniel 7:13–14. Ezekiel 2 uses the term *Son of man* differently, in the sense of son of Adam, meaning "mortal man."

54. John R. Donahue, *The Gospel in Parable: Metaphor, Narrative, and Theology in the Synoptic Gospels* (Philadelphia, 1988), 182. In the informal table of contents of his condensed "Life and Morals," Jefferson describes generically as "precepts" the portion of Luke 9 that he selects for inclusion. These passages concern decisive action and devotion to God. Jefferson excludes the verse in which Jesus says: "For the Son of Man is not come to destroy men's lives, but to save them." Yet he includes another: "Foxes have holes, and birds have nests; but the Son of Man hath not where to lay his head." In further references to the Son of Man, later on, Jefferson includes these disparate verses: "And as it was in the days of Noe [Noah], so shall it be also in the days of the Son of Man" (namely that God promised never again to send a catastrophe); and, with reference to the fire and brimstone in Sodom, "Even thus shall it be in the day when the Son of Man is revealed." This is directly followed by: "When the Son of Man cometh shall he find faith on earth?" And once again, "For the Son of Man is come to seek and save that which was lost." These all appear in Jefferson's rendition. See Luke 9:56–62; 17:26–36; 18:8; 19:10; *Extracts,* 185, 229–231.

55. *Extracts,* 189–191.

56. Ibid., 135, 173, 183.

57. Lehmann was first to pursue the synthesis, as he termed it, of Epicureanism and Christianity: "This combination of Epicureanism and Christianity which Jefferson professed has, on the surface, the aspect of a paradox which it was not to him." Lehmann, *Thomas Jefferson, American Humanist,* 142. The same notion is suggested by Carl J. Richard, who states: "Although Jefferson's chief guide for ethics was Jesus, it was Jesus viewed through an Epicurean lens." Richard, *The Founders and the Classics: Greece, Rome, and the American Enlightenment* (Cambridge, Mass., 1994), 189; also Yarbrough, *American Virtues,* 183; on the Epicurean outlook with regard to religious faith, see esp. Panichas, *Epicurus,* chap. 4, and Zeller, *The Stoics, Epicureans and Sceptics,* chap. 18.

58. William R. Herzog II, *Parables as Subversive Speech: Jesus as Pedagogue of the Oppressed* (Louisville, Ky., 1994), chaps. 3 and 4.

59. Andrew Burstein, "Immortalizing the Founding Fathers: The Excesses of Public Eulogy," in Isenberg and Burstein, eds., *Mortal Remains,* 91–107; Barry Schwartz, *George Washington: The Making of an American Symbol* (New York, 1987).

60. *Literary Commonplace Book,* 56.

61. Even during his retirement years, when he contemplated his own mortality, Jefferson used *heaven* colloquially as a substitution for God, in such phrases as: "find favor with heaven"; "may heaven give you"; "implore heaven to avert the evil," and so forth. During the War of 1812, he wrote James Monroe on the impracticality of raising a large regular army, saying: "We might as well rely on calling down an army of angels from heaven." (TJ to Monroe, October 16, 1814, TJP-LC.)

62. TJ to Adams, November 13, 1818, *Adams-Jefferson Letters,* 529.

63. TJ to William Short, April 13, 1820, *Extracts,* 391–392; TJ to Adams, August 15, 1820, *Adams-Jefferson Letters,* 567–568. Adams had prompted these remarks with his statement: "Matter is but matter; if it is infinitely less than infinitely little, it is incapable of memory, judgement, or feeling, or pleasure or pain, as far as I can conceive. Yet for anything I know, it may be as capable of Sensation and reflection as Spirit, for I confess I know not how Spirit can think, feel, or act, any more than Matter." Adams to TJ, May 12, 1820, ibid., 564. In a letter nearly three years later, Jefferson repeats for Adams his 1820 comment to Short: "Jesus tells us that 'God is a spirit.' 4 John 24. but without defining what a spirit is." TJ to Adams, April 11, 1823, ibid., 593. The most probing analyses of Jefferson's materialism are Sanford, *The Religious Life of Thomas Jefferson,* 147–152, 170; and Daniel J. Boorstin, *The Lost World of Thomas Jefferson* (Chicago, 1948), 112–119, quote at 113.

64. On this subject, he wrote to John Adams: "When I meet with a proposition beyond finite comprehension, I abandon it as I do a weight which human strength cannot lift." TJ to Adams, March 4, 1820, *Adams-Jefferson Letters,* 562.

65. Priestley, *An History of the Corruptions of Christianity,* 400–426.

66. TJ to François Adrian Van der Kemp, January 1, 1825, Ford 12:401. Though their correspondence built during Jefferson's last years, he and Van der Kemp (1752–1829) apparently never met. Jefferson wrote John Adams in 1816, after the Dutch scholar had taken up residence in New York, asking for details about him: "There is a Mr. Vanderkemp of N.Y. a correspondent, I believe, of yours, with whom I have exchanged some letters, without knowing who he is. Will you tell me?" Adams, who had met him in Leyden in 1780, replied at length on Van der Kemp's military background as well as his ministry. "His head is deeply learned and his heart is pure. I scarcely know a more amiable Character." See TJ to Adams, August 1, 1816; Adams to TJ, August 9, 1816, *Adams-Jefferson Letters,* 484–485.

67. Richard, *The Founders and the Classics,* 191.

68. Peter Gay, *The Enlightenment: An Interpretation,* vol. 2, *The Science of Freedom* (New York, 1969), 16.

69. Ernst Cassirer, *The Philosophy of the Enlightenment* (Princeton, 1951 [1932]), 105.

70. Vila, *Enlightenment and Pathology,* 31.

71. In a representative letter written to a Bostonian, late in his life, Jefferson compressed his Christian affirmation: He said he believed the ultimate value of Jesus was his reformist message, in having introduced "sublime and more worthy ideas of the Supreme being, teaching

[his countrymen] the doctrine of a future state of rewards and punishments, and inculcating the love of mankind, instead of the anti-social spirit with which the Jews viewed other nations." In this as in other similar correspondence, he did not mean to describe heaven or hell, but only to suggest that human beings answered in some way for their moral conduct on earth—yet his reference to a "future state" instructs us that Jefferson was interested in a religion that supposed beyond moral duty in life. TJ to George Thacher, Jan. 26, 1824, Ford 12:332–333.

72. Cassirer, *The Philosophy of the Enlightenment*, 67.

73. TJ to Adams, April 11, 1823, *Adams-Jefferson Letters*, 594.

74. TJ to Robert Skipwith, August 3, 1771, PTJ-Boyd 1:76–81.

75. TJ to Adams, April 11, 1823, *Adams-Jefferson Letters*, 594; Matthew 25:14, 21, 23; *Extracts*, 263, 265. From the Sermon on the Mount, as well, comes the line, "Rejoice, and be exceeding glad: for great is your reward in heaven." Matt 5:12, *Extracts*, 145.

76. TJ to Priestley, April 9, 1803, *Extracts*, 328.

Chapter 10

1. TJ to Dr. Kean, January 27, 1825, TJP-ViU.

2. Randall, 3:540; Malone, 6:469–470; TJ to Madison, October 14 and 18, 1825, TJP-LC and *Republic of Letters*, 1941–1942.

3. Sarah N. Randolph, *The Domestic Life of Thomas Jefferson* (Charlottesville, Va., 1978 [New York, 1871]), 425–426; TJ to Roane, July 18, 1822; Peale to TJ, December 28, 1813; TJ to Madison, October 18, 1825, all in TJP-LC; George Tucker, *The Life of Thomas Jefferson* (Philadelphia, 1837), 2:494.

4. TJ to Peyton, August 29, 1825; Peyton to TJ, September 3, 1825, TJP-MHS.

5. Herbert E. Sloan, *Principle and Interest: Thomas Jefferson and the Problem of Debt* (New York, 1995), chaps. 1 and 2, quote at 27. Jefferson did not believe that any one personal failing had brought on the crisis, but a far-reaching defect preexisting in the realm of economy. Regardless of how much blame we put on him personally for the loss of Monticello, we learn most by viewing Jefferson as one in a legion of once proud Virginia planters, all of them equally done in by conspicuous consumption (a way of life they inherited), unanticipated fluctuations in plantation agriculture, and bankers whose rules and operations they insufficiently understood. It was a dark moment for the South, belonging to a growing distrust that would lead away from Jeffersonian nationalism toward Jeffersonian sectionalism.

6. Malone 6:473–482; Sloan, *Principle and Interest*, 218–222; TJ to Cabell, February 7, 1826, TJP-ViU. In the past, Virginia had seen lotteries on behalf of public institutions, less frequently in sales of private property.

7. As reported in Jane Randolph to Cary Ann Smith, June 27, 1826, letter cited in Malone 6:496.

8. George Green Shackelford, *Jefferson's Adoptive Son: The Life of William Short, 1767–1848* (Lexington, Ky., 1993), 167. Short was taken unaware by Jefferson's predicament, and his biographer believes that the $500 was only a first installment, had not Jefferson died so soon after the lottery was announced. Jefferson had expressed his distrust of banks to Short, as one of "those gossamer castles." Ibid., 184.

9. Dorothy Porter and Roy Porter, *Patient's Progress: Doctors and Doctoring in Eighteenth-Century England* (Stanford, Calif., 1989), 150–151.

10. H. Kalant, "Opium Revisited: A Brief Review of Its Nature, Composition, Non-Medical Use and Relative Risks," *Addiction* 92 (March 1997): 267–278.

11. Rush to TJ, March 12, 1803, *Letters of Benjamin Rush*, 2:857.

12. Benjamin Waterhouse, M.D., *Cautions to Young Persons Concerning Health in a Public Lecture Delivered . . . Nov. 20, 1804* (Cambridge, Mass., 1805), 23.

13. Kalant, "Opium Revisited."

14. Alethea Hayter, *Opium and the Romantic Imagination* (London, 1968); Michael G. Cooke, "DeQuincey, Coleridge, and the Formal Uses of Intoxication," *Yale French Studies* 50 (1974): 26–40; Thomas W. Africa, "The Opium Addiction of Marcus Aurelius," *Journal of the History of Ideas* 22 (January–March 1961): 97–102.

15. Carl A. Trocki, *Opium, Empire and the Global Political Economy, 1750–1950* (London, 1999).

16. Paul C. Nagel, *The Lees of Virginia: Seven Generations of an American Family* (New York, 1990), chap. 15.

17. TJ to Lee, May 15, 1826, TJP-LC; *Inner Jefferson*, 223.

18. Lee to TJ, May 25, 1826; TJ to Lee, May 27 and 30, 1826, TJP-LC; Randall 3:660.

19. Dunglison to Madison, July 1, 1826, in *The Jefferson-Dunglison Letters*, ed. John M. Dorsey, M.D. (Charlottesville, Va., 1960) 66–67.

20. Samuel X. Radbill, "The Autobiographical Ana of Robley Dunglison, M.D.," *Transactions of the American Philosophical Society* 53 (1963): 32; Lee to Jackson, July 1, 1826, *Correspondence of Andrew Jackson*, ed. John Spencer Bassett (Washington, D.C., 1926–1934), 3:305–306; Randall 3:662–664; Merrill D. Peterson, *The Jefferson Image in the American Mind* (Charlottesville, Va., 1998 [1960]), 116–122.

21. Randall, 3:544.

22. *Inner Jefferson*, 143.

23. Randall, 3:543–544; TJ to Madison, February 17, and Madison to TJ, February 24, 1826, *Republic of Letters*, 1966–1968.

24. Andrew Burstein, *America's Jubilee* (New York, 2001), 241–249.

25. Randall 3:543, 545; Randolph, *The Domestic Life of Thomas Jefferson*, 427; Tucker, *The Life of Thomas Jefferson*, 2:495.

26. Randall, 3:544; Randolph, *The Domestic Life of Thomas Jefferson*, 428.

27. TJ to Adams, April 11, 1823; Adams to TJ, November 10, 1823, *Adams-Jefferson Letters*, 594, 602.

28. I have given ample evidence that the unintendedly ironic phrase "Jefferson survives" was contrived by eulogists who wished to do even more to enlarge the double apotheosis of Adams and Jefferson. See Burstein, *America's Jubilee*, chap. 11.

29. Adams to TJ, September 15, 1813, *Adams-Jefferson Letters*, 376–377.

30. *New-York American*, July 8, 1826; Webster, North Carolinian Henry Potter, and Wirt in *Selection of Eulogies. Pronounced in the Several States, in Honor of Those Illustrious Patriots and Statesmen, John Adams and Thomas Jefferson* (Hartford, Conn., 1826).

31. "Response to a Serenade," July 7, 1863, *The Collected Works of Abraham Lincoln*, ed. Roy P. Basler (New Brunswick, N.J., 1953), 6:319–320.

32. Simon Dein and Rob George, "The Time to Die: Symbolic Factors Relating to the Time of Death," *Mortality* 6 (2001): 203–211; see also David P. Phillips and Daniel G. Smith, "Postponement of Death Until Symbolically Meaningful Occasions," *Journal of the American Medical Association* 263 (April 1990): 1947–1951. This study tracks mortality "dips" and "peaks" around holidays of ceremonial importance to the decedent.

33. TJ to John Holmes, September 23, 1815, TJP-LC.

34. Anne C. Vila, *Enlightenment and Pathology: Sensibility in the Literature and Medicine of Eighteenth-Century France* (Baltimore, 1998), 39.

35. Garrett to Evelina B. Garrett, July 4, 1826, cited in Frank Edgar Grizzard, Jr., "Documentary History of the Construction of the Buildings at the University of Virginia, 1817–1828" (Ph.D. diss., University of Virginia, 1996), chap. 11.

36. The sample of hair, more red than white, is preserved at the James Monroe Museum, in Fredericksburg, Virginia.

37. *Jefferson's Literary Commonplace Book,* ed. Douglas L. Wilson (Princeton, 1989), 224–225.

38. Unpublished letter to Henry S. Randall, in Ellen Coolidge Letterbook, Special Collections, ViU.

39. Philip Alexander Bruce, *History of the University of Virginia, 1819–1919* (New York, 1920), 45.

40. In this sense, compare him to the trained physicians who, as philosophers, populate Roy Porter's recent *Flesh in the Age of Reason*: John Locke, Thomas Willis, Bernard Mandeville, Albrecht von Haller, and David Hartley.

41. Antonio Damasio, *Looking for Spinoza: Joy, Sorrow, and the Feeling Brain* (New York, 2003), 28. The author identifies, by the use of modern medical techniques, the way that emotions can be made "visible," whereas feelings, as mental images, remain private and hidden within the mind. Emotions are built-in mechanisms essential to human survival, part of the structure of life; feelings develop out of them.

42. Joyce Appleby, *Thomas Jefferson* (New York, 2003), 139.

43. TJ to Roger C. Weightman, June 24, 1826, in *Portable Jefferson,* 584–585. He was easily as eloquent in his September 12, 1821 letter to John Adams: "I will not believe our labors are lost. I shall not die without a hope that light and liberty are on steady advance. . . . In short, the flames kindled on the 4th. of July 1776. have spread over too much of the globe to be extinguished by the feeble engines of despotism." *Adams-Jefferson Letters,* 575.

44. E. M. Forster, *Aspects of the Novel* (New York, 1927), 48.

45. TJ to Abigail Adams, January 11, 1817, *Adams-Jefferson Letters,* 504.

46. Edward Young, *The Complaint, or Night Thoughts on Life, Death, and Immortality* (Glasgow, 1798), 41.

INDEX